KU-372-571

THE AGE OF
GREY AND PEEL

THE AGE OF
GREY AND PEEL

Being the FORD LECTURES for 1926

BY THE LATE

H. W. CARLESS DAVIS

REGIUS PROFESSOR OF MODERN HISTORY IN THE
UNIVERSITY OF OXFORD 1925–1928

With an Introduction
by
G. M. TREVELYAN

REGIUS PROFESSOR OF MODERN HISTORY
IN THE UNIVERSITY OF CAMBRIDGE

WITHDRAWN

CHESTER COLLEGE

ACC. No.
420692

DEPT.

CLASS No.
942.081 DAV

LIBRARY

CHESTER COLLEGE LIBRARY

OXFORD
AT THE CLARENDON PRESS

Oxford University Press, Amen House, London E.C.4

GLASGOW NEW YORK TORONTO MELBOURNE WELLINGTON
BOMBAY CALCUTTA MADRAS KARACHI LAHORE DACCA
CAPE TOWN SALISBURY NAIROBI IBADAN ACCRA
KUALA LUMPUR HONG KONG

FIRST PUBLISHED 1929
REPRINTED LITHOGRAPHICALLY AT THE
UNIVERSITY PRESS, OXFORD,
FROM SHEETS OF THE FIRST EDITION
1964

PRINTED IN GREAT BRITAIN

CONTENTS

INTRODUCTION

THE sudden death of Professor Carless Davis in the prime of life, and in the full vigour of his intellectual activity, came as a poignant grief to his many friends and a heavy blow to the whole English historical world. As a history teacher and an organizer of history teaching he had already performed large tasks, and was setting out on a task larger still amid a group of colleagues whom he had made his friends, and who looked for great things from his renewed residence at Oxford. As a writer he had already set his mark on medieval history, and was proceeding to set his mark on modern history as well.

The present volume, only an earnest of what he would have done in the next twenty years, is a valuable contribution to the study of the period in our political annals which perhaps comes nearest to rivalling in interest and importance the heroic age of Strafford and Cromwell. The special quality of this book seems to me to be the quality of summing up by a judge whose sympathies and criticisms are impartially extended to all parties in the case. He is an historian who sees the real issues both as they appeared to contemporaries and also as they appear to posterity. I hope this volume will be largely used by students of the period, for it will certainly help them to a right understanding of political issues between the accession of George III and the Repeal of the Corn Laws. The title—*The Age of Grey and Peel*—was chosen by the author.

Davis's own description of the book is given in this note :

'The following studies are in substance the Ford Lectures delivered before the University of Oxford in 1926. They are concerned with the parties and the ideas of English politics in the first half of the Nineteenth Century ; also with certain movements, intellectual, social, political, which originated outside party politics, but which in different fashions influenced party programmes. The general object of the studies is to show how general principles, often of very broad and vague description, were applied in practice.'

This volume, then, serves to fill up a lacuna in modern English historical studies—the absence of a full analysis of the ideas and character of the Whig and Tory Parties. Those two strange, perennial institutions, unknown abroad, were essential parts of the machine of English liberty and government. By neglecting to analyse them, constitutional histories fail to tell us how and why our constitution worked. Even political histories and text-books often talk about Whigs and Tories without explaining the terms. This volume helps to explain the ideas and movements which the two parties represented between 1765 and 1846.

These Ford Lectures were considerably revised by the author with a view to publication. My part, therefore, has scarcely amounted to editorship ; I have only gone through the manuscript and passed the proofs for press. With the help of the 'reader', I have detected and altered a few wrong references or missing dates and a few slips of the pen such as Davis must himself have corrected if he had lived. Otherwise I have done nothing, not even to the text of Chapter XII (on Sir Robert Peel), which was still in the unrevised state at the author's death. I have, however, cut down the long quotations in the notes to that chapter in accordance with the practice of the author in the revision of the other chapters.

I may be allowed to say that the work has been to me a labour of love, not only on account of the subject and its treatment, but because of my personal friendship with Davis and many of the colleagues who mourn him, a friendship which has been symbolized by my election to an Honorary Fellowship at his College of Oriel. For the purposes of this volume I may then pass as an Oxford history man.

G. M. TREVELYAN.

TRINITY COLLEGE,
  CAMBRIDGE.

THE ROCKINGHAM WHIGS AND THEIR POLICY, 1765-1782

THE great party which had been founded at the Revolution, on the principles of Sidney and Locke, and which under Walpole's leadership had developed a practical, coherent system of home and foreign policy, entered on a new and troubled phase of its existence when Chatham retired in 1761 from the war ministry, which he and Newcastle had organized. In the course of a generation the old principles were modified to meet the facts of a situation such as had been unimagined and inconceivable in 1688; for the three great questions of America, Ireland, and the French Revolution raised issues undreamed of by the classical Whig philosophers. On these questions the Whigs were again and again divided; and these differences of principle were aggravated by other and older causes of dissension—the private quarrels and the personal ambitions of Whig party leaders. So firmly organized are some of the Whig groups in this period, so open-minded are some of the Whig leaders whenever open-mindedness becomes a passport to high office, that we are tempted to regard the old Whig party as extinct, and to explain the manœuvres of the Whig groups, between 1761 and 1797, as nothing more than the jostlings and scrambles of conscienceless place-hunters. The truth is that every group was in part composed of place-hunters, and that no leader of a group could safely neglect what were regarded as the just and natural ambitions of his followers. When the leader himself was too weak to resist the pressure from below, or was cynical enough to rate the fortunes of his own connexion more highly than the public interest, the behaviour of a Whig group was indeed as bad as can well be imagined. But on the whole it is surprising how sensitive the leaders were to any charge of political inconsistency or double-dealing. Every group professed allegiance to certain principles and a certain system of policy. The explanation is, no doubt, that the most powerful

of groups became dependent upon outside support as soon as it
accepted office, and that the country gentlemen in the House of
Commons, who were still in great measure free to serve under
any banner that they fancied, had a healthy hatred and contempt
for turncoats. Principles, then, had still a value in practical
politics. Every Whig group did lip-service to the principles of
1688; no group prospered for long unless it had also a system
of policy which could be explained and justified to the country
members. The conflict of Whig groups for place and power
was also a conflict between systems of policy.

The earliest group of this kind which concerns our subject is
that which was known in 1739 as the Boy Patriots or the
Cobham party. This group, which revived, with needful modi-
fications, the foreign policy of William III, rested on the solid
basis of Grenville influence, but was fortunate enough to find
a leader of genius in the elder Pitt. It broke with Walpole
because he was too pacific; it fell tooth and nail on Carteret
because its leader considered that Carteret was making war in
the wrong way; it entered into an uneasy alliance with the
Pelhams in 1746, the basis of the arrangement being a promise
from the Pelhams that the war with France should be, for the
future, a war at sea and not on land. The party broke with
Newcastle in 1755, with the determination to found a new war
ministry, since Newcastle was not prepared to put the conduct
of the Seven Years' War in the hands of Pitt. Having failed to
keep power after it had been placed in their hands, they came
to terms with Newcastle in 1757. The essence of the bargain
was that Pitt should be responsible for all 'public measures',
and in 1757 the only public measures of any importance were
measures for defending the Empire. This magnificently successful coalition, between the Patriots and the main body of old-
fashioned Whigs, endured long enough to conquer Canada
and to save Frederick the Great from ruin. It came to an end
in October 1761 chiefly because the Nestors of Whigdom—
Newcastle, Hardwicke, Grenville, Ligonier, Anson—were unwilling that their ally should carry on the war indefinitely with
the object of humbling Spain as he had already humbled
France.

When Pitt and Temple left office, intent upon founding or

refounding a party hostile to the pacific Newcastle, George Grenville, the ablest of their parliamentary debaters, remained with Newcastle to fight the battle of Whiggism against the King and Bute, and to secure tolerable terms of peace with France and Spain. In 1763 Grenville joined forces with John, Duke of Bedford, to form a Whig Government from which both Pitt and Newcastle were excluded.

The next two years were the golden age of the Bedford group, although that group remained, for some years after the fall of the Grenville ministry, a solid phalanx which had to be reckoned with whenever a Whig ministry was in prospect. It can seldom have happened that men so honest as Bedford and Grenville have led followers so disreputable. The leaders stood for a policy of peace, retrenchment, and sound finance ; in fact, for the better part of Robert Walpole's system. Some of his followers were peers who, like Sandwich, Weymouth, Halifax, and Gower, thirsted for office, or who, like Marlborough, owned themselves too incapable for office but longed, each according to his rank, for the Garter, or Mastership of the Horse, or one of the sticks-in-waiting. Others of lower degree and humbler ambitions coveted snug places which carried more emolument than dignity, and paid their court to Mr. Richard Rigby, the business agent of the group, a hard-living and hard-drinking politician who repaired his fortune at the expense of the public by clinging to the office of Paymaster of the Forces for seventeen years more or less (1767–84). The Duke of Bedford was perhaps too great a nobleman to be curious about the personal characters of his political associates and dependents. As a leader he was too loyal to be other than grasping when it seemed his duty to secure for his friends the due rewards of their fidelity. Having so many clients to provide for, he was naturally anxious that the patronage and influence of the King should be diminished, always provided that every piece of patronage taken from His Majesty was put at the disposal of His Majesty's ministers. For himself he was not grasping, and it is greatly to his credit that he was willing in 1764 to stand aside in order that Pitt might come into office. They had differed about war policy three years before, but the Duke seems to have felt that there was no other Whig who could bear comparison with Pitt. In 1766 he would have brought over the Bedford gang to the support of Chatham's second ministry if the great man would only have consented to find places for a suitable number of the gang. At the end of 1767 he was more successful in his dealings with Chatham's successor and political heir, the Duke of Grafton, who had none of Chatham's scruples about patronage. The gang were sufficiently provided for, but Bedford himself took nothing. He and his friends had begun the quarrel with the American colonies by passing the Stamp Act of 1764; they returned to office in time to stiffen the attitude of the Duke of Grafton on the subject of Charles Townshend's American customs duties. This was not simply due to wounded pride. The Bedford Whigs had little respect for the rights of the individual, and still less for the royal prerogative. But they were whole-hearted in their support of the sovereignty of Parliament. They desired that the Empire should be ruled from Westminster.

The main Whig party had fallen upon evil days after the secessions of Chatham and the Duke of Bedford. But it was still, in the classic phrase, a 'numerous and respectable body', strong enough in numbers, and in the broad acres of its leading men, to challenge comparison with any rival group. Its efficiency was impaired by the fact that it still followed the old Duke of Newcastle, whom George III was not prepared to accept as his first minister on any terms. After his final quarrel with George Grenville and the Duke of Bedford, the King turned in despair to the old Whigs, since Chatham was not to be persuaded at that time; and, through the mediation of the Duke of Cumberland, an arrangement was made with the Marquis of Rockingham, the wealthiest and most popular of the younger peers of the orthodox tradition. He took office under discouraging conditions. Differences of political opinion, to say nothing of the King's private feelings, made it impossible that he should unite with the Bedford Whigs. Yet without extraneous support his Government could not hold its own in either House. He took the only steps that were possible to strengthen his party. He gave places in the Cabinet to three supporters of Lord Chatham —General Conway, Lord Camden, and the Duke of Grafton— in the hope, it seems, that the great man himself would eventually be secured as a colleague. In the meantime he established

a lien on the sympathies of the King's friends by letting the
Great Seal remain in the hands of Lord Northington, an
experienced courtier, and by inviting Cumberland to attend the
Cabinet meetings as a sort of minister without portfolio. A
ministry so constituted was far indeed from corresponding to
the ideal which Burke proposed to the Whigs some five years
later in his *Thoughts on the Present Discontents* (1770); its
members were held together by a common dislike for the policy
which Grenville and Bedford had pursued; otherwise there was
little hope that they would be animated by the 'common
opinions, common affections, and common interests' which Burke
postulated as the essential conditions of a sound political alliance.
In view of the anomalous position assigned to Cumberland and
of the inclusion of Lord Northington, we cannot even say that
the first Rockingham ministry was resolutely opposed to the
secret influence of the Crown in politics. Though Newcastle
remained discreetly in the background as Lord Privy Seal, the
new arrangements carry the imprint of his peculiar genius. The
same remark may be made of the legislation for which this
mixed ministry was responsible. The statesmanlike decision to
repeal the Stamp Act was balanced by the Declaratory Act,
which reasserted the right of Parliament to tax the colonies.
The hope was that the Declaratory Act would please the King
and the King's friends; but the main result of the Act was to
leave a loophole in the terms of pacification, a loophole of which
full advantage was taken in 1767 by Charles Townshend.

The fate of this ministry was sealed when the Duke of Cumberland died suddenly and unexpectedly on 31 October 1765.
The Rockingham Whigs might perhaps have saved themselves
by accepting Pitt as their leader. In February 1766 he was
willing to join their ministry upon those terms, and Rockingham
at that time was disposed to waive his personal dignity.[1] It
seems that he preferred this course to the alternative of making
terms with Grenville and with Bedford—so deep and so broad
was the cleavage at this time between the two main fragments

---

[1] See his message of 26 February 1766 to Pitt (*Chatham Correspondence*,
ii. 397). For his subsequent attitude see the *Grafton Memoirs* (p. 71).
He would not serve under Chatham unless assured that a substantial
number of his friends should come in.

of the old Whig party. The Repeal of the Stamp Act had
been carried with the help of Pitt's voice and vote, and Pitt was
perhaps the only man who was capable of defending the new
colonial policy against the country gentlemen and the King's
friends. But the followers of Rockingham were unwilling to
serve under Pitt, the sworn enemy of the old Whig system of
aristocratic influence and political corruption. And so the
golden opportunity was missed. For Pitt was the dynamic
force in the field of parliamentary politics, the only Whig statesman who was not *au fond* contented with the existing state
of the constitution. If Pitt had come into power in February
1766 it is just possible that he might have converted the old
Whigs to his plans for remodelling the government of British
India, for conciliating the still excited colonists, for forming
a new system of European alliances. Five months later, when
Rockingham was out and Pitt (now Earl of Chatham) was in
place, the latter was willing to recruit his Cabinet with as many
of the old Whigs (including Rockingham) as were prepared to
make their bargains individually. But an alliance concluded on
those terms would not have produced a coherent Whig ministry,
capable of holding its own and pursuing its leader's policy even
when that leader was stricken with disease.

The Rockingham party, then, became in the summer of 1766
a party in opposition. At first a half-hearted party, because
some of their number had accepted office under Chatham, and
there were still hopes that the rest of the leading men, even
Rockingham himself, might eventually be taken in *en bloc* upon
a formal treaty of peace. These hopes evaporated in the autumn
of 1766, and the Rockingham members of Chatham's ministry
seceded to rejoin their friends in opposition. For a time Lord
Rockingham and the Duke of Bedford made common cause
against the ministry. They were strong enough, when united,
to defeat the Government on a vital measure of finance.[1] But
on American matters they still acted separately, with the result
that Townshend's policy of taxing the colonies by means of
customs duties was carried by the votes of the King's friends
and the country gentlemen. At the end of the year the Bedford
Whigs, enchanted to find themselves at one with the Duke of

---

[1] By carrying a reduction of the land tax from 4*s*. to 3*s*. in the £.

Grafton on the American question, came to terms with him, and gave his ministry a new lease of life, without adding in any way to its stock of political wisdom. The new coalition established their supremacy in the House of Commons by a general election early in 1768, at which the price of rotten boroughs is said to have averaged £4,000. Some months before the election Burke had urged upon Lord Rockingham the importance of engaging the moneyed men of their party in the hunt for boroughs,[1] and it is evident that Burke's advice had been followed; otherwise the price of boroughs would not have soared so extravagantly. The old Whigs had no scruples then, or for many a long day afterwards, about buying votes or buying seats. But in 1768 they learnt by bitter experience the enormous advantage which a Government in power possessed through its control of Treasury influence and secret service money.

The election of 1768 was not so crushing a defeat as it at first appeared. The Grafton-Bedford coalition remained in office only for two years and then collapsed owing to dissensions within its own ranks and the odium which certain of its measures excited in the country. Its worst mistakes, those committed in handling the American situation, were condoned—the show of naval and military force at Boston, the imposition of the tea duty, the threat to bring colonial leaders as prisoners to England to stand their trial for treason were not unpopular in themselves. But the action of the House of Commons in the Middlesex election exasperated every elector in the kingdom against the King and against the Prime Minister, who was justly regarded as the King's tool in this matter. Junius, the most dexterous of Grafton's enemies, showed his acumen by indicting the Duke for gross political inconsistency. Had he not voted with Mr. Pitt and Lord Rockingham against the taxation of America? Had he not then permitted Townshend to impose new duties and the Duke of Bedford to devise measures of coercion for enforcing them? Had he not in turn deserted friend after friend, first Rockingham, then Chatham, and last of

---

[1] Burke, *Correspondence*, i. 143. It is no doubt with reference to this election that Junius wrote of the Duke of Bedford in 1769: ' I daresay that he has bought and sold more than half the representative integrity of the nation' (Letter XII).

all John Wilkes? Had he not become in the last resort the successor of Lord Bute as the King's first favourite and the leader of an administration composed of rats, 'the deserters of all parties, interests, and connexions'? These are fair samples of the charges which ruined Grafton with the public, which made his own colleagues ashamed to work with him any longer, and which undermined his majority in the House of Commons.

But the Rockingham Whigs were not allowed to benefit by Grafton's fall. In the King's opinion there was no need to change the system in America. What the times called for was a respectable figurehead who would assume responsibility for the policy of George Grenville and the Duke of Bedford and Charles Townshend. Rockingham would never play the part required. In July 1767, when pressed to help in forming a new ministry, he had laid it down as a prior condition that his American policy should be accepted;[1] to that policy he still adhered. He had his faults as a political leader, but he was at least entitled to the praise which Grafton bestows on him in retrospect. 'Lord Rockingham and many of his friends always wished to act on principle.'[2] It was this devotion to principle which condemned his party to sixteen years of wandering in the wilderness of Opposition.

It would be childish to pretend that they were in every respect the model of an Opposition. Most of them were very irregular in attending the debates of Parliament, even in the critical days when the Grafton ministry was tottering under the blows of Chatham's oratory. When North was firmly established in the saddle, a number of the leading men were in favour of secession from Parliament, and Rockingham and Richmond were with difficulty persuaded by Burke and Savile to abandon systematic absence in favour of occasional attendance.[3] Those who paid most attention to parliamentary business were sometimes guilty of a factious opposition, as for instance in the matter of the land-tax in 1766 and in their defence of the East India Company in the following year, when Burke took a line that cannot

---

[1] Rockingham to Lord Hardwicke, 2 July 1767 (*Rockingham Memoirs*, ii. 50, 57), and to the Duke of Portland, 15 September 1767.

[2] *Grafton Memoirs*, p. 143.

[3] Burke, *Correspondence*, i. 347, 349, 358-9, 361, 366.

be reconciled with his subsequent conduct as a minister in 1783. But on the whole the party had little to blush for while they were out of office. Burke was too sanguine in believing that in the years 1766-82 he and his friends elaborated a code of political principles sufficient for all emergencies that were likely to arise, at least in home affairs. But it is true that Burke himself converted the party to some leading principles of conduct which have become in course of time the commonplaces of the English party system. He was the only member of his party who, before 1782, showed any genius for political speculation ; but his associates were willing pupils, and learned much from him, though it is also true that some of the finer elements in his political creed eluded their comprehension. It is worth our while to collect from his letters and orations those doctrines which his own party did at once accept.

(1) The first was his doctrine of party. He persuaded his friends (though he never persuaded Chatham) that the party system was neither a disease of the body politic nor one of those expedients which must be accepted by practical men as necessary evils. Party, according to Burke, was not only useful as a means of securing the co-operation of public men who would be helpless and useless to the commonwealth so long as they were isolated individuals. It was a right and natural development in civilized society, being founded upon instincts and affections which are common to all right-minded men. It was also an elevating and a sobering influence in politics ; elevating, because a man must needs think more highly of his principles when he finds that they are not peculiar to himself, but shared by the friends whom he respects; sobering, because the man who commits himself to the business of carrying out a principle in concert with his friends will be strengthened in his loyalty to that principle by the fear of incurring hatred and contempt from those by whom he most desires to be esteemed.

' That versatility, those sudden evolutions which have sometimes derogated from the credit of all public professions, are things not so easy in large bodies as when men act alone or in light squadrons.' [1] The ideal party which Burke thus describes was something better than the party to which he belonged and

---

[1] *Letter to Dr. Markham* (1771).

the parties against which he fought. But it was a salutary ideal,
and it was gradually accepted as a counsel of perfection by the
great public men of Burke's generation. Burke himself lived to
be the apologist of a coalition which was clearly indefensible
from his own point of view ; but public opinion condemned the
Fox-North ministry in no uncertain fashion. ' The great Whig
families ', wrote Horace Walpole in April 1784, ' have lost all
credit in their own counties.' ' Such aversion to the coalition
and such a detestation of Mr. Fox have seized the country that,
even where omnipotent gold retains its influence, the elected
pass through an ordeal of the most virulent abuse.' [1] We know
that the gold of the King and the electioneering skill of
Mr. Robinson of the Treasury contributed heavily to the defeat
of the Whigs at the polls on this occasion ; but it is also clear
that independent electors were shocked by the factious character
of the coalition of Fox and North.

(2) The principles of managing a party in office had been
understood and practised in the time of Walpole. But Burke
seems to have made a new departure in urging that an Opposition should not play fast and loose with principles merely for
the purpose of embarrassing the Government in power ; and
that it should lose no opportunity of affirming its principles,
even though the prospect of converting the House or the country
might seem to be remote. Although in 1777 he assented, rather
reluctantly, to the practice of occasional attendance, admitting
that it was probably useless to speak and vote on measures
about which the majority were determined to make no concession, [2] his general view was that, in critical times, the Opposition
should be as regular in attending the debates as were the supporters of the ministry. In 1775 he sent to Rockingham a letter
which amounted to a bold rebuke of his chief's inveterate tendency to postpone the business of Parliament to more congenial
pursuits. ' This is no time for taking public business in their
course and order, and only as a part of the scheme of life, which
comes and goes at its proper periods and is mixed with its occupations and amusements. It calls for the whole of the best of

---

[1] Horace Walpole to Sir Horace Mann, 11 April 1784 (*Walpole's Letters*,
ed. Toynbee, xiii. 141).

[2] Prior's *Life* (ed. 1854), p. 165 ; *Correspondence*, i. 347, 359, 366.

us ; and everything else, however just or even laudable at another time, ought to give way to this great concern.'[1]

A chance correspondence with Sir Joshua Reynolds informs us of the function which Burke would assign to a systematic and temperate Opposition. Being asked by Sir Joshua what was the use of parliamentary speeches which would never turn a vote, he replied that although a bill which was ably opposed might pass into a law, yet in its progress the minister would become aware of the effect which the criticisms of his opponents have made on the minds of his supporters. 'There are many members who generally go with the minister who will not go all lengths.'[2]

The times in which Burke led the Opposition were not favourable for civil and regular relations between parties in Parliament. Yet on two occasions we find North formally notifying Burke of the arrangement of the Government's time-table. The first of these communications, dated 19 February 1775, is the more remarkable as it relates to a subject on which the Whigs neither gave nor expected courtesy in debate :

'SIR :—As I apprehend you would not choose to be absent from the House of Commons when any material question is proposed respecting America, I think it right to apprise you that I intend to propose a motion of importance to-morrow, in the committee upon the American papers. I am sorry that I am not able to give you a longer notice of it. I shall be much obliged if you will communicate this notice to such gentlemen of your acquaintance as may wish to be present.'[3]

The second of North's communications belongs to the summer of 1780 and relates to the sequel of the Gordon riots. Burke had written to his friend Lord Loughborough, recently appointed Lord Chief Justice, to urge that Government should lose no time in announcing how it would answer the fanatical petition of the Protestant Association ; and he sent to Loughborough three resolutions embodying the answer which he himself thought appropriate. Three days later North himself wrote to Burke ' to inform you of the conduct we mean to

[1] *Correspondence*, ii. 53.

[2] Prior, p. 166. Cf. Burke's *Correspondence*, ii. 95 (in 1789): 'We are in a minority, but then we are a very large minority, and I have never known an instance in which such a minority did not keep a majority in considerable awe.'

[3] Burke, *Correspondence*, ii. 23–4 (19 February 1775).

observe when the petition presented by Lord George Gordon shall be taken into consideration '. He sent with his letter a copy of the resolutions of the Government, adding that he had adopted one of those suggested by Burke and did not differ much from Burke about the other two. On Tuesday, June 20, ministers and Opposition presented a united front to the protestant agitators in the House of Commons. Burke and Fox both spoke against the petition, and the five resolutions which North had prepared were moved by Burke.[1]

An Opposition which claims to be recognized as part of the constitutional system is bound in honour to advocate no measures which it would not be prepared to carry when in office. Burke and Sir George Savile disapproved of the action of their followers in forcing Grafton and Townshend to accept a reduction of the land tax. Their view was communicated to Lord Rockingham in a blunt letter from Savile. 'Never let us drive a wrong or dubious point because we have numbers, and it will be a *strong point*, a devilish stroke, a fine topic of declamation '; the main question was whether anything less than a four-shilling land tax would meet the lawful liabilities of the nation.[2] The party acted on this principle in 1779 when North's measures for the relief of Irish trade [3] were before the House of Commons. It would have been easy to oblige the English commercial interest by taking a contrary course. But justice for Ireland had become an essential principle of Whig policy by that date. There was no principle which Burke had more at heart.

(3) To defend the liberties of the subject, especially against the prerogative or the corrupt influence of the Crown or even the privilege of Parliament, was a rule of conduct to which all sections of the Whig party were committed in varying degrees. The Rockingham Whigs were, however, conspicuously earnest in their attention to this duty. Chatham in 1766 had thought it a superfluous formality to obtain the ratification of a statute for his embargo upon the export of corn, considering the plain necessities of the situation. Grenville and Bedford had been

---

[1] *Op. cit.*, ii. 356–63 ; Prior, *Life of Burke* (ed. 1854), pp. 190–1.
[2] *Rockingham Memoirs*, ii. 36.
[3] 20 Geo. III, cc. 6, 10, 18.

perfectly willing to put that dubious patriot John Wilkes in his proper place by high-handed and irregular expedients. The Rockingham Whigs were uniformly opposed to measures which were termed 'strong' by their supporters and unconstitutional by legal critics. Their respect for rights of property was evinced in 1769, when they forced the Nullum Tempus Act (1769) upon the Grafton ministry, thus making sixty years of quiet possession of Crown lands a bar to any action for recovery on the part of the Crown.[1] In 1767, and again in 1773, Burke defended the proprietary rights of the East India Company, talking as though the whole question at issue was whether a great commercial corporation was to be robbed by an avaricious ministry, acting in concert with subservient majorities in Parliament. It is noticeable that this was one of the subjects on which the Old Whigs and the New Whigs did not see eye to eye. In 1772 the Duke of Richmond wrote to Burke, with reference to the Company's affairs: 'I think we shall not act wisely to be over-eager in taking a part. We have been much too ready in taking up the cudgels for everybody the ministers please to attack'.[2] In 1785 Fox denounced the doctrine that an electoral vote was a kind of property of which no elector should be deprived without due compensation. But the aristocratic leaders of the Whig party, the great oaks deeply rooted in the soil, were slow to abandon the older and more catholic definition of property as that which had a price. They held that the rights of property were as sacred as that of personal liberty. Property was the more sacred in their eyes because they held, with Harrington and Sidney, that it always had been and always ought to be the source of political power. To preserve the great estates from harm was the first duty of every friend of the constitution ; for the great estates were the bulwarks of political freedom. Liberty would be at an end whenever the revenues of the Government became greater than the revenues of the individual subjects.

(4) From considerations of this kind, Burke and Rockingham and the Duke of Portland were resolutely determined to avoid, or at the least to postpone, any interference with what Chatham styled 'the rotten part of the constitution'; that is, with the

[1] 9 Geo. III, c. 16.   [2] Burke, *Correspondence*, ii. 395.

defects of the representative system. Chatham might hold
parley with the followers of Wilkes and Tooke; Savile and
Fox and Richmond might hold out hopes to the Yorkshire
Association and the Westminster reformers; but they did not
carry with them the leaders of the party. Rockingham, it is
true, admitted with his usual moderation that it might not be
unjust in principle to disfranchise the close boroughs. But such
a reform was not urgent; it might be undertaken hereafter, but
certainly not in the immediate future. He warned one of his
supporters that the sixteen seats belonging to the close boroughs
of Yorkshire had after all their uses, which the Whig freeholders and gentlemen of that county could not afford to over-
look.[1] For his own part he had greater hopes of reducing
corruption. Burke was more outspoken:

'The bane of the Whigs has been the admission among them of the
corps of schemers who, in reality and at bottom, mean little more than
to indulge themselves with speculations, but who do us infinite mischief
by persuading many sober and well-meaning people that we have
designs inconsistent with the constitution. . . . The machine itself is
well enough to answer any good purpose, provided the materials were
sound. But what signifies the arrangement of rottenness.'[2]

As Fox and the Duke of Richmond and Lord Shelburne
were among the 'schemers', Burke's language boded ill for the
unity of the Whig party.

(5) The materials of the constitution were the electors of the
constituencies, their representatives in the House of Commons,
the hereditary peerage, and the Crown. To reform the electors,
at least by such means as Wilkes and Wyvill and Richmond had
in mind, was in Burke's opinion quite impossible. It would,
however, be a comparatively simple matter to improve the
political morality of the members of both Houses by sweeping
away the temptations which had undermined their political
virtue in comparatively recent times. It was particularly desirable to make this reform, since the means of corrupting the
political classes were vested in the Crown and it was the Crown
that reaped the ignoble advantages of the system of corruption.
The first draft of Burke's scheme of Economical Reform is
prefaced with the statement that

---

[1] *Rockingham Memoirs*, i. 398, 405.   [2] *Correspondence*, ii. 383.

'It takes away employments tenable with a seat and worthy of
a gentleman's acceptance, equal to those of fifty members of parliament; besides other innumerable retainers and dependents from
possession of emolument, from hope of obtaining it, and from fear
of the exercise of various powers of the Crown which are here proposed
to be taken away.'[1]

Burke's scheme was not allowed to pass into law until it had
suffered extensive mutilations. He had originally proposed to
sell the lands and to suppress the administrations of the Princi-
pality of Wales, the earldoms of Chester and Cornwall, and the
Duchy and County Palatine of Lancaster. These were spared
in the Economical Reform Act of 1782. That measure effected
some useful economies; it made away with a large number of
sinecures in the royal household; it abolished a smaller number
of public offices and boards, especially the office of Secretary
of State for the Colonies, the Board of Trade and Plantations,
the Lords of Trade and Police in Scotland. It cut down the
pension fund to £90,000 a year and the secret service fund to
£10,000. But still it was only an instalment of reform. Any
hope that Burke's policy would be carried farther by his party
was killed by one of the articles in the bargain which Charles
James Fox concluded with Lord North in 1783. 'They agreed
that nothing more was required to be done in reducing the
influence of the Crown by economical reform.'[2] This pledge
was given to North personally; but Fox seems never to have
recurred to Burke's plan when he was free again to take an
independent line of policy. Yet there is abundant proof in the
records of the Whig party that for the next fifty years at least
the sinecurists of the royal household were a formidable *bloc* in
the House of Lords and a cause of constant anxiety to Whig
premiers *in esse* and *in posse*. The truth was that Burke's
policy ceased to be attractive with the decline of the personal
power of George III. When the advantages of the corrupt
system were reaped rather by the ministers of the day than by
the sovereign himself, it became a serious question in Whig
circles whether it was wise to press for an economical reform
which would weaken the hands of any and every government.

[1] *Correspondence*, ii. 382.
[2] Adam's note of the interview between Fox and North 14 February 1783
(*Correspondence of C. J. Fox*, ii. 37).

It was arguable that the votes of lords in waiting were, like the Treasury boroughs in Ireland, and like the whole of the constituencies of Scotland—necessary buttresses and props of the executive.[1]

Much that now seems barbarous and archaic in the Whig creed of the eighteenth century becomes at all events intelligible when we read Burke's description (written in 1792) of the party to which he joined his fortunes in 1765:

'I understood it to be a party, in its composition and in its principles connected with the solid permanent, long possessed property of the country ; a party which, by a temper derived from that species of property, and affording a security to it, was attached to the ancient, tried usages of the kingdom ; a party therefore essentially constructed upon a ground-plot of stability and independence; a party therefore equally removed from servile court compliances, and from popular levity, presumption, and precipitation.'[2]

In this passage Burke describes accurately enough the inmost political conviction of the great Whig houses in serving whom he conceived that he was serving the country and the constitution. It is a sublimated form of feudalism, in which influence and social prestige take the place of homage as the links which bind the inferior ranks of society to their natural leaders. It is a view of the natural structure of society which derived from the Middle Ages as obviously as the Tory conception of the well-ordered monarchy, in which the hereditary sovereign is not only the symbol of corporate unity but the mouthpiece of the nation's will and conscience.

Passing from principles which relate to the constitution and internal government we may now consider the principles upon which the old Whigs desired to settle the relations of Great Britain with the colonies and Ireland.

(6) The Declaratory Act appears, as we have seen already, to have been adopted by the first Rockingham ministry as a measure of concession to the King and the country party. It was treated in America as a matter of no importance, as the statement of a legal right which was legally incontrovertible and never likely to be exercised. That, however, was not quite the

[1] *Rockingham Memoirs*, i. 398, 405.
[2] *Letter to William Waddell*, 31 January 1792

view of the Rockingham party, if we may trust the account
which is given by Burke, in 1774, of the policy which he and
his friends had contemplated.   They would not have been content with the indirect contributions which the colonies already
made to the Exchequer of Great Britain by submitting to the
restraints imposed upon American trade in the Navigation Acts.
They would have reserved to the Imperial Parliament the right
of taxing any colonies which would not contribute of their own
free will to the cost of the common defence of the Empire.
Burke justifies this intention in a stately passage which describes
the British Parliament as sitting and acting in two capacities.
The first is that of the local legislature of this island, providing
for all things at home, immediately, and by no other instrument
than the executive power.   He then continues :

   'The other, and I think her nobler capacity, is what I call her
imperial character; in which, as from the throne of heaven, she
superintends all the several inferior legislatures, and guides and
controls them all without annihilating any.   As all these provincial
legislatures are only co-ordinate to each other, they ought all to be
subordinate to her ; else they can neither preserve mutual peace, nor
hope for mutual justice, nor effectually afford mutual assistance.   It is
necessary to coerce the negligent, to restrain the violent, and to aid the
weak and deficient, by the overruling plenitude of her power.   She is
never to intrude into the place of the others while they are equal to the
common ends of their institution.   But in order to enable Parliament
to answer all these ends of provident and beneficent superintendence,
her powers must be boundless. . . . What ! Shall there be no reserved
power in the Empire to supply a deficiency which may weaken, divide,
and dissipate the whole? . . . But then this ought to be no ordinary
power ; nor ever used in the first instance.   This is what I meant,
when I have said at various times, that I consider the power of taxing in
Parliament as an instrument of empire, and not as a means of supply.' [1]

   This passage reminds us of Dante's ideal of the Holy Roman
Empire as the power which is responsible for the maintenance
of a *Pax Romana* within and without.   But to critical and
educated Americans it must have suggested unpleasantly the
Stuart doctrine of the difference between the ordinary and
extraordinary powers of the Crown.   Burke's theory of the
Empire was not carried in the heat of debate and thrown aside

---

[1] *Speeches*, i. 238–9.

when it had served the purpose of the moment. He revived it
on 22 March 1775, when he made his celebrated proposals for
conciliation with America. The gist of these proposals was
that the right of Parliament to tax the colonies should be upheld
as a bare principle ; that the inexpedience of imposing taxes on
the colonies through Parliament should be admitted ; and that
the colonies should be required by the Crown to tax themselves,
through their own assemblies, for the service of the Crown.
This capital concession was followed by proposals for giving
security of tenure to judges in the colonies, for reforming the
courts of admiralty, and for repealing the Boston Port Bill.

When we compare these proposals with the resolutions passed
by the American Continental Congress it is tolerably clear that
Burke's eirenicon, even if it had been approved at Westminster,
would have been coldly received at Philadelphia. It is true that
the delegates in the Congress admitted their cheerful consent
to the continuance of the navigation laws 'from a regard to the
mutual interest of both countries '. But on the subject of taxation
they were adamant :

'As the English colonists are not represented, and from their local
and other circumstances cannot be represented in the British Parliament, they are entitled to a free and *exclusive* power of legislation
in their several provincial legislatures, where their right of legislation
can alone be preserved, in all cases of *taxation* and internal polity,
subject only to the *negative* of their sovereign in such manner as has
been heretofore used and accustomed.'[1]

This passage concedes to the Mother Country the veto on
legislation, the control of sea-borne trade, and, by implication,
the responsibility for foreign relations, but refuses altogether to
the imperial Parliament the rights of supervision, mediation,
coercion, and taxation which Burke deems essential. Even
more significant is the language used by John Adams in January
1775, in replying to a colonial loyalist who, like Burke, desired
to maintain the political unity of the British Empire. This
loyalist assumed as self-evident that 'if we are a part of the
British Empire we must be subject to the supreme power of

[1] S. E. Morison, *Sources and Documents illustrating the American
Revolution* (1923), p. 120.

the state, which is vested in the estates in Parliament '. To which
Adams replies :

' Here again we are to be conjured out of our senses by the magic in
the words " British Empire " and " supreme power of the state ". But,
however it may sound, I say we are not a part of the British Empire ;
because the British Government is not an empire. . . . An empire is a
despotism, and an emperor a despot, bound by no law or limitation
but his own will ; it is a stretch of tyranny beyond absolute monarchy.
. . . The question should be whether we are a part of the kingdom of
Great Britain. This is the only language known in English laws '.[1]

Finally, it may be noticed that, only a month before Burke
moved his proposals of conciliation, Franklin, writing from
London to a friend who advocated reconciliation, had stated that
he apprehended more mischief than benefit from a closer union
between the colonies and the Mother Country. He was not
willing to leave foreign relations in the hands of Great Britain.
' I fear they will drag us after them in all the plundering wars
which their desperate circumstances, injustice, and rapacity may
prompt them to undertake.'

Burke's proposals were those of a constructive and far-sighted
statesman, and they appealed to American loyalists. But it is
scarcely to be believed that Burke's plan would have been more
acceptable to the men who led American opinion than the rival
plans of Lord North (in his resolutions of 20 Feb. 1775) or of
Lord Chatham (in his Provisional Bill of 1 Feb. 1775). All
three had the same vice, as the Americans regarded it, of insisting
on colonial contributions to the cost of imperial defence.

(7) It was not until the Rockingham Whigs came into power
for the second time that they were required to take any
momentous decisions respecting Ireland.[2] It is, however, noticeable that Burke and Savile joined forces with the friends of
Chatham in 1778 to procure a relaxation of the penal laws in
England ; and that Burke himself, probably with the approval
and support of his Whig friends, drafted the petition of the
Irish Catholics which led to the passing of Gardiner's Relief Act

---

[1] Morison, *op. cit.*, pp. 131–2.
[2] In 1779 Rockingham and Shelburne had called the attention of the
House of Lords to the grievances of Ireland (*Parl. Hist.*, xx. 635, 663).

by the Irish Parliament in the same year.¹ But these measures, taken in the name of religious liberty, had not committed the Whigs in any way to support the nationalist ambitions of the Irish Volunteers. The situation in Ireland had been menacing for two years before Lord Rockingham succeeded Lord North, and it is highly probable that Rockingham came into power with the formed decision to inaugurate a new system in Ireland. Nevertheless the situation in Ireland developed so rapidly and unexpectedly that he was taken unawares in April 1782, when Eden, the Chief Secretary, came over to England and, without seeing any of the new ministers, informed the House of Commons that in his view it was imperative to concede the demands which the Volunteers had formulated in the Dungannon resolutions (15 Feb. 1782). Fox, who led the ministerialists in the House of Commons, was taken by surprise, and told the House that one at least of these resolutions, that which called for the repeal of the Declaratory Act of 1720, and consequently for the renunciation of the claim of the British Parliament to legislate for Ireland, was of the most alarming character. But twelve days after this debate the Irish House of Commons unanimously endorsed the Dungannon resolutions, in spite of the efforts of the Duke of Portland, the viceroy whom Rockingham had sent over, to avert this blow. Portland, having surveyed the situation for himself, endorsed the advice that Eden had already given.² Perhaps the danger was not so acute as it appeared to these observers. Shelburne and his friends in the Cabinet were strongly averse to the repeal of the Declaratory Act without some other acknowledgement by Ireland of 'the superintending power and supremacy' of Great Britain.³ But their Whig colleagues thought otherwise. On reflection they concluded that the Irish grievances were similar to those of the American colonists and must be recognized as reasonable. Fox, in explaining the surrender to the Commons (17 May 1782), argued that the British Parliament could not with any show of justice legislate

¹ Burke, *Correspondence*, iii. 237–8, 293.
² *Rockingham Memoirs*, ii. 471 (Duke of Portland to E. Burke, 21 April 1782) : ' If resistance or half measures are adopted, I cannot and will not answer for the consequences.'
³ *Life of Shelburne*, iii. 152 (Charlemont MSS. i. 40).

for the inhabitants of a country which it did not represent—
a country, moreover, which possessed its own local legislature.
He went on to admit that the British Parliament had in the past
made tyrannous use of its pretended power 'to establish an
impolitic monopoly in trade'.[1] In his desire to blacken the
political character of North, Fox went still farther; he openly
defended the conduct of the Volunteers in pursuing a policy of
intimidation. They had, he told the House, first been driven to
violent counsels by the impossibility of obtaining justice in any
other way for the Irish commercial interest. Having been
successful in that instance (1780) it was not wonderful that the
Volunteers should henceforth put their trust in methods of
agitation. He and his colleagues were not to be blamed if they
found themselves obliged to make propositions which might be
humiliating to the pride of Great Britain. The blame must be
laid on the last administration, which had neglected to make
a more satisfactory settlement when they had the chance of
doing so. Thus far there is little in the speech to indicate that
Fox or his party welcomed the new change of system with any
confidence for the future. But Fox expressed more generous
feelings before he closed his speech. He predicted that Ireland,
having recovered the freedom of her trade and of her parliament,
would enter on a new and brighter stage of her history, in
which the Roman Catholics would be restored to the rights of
men and citizens. He hoped, in fact, as Rockingham also hoped,
that the leaders of the Volunteer movement were Whigs of the
English pattern; and he was ready for that reason to represent
the constitutional revolution in Ireland as a victory for the Whig
cause. This was a misconception which might easily have been
corrected if the Whigs had only reflected on the attitude which
the Irish nationalists adopted towards the Catholic claim of the
parliamentary franchise. The Catholic relief legislation which
passed the Irish Parliament in this year did not include this concession. On the contrary, as Eden sarcastically wrote to Burke,
it 'anxiously excludes five-sixths of the kingdom from any share
in that free legislation which the other sixth at the same hour
declare and swear to be the indefeasible right of the people of
Ireland'.[2] It was at Pitt's command that the Irish Parliament

---

[1] Fox, *Speeches*, ii. 69 ff.　　[2] Burke, *Correspondence*, ii. 459.

made this concession in 1793 after refusing it in 1792. It was
Portland and Fitzwilliam who in 1795 endeavoured to obtain for
the Catholics the right of sitting in the Irish Parliament. On
the whole the national party of the years 1780-2 felt and behaved
as a Protestant ascendancy, as a privileged minority who would
not willingly give any share of political power to the majority.
Burke as an Irishman saw from an early date the true character
of the Grattan Parliament. But Fox and his friends, both in
1782 and in 1799, were incorrigibly prone to assume that every
Irish opponent of North or Pitt was some kind of a Whig.

Up to this point we have traced the history of the evolution,
first of the Rockingham party, and secondly of the political
creed which it bequeathed to posterity. That party had barely
come into office for the second time before personal differences
and differences of principle appeared within its ranks. To the
growth of those differences the next chapter will be devoted.
The end of them was that Burke, who had refounded the Whig
creed between 1765 and 1782, placed his talents at the disposal
of a ministry which was never Whig and by degrees grew Tory
in extreme, to found a new variety of Toryism.

II

WHIGS, NEW AND OLD, 1782-1806.

BY 1782 the long and uphill work of opposition had become depressing and distasteful to the leading men of the original Rockingham group. They were not fitted for the light skirmishing which is nine-tenths of the duty of men out of power. In 1780 one of the Cavendishes confessed to Barré the weakness of the party: 'Our body has property, &c. but we have not those powers that enable men to take the lead in public assemblies.'[1] At that date Rockingham himself had begun to fail in vigour and in resolution. To the surprise of many of his friends he entertained overtures from Lord North, and actually outlined the moderate terms on which certain of his leading supporters (though not himself) might join the administration. North was assured that he could have the services of the Dukes of Richmond, Portland, and Manchester, of Fox and Burke and Thomas Townshend. These men would be prepared to support the continuance of the war in America and to let the question of American independence stand over. They would not demand the resignation of Lord North or of any of his colleagues, excepting only the detested Sandwich. Their main demand was that North should accept some of the economical reforms in which Burke was interested. Nothing came of these conversations, since the King objected to some of the articles of alliance. But it seems clear that Rockingham desired to go out of politics, and that certain of his followers would have preferred, if Rockingham retired, to serve Lord North in the hope of making North a reputable Whig. They had discovered, as Lord John Russell remarks, that 'between Lord North and the opposition party there was little diversity of principle or opinion'.[2] Current gossip held Burke responsible for this discovery.[3] But it is much more probable that Fox

---

[1] *Life of Shelburne*, iii. 103.　　[2] Fox, *Correspondence*, i. 251.
[3] *Life of Shelburne*, iii. 101.

took the lead in 1780, as he had already done in 1779, in opening correspondence with his old chief. Whoever was responsible,
the negotiations show an ominous cleavage in the ranks of the
Opposition. Lord Rockingham made no reference to Shelburne
and to the followers of Shelburne; though it was only a year
since he and Shelburne had formed a compact under which
Rockingham was to be the head of the next Whig administration and Shelburne was to serve under Rockingham. The *casus
foederis* did not arise in 1780; but Rockingham might perhaps
have shown more consideration for the interests of his powerful
ally.

The truth is that in 1780 there existed an acute difference
between Rockingham and Shelburne. It arose out of Rockingham's passive resistance to the Yorkshire scheme and every
other scheme of parliamentary reform;[1] it was aggravated by
Burke's criticisms of Shelburne's own proposals. Shelburne, of
course, in playing the reformer, only imitated the Duke of
Richmond, Sir George Savile, and Charles James Fox. But Shelburne was unpopular, while the Whigs with whom he shared
his heresies were respected and beloved. He was unpopular
because, rightly or wrongly, he was reputed a double-dealer;
because it was supposed that he intended to succeed or supplant
Rockingham; because he behaved more as an ally than as
a dutiful member of the party. Such principles as he professed,
whether in home or in imperial politics, appeared to be derived
from Chatham rather than from any legitimate Whig source.
Shelburne may have been grossly misjudged. If so, the Whigs
committed a great folly when they broke with him in 1783.
For he was intellectually well fitted for high office; always
susceptible to new ideas, extremely well informed on the great
questions of home and foreign policy, a sagacious diplomatist,
and, above all, capable of framing a policy on broad and generous lines. It was probably a great piece of good fortune for
Great Britain and for the United States that the peace treaties
of 1783 were negotiated by Shelburne rather than by Fox.

Those who have written of the celebrated quarrel between
these two great statesmen have usually omitted to notice that
they made up their differences after 1792; and that the recon-

---

[1] *Life of Shelburne*, iii. 74, 82, 104-5.

ciliation, which was at first one of political expediency, led in
a few years to a real friendship. This fact should in itself be
sufficient to dispel the legend that Shelburne was guilty of un-
pardonable behaviour towards Fox in 1782. At that time the
two were rivals in a double sense—rivals for the honour of
arranging the peace with America, and rivals for the succession
to Lord Rockingham. Fox seems to have been quite wrong in
maintaining that the negotiations with the Americans belonged
to the province of the Foreign Secretary. He may have been
right in supposing that the method of negotiation which he
desired—that of recognizing at the outset the unconditional
independence of the colonies—was superior to Shelburne's
method of treating recognition as a favour for which some
equivalent might be demanded. But he was grossly mistaken
in supposing that Shelburne meant to trick the colonists and
his own colleagues, and that he was delaying recognition in the
hope that some change of circumstances might make recognition
an unnecessary step. Though not exactly new to office in 1782,
Fox had never before held high office or found himself responsible for taking decisions on large issues. As Secretary of
State he showed abilities and diligence which astonished even
his admirers. But his promotion turned his head. Already he
regarded himself as the heir-expectant to Lord Rockingham,
and it was a shock to him when he discovered that Shelburne
nourished the same hope. With unconscious arrogance he
assumed that Shelburne's Whiggism could not be so genuine as
his own, forgetting it would seem that he himself had voted
with the Grafton ministry and had held office under North.
Shelburne's alliance with Rockingham was comparatively
recent; but those who had studied Fox's career most closely
were of opinion that his formal adhesion to Rockingham could
not be dated earlier than 1778.[1] Fox, it is true, had already
established his place in the first rank of parliamentary orators,
and was invaluable to the party in the House of Commons.
But he had still to give proofs of a well-balanced judgement and
of capacity to lead. Living in a small and exclusive clique of

[1] Lord Holland, quoted in Fox's *Correspondence*. There is, however, a
letter of 1776 from Fox to Rockingham (*Rockingham Memoirs*, ii. 297)
which indicates a close co-operation at that date.

friends and political admirers Fox had yet to learn how he was regarded by plain men who required plain everyday virtues of their statesmen. George III was by no means an impartial critic; but a great part of his subjects would have agreed with the attitude which he adopted towards Fox in the negotiations of 1780, to which reference has been made above. 'As for Mr. Fox, if any lucrative, not ministerial, office can be pointed out for him, provided he will support the ministry, I shall have no objection to the proposition. He never had any principle, and therefore can act as his interest may direct him.'[1]

It remains, however, to account for the readiness with which a number of the Whigs accepted Fox's estimate of Shelburne and rallied to the Duke of Portland, a right-minded, well-meaning peer, who controlled the Cavendish influence as well as that of his own great clan, but was perhaps the most mediocre statesman who was ever twice Prime Minister. Shelburne too had wealth and lineage; he was a great proprietor and the model of an improving landlord. He had also qualities of heart and head not to be discerned in Portland, which earned for him the respect and even the affection of men who were consummate judges of character, men so diverse as Chatham and Franklin, Hume and Bentham, Price and Romilly. He hated injustice; he was the advocate of oppressed minorities; he was keenly interested in all projects of social or political reform which had any substance in them. In spite of a defective education, he was a man of ideas and cultivated tastes, who attracted to himself some of the leading minds of his age. On most political questions of consequence—Ireland, America, religious toleration, the prerogative, political corruption—he held the views of an orthodox Whig. And yet he was unpopular in those very circles for which he seemed to be fitted by his sympathies and principles. Part of his unpopularity was due to faults which may have been superficial accidents, the consequences of his neglected youth. He was too civil and too flattering by half. His professions of political rectitude were too insistent and too unctuous. He claimed to be frank and transparent, but his colleagues never felt that they were in his confidence. What he intended, and by what means he would

[1] Fox, *Correspondence*, i. 253.

reach his goal, they rarely discovered from his words, and not always from his actions. If he was never detected in any flagrant treachery, on the other hand he was often guilty of small concealments, small misrepresentations and small contrivances for anticipating and circumventing opposition. It would have been well for his reputation if, in the matter of the peace negotiations, he had openly stated his own claims (which were considerable) to a principal share of the responsibility. He would have raised a storm, but the storm would probably have cleared the atmosphere of the Cabinet. He was more successful than any minister before the younger Pitt in managing the King; and he managed the King by the very sensible expedient of making concessions in small matters, in order that he and his colleagues might have their way in matters of more consequence. There was no harm in this, nor was it Shelburne's fault that he was the only member of the second Rockingham Cabinet with whom the King would maintain regular communications. But it did not escape the notice of Fox that it was Shelburne who allowed the King to put Thurlow into the Cabinet as Lord Chancellor; that the effect of this arrangement was to give Shelburne Thurlow's vote in all matters on which the Cabinet was divided; and that in return Shelburne seemed quite as solicitous as the Chancellor was to save the prerogative wherever possible. These were the circumstances which led Fox to allege that Shelburne was as much the King's man as North had ever been.[1] Fox and his personal friends thought that their suspicions were more than justified when the King, on the day after the death of Rockingham, instructed Shelburne to form a new administration, and this without taking advice from any member of Rockingham's connexion. Their suspicion would have been intensified if they had known that the King's private instructions (of 1 June 1782) to the future Prime Minister enjoined him not to become the slave of the Rockingham party, as Rockingham had been, but to insist on their acceptance of his policy, and to be ' the minister placed on a broad bottom '.[2]

[1] *Grafton Memoirs*, p. 322. The growth of the quarrel between Fox and Shelburne is amply related in Fox's *Correspondence*, i. 330 ff. For the affair of Thurlow's appointment see the same authority, i. 292.

[2] *Life of Shelburne*, ii², 149.

The results of Shelburne's promotion need not be described in detail. It is enough to notice how the Whig party was affected. Fox at once resigned ; his example was followed by Burke and Sheridan, by the Duke of Portland and Lord John Cavendish. Fox had hoped that no Whigs would consent to serve under Shelburne ; but the Dukes of Richmond and Grafton, Lord Keppel and Lord Camden, Barré and Conway and Thomas Townshend refused, not, it is true, without misgivings, to share in the secession. They had no exalted opinion of their new chief, but they were not convinced that he had been guilty of disloyal conduct. He seemed to be the only possible Whig Prime Minister, and in their view anything was better than forcing George III to fall back upon Lord North and the King's friends. With their help Shelburne carried on the government until the treaties of peace had been concluded. But his Whig supporters were never easy in their new situation. They were disgusted to find that important matters were settled by Shelburne, either on his sole responsibility or in conjunction with young Pitt, his Chancellor of the Exchequer. Shelburne on his side complained that the Whig ministers did not do him justice, and chafed at the necessity of answering their complaints and pacifying their scruples. He had inherited Chatham's conception of the rights and responsibilities of a Prime Minister. He was not prepared to be the chairman of a Board of Ten and to let the highest matters be settled by a show of hands. He looked about for other allies who could give him what he needed most—a majority in the House of Commons. Through Pitt he made an overture to Fox, whose following in the Lower House was reckoned at ninety more or less. The offer showed some magnanimity, for he and his friends had been insolently reviled by Fox in Parliament, immediately after the secession, as ' men whom neither promises could bind nor principles of honour could secure ', ' who would sacrifice fifty principles for the sake of power and forget fifty promises when these were no longer necessary to their ends '.[1] Evidently Shelburne was prepared to make some sacrifice of his own feelings to remain a Whig. But the overture was rejected, on the ground that Fox could not possibly bring himself to serve under Lord

[1] Speech of 9 July 1782 (Fox's *Speeches*, ii. 75).

Shelburne. After this the only question was, Which of the two rivals for the leadership of the Whigs would succeed in coming to terms with Lord North? Fox, unhappily for his party and his reputation, proved himself the more adept of the two in this species of diplomacy. While Shelburne bullied and threatened,[1] Fox offered to receive North as a partner upon equal terms. Their bargain was in some respects comparable to that which Chatham had struck with Newcastle ; and no doubt Fox's view of the bargain was that he, like Chatham, borrowed a majority for the purpose of carrying out a policy. But North in 1783 was more punctilious than Newcastle had been in 1757. He reserved to his own party the right of blocking any proposals for parliamentary or economic reform. It is true that the allies of 1783 had a working principle on which to base their coalition. They were pledged to resist the King's system ' of governing by departments '.[2] But this was a principle which could not be publicly avowed, whereas Chatham and Newcastle had been able to combine for an object which was public property and the most popular object that they could possibly suggest—the successful prosecution of a war with France.

Into this doubtful enterprise Fox carried the Duke of Portland, who became first minister after the King had applied in vain first to Lord North and afterwards to William Pitt. Burke was also drawn in ; and, though only in the subordinate position of Paymaster-General, he was second in influence only to Fox. He had little to do with arranging the coalition, and can hardly have been satisfied to find economical reform indefinitely postponed in consideration of North's objections. ' But ', wrote one of the authors of the coalition, ' if Burke had been averse, we must have dropped all idea of the thing as he bore the greatest sway.' He assented to it as a political necessity, but without enthusiasm, believing Lord North to be a man of personal integrity and Shelburne to be capable of any baseness. ' If Lord Shelburne was not a Catiline or Borgia in morals, it must not be ascribed to anything but his understanding.' We may safely ascribe to Burke's inspiration the celebrated India

[1] The threatening was done by Dundas acting as Shelburne's intermediary ; Fox's *Correspondence*, ii. 31-6.
[2] Fox's *Correspondence*, ii. 37-8.

Bills which were to supply the occasion of the King's fiercest quarrel with the Whigs, although it must remain uncertain how much of the contents of the bills should be ascribed to him.[1] India had been for some little time the special object of his interests ; he had written in 1783 two reports for a Select Committee on the administration of justice in Bengal, and these had acquainted him with some of the darker features of the Company's rule. It became his ambition, as he said in his speech of 1 December 1783, to ensure that India should be guarded against future robberies and oppressions, and he treated the whole subject of the first bill—the parliamentary commission of seven—as a mere detail of the scheme. As it happened, the debates and intrigues which were started by these bills centred on this detail. The second bill, however, did not escape the attention of William Pitt, and one of its clauses supplied him with the famous principle that 'schemes of conquest and extension of dominion in India are measures repugnant to the wish, the honour, and the policy of this nation'.[2] So far as India was concerned, all parties in England—the Whigs, the Tories, and the shareholders of the Company—were agreed in deprecating territorial conquests. But for the Whigs this rule was, as we shall see hereafter, only the application to a particular case of the wider principle that any further extension of the Empire was undesirable.

There are some other principles latent in the second bill

---

[1] There is a note from Mr. A. Pigot to Burke asking the latter ' to send me . . . so much of the bill, or instructions for the bill, as you have in the state in which it is'. This is endorsed in Burke's handwriting : ' From Mr. Pigot, who finished the India Bill from my drafts' (Burke's *Correspondence*, iii. 22). There were two bills : (1) ' For vesting the affairs of the East India Company in the Hands of Certain Commissioners '; (2) ' For the better Government of the Territorial Possessions and Dependencies of India '. Did Burke draw one, or both? Sir G. C. Lewis quotes Nicholl's *Recollections of the Reign of George III* (1820) for the statement of the law officers, Lee and Mansfield, that Burke prepared all the essential parts of the scheme.

[2] Pitt's India Act, 1784 (24 Geo. III, c. xxv). In the bill of 1783 it is provided, in more matter of fact language, that no native state shall be entered or invaded in a hostile or offensive manner unless it has attacked or is about to attack the territories of the Company ; also that no acquisitions of territory be made without the consent of the commissioners.

which illustrate the Whig political theory of that time. It was uniformly contended by Warren Hastings that British India would never be efficiently governed unless the Governor-General were invested with large discretionary powers. The one thing necessary was to select for this post a man of ' inflexible integrity ' and ' a judgment insusceptible of the bias of foreign suggestion ' and to give to that man a free hand.[1] To the Whigs it was inconceivable that an individual corresponding to this description should be found ; such powers carrying such temptations must infallibly corrupt the holder of them. The bill of 1783 provides that the Governor-General shall have no power of acting apart from the Council of Four with which he has been saddled by North's Regulating Act, and the Council shall never delegate its powers to the Governor-General. Furthermore, it provides that the Governor-General in Council shall have no discretionary power to override the instructions issued from home, whether by the Court of Directors or by the parliamentary commissioners. It is taken for granted that all considerations of efficiency in the government of British India must be subordinated to the paramount consideration of protecting native rulers from spoliation and securing the happiness of the subjects of British India.[2] The Whigs deserve all honour for insisting upon the obligations and responsibilities which this country had assumed by virtue of its acquisitions of Indian territories. Nothing could be more praiseworthy than their intention that the new system for India should be so framed as to exclude the possibilities of corruption and injustice. But it is extraordinary that they should put their reliance blindly in a strict centralization. The recent history of India had shown what mischief might be caused by mistaken orders from home and by the wilful abuse, for factious ends, of the checks which

---

[1] *Memoirs* (of 1786) *Relative to the State of India*, quoted in Muir's *Making of British India*, No. 60.

[2] See Fox's letter of 1783, quoted in *Correspondence*, ii. 219 : ' I never did act more upon principle than at this moment. . . . I have done no more than I was bound to do, in risking my power and that of my friends when the happiness of so many millions is at stake.' Also *Speeches*, ii. 239 : 'What is the end of all government ? Certainly the happiness of the governed. Others may hold other opinions, but this is mine and I proclaim it.'

the Council could impose upon the Governor-General.   At best
Lord North's scheme had provided a cumbrous and dilatory
executive at Fort William.   Pitt, who was by no means unsympathetic to the humanitarian aims of Burke and Fox, found
it advisable to increase the personal power of the Governor-
General in 1784 by reducing his councillors from four to three.
The India Act of 1793 [1] went farther still, empowering the
Governor-General to override his Council whenever he considered that the safety of British India was at stake.

It is generally believed that, in preparing the bill of 1783,
the Whigs were guided by Philip Francis.   He had returned
from India late in 1781, eager to prosecute his vendetta against
Warren Hastings, eager also to vindicate the constitutional
merits of North's conciliar system, which had enabled him for
nearly two years (1774–6) to balk the policy of the Governor-
General.   Before his return he had corresponded with Burke
on Indian affairs.   In 1785 he was taken into counsel by Burke
and Fox with reference to the impeachment of Warren Hastings.
But there is no evidence to connect him with ministers in 1783,
though there is a probability that the views of so staunch a
Whig would not be ignored on a subject with which Francis
was well acquainted.   Rightly or wrongly, Burke had decided
as early as 1780 that Hastings was a criminal and an oppressor.
He might apply to Francis for confirmatory evidence; but his
general view of the case was founded upon evidence obtained
by a Select Committee of the House of Commons which sat
while Francis was still in India.   To us it may seem amazing
that men of honour should associate with themselves a personal
enemy of Hastings to help in preparing the indictment.   Unfortunately for the party, the management of the process was left
too much in the hands of Burke.   Fox, at the very outset, gave
the timely warning that no charge ought to be preferred which
it was impossible to prove.[2]   Burke, however, who started to prepare the indictment with the truly preposterous conviction that
a great part of Hastings's public acts could only be explained
as the consequence of 'a corrupt, habitual, evil intention', was
in no mood to accept criticism of his evidence from friend or
foe; nor is there evidence that his friends made serious efforts

[1] 33 Geo. III, c. xxxii.   [2] Burke, *Correspondence*, iii. 38.

to restrain him.   Perhaps they felt, as Burke felt, that the verdict
of the Lords was a foregone conclusion,[1] that Hastings was in
no danger of losing life or liberty or status, and that on these
grounds there was no obligation to be scrupulously careful in
formulating the charges against a man whom they believed to be
utterly unscrupulous.   This is an explanation of their conduct ;
it is no defence.   If the indictment had been drafted by Pitt or
Wilberforce it would have been less sensational, but it would
probably have convinced the Lords.   There was prima facie
evidence that the accused had broken the law by accepting
presents ; also that in certain cases, notably those of Chait Singh
and the Begums of Oudh, he had descended to methods of
coercion or punishment which would have been venial if judged
by Eastern standards of morality and statecraft.   The real
question at issue was whether Oriental methods of government
were to be tolerated in British India for the future.   On this
question the Whigs, with the passive assistance of the Government, converted the public to their own view ; they did not
convince the House of Lords that Hastings ought to be treated
as a criminal simply because he had failed to emancipate himself
from the bad traditions which he found in being when he began
his Indian career.   How far they were responsible for the extraordinary delays of the impeachment is still uncertain.   One
thing alone is clear, that the speeches for the prosecution,
lengthy as they were, consumed a very small part of the time—
one hundred and forty-five days—which was devoted to the
hearing of the case.

We have been led, in discussing the Whig attitude on India,
far beyond the date at which the India Bills were wrecked by
the King's *coup d'état* of December 1783.   The seemingly
irresistible Coalition turned out of office on the strength of
an adverse vote in the House of Lords, a vote obtained by an
unprecedented appeal from the King to the fears and hopes of
wavering peers ; the address from the House of Commons
praying the King not to prorogue or dissolve Parliament ; the
dogged struggle of the new ministry in the Commons against
superior forces ; the general election of 1784, in which the abuse

---

[1] *Op. cit.*, iii. 39 : ' We bring before a bribed tribunal a prejudged cause '—
a characteristic exaggeration.

of the King's influence in the Lords was apparently approved by the constituencies; all these events have been described repeatedly. The development of the drama in the two Houses need not detain us; but the collapse of the Coalition at the hustings has been recently illustrated by the publication of the Robinson Papers, which reveal the plans and methods of Pitt's election agents. John Robinson, an experienced Treasury official, whose knowledge of the constituencies was extensive and minute, forecasted that his party could not hope much from the English counties; in the boroughs which were classed as open they might gain twenty-eight seats; but their main hopes would be the rotten boroughs of England and the constituencies of Wales and Scotland.[1] The total number of seats that might probably be secured he put at 369. He told Pitt and Dundas that the sum required for election purposes in England might be £193,500, and he indicated in explanatory lists of sects and patrons the various means of influence that were to be employed. Some patrons would expect cash, others office; but in many cases it would be necessary for Mr. Pitt or his henchman to open up 'communications' and to find out precisely what the vendor desired. Some, like Sir James Lowther and Mr. Edward Eliot, desired peerages and got them after the election, for placing whole blocks of seats at the disposal of the minister. Of the seats which were nakedly for sale fifty-six were purchased by ministerialist candidates, with the help of Robinson and his colleague George Rose; the prices ranged from £1,500 to £3,000 a seat; and to judge from Robinson's estimates the sum spent on constituencies of this class must have been near £130,000.[2] For the purpose of bribery in constituencies which were reputed to be open Robinson submitted an estimate of £35,000.[3] Unfortunately we have no balance sheet showing the actual as compared with the estimated expenditure. Nor do we know in what proportions the King, the ministers, and the Treasury contributed to the election fund, though we have

---

[1] *Parliamentary Papers of John Robinson* (ed. Laprade, 1922), pp. 66–105. The figures given above are obtained by adding together the two classes of seats which Robinson labels 'Pro' and 'Hopeful'.

[2] He allowed for an expenditure of £117,500 on fifty seats.

[3] *Op. cit.*, pp. 106 ff.

evidence that help was forthcoming from each of these several sources.[1]

Such were the methods by which the Coalition was overthrown. It went to the elections with a strength of 305 members, and of these 160 were defeated. Lord North was one of the survivors, and he remained a member of the Opposition in the lower house until 1791, when he removed, on his father's death, to the House of Lords, and practically disappeared from politics. In 1788 he was believed to have no more than seventeen adherents in the Commons;[2] and in 1789, when the Whigs rather prematurely decided who should have office in their next administration, the name of Lord North was omitted.[3] Thus the Whigs were able, soon after their *débâcle*, to rid themselves of this embarrassing connexion ; from time to time they united with North, as for instance in attacking Pitt's commercial concessions to Ireland (12 May 1785) and in resisting the limitation of the powers of the Prince of Wales when acting as a Regent (16 Dec. 1788). On the first of these occasions 155 persons voted against the Government; on the second 204, but in each case the minority must have been swollen by the temporary support whom a Whip would have denoted in the language of the day as ' hopeful ' or ' doubtful ', something midway between the ' pros ' and the ' cons '. On 8 June 1784, in a crucial debate on the Westminster scrutiny, which was a preliminary trial of strength between Ministers and Opposition, the latter numbered 117. On 12 February 1787, in a debate on the commercial treaty with France, the Opposition were 118 strong. With such a body of support, though not much more than one-fourth of the whole House, Fox was still an opponent whom the Government could not safely despise.

But in 1790, with the breach between Burke and Sheridan on the subject of the French Revolution, there appeared the first symptom of the approaching cleavage between the new and the old Whigs (Feb. 1790) ; a quarrel between Burke and Fox himself was only postponed by the strength of their private friendship. Late in the same year Burke published his *Reflections on the French Revolution*, in which he not only censured the

---

[1] Laprade in *E. H. R.*, xxxi, pp. 224 ff.   [2] *D. N. B.*

[3] Fox's *Correspondence*, iv. 283–5.

leaders of the French movement as enemies of the Church, of
private property, and of the essential principles of political
society, but also criticized the Revolution Club for applaud-
ing the French programme of reform. The Revolution Club,
founded as a Whig society to defend the principles of 1688,
was not in any way the mouthpiece of official Whig opinion,
but it represented accurately enough the sentiments of the
Nonconformists and the Whig left wing. Burke was immediately
answered in print by James Mackintosh, in those days an
impecunious physician, an ardent disciple of Horne Tooke, but
well-fitted by his education and intellect to answer Burke on
high questions. Fox refrained from replying to the *Reflections*,
but broke his silence in April 1791, when Burke had attacked the
new French constitution in another less celebrated pamphlet;[1]
and on this occasion Burke was shouted down by his own party
when he rose after Fox; and it became clear that there was
a settled design among certain Whigs to prevent him from
discussing the French Revolution in the House. As that subject
almost monopolized Burke's mind at that time, the decision
taken amounted to a sentence of excommunication, and inter-
preting it in that sense he renounced his friendship with Fox in
the course of the debate of 6 May on the Quebec Bill.

Burke had been treated with gross discourtesy, though not
by Fox. On the other hand, he had committed himself to some
principles which his old party could neither accept nor tolerate
without revising what they believed to be their traditional creed ;
and there was perhaps a feeling even in those days of loose
discipline that no man who challenged persistently the decisions
of his party-leader could be allowed to remain a member of the
party. Fox's chief newspaper, the *Morning Chronicle*, took
it for granted that Burke ought to resign his seat, and Windham
was the only Whig who openly took sides with Burke.

Burke did not resign his seat in Parliament, and he retaliated
on his old associates in the *Appeal from the New to the Old
Whigs* (1791), a closely reasoned demonstration that his opponents had deserted the historic faith of Whiggism in some
essential particulars. He attributed to the general body of the
Whigs three propositions concerning sovereignty which he

---

[1] *Letter to a Member of the National Assembly* (1791).

stigmatized as radically false.   He accused them of holding that sovereignty resides at all times in the general body of the people and is inalienable.   He accused them of admitting that a king may be deposed by his people, not only for gross misconduct, but even when no misconduct can be proved against him. Finally he accused them of allowing to the people the right of destroying, at their will and pleasure, the whole of the old forms of government, and of setting up a new government or remaining without any government at all.

It was easy to show the fatal consequences of these doctrines, and it was not difficult to show that they were expressly affirmed or implicitly assumed in such revolutionary manifestos as Paine's *Rights of Man*, or in the *obiter dicta* of Dr. Price and other Nonconformist Radicals.   But to attribute them to Fox or any of his leading followers in Parliament was wholly unjust.

Burke, however, soon found sympathizers, and this not only among the unbending Tories who looked to Mr. Jenkinson rather than to Mr. Pitt for a definition of their policy, so long as Pitt regarded with disfavour the invectives of Burke against the new French constitution and its authors.   But Lord Camden assured Burke that he concurred in the whole argument of the *Appeal* from the beginning to the end; [1] and Lord Fitzwilliam sent his thanks ' for the authorities you give me for the doctrines I have sworn by long and long since'. [2]   Camden was a member of Pitt's Cabinet, but still a Whig, and one of the main links that still connected Pitt with Whiggism.   Fitzwilliam, though more devoted to fox-hunting than politics, represented exactly the sentiments and principles of his uncle, Rockingham.   Others, like Portland, who were eventually to be convinced, kept silence in 1791 out of loyalty to Fox.   But such men were soon called upon to decide whether they would follow Burke or Fox in the gravest question of foreign policy; whether, with Burke, they would regard revolutionary France as the natural leader of all democratic factions, as a power pledged to destroy all European treaties, and bound by its own interests to disturb and distract all other governments; [3] or whether, with Fox, they should

[1] Burke, *Correspondence*, iii. 228 (Letter of 5 Aug. 1791).
[2] *Op. cit.*, iii. 334 (Letter of 18 Sept. 1791).
[3] See Burke's *Thoughts on French Affairs*, prepared in December 1791 for submission to the ministry, posthumously published in 1797.

welcome the new Republic as an essentially pacific and liberal
state, driven to aggression only by the ill will and threats of the
illiberal governments of Europe.

The decision had to be taken in 1792, under circumstances
which are fully related by Lord Malmesbury, who was at that
time a member of the Portland caucus. In June Burke was
emphatic in denouncing Fox's recent behaviour and warned the
caucus that the times required 'a union of all the abilities, all
the weight, and all the wealth of the country'. Pitt had come
to the same conclusion as Burke and was offering to take in the
Portland Whigs on liberal terms, allowing to them four places
in the Cabinet and the lord-lieutenancy of Ireland. Portland
was favourably inclined to the plan, if Fox could be brought
into it with an office befitting the Whig leader in the lower
house. But the followers of Portland were uneasy. As one of
them puts it, they differed from Pitt on most current questions,
and from Fox on all.[1] Even Portland himself was of the opinion
that Fox would never be reliable unless he could be detached
from his new friends, and particularly from Grey and Lambton.
To increase the difficulties of the situation Fox insisted that, if
the Whigs were to join with Pitt, they must join on equal terms
and under a neutral prime minister. Fox professed reluctance
to take office as Pitt's colleague, even on these terms. But he
was incensed when Pitt, who had proposed to give Fox the
Foreign Office, suddenly announced that his friends would not
agree to the inclusion of Fox in the arrangements. His dis-
satisfaction with the policy of the Government appears to have
been exacerbated by the belief that Pitt was essentially treacherous.
In this ominous frame of mind he came to the winter session of
1792, inclined, as he himself confessed, to oppose almost any
policy that his great rival might propose. Two days before the
debate on the Address he dined with Portland (Dec. 11) and
some leading members of the party to discuss the line of action,
especially with reference to a recent proclamation which called
up part of the militia. All present, except Fox, agreed that it
was a reasonable precaution, having regard to the French decree
about the Scheldt. But Fox denounced the militia proclamation

---

[1] *Malmesbury Diaries*, ii. 459 ff. The questions referred to are Parliamentary Reform, the Slave Trade, the Test Act, relations with France.

as a trick, and refused to treat the Scheldt as a *casus belli*. Accordingly on 13 December he moved an amendment to the Address and found himself supported by no more than fifty members. Of these fifty, says Lord Malmesbury, twenty-one were reformers, an equal number were men who stood by Fox less because they liked his amendment than from personal friendship and the desire to keep him as a leader; the remainder were members for Lord Lansdowne's boroughs; and it was noticed that Lord Lansdowne (Shelburne) spoke forcibly against the Address in the House of Lords. This was the first step towards a *rapprochement* between Fox and Lansdowne. But the amendment was also the first step towards an open breach between Fox and the old Whigs.

The Duke of Portland delayed the breach as long as possible, and much longer than was agreeable to Burke and Windham and Lord Loughborough.[1] But by the beginning of 1794 the two sections of the Whigs were speaking on different sides in both the Houses, not only when the war policy was in question, but even on such subjects as the Scottish trials for treason. There had been a time when the sentences on Muir and Palmer would have moved every Whig of any shade to righteous indignation. But the Portland Whigs had come to the view that Pitt must be supported at all costs against the French peril and against domestic clubs or factions. On 7 July 1794 they at length concluded their treaty of coalition with Pitt,[2] the Duke of Portland becoming Home Secretary, Lord Fitzwilliam President of the Council, Earl Spencer Privy Seal, and Windham Secretary at War. It was a firm alliance which outlasted Pitt's administration. The Portland Whigs and the New Whigs did not come together again until 1806.

The small group which was led by Fox remained fairly constant in numbers and in composition. In the House of Lords it had the services of some acute debaters, Lauderdale, Stanhope, the Duke of Bedford, and Lord Lansdowne. In the House of Commons Fox, Sheridan, and Grey were their only orators of note. The latter came into Parliament in 1786 as one of the

---

[1] *Malmesbury Diaries,* ii. 481, 487.

[2] The precise date is given in a letter from Pitt to Lord Liverpool, announcing the coalition (Add. MS. 38192, fo. 95).

members for Northumberland, first distinguished himself in
the debates on Oczakow in 1791, and from 1792 stood out as the
leader of the little band of Whig reformers, which included
Lord John Russell (afterwards sixth Duke of Bedford), William
Lambton (the father of the first Lord Durham), and Samuel
Whitbread.   In 1796 the party secured a notable recruit in the
person of George Tierney, but it had little attraction for the
rising politicians of the war period ; and George Canning, who
was educated in the Whig tradition, enlisted under Pitt in 1793,
when the time came for offering his allegiance to one or other
parties.

Occasionally the party secured temporary allies.   In 1795,
when Wilberforce was disappointed in his efforts for suppressing
the slave traffic, he twice gave his support to Whig peace
motions, with the result that the voting strength of the minority
leaped up to eighty-six.[1]   In 1797 no less than ninety-one members voted for Grey's scheme of parliamentary reform—a subject
on which many ministerialists had cause to feel compunction,
when they remembered the pledges which they and Pitt had
given on this subject in the past.   But these successes were not
symptoms of any real growth of the new Whig party.   Their
favourite topics were the iniquities of the war policy, the untrust-
worthiness of the allies, the violence done to the liberties of the
subject by Pitt's coercive legislation.   These topics became stale
and tedious with repetition.

It would be purposeless to follow year by year the intermittent and unprofitable conflicts of Fox and his friends with
Pitt's majority.   That majority was not always solid and un-
shakable before 1793.   During the years of peace Pitt was in an
ambiguous position—a Whig minister who was forced to rely
largely upon Tory colleagues and Tory votes ; and he was
obliged to pay great attention to the views of Dundas (who
controlled Scotland and the East India Company) and of
Jenkinson, the manager of the compact group of King's friends.
In 1784 and 1785 he found himself deserted by his own majority
when he revived his father's plans of parliamentary reform ; and

---

[1] See for this temporary schism between Wilberforce and Pitt the *Life of
Wilberforce*, ii. 90 ff.   They were reconciled in 1796, and the Whigs only
secured fifty votes for their peace motion of that year.

in the second of these years he only saved his measure of relief
for the commercial interest in Ireland by accepting amendments
which restricted Irish trade with the colonies and with India.
But as the European situation became blacker the parliamentary
difficulties of his administration diminished, and he had little to
fear in either House so long as his war measures were approved.
It is hardly wonderful that the Whigs fell into the habit of
insinuating that Pitt prolonged the war in order to perpetuate
his own ascendancy; or that by 1797 they were reduced to
a condition of despair and apathy on finding that hopes of
peace were more remote than ever before.

Much time and ingenuity were devoted by the Whigs to the
business of impugning the motives and the efficiency of the men
in power.   But they were at a disadvantage for several reasons.
Like all critics of all war ministries, they depended for their
information chiefly on the men whom they were criticizing. Until
their reconciliation with Lord Lansdowne (Shelburne), which
began in 1795,[1] the Whigs had no adviser who possessed a considerable knowledge of European politics.   Both in the debates
on the Eden Commercial Treaty with France (1787) and in the
Oczakow crisis of 1791 the Whigs had shown themselves sur-
prisingly ill informed; in the second of these cases they had
committed the folly of sending an unofficial envoy to St. Peters-
burg and of framing his instructions on the hypothesis that
Russia was 'a rising naval power' whose navy might be useful
to us in the event of another war with France.[2]   Last, but not
least, they were encumbered with a general belief that foreign
alliances, like English party combinations, could never be
honourable or useful unless they were founded on a basis of
abstract principles.

The Whigs in fact were doctrinaires in matters of foreign
policy, and Fox succeeded in creating a tradition that no policy
could be respectable unless it was inspired principally by considerations of morality or public law.   In his view the wars

[1] Fox's *Correspondence*, iii. 112 (Fox to Lord Holland 16 June 1795):
'We have so far explained ourselves to one another that we agreed, if any
opening came from the Court to either of us, that we would mutually
communicate and consult.'

[2] See *Dropmore Papers*, ii. 114, 142, 211 ; Fox's *Correspondence*, ii.
383-7.

with Revolutionary France had originated with an iniquitous compact between Prussia and Austria to destroy the hard-won liberties of the French ; and in proof of this theory he was accustomed to quote the indefensible and entirely unauthorized proclamation of the Duke of Brunswick (of 25 July 1792). He took it for granted that Pitt was either the dupe or the accomplice of the two ' despotic powers '. He assumed that no republic could possibly be unenlightened enough to embark upon wars of aggression and conquest. And he passed to the further assumption that the Dutch Republic could not be so foolish as to think itself in danger from the ambition of the French Republic. When France accepted the rule of a First Consul, Fox was quick to change his ground. The position of a usurper must be so precarious that he would not dare to wage a war of aggression, injurious to the pockets and offensive to the moral rectitude of his republican subjects. It was a strange doctrine to be held by a statesman who, until 1789, had argued that the Bourbon monarchy, however insecurely rooted, always would be the most dangerous enemy of England. As the Treaty of Pillnitz receded into the past, and as it became evident that continental coalitions were only efficient when held together by British gold and British diplomacy, Fox came to the conclusion that Pitt was the arch enemy of European peace. In a speech of 30 December 1796 he argued that this country was really fighting for colonies and commerce. Was it not ridiculous to suppose that we had combined with the despoilers of Poland merely to prevent a French annexation of Belgium ? On 3 February 1800 he maintained that it was rank hypocrisy to pretend that the French were more criminal, in the eyes of public law, than the Austrian Emperor who had accepted Venice as a gift from Buonaparte, or the Tsar who had appropriated Malta and had intimidated Denmark. One might almost say that he was determined to deny to his own country the right of self-defence.

What then was the secret of the spell which Fox cast over his contemporaries and of the veneration in which he was held by at least two generations of Whigs? He was not great as a man of affairs. As a leader of his party he was indolent. His mind was critical rather than constructive ; and his speeches, unequalled as exhibitions of dialectic, are wanting in the systematic theory of social organization which gives solidity and consistency to every speech and every pamphlet of Edmund Burke. Fox gave the best of himself to the House of Commons, and it is surprising how little is revealed in his familiar letters that we did not know already from his speeches. Perhaps the explanation of his influence is that he represented the noble illusions and aspirations of the century in which he grew to manhood. He believed that the individual, when uncorrupted by vicious government, or by the bad traditions of the society in which he lives, is by the very law of his nature just, reasonable, benevolent, pacific. He believed further that men, being endowed by nature with these virtues, should be left as much at liberty as possible to pursue their own interests in their own fashion; that in a state of freedom truth would always prevail over folly, passion, and deceit, and men would always realize that true happiness is not to be secured by destroying the happiness of their fellows. It was unthinkable that one free nation would oppress another, just as it was unthinkable that any right-minded individual would pick the pocket of his neighbour. Those who held such views assumed too readily that the virtues taught by the Christian religion were inherent in the natural man. Burke was wiser, because he had studied human nature more closely, because he had noted the centrifugal, aggressive, combative instincts of the natural man. But it is always pleasant to imagine that the golden age is the natural and normal state, to which society can return simply by casting away the whole apparatus of corrective and formative institutions. If Fox had ever thrown his ideas about human nature and society into a systematic form, the large and dubious assumptions of his optimism would have been obvious to his hearers. But these ideas, when revealed by hints and suggestions piecemeal and incidentally to a political argument, threw a golden haze over his main argument. They were familiar ideas, the commonplaces of the *philosophes*; but in the mouth of a consummate orator and man of affairs they acquired a new significance and became more plausible.

On two great themes, however, Fox was comparatively systematic.' Again and again in his speeches he discusses and defines the liberties of the individual and the rights of a free people. Here, if anywhere, are his positive contributions to Whig doctrine, and it is necessary to consider what he actually contributed.

It is evident from his speeches on the war with France that he had paid some attention to some of the theories of international law. In 1794 he quoted Vattel to the House of Commons as the most eminent writer in that science with whom he was acquainted, and the sum of what he has to say about the rights of free states is to be found in a few passages of Vattel. Nations, says Vattel, are naturally equal, subject to the same obligations, possessing the same rights; a small republic is just as much a sovereign state as the most powerful kingdom (Préliminaires, § 18).[1] When two nations are at war, all the others, so far as they are not bound by treaties, are free to remain neutral; it would be a gross infraction of their independence if one of the belligerents should apply pressure to make them abandon their neutrality (Bk. III, § 106).[2] Every nation has the right to adopt whatever constitution seems good to it, to make reforms, to change its constitution and even to depose its king; in proof whereof Vattel cites the example of the English nation in 1688. No foreign nation has any right to interfere in the government of an independent state; for the right of self-government is a corollary of independence. Neither may one nation attempt to impose by force upon another a better civilization, a better religion, or even a better code of morals. Grotius was wholly wrong when he alleged that a sovereign may justly take up arms to punish nations which are guilty of enormous crimes against the law of nature (Bk. I, § 32, Bk. II, §§ 7, 54-7, 196-7). The only just causes for which one state may declare war upon another are to defend itself, to obtain compensation for an injury, or to exact vengeance for a wrong which is irre-

[1] Cf. Fox, Speech of 24 March 1795 (with reference to Genoa and Switzerland) : ' It is only to the weak and defenceless that we talk big ; to the great and powerful we apologize and agree to pay for all the injustice we have done them.'

[2] Cf. Fox, *op. cit.*: ' If any one principle in the law of nations be more clearly and generally acknowledged than another, it is that of a right in every nation, which no treaty obliges to the contrary, to preserve a complete neutrality.'

parable (Bk. II, § 28),[1] or to help an ally when the *casus foederis* arises without injustice on his part (Bk. III, § 88).[1]

It is significant that Fox, in his references to international affairs, ignores entirely one side of Vattel's teaching which makes a special appeal to modern consciences. This is the doctrine that all nations are members of a great society, established by nature herself, and by virtue of this union are bound to co-operate with one another *pour se perfectionner, elles et leur état*; so that their reciprocal obligations, one to another, are by no means entirely negative. It is the duty of each not merely to respect the liberty of all the rest, but to render to its fellow members what services it can offer without neglecting its duty to its own citizens; and all have a common duty to discharge in repressing the attempts of any nation to violate the laws of the society (Préliminaires, §§ 11 ff.). The Society of Nations had no meaning for Fox, because he was wedded to the traditional English ideal of isolation and detachment. In fact he deprecated the supposition that England could have interests in common with any powers which had not accepted the English ideal of free constitutional government. It might be worth her while to defend constitutional liberty upon the Continent, in Holland, for example, in Switzerland, or even in France. But a Concert of Europe, in which despotic monarchies would necessarily predominate, seemed to Fox a detestable prospect; and his successors used precisely the same language when they found Great Britain more or less implicated, through the policy of Castlereagh, in a European Concert.

On the liberties of the individual Fox had no need to consult a foreign text-book. His mind was saturated with the doctrines

---

[1] Parallel passages in Fox's speeches are—(1) 21 January 1794 : 'However we may abhor the conduct of Frenchmen towards Frenchmen, whatever indignation we may feel against crimes at which humanity shudders, the hatred of vice is no just cause of war between nations'; (2) 1 February 1793 : 'The general maxim of policy always is that the crimes perpetrated in one independent state are not cognizable by another'; (3) 1 February 1793 : 'Admitting that the French are all atheists, are we going to war with them in order to propagate the Christian religion by means contrary to the precepts of Christ?'; (4) 12 February 1793 : 'War should never be undertaken when peace can be maintained without breach of public faith, injury to national honour, or hazard of future security.'.

of Locke and Sidney; he showed a sturdy confidence in the established rules of law and in the respect of Englishmen of every class for the decisions of the court. He would not admit that any danger from abroad, or any new political agitations in this country, could justify new restrictions upon the freedom of speech and freedom of association. ‘If any doctrines are published tending to subvert the Constitution in Church and State, you may have cognizance of the fact in a court of law.’[1] In resisting the first of Pitt's acts for the suspension of the Habeas Corpus Act he warned the House of Commons that,

‘The evil they were pretending to remedy was less than the one they were going to inflict by the remedy itself. We were going to give up the very best part of our constitution, and that which every man was entitled to do, and which he was now doing—delivering the sentiments of his heart upon the affairs of government, for the benefit of the public—would be at an end at once.’[2]

In 1795 he joined issue with the Government on a clause of the Treasonable Practices Bill, which made it a transportable offence to publish designs for putting restraint upon the King or levying war against him. The penalty seemed to him excessive and outrageous, an attempt to burke any discussion of proposals for a change in the constitution.

‘If ministers were determined by means of the corrupt influence they possessed in the two Houses of Parliament to pass the bill, in direct opposition to the declared sense of a great majority of the nation . . . if his opinion were asked by the people as to their obedience, he should tell them that it was no longer a question of moral obligation and duty, but of prudence.’

Even at this date he was still prepared to admit that certain restrictions on freedom of speech were inevitable in a free government. But on 23 May 1797 he used language which suggests that he would deprecate almost any kind of restriction.

‘Do you think that you have gained a proselyte where you silence a declaimer? No: you have only, by preventing the declaration of grievances in a constitutional manner, forced men to more pernicious modes of coming at relief. In proportion as opinions are open they are innocent and harmless. Opinions become dangerous to a state

[1] Speech of 13 December 1792.
[2] Speech of 16 May 1794.

only when persecution makes it necessary for the people to communicate their ideas under the seal of secrecy.'

Whether this robust complacency was justified in the circumstances of the time—this speech was delivered during the mutiny at the Nore—must remain an open question. But it was an attitude which the political heirs of Fox approved and practised in quieter times with good effect. It never commended itself to the right wing of the Whig party, whose views are illustrated by the policy of George Grenville in dealing with Wilkes, and by that of William Lord Grenville in 1819. The right wing were always a majority. But the views of the left wing, right or wrong, have had the greater influence in shaping British history; for to the left wing we owe, for good or ill, such changes as the Whigs effected in the spirit and the forms of the working constitution.

III

RADICALISM AND REFORM, 1769–1792

THE age of Grey and Peel begins in the eighteenth century, for Grey was born in 1764 and Peel in 1788. The political ideas of both statesmen were largely inherited from that century ; for Grey served his parliamentary apprenticeship under Charles James Fox, and the young Peel grew up in a circle which idolized William Pitt. The two great legislative measures with which the names of Grey and Peel will always be associated, the Reform Act of 1832 and the Repeal of the Corn Laws in 1846, represent the triumph of eighteenth-century ideas. Therefore, in dealing with the two political generations which are represented by these statesmen, we cannot avoid paying some attention to that most fruitful and formative century, the age of Montesquieu and Beccaria and Rousseau, of Priestley and Bentham and William Godwin. Whoever reads, for example, the reformist literature of the years 1815–32, or the discussions of fiscal policy in Parliament in the same period, will be at once impressed with the stale and threadbare presentation of the arguments on both sides of the question. The orators and the pamphleteers alike are oppressed by recollections of what had been said on the same subject years before.

In this chapter I propose to outline the history of the idea of parliamentary reform, up to the time when that idea was adopted by the Whigs as a point in their party programme. Such an outline explains much that would otherwise be obscure in the Act of 1832 — a most curious compromise between old theories and new conditions of existence. In this legislation the legacy from the past is the more remarkable because it was offered to, and was eagerly accepted by, a popular party which stood for a new and revolutionary ideal of government. When the extension of the franchise was first mooted, the grand argument was that Parliament ought to be, above all, a ' barrier against corruption ', a brake to check the vicious propensities of the Crown, its ministers, and the landed aristocracy. But in the age after

Waterloo the tendency of reformers was to think of Parliame
as a more constructive force, as the grand artificer of natior
life, as representing the collective conscience and the spokesman
of the general will. No doubt it was the fear of giving too much
rein to this idealism that led the Whigs to limit the elective
franchise as they did. There is no reason to wonder at their
attitude. But their panacea would hardly have served its purpose, but for the fact that the general lines of their Reform Bill
had the support of great historic names, above all of Chatham,
of Chatham's son, of Charles James Fox, and of Lord Grey.
Under the spell of traditions old remedies were assumed to be
adequate for the healing of a new malaise; or at least this assumption was accepted by the great majority of those who
desired any kind of parliamentary reform.

The Nonconformist Pamphleteers

But in the eighteenth century the views of the two Pitts and
Fox were by no means the only views on parliamentary reform
which had powerful support. The Pitts and Fox desired above
all to diminish the number of close constituencies, and stopped
short of discussing the abstract question, who ought to have the
right of voting at elections? But this question was raised and
very acutely argued by thinkers who derived their fundamental
principles partly from the sects of the Commonwealth period,
partly from such foreign writers as Beccaria and Rousseau.
Arguing in favour of manhood suffrage, with some trifling
exceptions, they arrived at the principle, ' that a majority of men
told by the head are to be considered as the people, and that as
such their will is to be law '.[1] Among these thinkers, who were
largely dissenters of the old stock, Joseph Priestley, Richard
Price, and (longe impar but widely read) the Nonconformist
schoolmaster James Burgh, of Newington Green, the author of
three volumes of Political Disquisitions (1774–5),[2] which supplied a whole armoury of useful facts to contemporary critics of
the British constitution. The influence of these men is not to

---

[1] Burke, Appeal from the New to the Old Whigs (ed. Raffety), p. 100.

[2] This work was reprinted at Philadelphia in 1775; the third volume contains a list of those who ' encouraged ' the American publisher; in this list
occurs the names of George Washington and Thomas Jefferson.

be measured wholly by the circulation of their books and pamphlets. They had influential friends in politics who by no means despised the value of such allies. They had also considerable opportunities of moulding opinion within their own religious societies. Some of them preached political sermons. Some of them taught in those Nonconformist academies which supplied a higher education both for theological students and for other youths who were excluded by the tests from Oxford and from Cambridge.

These academies still await their historian,[1] and the materials hitherto published supply at best a fragmentary account of those which had the longest lives, and there were others which, beginning as private ventures and acquiring no endowment, expired with the decease of the individual teachers by whom they had been founded. But there were others which, thanks to the munificence of local congregations, or to support from a trust fund, acquired comparative stability. From 1715 to 1819 the Nonconformists of the Midlands maintained an academy which, in spite of being several times shifted from one town to another, maintained a fairly continuous tradition of sound learning. Originally established at Kibworth in Leicestershire, it was transferred to Northampton in 1729, to Daventry in 1752 ; brought back to Northampton in 1789 ; finally, in 1799, removed to Wymondley in Hertfordshire. It counted among its teachers Philip Doddridge, who was its head from 1729 to 1751, and Thomas Belsham ; among its pupils Joseph Priestley, and also John Aikin, the elder, afterwards one of the pillars of the Warrington Academy, and Caleb Ashworth, who succeeded Doddridge and raised this midland academy to its highest pitch of efficiency between 1752 and 1775. As it happens, this academy produced comparatively few pupils of note. But an imposing and very varied list might be compiled of eminent men of the eighteenth century who were educated at institutions of this type.[2] They were not exactly forcing-houses for the manu-

[1] Some useful information is given by Miss Irene Parker, *Dissenting Academies in England* (1914).

[2] Daniel Defoe, Isaac Watts, Samuel Wesley, Robert Harley, Henry St. John, Simon Harcourt, Richard Price, William Godwin, William Hazlitt, Gilbert Wakefield, Thomas Malthus, are cases in point. No doubt the list could be extended.

facture of politicians of a particular type ; but from time to
time they produced teachers who held strong political opinions,
and who trenchantly criticized the existing order in the class-
room and outside it. When Priestley was a tutor at the Warrington academy he wrote (1761–7) three courses of lectures on
history, a subject to which the better academies paid more attention than was usual in the homes of Anglican learning. Priestley's
lectures became celebrated and were afterwards published by
request. They are not very good lectures, but they deserve to
be studied as an index to his opinions at that early date. The
most striking passage in them is a dissertation on the hard lot
of those who are excluded by law from any share in political
power. What it comes to, though Priestley does not make his
point so openly, is that no Englishman is really free unless he
has the parliamentary franchise.

'It may appear at first sight to be of little consequence whether
persons in the common ranks of life enjoy any share of political
liberty or not. But without this there cannot be that persuasion
of security and independence which alone can encourage a man
to make great exertions. A man who is sensible that he is at the disposal of others, over whose conduct he has no control, has always some
unknown evil to dread. He will be afraid of attracting the notice
of his superiors, and must feel himself a mean and degraded being.
But a sense of liberty and a knowledge of the laws by which his conduct must be governed, with some degree of control over those who
make and administer the laws, gives him a constant feeling of his own
importance, and leads him to indulge a free and manly form of thinking, which will make him greatly superior to what he would have been
under an arbitrary form of government.'[1]

Perhaps Priestley, when he wrote this passage, had in mind
the hard case of the Irish Catholics, whom an Irish act of 1727
had definitely deprived of the parliamentary franchise. At all
events, when he shortly afterwards produced a treatise upon
liberty, he placed it in the hands of a Dublin publisher. It is
entitled *An Essay on the First Principles of Government, and
on the Nature of Civil and Religious Liberty*, and it was published in 1768. In the preface Priestley claimed that he had put
together 'a more accurate and extensive system of morals and

[1] *Lectures on History and General Policy* (Birmingham, 1788), pp. 282–3.

policy than was adopted by Mr. Locke and others who formerly wrote upon this subject.'

Priestley seldom acknowledges the source from which he derives an idea, but he quotes in this work from Rousseau, whose *Contrat Social* had appeared in 1762. He had also read some of the works of Montesquieu, and his lectures show that he had made a careful study of Hume's *Political Discourses*. Thomas Cooper, his first biographer, thinks that he may have used a collection of passages made from the works of Jesuit writers, by order of the Parlement of Paris in 1757, to illustrate their views on the sovereignty of the people; but this is a mere guess. Whatever Priestley's sources, his system has all the marks of an eclectic compilation. It attracted attention, not because the author had anything to say that was absolutely new, but because he expressed his views with lucidity and vigour. Bentham tells us what a profound impression was made upon him, when he read the book at Oxford as an undergraduate, by the passage which explains that all laws and institutions must ultimately be judged by their effect on 'the good and happiness of the members, that is the majority of the members, of any state'.[1] Yet Bentham might have found the same doctrine, less vigorously explained, in Hume's *Political Essays*, especially in that on the social contract. And if Bentham had read Priestley with more care he would have found in Priestley's *Essay* the doctrine of natural, equal, and inalienable rights of the individual—a doctrine which Bentham, and many others since Bentham, have regarded as incompatible with the principle of 'the greatest happiness of the greatest number'.[2]

To ordinary readers it must have seemed that the most audacious feature of the *Essay* was its definition of political liberty, as 'the power which the members of the state reserve to themselves of arriving at the political offices, or at least of having votes in the nomination of those who fill them'. It is true that Priestley at once proceeds to qualify his general statement. Only minute states like Genoa or Venice can allow complete political liberty to all their citizens, and the day of such states is over, since they cannot defend their liberty against great

[1] Bentham, *Deontology*, i. 300.
[2] See *Fragment of Government* (ed. Montagu), § 19.

powers such as now exist. In larger states the highest
should be the monopoly of 'persons of considerable fo
who are likely to be better educated than their social in
and also have a larger stake in their country's welfare. It is
inexpedient that the lowest classes should have any voice in the
elections to high offices of state. For such elections the franchise should be given only to men of property. If any one
complains that natural rights are infringed by such restrictions,
the answer is that the natural rights of any individual can only
be respected so far as they are consistent with the happiness of
the majority. Priestley's essay was not intended as a revolutionary manifesto. Like Montesquieu he repudiates the doctrine
that there is one ideal constitution which can and should be
adopted in any and every state without regard for local circumstances or the principle of expediency. But there are traces
here and there of that spirit which shocked Burke, a good many
years later, in the writings of Nonconformist politicians as a
class. In discussing the right of revolution Priestley is emphatic
and specific to a degree which would shock any Whig of conservative tendencies. Though it is inexpedient, says Priestley,
to make small grievances the excuse for revolution, yet when
the officers of the State become flagrantly oppressive, and it is
possible to overthrow them without much risk of confusion,
what in God's name are the principles that ought to restrain an
injured and insulted people from asserting their natural rights?
And supposing the circumstances to be such that the people
cannot formally combine in issuing a mandate to a deliverer of
their own choice. Why, then, every man who has the power of
calling the oppressor to account may proceed to act as the
agent and avenger of the people. It is curious that this variant
of the old defence of tyrannicide, this claim that the tacit and
presumed support of the majority is good and sufficient authority
for any one who has the will and power to start a revolution,
attracted little attention in 1768. Twenty-three years later the
situation which Priestley had thus imagined did arise in France,
and Priestley had the courage to defend his old opinion. He
justified, as against Burke's indictment, the revolutionary claims
and behaviour of the National Assembly, arguing that where no
ordinary means of redressing grievances exist the people must

have recourse to means which are extraordinary ; if thirty
millions find that their interests conflict with those of a small
minority, they have the right, as the majority, to come to a
judicial decision on the matter in dispute, and also to put their
sentence into execution.[1] The National Assembly had received
no formal mandate from the thirty million malcontents, but it
might legitimately regard their approval and support as assured.
It was not Priestley's habit to water down his theoretical conclusions when they were distasteful to the majority of his own
countrymen.

In 1772 Priestley became the librarian of Lord Shelburne, and
was admitted to a coterie of Shelburne's friends which included
Benjamin Franklin, David Hume, and Dr. Richard Price. It
must remain an open question whether Shelburne cultivated
the friendship of these intellectual free-lances out of a spirit of
pure intellectual curiosity.[2] But if he hoped to make use of
Priestley's pen for the purposes of party warfare he was soon
undeceived. That versatile and independent intellect was for
the moment weary of politics. He wrote in 1774 (at Franklin's
request) an *Address to Dissenters* on the subject of the
approaching rupture with America. But the discovery of oxy-
gen, the examination of the nature of the soul and of matter,
and the vexed points of gospel history were his main pre-
occupation until in 1780 he quitted Shelburne's service. But
Price gave more satisfaction to his friend and patron. Like
Priestley, he was a product of the Nonconformist academies, and
an adventurer in several different fields of speculation ; but his
intelligence was more practical—witness his publications on the
vital statistics of insurance companies and on the national debt
—and he combined with a taste for political philosophy the
rhetorical skill of an accomplished preacher. In his *Observations
on Civil Liberty* (1776)—perhaps the most influential of all the
pamphlets suggested by the American Revolution—he gave to

---

[1] *Letters to the Right Hon. E. Burke occasioned by his Reflections on the
Revolution in France* (Birmingham, 1791).

[2] Priestley himself was puzzled by the offer and wrote to Price saying that
he could not hope to be of use to Shelburne on political matters (Fitz-
maurice, *Life of Shelburne*, i. 435). Shelburne, however, was interested in
Priestley's scientific work.

some of Priestley's political ideas a vogue which they would
scarcely have obtained without his advocacy; and he went
beyond Priestley when he stated in this pamphlet the general
case for a reform of the House of Commons.

' If the persons to whom the trust of government is committed . . .
are chosen for long terms by a part only of the state ; and if, during
that term they are subject to no control from their constituents, the
very idea of Liberty will be lost, and the power of choosing representatives becomes nothing but a power, lodged in a few, to choose at
certain periods a body of Masters for themselves and for the rest of the
community.   And if a state is so sunk that the majority of its representatives are elected by a handful of the meanest persons in it, whose
votes are also paid for ; and if also there is a higher will [1] on which even
these mock representatives themselves depend and that directs their
voices, in these circumstances it will be an abuse of language to say
that the state possesses liberty. . . . And rather than be governed in
such a manner, it would perhaps be better to be governed by the will
of one man without any representation.   For a representation so
degenerated would answer no other end than to mislead and deceive,
by disguising slavery and keeping up a form of liberty when the reality
was lost. . . . Nothing can be more absurd than the doctrine which
some have taught with respect to the omnipotence of Parliament.
They possess no power beyond the limits of the trust for the execution
of which they were formed.   If they contradict this trust they betray
their constituents and dissolve themselves.'

There is in this passage an adroit mixture of new and old
proposals for reform.   The abolition of the Septennial Act, the
extirpation of bribery at elections, the limitation of the corrupt
influence of the Crown in the House of Commons, are all indicated in general terms as useful objects to be aimed at ; and so
far Dr. Price was only expressing views that had long been held
by many moderate politicians.   But coupled with these proposals
we find the doctrine that it is the business of the members of the
House of Commons to voice the opinions of their constituents,
and to fulfil a trust or a mandate which has been imposed on
them by the popular will.   This novelty is not made too clear—
either because Price was too discreet, or because he had not
thought enough about the subject, to make his meaning perfectly plain.   We are reminded of the dry epitaph with which

[1] George III.

Priestley honoured his friend and expositor in the course of
a funeral sermon.[1] 'The National Assembly of France have
justly styled him the Apostle of Liberty. Not that he added
much to the clearness of its principles, but strongly feeling their
force, he inspired all his readers with the same ardent love of it
and zeal for it.'

In effect Dr. Price at this period was more concerned to frame
a practicable policy of reform than to discuss abstract principles.
He identified himself with the party which in London and in
Yorkshire was agitating for definite and limited changes in the
character of the English House of Commons. This attitude he
openly avowed in 1783 when he, like several other persons of
distinction, was consulted by the Irish Volunteers with regard
to the best means of reforming the Irish Lower House. His
answer is that in theory every independent man ought to have
a vote, but that even in America it had been found desirable to
limit the franchise, conferring only on those who paid taxes
and possessed property ; that, so far as England was concerned,
he would be content, for the time being, with the scheme of
transferring one hundred seats from the boroughs to the counties,
as proposed by the Yorkshire Association.[2] We have it from
Wyvill, the founder of that Association, that the Nonconformist
body throughout England were practically unanimous in supporting the Yorkshire scheme.[3]

The Nonconformist leaders were attracted by new and extreme
speculations on the subject of natural rights, the more so because
they felt no sentimental reverence for the established order of
things, but rather exaggerated its defects. They represented
a minority which felt that it was still unjustly treated by the
ancient laws of the land. But they were cautious, not to say
timid, when confronted with radical schemes of reform. They
believed up to a point in the dogma of Equality. But they also
felt that it was safest to leave the work of government in the
hands of an aristocracy, and to withhold the franchise from men
who had not a substantial property qualification. They were

---

[1] *Discourse on the Death of Dr. Price* (1791).

[2] This reply is printed in *A Collection of Letters to the Volunteers of
Ireland* (London, 1783).

[3] C. Wyvill, *Defence of Dr. Price and the Reformers of England* (1792).

in fact more Whiggish and less 'enlightened' than they knew. But they may claim some credit for having cleared the minds of their own followers and helped to form a habit of political discussion and criticism. It was largely through their publications that the English middle classes acquired some knowledge of the leading ideas of Montesquieu and Rousseau. The scoffers might suggest, with some show of justification, that divines like Price preached radical opinions as though they were articles of religion. This is true up to a point, but the radicalism which Price recommended to his congregations was an attitude of mind rather than a collection of political nostrums. In a sermon preached at Hackney in 1779 he defined the Christian Radical in the following terms: —

'A righteous man is the best member of every community, and the best friend to his species, by being the most irreconcilable to slavery, the most sensible to every encroachment on the rights of mankind, the most zealous for equal and universal liberty, and the most active in endeavouring to propagate just sentiments of religion and government. In short a virtuous man must be a firm and determined patriot.'[1]

There is no reason to suppose that the political views of the Nonconformists were materially changed by the French Revolution, which, in its earlier stages, they applauded as another glorious victory for the principles of 1688. The Revolution Society, of which both Price and Priestley were members, was an old Whig club, and its dinners in commemoration of the fall of the Bastille were very harmless celebrations. In the heat of controversy with Tory critics of the French Revolution it was inevitable that Price and Priestley should restate and even exaggerate certain features of their old creed which had remained in the background before 1789; but we cannot convict them of holding the extreme view of popular sovereignty which Burke imputed to the New Whigs indiscriminately, the view 'that the people are essentially their own rule, and their will the measure of their conduct'.[2] This view, no doubt, was held by those students of the Hackney College who in 1791 entertained Thomas

---

[1] *Sermon delivered to a Congregation of Protestant Dissenters at Hackney* (1779).

[2] *Appeal from the New to the Old Whigs* (ed. Raffety), p. 53.

Paine at a republican supper, and sang 'Ça Ira' when other
people were singing 'God save the King',[1] thereby provoking
Burke to the remark that this academy was the new arsenal in
which subversive doctrines and arguments were forged. It is
possible that the misbehaviour of the Hackney students was
inspired by the teaching of that eccentric revolutionary, Gilbert
Wakefield, who was their classical tutor in 1790 and 1791.
Wakefield's sympathy with the French Revolution grew to be
fanatical, and in 1799 he incurred a sentence of imprisonment
for arguing in print that the labouring classes had nothing to
lose by a French invasion. But Wakefield represented no one
and was a little mad.

Price and Priestley did something to promote the growth of
radicalism as a school of speculative thought. But when we
search for the origins of those programmes of radical reform
which were so hotly discussed in the country and in the House
of Commons between 1769 and 1786, it at once becomes apparent
that the Supporters of the Bill of Rights, the Society for Constitutional Information, and the Yorkshire Association owe very
little to Price and Priestley. These thoroughly English patriots
were nurtured on Whig literature, and especially on that part
of it which was written by the Whigs of the extreme left, or by
old commonwealth men. The favourite works of this kind were
edited anew by Thomas Hollis, rather expensively, and in the
cheapest possible forms by the London Association and the
Society for Constitutional Information. Among them were
the prose writings of Milton, Ludlow's *Memoirs*, Needham's
Excellency of a Free State (1656), Algernon Sidney's *Discourses*,
Henry Neville's *Plato Redivivus*, the political works of Locke,
and Lord Molesworth's *Principles of a Real Whig* (1711).
None of these works defended the extreme Levelling position,
as we find it in the original edition of the *Agreement of the
People*. Most of them accepted the principle that political
power should go with property, and avowedly believed that
the rule of an aristocracy was what England needed. But in
Sidney there was a good deal of doctrine that Burke and all
quiet Whigs regarded as subversive. Sidney argued that

[1] H. McLachlan, *Letters of Theophilus Lindsey* (1920), pp. 39, 41.

magistrates who abused their power and were too powerful to
be restrained by the law courts could legitimately be brought
to account by the weapons of sedition, tumult, or war;[1] that
a king was not the master but the servant of the commonwealth,
and like any other servant might be dismissed if his masters
were not satisfied with his service, however well and truly that
service has in fact been rendered.[2]   Sidney also insisted upon
the right of the people to change the ancient forms of government:—

' If it be lawful for us . . . to build houses, ships, and forts better
than our ancestors, to make such arms as are most fit for our defence,
and to invent printing, with an infinite number of other arts beneficial
to mankind, why have we not the same right in matters of government,
upon which all others do most absolutely depend? . . . Why should
men be for ever compelled to continue under the same form of
government that their ancestors happened to set up in the time
of their ignorance.'[3]

But Locke too, though milder than Sidney in his language, had
written passages which were grateful to restless critics of the
established order.   Locke assigned to the individual certain
inalienable rights, such as that of property, which in his view
no legislation could take away ; he taught that *salus populi* was
the grand and fundamental law of every state; and he defined
the cases in which the right of resistance to the Government
might legitimately be exercised and the forms of the Government altered in accordance with the views of the majority.[4]

Before 1769 this literature, so widely circulated and so devoutly
perused in Whig circles, had not stimulated its readers to demand
any extensive changes in the constitution.   Now and then we
find a pamphleteer recommending annual parliaments as a
remedy for political corruption, or pointing to the rotten
boroughs as a disease of the body politic.   The anonymous
author of *The Act of Governing by Partys* (1701), generally
supposed to be John Toland, adds to these two desiderata
a plea for giving representation to those unrepresented towns
('as Leeds, Halifax, Manchester, Newbury, Croydon') whose
population and taxable wealth are really considerable.   But this

---

[1] *Discourses*, c. ii, § 24.   [2] *Ibid.*, c. iii, §§ 16, 41.
[3] *Ibid.*, c. iii, § 7.
[4] *Second Treatise on Civil Government*, cc. xi, xiv, xix.

writer, anticipating the author of the *Patriot King*, regards the system of party government as the grand malady, and suggests that this can only be abolished by a wise.and independent use of the sovereign's prerogative in choosing ministers. Such a reform as this never found favour in Whig circles; and it was the attempt of George III to reform national politics by the methods of a patriot king, carried to their logical conclusion, that stirred up one section of the Whigs to demand that the House of Commons should be reformed in such a way as to make it independent of ministers who owed their places to the arbitrary pleasure of the King.

By a most curious chapter of accidents John Wilkes became the standard bearer of this reformist movement, whose leaders organized themselves (20 Feb. 1769) immediately after Wilkes had been for the second time elected by the Middlesex freeholders and for the third time expelled from the House of Commons. The new society, called ' Supporters of the Bill of Rights ', produced in July 1771 a set of eleven articles, which ought to be subscribed by every candidate for Parliament. Four of these articles relate to constitutional reforms and are interesting as an index to the views of the city Whigs—Sawbridge, Oliver, Beckford, Townshend—to whom the society owed such influence as it possessed.

No. 2. You shall promote a law subjecting each candidate to an oath against having used bribery or any other illegal means of compassing his election.

No. 3. You shall promote, to the utmost of your power, a full and equal representation of the people in Parliament.

No. 4. You shall endeavour to restore annual parliaments.

No. 5. You shall promote a pensions and place bill enacting, That any member who receives a place, pension, contract, lottery ticket, or any other emolument whatsover from the Crown, or enjoys profit from any such place, pension, &c., shall not only vacate his seat, but be absolutely ineligible during his continuance under such influence.[1]

Three of the four articles which we have quoted contain little or nothing that was novel in 1771. Bribery at elections had

---

[1] For the full text of the eleven articles see *Letters of Junius*, Private Letter, No. 66, footnote.

been made a statutory offence by an Act of 1694 (7 Will.
The proposed bill against place-men and pensioners v
stantially an attempt to restore in its pristine severity
of the Act of Settlement; it would have excluded the King's
ministers from the House of Commons, but Junius, in other
respects a severe critic of the eleven articles, does not take this
point, and therefore may be presumed to have thought that
this divorce between the executive and the Lower House was
feasible and salutary. Annual parliaments had been recommended by Henry Neville and by Sidney; this reform would
undoubtedly diminish the influence of the Crown, and it was
resisted by independent politicians chiefly on the practical
ground that they would be ruined by the expense of annual
elections, even if, by some miracle, the practice of buying the
votes of the electors could be suppressed. Chatham had been
induced in this very year to advocate triennial parliaments, but
he only recommended them as a heroic remedy for an intolerable
state of affairs (1 May 1771).[1]

But the demand for a full and equal representation of the
people had a more imposing sound. A full representation
might mean manhood suffrage, a proposal which since 1647
had been generally deprecated by serious thinkers; at the least
it suggests a householder franchise. Equal representation would
naturally suggest a redivision of the country into constituencies
of equal size. This expedient had been seriously suggested by
David Hume in his essay on *The Idea of a Perfect Commonwealth*. But Junius, who was probably well informed of the
intentions of the London reformers, assumes that they would
only press for the disfranchisement of rotten boroughs, and for
the separate representation of those large commercial or manufacturing towns which were still merged in the counties. This
was more than Chatham was inclined to recommend. Eighteen
months previously he had announced his desire that every
county in England and Scotland should receive one additional
member; but at the same time he had deprecated any interference with close boroughs :—

'These boroughs, corrupt as they are, must be considered as the
natural infirmity of the constitution. Like the infirmities of the body

[1] *Chatham Correspondence*, iv. 174.

we must bear them with patience. . . . The limb is mortified, but the amputation might be death.' [1]

It might be death to the constitution because the rights of borough patrons and borough electors were private property which ought not to be invaded by any Act of Parliament; also because, the degrees of corruption being infinite, Parliament would be called upon to exercise a most difficult and dangerous discretion in distinguishing between the constituencies which were to be spared and those which were to be abolished. All this is clearly explained by Junius in defending the proposals of Chatham and criticizing the counter-proposals of the supporters of the Bill of Rights. In 1785 the son of Chatham was prepared to cut the Gordian knot by offering pecuniary compensation to the electors in any close borough where two-thirds of the electorate were ready to take a price for the extinction of their franchise. But on that occasion Fox defeated the scheme, taking the line that an elector's vote ought not to be treated by the legislature as a form of marketable property. It is indeed remarkable that the opinion of the best Whigs on this subject should have changed so greatly in the course of fifteen years.

The supporters of the Bill of Rights were weakened in 1771 by a quarrel between Wilkes and Horne Tooke, which led to the latter's secession and to the establishment of a rival club, the Constitutional Society. But in March 1776 Wilkes asked leave of the House of Commons to introduce a measure of parliamentary reform. This was to have been framed on the lines proposed by Chatham six years previously, and would not have been a sweeping measure. But it was significant that Wilkes, an excellent judge of the trend of opinion among the unrepresented classes, saw fit to introduce into his speech a strong plea for universal suffrage.

'The meanest mechanic, the poorest peasant and day labourer has important rights respecting his personal liberty, that of his wife and children, his property however inconsiderable, his wages, his earnings, the very price and value of each day's labour, which are in many trades

[1] Speech in the House of Lords, 22 January 1770. (*Chatham Correspondence*, iii. 406-8).

and manufactures regulated by the power of Parliament.   Every law
relative . . . to every contract with a rapacious or unjust master is
of importance to the manufacturer, the cottager, the servant. . . .
Some share therefore in the power of making those laws which deeply
interest them . . . should be reserved even to this inferior but most
useful set of men in the community. . . . Without a true representation
of the Commons our constitution is essentially defective, our Parliament
is a delusive name, a mere phantom, and all other remedies to recover
the pristine purity of the form of government established by our
ancestors would be ineffectual.' [1]

It need hardly be said that this passage, the most striking in
Wilkes's speech, was not the creature of his own brain.   The
argument is taken from a work compiled by James Burgh,
a Scots schoolmaster, who was a disciple of Dr. Price and his
neighbour at Newington Green.[2]   The dogma of equality was
in the air just then, and in 1776 it was affirmed in two well-
known American manifestoes.   The Virginia Bill of Rights
asserted ' that all men are by nature equally free and independent
and have certain inherent rights', and the Declaration of
Independence that ' all men are created equal . . . endowed
by their Creator with certain inalienable rights'.   But there
can be little doubt that the men who framed these statements
were chiefly concerned to stigmatize hereditary rank and privilege as offences against the law of nature.   The most radical
of the new state constitutions in America was that of Pennsyl-
vania; and in this constitution the law of the franchise runs as
follows :—

' Every freeman of the full age of 21 years, having resided in this
state for the space of one whole year next before the day of election
for representatives, *and paid public taxes during that time*, shall enjoy
the right of an elector.' [3]

Burgh and Wilkes were therefore prepared to go farther than
the American colonists in extending the franchise.   So too was
Major John Cartwright, formerly of the Royal Navy, but at this

[1] *Parl. Hist.*, xviii. 1288-98.
[2] *Political Disquisitions* (3 vols., 1774-5), by James Burgh, vol. i, p. 37.
Burgh is, however, content to press for a householder suffrage.
[3] For these documents see S. E. Morison, *The American Revolution*,
pp. 149, 151, 162.

date a landed proprietor and an officer of the Nottinghamshire militia. Cartwright is one of the connecting links between the reformers of this period and the Radicals of the nineteenth century. He began his career as a political controversialist in 1775 and pursued it for nearly fifty years. His literary output was prodigious, but can be summed up in half a dozen propositions which became eventually the Six Points of the People's Charter. He was not highly intelligent, and he was not well educated. His works are liberally peppered with references to authorities whose doctrines he had by no means assimilated. He believed, as not a few legal historians of the seventeenth and eighteenth centuries believed, that the Anglo-Saxon constitution had been a pure democracy,[1] and this form of government he thought could be restored by means of annual parliaments, elected through equal constituencies, by an electorate composed of all men of full age and sound mind, not being convicted criminals. This programme he expounded in a pamphlet, *Take Your Choice* (1776), which supplied the Duke of Richmond with the basis of his abortive Reform Bill of 1780.

Cartwright, in spite of a talent for robust denunciation of abuses, was in no sense a revolutionary. He desired to retain the hereditary monarchy and the hereditary House of Lords. He was in favour of a stiff property qualification for membership of the House of Commons.[2] The property qualification he dropped in the draft Reform Bill which he published in 1780, and he introduced then for the first time the payment of members as a fundamental of his programme. But the Duke of Richmond held fast to the scheme of 1776, which he regarded as essentially conservative in character.[3] He proposed it not to

---

[1] Cartwright quotes in particular Samuel Johnson's *Essay concerning Parliament at a Certainty* (1693) and Ruffhead's preface to the *Statutes at Large* (1760-5).

[2] See *Take Your Choice*, p. 69: 'For a county member the qualification should be a landed estate, and £400 a year might be sufficient; for London it might be the same, or property in the kingdom of £12,000; for other cities and towns £300 per annum in land, or £9,000 in other property.'

[3] That is he kept to the principle of a property qualification; but he proposed to retain the existing statutory qualification.

undermine but rather to restore the influence of his own order, and he avows this object very frankly in his *Letter to Lieut.- Colonel Sharman* (1783), a pamphlet which long was regarded by reformers as the classical defence of manhood suffrage. Richmond's main argument was that the time for half-measures (such as those of Chatham) had gone by. The people had become aware that the only effect of a half-measure would be to modify the distribution of political power between those classes by whom it was already engrossed. Manhood suffrage would not, as some feared, bring about mob rule. When every man possessed a vote, all would be equally secure against oppression ; but it did not follow that all would have equal power ; for men of superior fortunes would always exercise a superior weight and influence ; ' and I think ', the Duke adds, relapsing on a commonplace of eighteenth-century Whiggism, ' that as education and knowledge generally attend property, those who possess them ought to have weight and influence with the more ignorant. But the essential difference will be that, though the people may be led, they cannot be driven.' He argued that, so long as a property qualification was required from the elected representatives of the people, those representatives could be trusted not to become the slaves of their constituents ; but here he ignores the fact that evasions of the law of qualifications had been not infrequent, and were still possible, although an Act of 1760 had prohibited some of the methods of evasion. Richmond stoutly opposed the introduction of the ballot, although this expedient was, in Cartwright's view, a fundamental ; to Richmond it appeared that secret voting gave an advantage to the liar and the hypocrite, without benefiting the honest man.[1]

Richmond had, it seems, full confidence in the disposition of the classes which he proposed to enfranchise. The masses, he held, would be content to use their votes to protect their personal security and personal interests. He was not afraid that revolutionary or communistic instincts would be aroused in them by the consciousness of political power. He was much more afraid of the propertied men who would sit in the reformed House of Commons. The most remarkable of his proposals in this

---

[1] Richmond's bill was printed in pamphlet form—*An Authentic Copy of the Duke of Richmond's Bill* (1783).

pamphlet was that the activity of that House should be much restricted. The work which it is necessary that Parliament should do, is, he contends, quite trivial in amount. The main business of any government must always be to administer and to enforce existing laws. There is no good reason why any session of Parliament should last for more than two or three months. In that time it should be possible to review the expenditure of the past year, to vote supplies for the forthcoming year, to redress the grievances of petitioners and to pass the few new bills that are really required. Limited to a short session, and tied down to an unambitious programme, the House of Commons could neither set up a tyranny of its own nor become the instrument of a tyrannical executive.

It is remarkable that this adventurous reformer transferred his allegiance to the younger Pitt four months after publishing a vindication of his own drastic scheme. Some ingenious critics have suggested personal motives of a trivial and unworthy kind for this change of front. The ingenuity is quite gratuitous, unless we make two assumptions, each of which is very questionable: first, that Pitt was only playing with the idea of reform in 1783, and secondly that Richmond had detected the hypocrisy of Pitt's public declarations. The truth is that practically all the reformers, whether their views were moderate or extreme, regarded Pitt at this time as the most trustworthy champion of their cause. They cannot have hoped that Pitt would ever go so far as Richmond had gone in 1780. But it seemed very likely that he might persuade Parliament to give them a part of what they desired. The events of the past three years had caused them to despair of real assistance from any other leading parliamentarian.

This becomes clear if we follow the history of the Yorkshire Association, founded in 1780, through the exertions of that indefatigable, honest, and muddle-headed agitator, Christopher Wyvill, who played in the camp of the moderate reformers the same sort of role that Cartwright filled in that of the extremists.

Wyvill had been ordained before he became, by marriage with a Yorkshire heiress of his own family, a country gentleman. His tastes were political, but his orders prevented him from

seeking election to Parliament, and he consoled himself with
plans for organizing the county electors of England in support
of a political programme which he himself had drafted. The
points of this programme were economical reform, the addition
of at least one hundred county members to the House of
Commons, and triennial parliaments. It was approved by a
number of Yorkshire peers and members; and it was taken up
by the Whig freeholders of twenty-five other counties, including
Middlesex. In February 1780 Sir George Savile presented to
the House of Commons a Yorkshire petition founded on Wyvill's
programme. Lord Rockingham declined to consider it, on the
ground that Burke's measure of economical reform would do
more to purify the House of Commons than any tinkering with
the franchise or with the duration of parliaments;[1] and the
Duke of Portland raised the odd objection that an addition to
the county representation would make county elections more
corrupt than ever.[2] But Wyvill was obstinate, and produced
a plan for the closer co-operation of the reformers in Yorkshire
with those of other counties. The plan was not of his own
devising. It was propounded by Dr. Jebb in 1779 in an *Address
to the Freeholders of Middlesex*, and may have been devised in
the councils of the Society for Constitutional Information. At any
rate it was a plan of which the main was much used by the Corresponding Societies, the Hampden Clubs, and the political unions
of the next fifty or sixty years. Jebb suggested that the reformers
of each county should appoint a small standing committee with
full powers to negotiate, and to arrange plans of common action,
with similar committees appointed elsewhere. The programme
of reform being settled by agreement, the next step would be
to embody it in a monster petition. The associated committees,
said Jebb, could then speak to the House of Commons in the
name of the whole country, they could warn members of the
House to remember their duties as delegates and servants of
the people. On 3 January 1781 the Yorkshire Association
followed Jebb's advice to the extent of appointing Wyvill and
two others as a standing committee authorized to negotiate

---

[1] Rockingham to Pemberton Milnes, 28 February 1780 (*Rockingham
Memoirs*, ii. 395 ff.).

[2] *Op. cit.*, ii, p. 412.

with other counties, first as to a petition for economic reform, and secondly as to ways and means of securing additional representation for counties. The result of these negotiations, which in their later stages had the support of the Duke of Richmond and other ministerialists, was that the reformers induced Pitt, then a private member, to move in the House of Commons for a measure of moderate and substantial reform. They had to fall back upon this young and untried heir of a great name because there was no hope of persuading Rockingham to inscribe reform upon the banner of his party. The supporters of Pitt's reform schemes, in Parliament and outside it, were a motley but not unimpressive host. He had Richmond on his side, and Fox and Sheridan and Shelburne and Sir George Savile; he had also Wilkes and Sawbridge and Cartwright and Horne Tooke. And Pitt, though he carefully avoided committing himself on details, indicated quite clearly that his scheme would not spare the close boroughs which Rockingham was defending in the name of the rights of private property.[1] Even in those days he appeared to reformers more democratic than Fox, although Fox had been active in the preliminary stages of the campaign, while Pitt was holding aloof; and Fox's reputation as a reformer was naturally damaged by the coalition with North in the following year. It was hard to believe in the reforming zeal of a minister who had as his principal partner the man held most responsible for the parliamentary corruption of the years 1770–82. Fox himself supported Pitt's reform motion of 1783, but most of his colleagues divided against it, and Fox must have been aware from the first that there was no danger of Pitt securing a majority.

Hence at the general election of 1784 the reformers of Yorkshire threw in their lot with Pitt on the faith of a pledge that he would do his utmost to carry a measure of parliamentary reform. Their support must have been particularly welcome, as the Government's election manager was very doubtful of the Yorkshire electors, both in the boroughs and in the county, and the Coalition were regarding Yorkshire as their sheet anchor.[2]

---

[1] See Romilly's *Life*, i. 222, for a quotation from this part of Pitt's speech. The newspaper reports of this debate were very bad.

[2] *Life of Wilberforce*, i. 51 ; *Robinson Papers* (1922), pp. 67, 72–3.

The Yorkshire freeholders loyally fulfilled their side of the bargain by bringing in Wilberforce and Duncombe for the county in the teeth of the great Whig peers, and another Pittite was elected for the city of York. It was thought at the time that the example of Yorkshire accounted for many of the seats which were captured by Pitt's followers in other counties. Pitt on his side behaved correctly enough. He would not stake the fruits of his victory on a reform bill, and in fact his majority would have crumbled at once if he had taken this quixotic step. But he produced his scheme in the session of 1785, and he carried it to a division. It was no doubt something less than a half-measure. Already in 1783 he had confessed that it was difficult to abolish all close boroughs without endangering the constitution. In 1785 he proposed that only thirty-six should be abolished, none of them without the consent of the electors, who would be duly compensated for the loss of their votes. All that he proposed by way of enlarging the electorate was that copyholders should receive the county franchise, whereas the Yorkshire Association would have liked to enfranchise all ratepaying householders. But Pitt's scheme satisfied the Association as a first instalment of reform, 'not sufficiently extensive perhaps in the proposed communication of the Right of Suffrage, but capable of receiving that extension hereafter, without the slightest derangement of the System'. They regarded the defeat of Pitt's motion as a proof that the times and the House of Commons were not propitious to any second attempt in the near future. They expressed themselves as content both with the scheme and with Pitt's advocacy. They would wait until he saw a more favourable opportunity. The Yorkshire Association dissolved itself in 1786. But less moderate reformers were not so patient, and in 1793 Wyvill made an urgent appeal to the minister. Something must be done to counter the activities of those who desired the Duke of Richmond's scheme or a republican system of government; and what had been a sufficient concession in 1785 would no longer suffice. Would Pitt revive his scheme, with an amendment granting the householder franchise in the counties?[1] To this appeal Pitt

[1] Wyvill, *Letter to the Right Hon. William Pitt* (1793).

turned a deaf ear, for intelligible and possibly adequate reasons. But Grey responded to it by moving his first reform motion in that very year. It was too late to reassemble the Yorkshire Association; but Wyvill at all events rallied to Grey, and in 1801 published a letter to John Cartwright urging that veteran and his supporters to be content with the programme of the New Whigs.

IV

THE RIGHTS OF MAN AND THE POPULAR SOCIETIES

SO far we have come across no sinister, revolutionary elements in the reform movement of the eighteenth century. But there still remains to be considered the last stage of the movement which frightened Burke, frightened Pitt's Government, and exasperated to madness the Tory middle-classes, driving them to organize ' Church and King Clubs ' or ' Associations for Preserving Liberty and Property '. If we look only to the intentions of those who organized the popular societies, the fears of their opponents were quite baseless. But if we remember how rough were the recruits of the societies, how little fitted for command the men who raised them, and how inadequate the machinery in all the towns of Great Britain for repressing organized breaches of the peace, it is not altogether surprising that some ill-considered legislation was passed and some insignificant persons were too hastily prosecuted on account of supposed designs which they were certainly not capable of putting into action.

The organization and history of these societies have been so carefully traced by Dr. Veitch that there is no need to dwell upon these topics here. But a few words are necessary to explain the aims and methods of those which figured in the political trials of Pitt's reign of terror.

In 1794 the law officers of the Crown, in preparing the case against Horne Tooke, appear to have supposed that a club with which he was closely connected, the Society for Constitutional Information, was the directing force behind the popular agitation. This club had been founded in 1780 by Major Cartwright, Horne Tooke, and Dr. John Jebb to promote the discussion of reformist ideas and the circulation of reformist literature. All three belonged to the left wing of the reform movement and were notable pamphleteers. Tooke had been sentenced in 1777 to a year's imprisonment for acting, two years before, as the treasurer of a public subscription raised for the families of those

American soldiers who had been 'inhumanly murdered' in the battle of Lexington. Jebb, who had been a Fellow of Peter-house and an Anglican incumbent, was at this time a qualified medical practitioner, a unitarian in theology, and a prison re-former; he died in 1786. Up to that date, or even later, the Society for Constitutional Information was inconspicuous. Its leaders, in spite of their advanced views, adhered to Pitt's pro-gramme of reform and waited patiently for its resuscitation. They sympathized, like the Nonconformist politicians, with the aspirations of the French National Assembly; but in 1790 the Society voted, on the motion of Horne Tooke, that the British constitution required no violent measures of reform. The annual income of the society, which was derived from guinea subscriptions, amounted to £60, and its annual expenditure was stated to be about £50; but it is probable that other funds were available for the expense of propaganda, as the society circulated a considerable quantity of pamphlets. The average attendance at the weekly meetings was about ten, but there had been occasions when as many as thirty persons were present. Up to the summer of 1792 the meetings were held at the private house of the secretary in Chancery Lane. But at that time the venue was changed to the famous Crown and Anchor tavern in the Strand. The society reprinted Paine's *Rights of Man*, and it presented sympathetic addresses to the Jacobin Club in Paris and to the National Convention. On 18 January 1793, but before France declared war on England, the society elected Roland, St. André, and Barrère as honorary members. It was therefore publicly identified with the most radical school of thought that then existed in England. It originated no new doctrines, but it assisted in circulating a type of literature which was incendiary in its language and in its conclusions. It gave advice and countenance to a number of political associations, both in London and in the provinces, of which a few were re-cruited from the middle-class alone, but more were of a mixed character or altogether popular in their constitution. The members of the Society for Constitutional Information were men of mediocre abilities and politically insignificant;[1] but they

[1] Next to Cartwright and Horne Tooke, the best-known member of the S. C. I. is Thomas Holcroft, the dramatist, who joined it in November 1792.

were educated men, possessing some knowledge of constitutional law and some experience of the art of agitation. They were largely, though not solely, responsible for giving a vogue to that new political philosophy which Burke denounces in his *Letter to Captain Mercer* (1790) and in his *Appeal from the New to the Old Whigs* (1791).

The main features of this philosophy were: an implicit confidence in the wisdom of the people; a conviction that this wisdom is expressed in the opinions of the numerical majority of the people; a claim, on behalf of the people, that they are and always should be the effective sovereign, and that no other authority in the State has any right to a share in the government, unless it is appointed by the people and responds obediently to every new decision of the general will—that is, to every vote of the numerical majority. Those who held to this philosophy were bound by their own logic to regard the monarchy and the House of Lords as political monstrosities and the House of Commons as an institution which could claim no legitimate power until it should be elected in such a manner that it automatically and inevitably expressed the general will.

Most, if not all, of these opinions are to be found in the pamphlets of Priestley, Price, and Cartwright. But they did not become widely popular in England until they were restated by Thomas Paine in the first and second parts of his *Rights of Man*, published in 1791 and 1792. This work was at once acclaimed by the Society for Constitutional Information, which passed a vote of thanks to Paine on 23 March 1796, ten days after the publication of the first part, and caused the vote to be published in the London and provincial papers.[1]

The cue was taken by a number of provincial societies which

According to Hazlitt (*Memoirs of T. Holcroft*, Bk. IV, c. 3), ' he never interfered with the framing of a single resolution ', but on 11 April 1794 he was one of the representatives of the S. C. I. at a conference with delegates of the London Corresponding Society (*Trial of Thomas Hardy*, i. 71). He was not a member of the Corresponding Committee of the S. C. I. He was indicted for High Treason in 1794, but discharged without a trial after Hardy had been acquitted. Holcroft, along with Godwin and Brend Holles, helped Paine in the publication of the *Rights of Man* (1791).

[1] See the society's minute, printed in the *Trial of Horne Tooke* (1795), i, p. 145.

first emerged from their obscurity to advertise Paine's book. One of these was the Manchester Constitutional Society, founded in October 1790 to resist the older Church and King Society of the local Tories. The leader of the Manchester constitutionalists was Thomas Walker (father of the better-known 'Original' Walker), who was a prosperous cotton merchant and sufficiently important to serve as borough-reeve in 1791. He showed the courage of his opinions, in 1793, when he allowed his house to be used as the meeting-place not only of the Constitutional Society but of two humbler reform clubs when the magistrates and the local Loyal Societies had made it impossible for reformers to hold their meetings on licensed premises. In 1794 he came unscathed through the ordeal of a prosecution of conspiracy, which illustrates the blind malignity of party warfare as it was then conducted in Manchester. The only witness brought against him was a wretched Irish weaver, a member of one of the clubs to which Walker had shown hospitality. This man, it was proved at the trial, was induced to turn informer by a clerical magistrate who had coerced him with threats and had stimulated his imagination with rum (paid for by the Manchester Loyal Association) until he produced a tale which he owned to be a tissue of perjuries even before the trial began.[1]

Walker was a reformer of the old Wilkite pattern. But he had as his political mentor a friend who was more extreme, more philosophic, and more addicted to sensational rhetoric. This was the well-known Thomas Cooper of Bolton, at that time a prosperous calico printer and an energetic pioneer in the campaign against the slave trade. In chemistry and in politics Cooper was an apt and admiring pupil of the great Dr. Priestley. He thought Priestley's *Essay* the first plain and unanswerable book on the principles of civil government; and he had recently enlivened the proceedings of the Manchester Literary and Philosophic Society by a paper in which he denied that superior abilities or attainments carried with them the right of ruling, clinching his demonstration with the statement that 'public affairs do not require more than ordinary talents', and with a

---

[1] See Walker's narrative in *A Review of Political Events* (1794), pp. 118, 120; and also Gurney's report of the Trial of Thomas Walker (1794), *passim*.

warning against the evils of competition for office and for power. It would be hard to find anywhere a more thorough-going defence of the principle of political equality in its extremest form. We may conjecture that Cooper, not Walker, was responsible for a resolution which the Manchester Constitutional Society passed on 13 March 1792, thanking Paine for the publication of the second part of the *Rights of Man*, and expressing the hope that this book would not only lead to a complete reform of the representation, but would also further ' those other great plans of Public Benefit which Mr. Paine has so powerfully recommended '.[1]

It would be interesting to know how many of those who voted in favour of this unanimous resolution had read the work which it commended. For in it Paine suggested the desirability of abolishing the monarchy, of reforming Parliament by direct action on the part of the unrepresented, and of extirpating the aristocratical system by means of a progressive income-tax. We may take it for granted that Thomas Walker did not understand the true nature of Paine's practical advice to the English people ; he was no doubt content to accept the new book at the value which was put upon it by Thomas Cooper and the experts of the Society for Constitutional Information.[2]

At the time of the Manchester meeting Cooper was in Paris endeavouring to promote the cause of Fraternity, and on April 13 he presented to the Jacobin Club, on the part of the Manchester Society, an address requesting the favour of a regular correspondence, and affirming that the cause of the French people was that of all mankind. On the face of it there was nothing illegal, nothing revolutionary, in complimenting the French nation on a newly acquired form of constitutional government, and Cooper's conduct was defended in Parliament by Sheridan against the strictures of Burke. But something more than Sheridan's eloquence was needed to convince the majority of

---

[1] The resolution is printed in a pamphlet called *Common Sense* (Lancaster, 1794), written by an opponent of the society.

[2] In May, after Burke had called attention to Cooper's proceedings, Walker published a statement to the effect that the aim of his society was to restore the constitution to its original purity by bringing its practice into consonance with its principles.

Englishmen that those who fraternized with the Jacobin Club desired only moderate changes in the British constitution. The prejudice which Cooper had excited by his action was enhanced by the folly of the Society for Constitutional Information which, in May 1792, presented to the Jacobin Club another address in which the society expressed its regret that the neighbours of France had not seen fit to recognize the Rights of Man.[1] It is difficult to avoid the conclusion that the main objects of the society in taking this step were to irritate those who were in sympathy with Burke, and to show the country that London reformers were as bold as those of Manchester. But these empty and mischievous demonstrations did irreparable harm to the cause which the reforming societies really had at heart. They confirmed the impression that unrepresented English-men would no longer be content with such a reform as Pitt had promised in 1783, or even with the more drastic scheme of Cartwright and of Richmond. Tories in general came round to the view that the real object was, as Burke suggested, to substitute for the rule of hereditary wealth the rule of attorneys, shop-boys, clerks, and rustics from the plough.[2]

The Government, however, kept its head for the time being. When Thomas Cooper defended himself against Burke's asper-sions in a very bitter pamphlet, which incidentally denounced all privileged orders, and asserted the right of every people to alter its forms of government at pleasure, he offered the Government an opportunity for indicting him on a charge of seditious libel. Yet the Attorney-General was content to inform Cooper that if the pamphlet were republished in a cheap form for popular circulation he would be prosecuted.[3] The incident shows that the much-abused proclamation of 21 May 1792, against wicked and seditious writings, was not the prelude to any unscrupulous campaign against the freedom of political discussion. Indeed, on the very day when the proclamation was issued, Fox's Libel Act passed the third reading in the Lords. Nothing would have been easier or more natural, if a strict control of the

---

[1] *Trial of Horne Tooke* (1795), i. 54.
[2] *Letter to William Weddell*, 31 January 1792.
[3] Malone, *Public Life of Thomas Cooper* (1926), pp. 45–53.

Press had been desired, than to procure the rejection of this measure.

The truth is that the popular societies, as distinct from those formed of educated men, were still inchoate. There was a Sheffield Society of Working-men, which was said to be two thousand strong. Reports as to the character of the members are singularly discordant. To one observer of reforming tendency they appeared a body of 'well-behaved men' who had combined for the purpose of political discussion. He admits, however, that they had all been reading the first part of the *Rights of Man*.[1] A king's officer, who was in Sheffield a few months later, and saw the society celebrate the victory of Valmy with a procession and a display of tricolors, calls them 'as resolute and determined a set of villains as I ever saw'.[2] Like the Manchester constitutionalists, those of Sheffield thanked Paine for his second volume, and especially for his proposal of a graduated income-tax. But what appealed to them was the use to be made of the proceeds of the tax—'the affectionate concern he has shown on behalf of the poor, the infant and the aged.' At its inception the Sheffield Society had the support of some men of property and was able to found a reform newspaper, the *Patriot*, in 1792. But at the end of 1793 this venture had proved disastrous, and the secretary made a dismal report on the financial position. 'We have many thousand members, but the vast majority of them being working men, owing to the war, which has deprived many of them of all employment, and almost everyone of half his earnings, we have been crippled more than any other in the kingdom. . . . Our funds are not only exhausted but the Society is considerably in debt.'[3]

Another much-advertised association was that of the United Constitutional Societies of Norwich, which, in March 1792, informed the Society for Constitutional Information that 'it is our wish that all the societies of a similar kind in England were only as so many members strongly and indissolubly united in one political body', and in May asked leave to correspond regularly through delegates with the Society for Constitutional

[1] H. MacLachlan, *Letters of Theophilus Lindsay* (1920), p. 132.
[2] Stanhope, *Life of Pitt*, ii. 175.
[3] *Trial of Horne Tooke*, i, pp. 291-4.

Information. The Norwich organizers, more modest than those of Sheffield, only claimed a membership of 'some hundreds'. The members were reading, in 1792, the *Rights of Man*, Mackintosh's *Vindiciae Gallicae*, and Joel Barlow's *Advice to the Privileged Orders*. Their most definite aspiration was for parliamentary reform. The hypercritical might detect a subversive tendency in another of their objects, which was 'to lessen the numbers of the unproductive . . . and to do away such institutions and imposts as abridge the means of maintenance by resisting the demand for labour or sharing its reward '. But the author of this formula perhaps was asking for no more than the abolition of placemen and pensioners, a relaxation of the laws of settlement and a reduction of taxes.[1] Finally, among the societies which attracted the attention of the Law Officers is mentioned the Southwark Society of the Friends of the People, which came into existence in April 1792 for the purpose of investigating the rights of man and promoting a reform of the representation on the basis of manhood suffrage. A member of the Society for Constitutional Information, one Samuel Favell, took the chair at the inaugural meeting, and to his influence, rather than to any special malevolence or ability in the Southwark reformers, we may ascribe the acrid tone and the balanced rhetoric of its first manifesto:

'We are told that we have a Constitution—If it permits these abuses, it is either not a good one, or good only in part, and defective in its principles, construction, and effects. The continual applause bestowed upon it by Placemen, Pensioners, Government Contractors, Court Expectants and the hired editors of Prostituted Newspapers, has justly excited our suspicion either of its excellence or its existence. It may be good for them and not for us; and as we are no longer able to be amused with a Name, or a Phantom, we will direct our enquiries to the fact.'[2]

But there is fragmentary evidence, in 1792 and 1793, of a lively and even an active interest in the reformers' programme at many other places than those already mentioned. At Wakefield in Yorkshire there was a brisk war of manifestoes and counter-manifestoes between Tories and Reformers, which pro-

---

[1] See *Trial of Horne Tooke*, i. 192, 194.
[2] *Trial of Horne Tooke*, i. 182-4.

duced at least one weighty defence of the doctrine of political equality, obviously the work of a well-practised pen :[1]

'The perverse sense imposed on the word Equality by the Folly or Fears of some of our Countrymen is as dangerous as it is absurd ; and they may probably see the day when they may repent having infused into the minds of the People a notion that the Equality to be contended for is an Equality of wealth and possessions. . . . The Equality insisted on by the Friends of Reform is an Equality of Rights, or in other words that every person may be equally entitled to the Protection and Benefits of Society ; may equally have a voice in the Election of those who make the Laws by which he is affected in his liberty, his life or his property ; and may have a fair opportunity of exercising to advantage any talents he may possess. By an Equality of Rights is further meant that every person, whatever be his property, shall have an equal liberty of examining the Principles of Government, since he is equally interested in knowing that the portion of his income is well managed which he gives up to the Public.'

Even more curious is the record of a meeting held at Partick, near Glasgow, on 22 November 1792 :

'The inhabitants of the village of Partick and its neighbourhood, animated with a just indignation at the honour of their town being stained by the erection of a Burkified Society, have formed themselves into an association under the name of The Sons of Liberty and the Friends of Man.'

These Sons of Liberty resolved to co-operate, in defence of the Rights of Man, 'with the respectable assemblage of the Friends of the People in Glasgow and with the innumerable host of reform associations in Scotland, England, and Ireland'. The originator of this demonstration was indicted, but managed to escape arrest ; otherwise we might be more fully informed of the state of feeling in Partick and even in Glasgow.

To link together all such local efforts in the pursuit of common aims was the object, from its inception, of the London Corresponding Society, which was formed in January 1792. The society elected a committee to conduct its correspondence, and in May issued a lengthy statement of its principles, which differed in no respect from those of the other associations already described, and clearly announced that the society abhorred all

[1] These are collected in a volume of pamphlets in the John Rylands Library (No. 25059. 16).

violence and tumult. Although it was no more democratic than the Sheffield and Norwich societies, it attracted the attention of the Government, partly because it avowed the intention of concerting a policy with similar bodies, partly because it was, on paper at least, well organized for action. By August the members were organized in companies or branches, each of which held its own independent meetings. Each branch elected one delegate to serve on the executive committee, which met once a week; and the chairman of the society was elected by this committee. From an early date the society was in correspondence with Manchester, Stockport, Norwich, Sheffield; and some at least of its members hoped to avert the outbreak of a war with France by inducing all the reform societies to join in 'animated (but safe) declaration, assuring the French that we entertain the most friendly dispositions towards them'. A declaration to this effect was actually presented to the French National Convention on 7 November 1792, and it contained an assurance that the King of England would not be allowed to use British armies against the French, as he was already using those of Hanover.[1]

On 18 November yet another address was presented to the Convention, by John Frost and Joel Barlow. Both acted as deputies of the London Corresponding Society, and Frost was its secretary. The addresses were not illegal; Frost, who was a qualified attorney and a leading member of the Society for Constitutional Information, appears to have been adept in going to the verge of illegality without ever crossing it. Neither did the Corresponding Society transgress the law when, on 15 March 1793, some weeks after France had declared war upon Great Britain, it defiantly passed a vote of thanks to Barlow and to Frost for presenting the address, and begged Frost to rest assured 'that our regard for him is not lessened but increased by the prosecutions and persecutions which his faithful and due discharge of that commission may bring upon him'.[2] But it was natural that ministers should suspect some sinister design in these plain intimations to the French that the attitude of the British people was very different from that of the British Govern-

---

[1] Holland Rose, *Pitt*, ii. 67, quoting Munro's report to the Foreign Office.
[2] *Trial of Horne Tooke*, i. 261.

ment. In February 1793 Frost was indicted for sedition on the strength of a chance conversation in a tavern which, if correctly reported, showed that he was in favour of abolishing the monarchy, and in May he was sentenced to six months' imprisonment, to stand in the pillory for one hour, and to be struck off the roll of attorneys. The case is memorable as the first state trial in which Lord Eldon (at that time Sir John Scott, and newly appointed attorney-general) was officially concerned, and the first in which a Radical reformer had the advantage of being defended by Erskine. The action of the Government, in prosecuting Frost for a statement of political principles which might have been made with impunity on any other occasion in the past eighty years, was ill judged and created a most dangerous precedent ; and the approval of it by a common jury showed that Fox's Libel Act was not likely to be, under all circumstances, a guarantee of the freedom of political discussion. It is unnecessary to shed tears over Frost. His friends alleged that his constitution was undermined by his imprisonment in Newgate, but he survived it for nearly fifty years. Three Whig ministries held office in that period, and none of these appears to have taken any steps to obtain the replacement of his name on the attorneys' roll.

The courts of Scotland were perhaps no more pedantic than those of England in applying the old law of sedition ; but in Scotland the judges made not the slightest affectation of impartiality, and the sentences which they passed on political offenders in 1793 can only be described as barbarous. In August 1793 Mr. Thomas Muir of Hunterspill was sentenced to transportation for fourteen years on account of seditious speeches. Like Frost, he was bred a lawyer ; he was also a graduate of Glasgow University ; and it was probably on account of these distinctions that he was singled out for attack by the law officers, who in Scotland as in England were not unnaturally disposed to regard superior education as an aggravating circumstance in the record of any political suspect. Muir was concerned in the foundation of the Glasgow Society of Friends of the People (Oct. 1792), to which reference has already been made,[1] and he attended a convention of delegates of reform societies which was held in

[1] *Supra,* p. 79.

Edinburgh shortly afterwards. He was accused in the indictment *inter alia* of having denounced, in public speeches, the legislature as corrupt, and the monarchy as useless and expensive; of having recommended the works of Paine to various persons, and of having read to the Edinburgh Convention a seditious address from the Society of United Irishmen. It is probable that the last of these three counts told heavily against the prisoner, for a reason which could not be disclosed in court. The United Irishmen, organized a year previously (Oct. 1791) by Wolfe Tone, were ostensibly no more than parliamentary reformers of the standard pattern. But the Government knew, from intercepted correspondence, that Tone's ultimate object was the separation of Ireland from Great Britain; and there was some reason to suppose that the United Irishmen were only a screen concealing the operations of a secret and more dangerous body.[1]

But the proceedings against Muir were marked with a degree of animus which no evidence, secret or disclosed, could warrant, and Lord Braxfield's summing up was a violent profession of political faith. He started from the general principle that the British constitution, being the best that had ever existed since the creation of the world, could not possibly be changed for the better. What business had the prisoner to upset the minds of ignorant country people[2] at a time when the spirit of sedition was abroad? He ought to have known that such a rabble had no right to be represented in the legislature. The government of a country should always be a kind of corporation, like the government of a chartered borough. In this country the Government was the landed interest, which alone had a right to be represented. ' As for the rabble, who have nothing but personal property, what hold has the nation of them? What security for the payment of their taxes?'[3] The impropriety of these remarks was the more flagrant because the evidence of the principal witness against the prisoner was open to considerable suspicion. Romilly, than whom no one could have been better qualified

---

[1] Lecky, *History of Ireland* (ed. 1892), iii, pp. 13–16.

[2] Muir had made reform speeches at Kirkintilloch, Milton, and other country places.

[3] Quoted from the Report edited by James Robertson (Edinburgh, 1793).

to give an opinion on the conduct of the trial, was present as a spectator, and wrote severely of the judges both to Dumont and to Bentham.[1]

The trial of Muir was followed, at a short interval, by that of the Rev. Thomas Palmer of Dundee (Sept. 1793). Palmer was an Englishman of good birth, educated at Eton and Cambridge, a former fellow of Queens' College, Cambridge, who had renounced his Anglican orders ten years before this time, in consequence of the impression that Priestley's theological writings had made upon his mind. Since 1783 he had established his reputation in Scotland both as a preacher and as an energetic organizer of the Scottish Unitarians. The offence for which he was indicted was that of assisting in the preparation of an Address to the People which was issued by The Friends of Liberty, a Dundee society of working-class reformers. Though he took some pains to moderate the language of the draft which was submitted to him, he left in it some sentences which were palpably seditious, and one which used violent language about the war with France:

'You are plunged into a war by a wicked Ministry and a compliant Parliament, who seem careless and unconcerned for your interest, the end and design of which is almost too horrid to relate—the destruction of a whole people, merely because they will be free.'

But the court was not satisfied with calling the attention of the jury to these passages. The Friends of Liberty had stated that universal suffrage was their chief object. Lord Abercromby, in summing up, told the jury that universal suffrage would be tantamount to a total subversion of the constitution. The sentence was one of transportation for seven years. After it had been passed Palmer addressed the court in a speech of manly eloquence, claiming that his whole object had been to increase the sum of human happiness, and professing his willingness to bear any sufferings which he might incur in the pursuit of that ambition. Speaking as a lawyer Lord Cockburn remarks that although the language of the Friends of Liberty was

---

[1] *Memoirs*, ii. 23 (to Dumont): 'I am not surprised that you have been shocked at the account you have read of Muir's trial; you would have been much more shocked if you had been present at it, as I was.' For the letter to Bentham, see the latter's *Works*, xix, p. 295.

seditious, Palmer had not been proved guilty of a seditious intention. He was, indeed, a man of quite a different stamp from Frost.[1]

These trials produced, as well they might, an outburst of indignation, not unmixed with fear, from the reformers of England and Scotland. The London Corresponding Society would have received short shrift from Braxfield or from Abercromby; for in its first considerable manifesto (24 May 1792) the society had declared ' that the Nation is unrepresented and that the present system [of representation] is totally unconstitutional '.[2] The reformers of the London Corresponding Society could hardly be aware of the fact that the law of Scotland was more elastic in regard to treason and sedition than was that of England. They thought that what had happened to Muir at Edinburgh and to Palmer at Perth was a warning and a threat to themselves. True, they had avoided, and had advised other societies to avoid, such fundamental and perilous topics as monarchy, democracy, and religion.[3] But they had come to the point of believing that mere innocence would not protect any reformer from the malice of ministers and judges who were identified with the interests of the privileged classes. By July 1793 they were genuinely afraid that Hanoverian troops would be brought over to cow them, and we find them solemnly advising their correspondents, in such a case, to show the foreign mercenaries ' that their opponents are neither mob nor rabble, but an indignant, oppressed people, in whom is not yet entirely extinct the valour of their forefathers '.[4] In October they elected two delegates, Maurice Margarot and Joseph Gerrald, to represent them at the second Edinburgh Convention, and gave to these emissaries the ominous instruction, ' that it is the duty of the People to resist any act of Parliament repugnant to the original principles of the Constitution, as would be every attempt to prohibit associations for the purpose of reform '.[5]

---

[1] See Skirving's report of the trial (Edinburgh, 1793); also Cockburn, *Trials for Sedition in Scotland*, ii. 190.

[2] *Trial of Thomas Hardy* (Gurney, 1794), i, pp. 206-8.

[3] See the warning of the L. C. S. to the Norwich Societies, November 1792, in the *Trial of Thomas Hardy*, i. 225.

[4] *Ibid.*, i. 251.   [5] *Ibid.*, i. 266.

What was the purpose of the second Edinburgh Convention, or, as it was called by its promoters, the British Convention of the Delegates of the People? The original aim of William Skirving, who managed the negotiations with the English reformers, was nothing less than to prepare a definite and comprehensive scheme of reform, so that it might be put into execution as soon as the existing Government had collapsed, which he thought must happen soon. But this bare summary does less than justice to the flamboyance of his style. He wrote to the London Corresponding Society as follows:

' Let us provide every stake and stay of the tabernacle which we would erect, so that when the tabernacles of oppression in the palaces of ambition are broken down, under the madness and folly of their supporters, we may then, without anarchy and all dangerous delay, erect at once our tabernacle of righteousness. ... If the present Ministry fail who, after them, shall be trusted? It requires little penetration to see the anarchy and discord that will follow ; it will be such that nothing short of a general union among the people themselves will be able to heal ; haste therefore to associate, at least be ready to associate.' [1]

But when the delegates actually met in Edinburgh (29 Oct. 1793), there were no signs of any imminent dissolution of the existing order. The Convention went to work on humdrum lines, approving the Duke of Richmond's scheme of reform, and agreeing to petition the King that he would terminate the war with France. It was only the delegates from the London Corresponding Society and the Society for Constitutional Information who at length gave a sensational turn to the proceedings. On 28 November Sinclair, who represented the Society for Constitutional Information, moved a resolution defining the various emergencies which ought to be met by the summoning of a British Convention. These were a foreign invasion, the landing of foreign troops, the passing of a Convention Act, or the suspension of the Habeas Corpus Act. Maurice Margarot, president of the London Corresponding Society, moved on the same day and on 4 December two supplementary resolutions which provided for the prompt

[1] *Ibid.*, i. 247.

summoning of emergency conventions.   The first of these resolutions ran :

'That a Secret Committee of three and the Secretary be appointed
to determine the place where such Convention of Emergency shall
meet.   That such place shall remain a secret with them and the
Secretary of this Convention, and that each delegate shall at the break-
ing up of the present session be entrusted with a sealed letter contain-
ing the name of the place of meeting.   This letter shall be delivered
unopened to his Constituents . . . and preserved in the same state
until the period shall arrive at which it shall be necessary for the
delegate to act.'[1]

Margarot's second resolution was to the effect that any illegal
dispersion of the present Convention should be taken by the
delegates as a signal to meet together at the place appointed by
the secret committee.[2]   These were the resolutions which decided
the Lord Advocate and the Solicitor-General to disperse the
Convention and arrest the leaders.   This was done on 4 December, the day after the resolutions appeared in print in the *Edinburgh Gazetteer*.   From the fact that the law officers got their
information in this way it may be inferred that no system of
espionage had been established.

Three prosecutions were instituted as the result of these proceedings, and Margarot, Skirving, and Gerrald were sentenced
to transportation.   The two first were insignificant personages.
Margarot is described by an eyewitness, at that time fifteen
years of age, as 'a little, dark, middle-aged man, dressed in
black with silk stockings and white metal buttons, something
like one's idea of a puny Frenchman—a most impudent and
provoking body'.[3]   Skirving, whose rhetoric has already come
before our notice, had been trained for the ministry of the
Secession Church, but had afterwards become a farmer ; he bore
a respectable character.   He was charged with seditious utter-

---

[1] Professor Holland Rose suggests (*Pitt*, ii. 182) that Sinclair, who afterwards turned King's evidence, may have been acting as an *agent provocateur*.
This may be so, but the germ of his resolution is to be found in the instructions of the L. C. S. to its delegates ; and a similar resolution was adopted
by the L. C. S. itself on 20 January 1794 (*Trial of Hardy*, i, pp. 351–6).

[2] *Ibid.*, i. 321.

[3] *Journal of Henry Cockburn*, ii. 239–41, and *Trials for Sedition*, ii.
23–5.

ances and the circulation of seditious literature ; also of being
the secretary of a seditious society.   To prove his guilt the
judges were driven to reassert the doctrine that it was illegal to
agitate in any way for universal suffrage or annual parliaments.[1]
Gerrald's case excited more sympathy.   He seems to have been
a ne'er-do-weel, but he was better educated than his associates,
was in a state of health so precarious that he could not hope to
survive his sentence, and yet refused to entertain the suggestion
of his friends that he should break his bail and take to flight.
He defended himself with ability and eloquence, being evidently
more concerned to explain his views than to rebut the charges
against him.   At one point he said : ' Whatever may become of
me, my principles will last for ever.   Individuals may finish, but
truth is eternal.'   Braxfield's rejoinder was equally characteristic.
' Supposing that he acted from principle and that his motives
are pure, he becomes a more dangerous member of society than
if his conduct were really criminal. . . .   A man acting from
criminal motives is not so dangerous a member of society as a
man who thinks he is acting from principle.'[2]

The Scottish ' martyrs ', who are commemorated by a monument on the Calton Hill erected in 1844, were indeed to be
pitied.   Skirving and Gerrald died soon after their arrival in
New South Wales.   Muir was rescued by American sympathizers
in 1796, and in 1798, after many wanderings, became the guest of
the French Government at Paris, where he died in the same year.
Palmer served his full term of transportation, was taken prisoner
of war by the Spaniards in the Ladrone Islands on his homeward
voyage, and died in prison.   Margarot alone returned to England
safely after serving his full sentence (1807).   It is singular that,
while he was suspected by his fellow prisoners of being an
informer, he was also disliked by two successive governors of
the colony, and was exiled by Governor King to the island of
Tasmania for two years.   He died in 1815.

The untimely end of the British Convention excited in the
London Corresponding Society a panic which, though not wholly
unreasonable, led to extremely ill-judged actions.   At a meeting
held in a Strand tavern on 20 January 1794 the society issued

---

[1] Cockburn, *Trials for Sedition*, ii. 222, 261.
[2] *Ibid.*, ii. 42, 82, 89.

a fiery Address to the People, in which they denounced the war
with France and the political trials of the autumn, and hinted not
obscurely at the need for preparing to resist oppression by force :

'Can you believe that those who send virtuous Irishmen[1] and
Scotchmen fettered with felons to Botany Bay, do not meditate and
will not attempt to seize the first moment to send us after them. . . .
We must now chuse at once either liberty or slavery for ourselves and
our posterity.   Will you wait till Barracks are erected in every village,
and till subsidized Hessians and Hanoverians are upon us? . . . We
must have redress from our own laws and not from the laws of our
plunderers, enemies, and oppressors.'

The same meeting imitated the British Convention by resolving that in case of emergency a General Convention of the
People should be summoned.   The emergency would be held
to have arisen as soon as any bill or motion inimical to the
liberties of the People should be presented in Parliament ; as for
example a bill to authorize the landing of foreign troops in
Great Britain or Ireland, or to suspend the Habeas Corpus Act,
or to proclaim martial law, or to prevent the People from meeting in Societies of Constitutional Information.   Hardy, as the
secretary of the London Corresponding Society, at once issued
a circular to the affiliated societies, asking whether they approved
of the plan for a Convention, and how many delegates each of
them was prepared to send.   The most cordial responses came
from an open-air meeting which was held at Halifax on 21 April
1794 by ' the Reformers of Halifax, Leeds, Wakefield, Huddersfield, Bradford ', and which voted in favour of sending delegates
to attend a convention at Bristol.[2]

Of the illegality of these proceedings there could be little
question ; for a Convention summoned under the circumstances
which the Corresponding Society anticipated could only be
intended to traduce and intimidate the Houses of Parliament by
resolutions, petitions, and possibly by ulterior measures of a
more violent character.   Whether the Corresponding Society
could have stirred up a formidable demonstration is much more

---

[1] The trial of Hamilton Rowan, secretary of the United Irishmen and one
of the Irish delegates at the Edinburgh Convention, for seditious libel was
then impending, but he was in no danger of transportation.

[2] *Trial of Hardy*, i. 351–6, 404, 413.

doubtful. Dundas, then Home Secretary, believed that he
evidence of a serious plot in Scotland, and of pikes being ma
factured wholesale in Sheffield for the reformers. The operations of the Sheffield pike-makers were, however, limited to the
manufacture and sale of a few dozen pike-heads, and the magistrates of Birmingham were confident that their community was
guiltless of any such trade.

In the Scottish conspiracy, which was duly investigated in
a Scottish court, seven persons were found to be implicated, and
one was executed for high treason. He confessed to a design,
of the same type as those which were many years afterwards
framed in London by Despard and Thistlewood, for getting
possession of the government of Edinburgh; the first step was
to have been the summoning of a general convention of the
people of England, Scotland, and Ireland. But while the existence of the design was verified, the portentous emphasis with
which Dundas had announced it was shown by the revelations
at the trial to be ridiculous. The seven conspirators represented no one but themselves and were individually contemptible.

This being the position, the ministry damaged a good case and
incurred unnecessary odium by taking the English Jacobins too
seriously. In May 1794 the Habeas Corpus Act was suspended
in order to enable the Government to confine political suspects
without trial for an indefinite period. In the autumn Hardy,
Horne Tooke, Thelwall, and ten others were indicted for high
treason, although a charge of sedition would have been more
appropriate. But with the acquittals of the three whom we have
named the whole campaign collapsed. They had been prisoners
for about five months before they were acquitted, and they no
doubt were seriously alarmed as to the possibility of conviction;
to that extent they were 'martyrs' of their cause. But they had
been playing with edged tools, and Tooke at least could not
claim the indulgence due to want of education and experience.
The Government can hardly be censured on any moral grounds
for deciding to prosecute those who admittedly were organizing
agitation at a time when it was thought probable that the French
might attempt a landing. On the other hand, Pitt's decision to
support the excessive and unjustifiable sentences passed in the
courts of Scotland is one of the chief blots on his political career.

It was fortunate for his reputation that Dundas, his evil genius, left the Home Office in the summer of 1794, and was succeeded by Portland, the leader of the Rockingham Whigs, whose wise administration deprived the coercive acts of 1794-9 of half their sting.

The later history of the London Corresponding Society is obscure. There was an outburst of jubilation after the acquittals of 1794. On 4 February 1795 the society dined at the Crown and Anchor tavern in honour of Hardy, Tooke, and Thelwall; and Lord Stanhope, a Revolution Whig of the old stamp, took the chair. The society had high hopes of 'Citizen Stanhope'; but his interest in their doings seems to have been transitory, and was perhaps prompted by his personal resentment that his own private secretary, the Rev. Jeremiah Joyce, had been one of the thirteen persons indicted. On 29 June 1795 the society held an open-air meeting in St. George's Fields to affirm the necessity of annual parliaments and universal suffrage and to petition the King for a peace with France.[1] According to a report published by the society it was attended by upwards of 100,000 persons.[2] This figure may be dismissed as a gross exaggeration in view of the fact that in 1801 the population of Middlesex was returned as 818,000 souls, and that in 1811 the population of London including Westminster and Southwark was 1,050,000. This meeting did not excite any special alarm, and its petition, which had been left at the Home Office, was simply ignored by the Duke of Portland. A more ominous meeting of the society assembled in Copenhagen Fields, Islington, on 26 October. The chairman on this occasion was John Binns, a young Irishman who had lately come to London and was working as a plumber. He moved from the chair an Address to the Nation and a remonstrance to the King for his neglect of the society's petition.[3] This demonstration was used by ministerialists as an argument for passing the Treason and Sedition Acts which became law in November. As the effect of these measures was

---

[1] *Summary of the Proceedings . . . Monday, 29 June 1795.*

[2] *Correspondence of the L. C. S.* (1795), p. 29.

[3] *Account of the Meeting . . . 26 October 1795.* The society had already published a protest directed to the Duke of Portland, *A Summary of the Rights of Citizenship* (1795).

practically to gag the reform societies and their lecturers, they were naturally the cause of further mass-meetings. That of 12 November 1795, held while the fate of the bills was still uncertain, so alarmed Pitt and Portland that they appealed to the Commander-in-Chief for reinforcements of cavalry, which were to be quartered on the outskirts of London in readiness for any crisis. But two subsequent mass-meetings, on 2 December and 7 December, passed off without any serious incident.

The new Acts soon produced a calmer atmosphere; and the only notable meeting of 1796 was one held at Birmingham on 11 March. Two delegates of the London Corresponding Society were present—the redoubtable Citizen Binns and John Gale Jones, a surgeon without a practice, who had recently become one of the society's leading orators. At this meeting, which was forcibly dispersed, Jones used language which, in the opinion of a Warwickshire jury, was calculated to instigate resistance to the Treason and Sedition Acts; and in 1797 he was sentenced to a term of imprisonment, though his companion was acquitted.[1] During the mutiny of the fleet the society remained inactive, so far as the Home Office could discover, although there was some evidence implicating the United Irishmen. But it was probable that the leaders of the mutineers had learned the art of organization from the reform associations; both at Spithead and at the Nore the supreme control was vested in a central committee of elected delegates; and there is evidence that a Constitutional and Corresponding Society was in being at Portsmouth in 1795.[2] Pitt on 2 June 1797 indicated to the House of Commons his belief that the seamen had been incited by traitors, 'enemies to the fundamental interests of this country', leaving it uncertain whether the traitors in question were English or Irish. The Bow Street magistrates at the end of July proclaimed as unlawful a general meeting of the London Corresponding Society which was advertised to take place on 31 July.

---

[1] Curiously enough, the trial of Binns is in the *State Trials*, vol. xxvi, but that of Gale Jones is omitted.

[2] *Correspondence of the London Corresponding Society* (1795), pp. 75–9. The evidence implicating the clubs is fully discussed by C. Gill, *Naval Mutinies of 1797* (1913). For the Home Office inquiry at Sheerness see J. H. Rose, *Pitt*, ii. 316 f.

The society, having asked in vain for the reasons of the magistrates, persisted in assembling at the advertised time and place; whereupon the magistrates appeared on the ground with a considerable force of constables and soldiers, ordered the crowd to disperse, and arrested Citizen Binns with five others.[1]

Binns appears to have escaped any serious consequences on this occasion; but in February 1798 he was involved, innocently perhaps, in more serious proceedings. Arthur O'Connor, one of the leading members of the United Irishmen, came over to London with the object of finding his way to France, where he proposed to confer with the generals of the Directory respecting a plan of operations in Ireland. It was proved that Binns went down from London to Deal in order to hire a boat which would land O'Connor at a French port; that O'Connor and Binns were joined at Margate by an Irish priest, O'Coigly, who was the bearer of a communication from 'the Secret Committee of England' to the Directory. All three were apprehended on their way from Margate to Deal, and were tried for High Treason. O'Coigly was found guilty and executed in due course. O'Connor and Binns were acquitted, though it is probable from the evidence that they could have been convicted on several charges less grave than treason. Binns had been a humble but energetic accessory in arranging for the voyage of his friends to France; he had shared his London lodgings with O'Coigly, and appears to have received O'Connor's letters at that address; when arrested he was found to be in possession of a cipher.[2] When we add to these circumstances the fact that Binns's lodgings were in the house of Thomas Evans, the secretary of the Corresponding Society, it is not surprising that the society was held to be compromised by the affair. Binns was arrested, shortly after the trial, under the Habeas Corpus Suspension Act, and he remained in prison until 1801. The premises of the society were raided on 19 April 1798, during a session of the General Committee, which had met, for the third time in that month, to consider whether the members of the society should allow themselves to be enrolled for the defence of the country, in the event of an act being passed to

[1] *Narrative of the Proceedings . . . July 31, 1797.*
[2] *State Trials*, xxvi and xxvii.

make such service compulsory. The meeting was dispersed, and several members of the committee were arrested and committed to Newgate, after they had been interrogated before the Privy Council.[1] They remained in prison for three years. The papers of the society, which were seized at the same time, were found to include an Address to the United Irishmen which had been passed by the society in January. The natural consequence was that the Corresponding Societies Act of 1799 suppressed, as unlawful associations, both the Corresponding Society and the United Irishmen.

This Act was so important as a check upon reform agitations for many years to come that its chief provisions deserve to be carefully noted. It enumerates a number of tests by which a society may be proved illegal. These were; (1) the imposition upon the members of any oath not required or authorized by law; (2) the concealment of the names of the members, or of any part of them, from the society at large; (3) the appointment of any committee so chosen that the names of its members are unknown to the society at large; (4) the appointment of officers or delegates in such a way that their names are unknown; (5) the organization of divisions or branches of the society, with liberty of separate action or with separate officers.

It only remains to notice the end of several other societies, and of certain leaders of the reform party.

The Manchester societies ceased to meet in the summer of 1793, and do not appear to have revived after the acquittal of their leader, Thomas Walker, in 1794. The Sheffield Constitutional Society suffered a heavy blow in 1795 when young Mr. Henry Yorke, their leading orator, was found guilty of seditious utterances at a meeting on the Castle Hill, and was sentenced to be imprisoned for two years and to pay a fine of £200. Thomas Walker took no further part in politics, and his friend Thomas Cooper left England to settle in America, where he was joined in 1794 by his master Dr. Priestley. Henry Yorke became during his imprisonment a moderate Tory and a

---

[1] *Proceedings of the General Committee . . . on the 5th, 12th, and 19th of April 1798.* For a knowledge of this pamphlet, and of those already cited for the acts of the L. C. S. in and after 1795, I am indebted to Sir Charles Firth.

supporter of the war with France. After his release he took to the study of literature and history, and he was admitted a student of the Middle Temple in 1801, though he never was called to the bar. In Scotland there were some feeble attempts to reorganize the reformers after 1793. The Friends of Liberty are heard of at Dundee in 1795, and this town was in 1797 the meeting-place of a delegates' convention of the Society of United Scotsmen, which was formed in that year, with branches in the counties of Fife, Forfar, and Perth. George Mealmaker, a weaver of Dundee, was sentenced, early in 1798, to be transported for fourteen years, because he had circulated the literature of the society and had administered to another weaver the oath required from its secretary. Later in the year two other weavers, Black and Paterson, both of Dunfermline, were indicted for similar offences. Black absconded, and Paterson was transported for five years.[1]

The later history of some London reformers is not uninteresting. Horne Tooke survived until 1812, in comfortable circumstances, the recipient of an annuity of £600 a year, which had been bought for him by his friends. He stood for Westminster in 1796, and was actually returned for Old Sarum in 1801, when his return led to the passing of the Act 41 Geo. 3, c. 63, by which the clergy of the Established Church are disqualified from sitting in the House of Commons. Until his death he remained influential as an exponent of reformist doctrines. Sir Francis Burdett was his disciple, and his political parties on Sunday evenings at Wimbledon were frequented by Whigs and Reformers of every shade. Thomas Holcroft took no further part in politics, and returned to his literary pursuits— no longer a fashionable dramatist, since his political views had made his writings unpopular, but labouring under a load of debts and the handicap of bad health. He was on friendly terms with many Whigs of Fox's party; we find him advising Sir Francis Burdett, and reproaching Erskine with the behaviour of the Whigs towards the popular party in 1794. They respected him, but did nothing for him. John Thelwall persisted in his political lecturing until 1798, in spite of the Seditious Meetings Act of 1795 which required that every lecture-hall should be licensed by two magistrates; he was accustomed to

[1] These cases are reported in *State Trials*, xxvi.

set forth his political opinions in the course of lectures upon
Roman History.   But in the years 1798–1800 he found it safer
to abstain from lecturing at all, and from 1800 to 1818 he was
content to make a livelihood by lecturing and teaching as an
elocutionist.   Hardy and Evans sank back into the obscurity
from which they had emerged in the crisis of the societies.
Despard, one of those members of the Corresponding Society
who were arrested in April 1798,[1] was almost continuously
a political prisoner from that date until 1800, and emerged from
prison only to enter on the hare-brained and desperate plot
which was detected in 1802.   He was a man of superior rank
and education, and it is hardly possible to explain the folly of
his plot except on the supposition that his mind was disordered.

[1] The author of the life of Despard in the *D. N. B.* has overlooked
Despard's connexion with the L. C. S.   See, however, the life of Francis
Place by Graham Wallas.   Despard is the object of a special study, *The
Unfortunate Colonel Despard,* by Sir Charles Oman.

V

THE WHIGS AND THE REFORMERS, 1792-1800

THE Radicals of the eighteenth century do not seem to have been aware that two at least of their favourite demands—manhood suffrage and equal constituencies—had been put forward by Lilburne and the Levellers in 1647.[1] They reverenced Lilburne's memory, but all they knew of his history was what they could learn from Clarendon or from the *Biographia Britannica* (1760). In their eyes Lilburne was simply the honest and fearless defender of the people's rights against a despotic House of Commons and a military dictatorship. It is probable that the Radicals derived their doctrine of Equality at second or third hand from the literature of the Levelling movement; for, as we have seen, the first political pamphlet of the eighteenth century in which the doctrine is clearly stated is the *Essay* of the unitarian Priestley.

'Every government whatever be the form of it, is originally and antecedent to its present form an equal republic. . . . Every man, when he comes to be sensible of his natural rights, and to feel his own importance, will consider himself as fully equal to any other person whatever. The consideration of riches and power, however acquired, must be entirely set aside, when we come to these first principles.'

This is an eighteenth-century version of the views of Rainborough and Sexby. But Priestley's admirers thought his doctrine new and original, and Priestley himself was probably more conscious of indebtedness to Rousseau than to any English thinker.

The Whigs, on the other hand, made it their boast that their main principles were borrowed from publicists and statesmen of the seventeenth century. The list of their political classics begins with Harrington's *Oceana* (1656), and the authors to whom scholarly Whigs most often appealed were Sidney, Henry Neville, and John Locke. So long as they remained

---

[1] *Case of the Army Truly Stated* (1647); *First Agreement of the People* (1647).

true to the teaching of these masters they were bound to resist
the doctrine of Equality ; but on the other hand they could not
dispute the right of the people to rise against an oppressive
sovereign.

They were bound to reject Equality because the Whig classics
took it for granted that ' empire follows the balance of property ' [1]
and ought to do so. ' Force or fraud ', Neville says, ' may alter
a government, but it is property that must found or eternise it.'
And, speaking generally, .it is assumed by the whole school
that the qualification for the electoral franchise and for a seat in
Parliament ought to be landed property. The rule of the landless mob would be not a democracy but mere anarchy, according
to Neville, and Sidney holds that

' Those governments in which the democratical part governs most do
more frequently err in the choice of men or the means of preserving
that purity of manners which is required for the well-being of a people
than those wherein aristocracy prevails.' [2]

But the right of resistance to oppression is assigned by these
theorists in the last resort to the people at large; to whom,
Sidney frankly acknowledges, an unfettered discretion must
be allowed in deciding whether insurrection is justifiable and
necessary :

' Men who delight in cavils may ask, Who shall be the judge of these
occasions ? And whether I intend to give the people the decision of
their own cause? To which I answer that, when the contest is between
the magistrate and the people, the party to which the determination is
referred must be the judge of his own case, and the question is only
whether the people of Rome should judge Tarquin or Tarquin judge
the people.' [3]

' If the safety of the people be the supreme law, and this safety
extend to, and consist in, the preservation of their liberties, goods,
lands, and lives, that law must necessarily be the root and beginning of
all magistratical power, and all laws must be subservient and subordinate to it. The question will not be what pleases the king, but what is
good for the people.' [4]

---

[1] This phrase first occurs in *A Letter from an Officer of the Army in
Ireland* (1653), which has been variously attributed to Henry Neville,
Wildman, and Ludlow.

[2] *Discourses concerning Government*, c. 2, § 19.

[3] *Op. cit.*, c. 2, § 24.　　　　　　　　[4] *Op. cit.*, c. 3, § 16.

Locke, reaffirming the right of resistance, goes a step beyond Sidney, by arguing that the right is inalienable,

'God and Nature never allowing a man so to abandon himself as to neglect his own preservation.' [1]

He soothes his readers by reminding them that the inconvenience of an unjust government must become extreme before the majority will be convinced that a revolution is the only way of amending it. He might have added the comfortable argument, which was never far from the minds of Whig statesmen, that the unenfranchised could be trusted, in such matters, to follow the wishes of the lords of the soil.

Locke's commentators, however, were not content to see the new Whig system protected only by general probabilities or by considerations of expediency in the minds of the sovereign people. We find Sir Robert Walpole, for example, arguing, in the Sacheverel case, that

'Resistance ought never to be thought of but when an utter subversion of the laws of the realm threatens the whole frame of our constitution, and no redress is otherwise to be hoped for.'

Burke's comment on this and other speeches of the same tenor is that the Whigs of that day desired to assert the perpetual validity of the Revolution settlement; and of this intention he approved.[2] But there were many Whigs in the reign of George III who preferred the opinion of Sidney to that of Walpole. And Sidney had argued that changes in the constitution were only natural and right:

'If it be lawful for us . . . to build houses, ships, and forts better than our ancestors, to make such arms as are most fit for our defence, and to invent printing, with an infinite number of other arts beneficial to mankind, why have we not the same right in matters of government upon which all others do absolutely depend? . . . Why should men be for ever obliged to continue under the same form of government that their ancestors happened to set up in the time of their ignorance?'[3]

It is remarkable what pains were taken in the eighteenth century to make the older Whig classics accessible. The

---

[1] *Second Treatise on Civil Government*, c. 14.
[2] *Appeal from the New to the Old Whigs.*
[3] *Discourses concerning Government*, c. 3, § 7.

eccentric Thomas Hollis (1720–74), a Whig lawyer and a man
of considerable fortune, went to considerable expense in re-
publishing the works of Sidney, Locke, and Neville in the years
1763–73. His chief assistant in the first stages of this enterprise
was Richard Baron (d. 1766), a native of Leeds, educated in
Glasgow, who, in 1751–3, had published a good deal of the
political writings of the Commonwealth men, especially Ludlow's
Memoirs, Milton's prose-works, and Sidney's *Discourses*. Holles
and Baron passed for republicans; that is to say, they emphasized
the doctrine of the sovereignty of the people. To the same
school belonged the followers of Wilkes and Cartwright and
the Duke of Richmond. It was possible in those days to be
a very good 'republican' without incurring the suspicion of
subversive tendencies. For many republicans held that, whatever theories prevailed, property would still guide the ship of
state. Only, to ensure this happy result, it was essential that the
property qualification for members of the House of Commons
should be retained, and that members should insist on voting in
accordance with their own convictions, no matter what the wishes
of their constituents might be. On this question the adventurous
Sidney held the same language as Burke. Sidney says:

'It is not for Kent or Sussex, Lewes or Maidstone, but for the whole
nation that the members chosen in those places are sent to serve
in Parliament; and though it be fit for them as friends and neighbours
. . . to hearken to the opinions of the electors for the information
of their judgments . . . yet they are not strictly and properly obliged to
give account of their actions to any, unless the whole body of the nation
for whom they serve, and who are equally concerned in their resolutions, could be assembled.'[1]

There were some statesmen on the Whig side who thought
that rotten boroughs, controlled by men of great property, would
always be needed, however Parliament was reformed, to ensure
the stability of ministries and to keep the House of Commons
from changing its composition too suddenly and violently at
general elections. But twenty years of the personal ascendancy
of George III had shown that the Whigs were not likely to gain
power or to keep it by the help of rotten boroughs. The Whig
landowners did not own a sufficient number of such boroughs;

[1] *Op. cit.*, c. 3, § 44.

nor, if it came to buying boroughs, could they afford for long
to compete against the combined resources of the Tories and
the Privy Purse. By 1780 it had occurred to Charles James Fox,
as it had already occurred to William Pitt, that a minister who
was prepared to press for a moderate reform of the House of
Commons might not only secure popularity in the present, but
might also be preparing for himself and for his party a hold
upon the constituencies which would enable him to govern
without regard for the caprices of the King or the goodwill
of the borough-owners.   But Fox, with characteristic levity,
after obtaining election for Westminster in 1780, on the strength
of a definite programme of reform, sacrificed his pledges in
1783 in order to secure the alliance and co-operation of Lord
North.   He agreed with North that reform should be an open
question in the Cabinet; and although he himself and his supporters spoke in favour of Pitt's reform motion, it was a foregone
conclusion that the motion would be rejected.

The younger Whigs may have felt that the compromise had
been ignominious.   They certainly felt, after the Coalition had
fallen and Pitt was firmly in the saddle, that something should
be done to restore the alliance between the Whigs and the
popular party.   Hence the foundation in April 1792 of the
Society of the Friends of the People.   Its leading members
were Charles Grey, Henry Erskine, and the Lord John Russell
of that day.   James Mackintosh, then the Marcellus of the
Whigs in Scotland, acted for a time as secretary, and is said to
have composed the Address to the People which the society
issued soon after its formation.   The objects in view were
announced in reserved and decorous language : ' First to restore
the freedom of Election and a more equal representation of the
People in Parliament.   Secondly to secure to the people a more
frequent exercise of their right of electing their Representatives.'
The Address threw no further light upon the projects of the
society, but announced with bewildering catholicity that the
principles of the society were those of Locke and Blackstone,
Chatham and Sir George Savile, the Duke of Richmond and
the Marquis of Lansdowne (i.e. Lord Shelburne), Mr. Pitt and
Mr. Fox.   No innovations would be proposed; but the society
hoped to reinstate the constitution upon its true principles and

original ground. The members had pledged themselves to oppose any unconstitutional or irregular agitation. But a motion for introducing a reform biil would be moved at an early date by Mr. Charles Grey and would be seconded by the Hon. Thcmas Erskine.[1]

This manifesto was rather prematurely taken by Major Cart-wright as an expression of sympathy for his own political ideas; and he wrote, on behalf of the Society for Constitutional Informa-tion, to solicit the alliance of the Friends of the People. Lord John Russell corrected his error in a vein of ponderous sarcasm. He explained that he and his friends had no faith in the theories of Paine. 'We view man as he is, the creature of habit as well as of reason. We think it therefore our bounden duty to oppose extreme changes.' The letter ended with a blunt statement that the Friends of the People desired no further intercourse with Cartwright's society.[2] It was harder to answer the London Corresponding Society, which bluntly asked the Friends of the People, a few months later, 'what measures you mean to pursue, when you mean to begin, and how far you intend carrying your proposed reforms?' The reply was brusque, and at the same time indicative of embarrassment. 'We never can be supposed to have surrendered to any other body of men the exercise of our own discretion, with respect both to the plan which we deem most effectual for the purpose, and the time which we may think most favourable for offering it to the public; at present we think that to make public our views on these subjects would be to furnish arms to our enemies and to injure the cause in which we are engaged.'[3]

The truth was that the Friends of the People did not yet know what they intended to propose, because they did not know how much reform the average Whig elector was prepared to swallow. On 30 April 1792, when Grey gave notice in the House of Commons that he would move a reform motion in the following session, Burke raised his voice to insinuate that Grey's object was to remodel the House on the pattern of the National

---

[1] See the pamphlet *Society of the Friends of the People* (1793) issued by the society itself.
[2] Printed in the *Trial of Horne Tooke*, i, pp. 185–90.
[3] Printed in the *Trial of T. Hardy*, i, pp. 221–31.

Assembly, and Burke expressed accurately enough the feelings of the Portland Whigs. Even among the friends of Fox there were some who lamented, with Lord Holland, that Grey's impetuosity, Lauderdale's restlessness, and the ambition of certain younger Whigs, Whitbread, Lambton, and Tierney, were drawing the party into strange courses. But these alarming conspirators were almost naive in their open-mindedness. Late in 1792 Fox asked Tierney what specific reforms the Friends of the People would propose. 'I assured him', writes Tierney to Grey, 'that we had no specific plan yet drawn out, and that we should esteem it a very particular favour if Fox would give us his ideas, as I was convinced the majority of our Society were above all things anxious to act cordially with him'.[1] In the session of 1793 Grey merely moved for a Committee on the Franchise, without explaining his own views. Only in 1794 do we find him avowing a preference for a householder franchise,[2] or, as it was commonly called, a 'scot and lot franchise'; and in May 1795 the Friends of the People, at their last meeting, adopted Grey's plan in the form of a resolution, 'that every householder in Great Britain paying parish taxes, except peers, should have a vote at the election of one member of parliament'. Fox came slowly, and, it must be added, rather languidly into agreement with Grey. In 1796 Fox wrote to his nephew, Holland, that perhaps parliamentary reform would have to come about before the House of Commons could recover its due influence in the Government. He continued:

'We as a party, I fear, can do nothing, and the contest must be between the Court and the Democrats. These last, without our assistance, will either be too weak to resist the Court—and then comes Mr. Hume's Euthanasia, which you and I think the worst of all events —or, if they are strong enough, being wholly unmixed with any aristocratic leaven, and full of resentment against us for not joining them, will probably go to greater excesses and bring on the only state of things which can make a man doubt whether the despotism of a monarchy is the worst of all evils.'[3]

This confession of faith might have been literally adopted by his friend Grey on taking office in 1830. It may not unfairly

[1] Trevelyan, *Lord Grey*, p. 61.   [2] *Op. cit.*, p. 94.
[3] *Correspondence of C. J. Fox*, iii. 135.

be described as exhibiting the normal attitude of the New
Whigs, whom Burke feared so greatly, when they were face to
face with a popular agitation.   But by 1796 it was too late for
Fox to put this rule of action to the test.   For, as we have
already seen, the Acts of 1795 had robbed the popular societies
of their most damaging weapons, and the Whigs, by reason of
their fanatical opposition to the war, were losing all credit in
the House of Commons and outside it.   In fact the gesture of
sympathy for the Radicals was delayed until 26 May 1797, when
Grey at length produced a concrete scheme of parliamentary
reform.   It provided for triennial parliaments, the abolition of
rotten boroughs, and an increased number of county members;
for a household franchise in the boroughs; for the extension of
the county franchise to certain classes of leaseholders and copyholders; for the creation of single-member constituencies and
the abolition of plural voting.   The speech of Grey appeared to
Charles Abbot, who did not sympathize with Grey's views and
disliked him as a man, both moderate and discreet.   Grey
claimed for his measure that it was founded on practical
expediency, not upon any doctrine of natural and inalienable
rights, nor upon the opinion that anomalies and inequalities in
the representative system were essentially unjust.   The House
of Commons had become negligent of its duties and submissive
to the ministers in power, and the consequences of this temper
had been disastrous to the country in the past five years.   'In
a war remarkable only for misfortune, and distinguished on our
part solely by disgrace, the House of Commons have suffered
ministers to go on from failure to failure, adding misconduct to
misfortune and madness to folly.'   The House had also failed
to defend the liberties of the subject when these were attacked
by the executive; and it had accepted, without censure or investigation, the mandate of the Privy Council under which the
Bank suspended cash payments and an unparalleled shock was
inflicted on the public credit.   For these reasons he desired to
obtain a full, free, and fair representation of the people in the
House of Commons.   And he desired to fix the property
qualification for a member of the House so low 'that no man,
however mean, may not hope, by honest industry and fair
exertions, to obtain a seat in the House of Commons'.   The

present House had brought the country nearly to the end of its resources, and it would be wise to put a reform in hand which would remove every just cause of complaint in this country before new trials presented themselves, as, for example, a rising in Ireland. The boldest passage of the speech, because the most open to misrepresentation, came near its close:

'In France a revolution has taken place; the principles at least in which it originated, whatever others may think, I shall always defend. . . . For my own part I entertain a sanguine hope that in the end it will tend to the diffusion of liberty and rational knowledge all over the world.'[1]

Fox, who reserved himself till the end of the debate and ranged at large over all the misdeeds of ministers since 1784, reminded the House that, since 1782, he had supported every motion for parliamentary reform, by whomsoever proposed. But he had never believed it a matter of great urgency until the present time. Grey's motion, in his view, made it possible to escape from the alternatives to which the country stood exposed—on the one hand a base and degraded slavery, on the other a tumultuous, though short-lived, anarchy. The history of Ireland since 1791 showed the unwisdom of irritating those who demanded moderate charges by an impolitic and unjust refusal. Ministers pride themselves on the confirmation which their policy had obtained at the last general election. But general elections had given no index of the true feeling of the country during the American War; and under the present form and practice of elections it would be unreasonable to anticipate that a general election would produce any considerable change. The petitions for reform which had come up from Middlesex, London, Westminster, Surrey, Hampshire, York, Edinburgh, and Glasgow were much more significant than a general election. There was much more argument on this level in the speech; but intercalated between his criticism of the ministerial case and his reasoned defence of Grey's measure there is one of those flights of eloquence which stamp Fox as one of the great idealists of English history:

'Now, Sir, though I do not wish to imitate France, and though I am persuaded you have no necessity for any terror of such imitation being

[1] *Parl. Hist.*, xxxiii. 644–52. Cf. the *Diary of Lord Colchester*, i. 104–5.

forced upon you, yet I say that you ought to be as ready to adopt the virtues, as you are steady in averting from the country the vices, of France.   If it is clearly demonstrated that genuine representation alone can give solid power, and that in order to make government strong the people must make the government ; you ought to act on this grand maxim of political wisdom thus demonstrated, and call in the people, according to the original principles of your system, to the strength of your government.   In doing this you will not innovate, you will not imitate.   In making the people of England a constituent part of the government of England, you do no more than restore the genuine edifice designed and framed by our ancestors.   An honourable baronet [1] spoke of the instability of democracies. . . . When we look at the democracies of the ancient world, we are compelled to acknowledge their oppressions (? oppressiveness) to their dependencies, their horrible acts of injustice and ingratitude to their own citizens ; but they compel us also to admiration by their vigour, their constancy, their spirit, and their exertions in every great emergency in which they are called upon to act.   We are compelled to own that it (sc. democracy) gives a power of which no other form of government is capable.   Why ?   Because it incorporates every man with the state, because it arouses everything that belongs to the soul as well as to the body of man : because it makes every individual feel that he is fighting for himself and not another ; that it is his own cause, his own safety, his own concern, his own dignity on the face of the earth and his own interest on the identical soil which he has to maintain, and accordingly we find that, whatever may be objected to them on account of the turbulency of the passions which they engender, their short duration and their disgusting vices, they have exacted from the common suffrage of mankind the palm of strength and vigour.' [2]

But, before Fox made his appeal to the House, Government in the person of Pitt himself had announced its determination to resist Grey's plan.   The minister spoke at some length and with an evident desire to defend his own consistency, which Grey had very naturally called in question :

'Whatever may have been my former opinion, am I to be told that I am inconsistent, if I feel that it is expedient to forego the advantage which any alteration may be calculated to produce, rather than afford an inlet to principles with which no compromise can be made ; rather

[1] Probably Sir William Young, who had spoken earlier in the debate, in opposition to the motion ; but the report of his speech in the Parliamentary history does not contain this remark.

[2] *Parl. Hist.*, xxxiii. 714–15.

than hazard the utter annihilation of a system under which this country has flourished in its prosperity, by which it has been supported in its adversity, and by the energy and vigour of which it has been enabled to recover from the difficulties with which it had to contend.'[1]

Pitt expressed the opinion that Grey's plan would not content the followers of Paine—and these, he remarked, were the only persons in the country who were demanding a reform of the representation as an immediate necessity. Their object was simply to destroy the constitution; and if they supported Grey's scheme it would be with a view to that object. The proposed household franchise was, in his opinion, too much like universal suffrage to be safe. He argued that, under the existing system, the sense of the people was adequately expressed at the elections of county members and members for populous boroughs. How would universal suffrage improve the position? Would any man contend that Manchester and Birmingham suffered any disadvantage from having no representatives?

'It is not the harsh uniformity of principles, each pushed to its extreme, but the general complexion arising out of the various shades, which forms the harmony of the representation and the practical excellence of the constitution, capable of improving itself consistently with its fundamental principles. Who will say that this beautiful variety may not have contributed to the advantage of the whole?'

More cogent than this nebulous aestheticism was Pitt's references to the circumstances of the moment, 'when it is admitted by the learned gentleman himself[2] that radical discontent is prevalent in the country, and when it is undeniable that the men who talk of liberty aim merely at licentiousness'. Pitt had in mind, though he did not mention, the mutineers of the fleet. Grey's motion was defeated by 256 votes to 91. It was a crushing defeat, for the Whigs were at full strength on this occasion. They had not expected any other result, and they had arranged, before the debate began, that they would secede from both Houses after the division. This rash and unstatesmanlike plan was adopted, according to Lord Holland, as the result of a vote taken in a meeting of the party, and Grey was the prime mover, Fox acquiescing 'from indolence rather than judgment'.[3] It is

---

[1] *Parl. Hist.*, xxxiii. 673.
[2] i. e. Erskine, who had seconded Grey's motion.
[3] *Memoirs of Whig Party*, i. 84.

remarkable that Grey should have done his party this disservice and simultaneously have given to it a claim upon the trust of the unrepresented classes, which thirty-three years later was to make him the most popular of Whig ministers since Walpole.

The secession did not mean continuous absence from the House of Commons, nor was this what the leaders had intended. Grey, at the close of his speech on May 26, said that 'though he should always be present in future to vote for or against any measures by which the interests of his constituents might be affected, after that night he should not think proper to trouble the House with any observations'. And Fox said that he did not think it consistent with his duty totally to secede. 'Whenever it shall appear that my efforts may contribute in any degree to restore us to the situation from which the confidence of this House in a desperate system and an incapable administration has so suddenly reduced us, I shall be found ready to discharge my duty.'[1] In fact Grey spoke no more until February 1799, when he made two speeches on the proposed Union with Ireland. Fox, at the desire of his own constituents, spoke twice in the winter of 1797–8 against the proposed increase of the assessed taxes. In April 1798 he spoke in a debate on the Slave Trade, and in June 1798 protested against a policy of coercion in Ireland. In 1799 he did not speak at all. The only speech of his in this period which calls for special mention is that of 4 January 1798, in which he re-emphasized his new attitude towards parliamentary reform. At one time he had thought such a reform useful but not a matter of absolute necessity. Now he thought that it was absolutely impossible to correct abuses until there had been a reform. He would never try to bring about reform otherwise than through the House of Commons. For the present he despaired of converting the House, and would therefore stay away from the debates. But he hoped for a time when the public would express an opinion on the subject in such a way that the House would realize the wisdom and the necessity of reform. 'But why should I, by my attendance from day to day, give countenance to the idea that there is in this House a free unbiassed opinion, and that it is not under the influence of the Crown ?'.[2]

[1] *Parl. Hist.*, xxxii. 652, 732.   [2] *Ibid.*, xxxiv. 1233, 1237.

We may at this point pause to examine the composition of the Whig party in both Houses. In the House of Lords the Dukes of Norfolk and Bedford and Devonshire, the Marquess of Lansdowne, the Earls of Derby, Guilford, Moira, Earl Fitzwilliam, Lord Holland, and Lord King had some pretensions as debaters. In the House of Commons Sir Francis Burdett, Curwen, Erskine, Sheridan, Tierney, Western, and Whitbread were the most efficient after Fox and Grey. Sheridan and Tierney were much in evidence during the secession, and Tierney gave much offence to his brother Whigs by the regularity of his attendance, and the persistency with which he thrust himself forward. Clear headed, and coming of a business stock, he had the making of a leader in the lower House, and might have become a competent Chancellor of the Exchequer. But his mind was that of a subaltern, and the best to be hoped of him was that he would harass the Government on questions of finance and the liberty of the subject. Many years were to elapse before he was given a trial as a leader, and when his chance came he failed to control the unruly team that he was asked to drive. Erskine and Sheridan were excellent as orators, but wanting both in character and in the capacity for diligent attention to routine.

The only Whig member in a subordinate position who appeared to have energy and ideas was the brewer Samuel Whitbread, schoolfellow and brother-in-law of Charles Grey, who had entered the House of Commons in 1790 as member for Bedford. In 1795 Whitbread came forward with a proposal that magistrates should be empowered to fix a minimum wage for agricultural labourers; he had been impressed by the investigations of Dr. Richard Price, who had shown reasons for believing that prices of the necessaries of life were rising faster than the wages of labour. Whitbread's contentions excited interest enough to elicit a reply from Pitt; and, what was more, a half-promise that the laws of settlement, so far as they bore hardly on the poor, should be relaxed, and that parish relief should be proportionate to the size of the applicant's family. Pitt, indeed, went so far as to draft a bill for the amendment of the Poor Laws; but his measure was resisted by his own supporters, and it was left to the justices of the peace to carry out

the less useful of Pitt's two suggestions.[1]   On 11 February 1800
Whitbread returned to the charge, and asked for leave to revive
his former bill since nothing had been done by the minister.
Leave was granted after Whitbread had explained that his object
was simply 'to empower magistrates for a limited time and
within a limited extent to determine the sum below which the
wages of a working man in full vigour should not be reduced',
and that it was only fair to make this change in the law, since
the labourer was prevented by the statutes against combinations
from uniting to raise their wages against the masters.   This bill
was thrown out on the second reading, probably because the
House agreed with Pitt that the distress of the poor would be
best relieved by the overseers in the parishes, because no
uniform wage could be fixed which would be adequate to meet
all cases of hardship.[2]

[1] *Pitt's Speeches* (ed. 1817), ii. 129–37 (Speech of 12 Feb. 1796).
[2] *Parl. Hist.*, xxxiv. 1426 ff.

VI

THE WHIG PARTY, 1801–1819

OF all the preceptors to whom the Whigs were indebted for their political education Napoleon Bonaparte was the most effective. He obliged them to admit that the enemies of England, as well as her friends, might sometimes behave unjustifiably; that war is sometimes an unavoidable necessity in this wicked world; and that there are evils, worse even than the loss of commerce or submission to military discipline, to be endured by nations which pursue the policy of peace at any price. They were also compelled to admit that, admirable as the leading ideas of the French Revolution might be when applied to the government of the French people, there was no valid reason why France should be allowed to dominate Europe, and much to be said in favour of the Governments and peoples who were prepared to resist a French hegemony imposed by military force.

These lessons were not quickly learned. The Peace of Amiens was criticized by Fox in the old factious spirit. ' I do not like it any the worse for being so triumphant a peace for France ... The triumph of the French government over the English does in fact afford me a degree of pleasure which it is very difficult to disguise.'[1] When difficulties arose about the fulfilment of the terms, he accepted Napoleon's complaints and reproaches as undeniably just. It was our plain duty to evacuate Malta and Alexandria. How hypocritical of Addington to simulate a concern for the liberties of Switzerland, considering that we had never stirred a finger to save Poland. As for the incorporation of Piedmont with France, that was ' literally nothing '. Napoleon's behaviour to Switzerland and Piedmont was no doubt abominable; but in what way were British interests imperilled by it? And even if we had a case on which we might legitimately stand, was it not obvious that the only result of a new war would be to increase the power of Napoleon?

---

[1] *Correspondence*, iii. 345, 349.

But already his followers were beginning to think for themselves upon these subjects. Grey came to the conclusion that Napoleon wished for war.[1] It was true that the recent annexations of France were not contrary to the letter of the Peace of Amiens. ' But there may be a way of using power so threatening and so insulting as at last . . . to force resistance. And he appears to me to be determined . . . to push us point by point until we shall be compelled to take some measure which may give him a pretence for the hostilities which he meditates.'[2] Grey was already designated by Fox as the future head of the Whig party, and indeed the older statesman assumes in their correspondence of this date that it would be for Grey to settle the future orientation of Whig policy.[3] This arrangement and Grey's views on foreign policy seem to have been an open secret; for in April 1803 Addington made overtures to Grey for a junction of their respective parties. The offer was in effect refused, since Grey replied that, if he was to come into office, there must be a Whig majority in the Cabinet and Fox must be included.[4] But when the rupture with France was discussed in the House of Commons (May 23) Grey announced that his party, without approving of the manner in which ministers had conducted the negotiations, would nevertheless not oppose the war. As a consequence the Whigs found themselves, for the first time for many years, substantially in agreement with Mr. Pitt—approving of the war-policy, but ready and even eager to indict Addington for the bungling character of his war measures. They had become one element in an opposition party which agreed on hardly anything but foreign policy.

There was now no valid objection to an alliance of the Whigs with the following of William Grenville, round whom had gathered all the more Whiggish members of Pitt's old majority. The Grenvillites were first and foremost a war party. They were out of humour with Pitt, because they held that Pitt was unduly tolerant of Addington's shortcomings. If Pitt would not

---

[1] *Correspondence*, iii. 385, 388, 404. *Speeches*, vi. 395 (Piedmont). See also the speech of 21 May 1803 for the question of Malta.

[2] Trevelyan, *Lord Grey*, p. 129.

[3] Fox's *Correspondence*, iii. 373 (Letter of 29 Nov. 1802).

[4] *Life and Opinions of Earl Grey*, pp. 75–6.

take office himself, the next best course, so Grenville held, was
that a coalition ministry should be formed on the broadest basis
possible to make war as war should be made. As a preliminary
measure they made overtures to Fox, who was left by his
colleague to lead the Whigs single handed in the sittings of
the winter of 1803-4; and a bargain was struck between Fox
and Grenville in the month of January. The contracting parties
announced, through the newspapers, that their alliance was not to
be called a coalition; it was simply an agreement to co-operate
in opposition, and that it would not call for any sacrifice of
principles on either side. They did not, however, announce
that the ultimate object was to form a new administration in
which followers of both Fox and Grenville would serve, and
in which differences of opinion would of necessity have to be
adjusted by mutual concessions. That secret was only disclosed
to the followers and parliamentary friends of the two leaders.
Fox of course communicated it to Grey; Grenville, from a sense
of personal loyalty, communicated it to Pitt.[1] The latter was
not offended or perturbed. He probably assumed that he could
step into Addington's place at any time he chose, and thought
that, with Addington's followers to support him, he could easily
defeat the new coalition. Events soon showed that this was
indeed the case. For in April Addington decided to resign
rather than continue to fight the combined forces of Pitt and
the coalition with a diminishing majority; and the King then
sent for Pitt.

There was still a possibility that the Fox-Grenville coalition
might be taken into partnership by Pitt, whose great ambition
was always tempered by good sense and moderation. An idea
was abroad that the times called for a ministry formed on a
broad basis, and Pitt was willing to try the experiment provided
that he was unequivocally the First Minister. He was, however, not prepared to force this plan upon the King, whose
sanity was at this time precarious; and he cannot have been
greatly surprised when the King stipulated that Fox should be
excluded from the new arrangements, or when Grenville declined
to accept office in a Cabinet which would, as he put it, be

---

[1] Fox, *Correspondence*, iii. 449 (Letter to C. Grey, 29 Jan. 1804); *Windham Papers*, ii. 231; *Dropmore Papers*, vii. 212 (Grenville to Pitt 31 Jan.).

founded on a principle of exclusion.[1]   Without any loss of time
Pitt turned to an alternative policy which he had framed before
the ministerial crisis actually occurred.   He formed a Cabinet
of his own friends, supplemented by members of the late administration; among the latter were the Duke of Portland, Lord
Castlereagh, Lord Hawkesbury, and Lord Eldon; of the former
Lord Melville alone was likely to be a source of strength.   It
was on the whole a Tory administration, and little calculated to
reassure the country.   Castlereagh and Hawkesbury had yet
to prove their worth as the managers of a great war, and at
this date were regarded by Lord Grenville, a tolerably competent
critic, with supreme contempt.[2]

During these negotiations Fox had very honourably intimated
to his own followers and to Grenville his wish that they should
accept Pitt's invitation.   It was only to be expected that the
Whigs should reject the suggestion.   'No earthly consideration',
writes Grey to his wife, 'should make me accept office without
Fox';[3] and, again, when Fox had endeavoured to reopen the
negotiations with Pitt, Grey writes, 'I put an absolute veto on it,
and we are all excluded'.   The Whigs, however, were a little
surprised and sincerely touched by Grenville's loyalty, which
they apparently thought to be in excess of any engagement
that he had formally given in his contract of alliance.

From this date until 1819 the Grenville group were regarded
as true Whigs, and their leader shared the leadership with Fox
and Grey successively.   They were very distinctly a conservative
wing of the party, always zealous for the efficient prosecution
of the war, always averse from parliamentary reform or any
other measure which trenched upon the old Whig theory of the
constitution.   Nor were they easy to deal with.   Lord Grenville
inherited from his father the legal ingenuity which had devised
the American Stamp Act, and the pertinacious obstinacy which
had driven George III, in his apprentice days, to the verge
of distraction; and though Lord Grenville was himself comparatively disinterested, he was surrounded by relatives and

---

[1] Stanhope's *Pitt*, iv. 141 (Pitt to Melville, 29 March 1804); *ibid.*, Appen-
dix, pp. i–xiv; *Dropmore Papers*, vii. 222 (Grenville's refusal of Pitt's offer).
[2] *Dropmore Papers*, vii. 333.
[3] Trevelyan, *Earl Grey*, p. 136.

connexions who approached politics with a strong and simple determination to better the fortunes of their clan. Apart from its voting strength the Grenville connexion was never an asset to the Whigs, and its influence goes far to explain the failure of the Whigs, after 1807, to maintain the role of a popular party.

There was not a large choice of fundamental measures on which Fox and Grenville could agree, and for which their followers would cheerfully co-operate. They found one in the Catholic question, on which, to do them justice, both felt strongly, and in 1805 they undertook the management of the Catholic agitation in Parliament, after Pitt had been approached by a deputation of the Irish Catholics and had positively refused to support the petitions which they had prepared. These petitions were presented on the 25th of May by Grenville in the House of Lords and by Fox in the House of Commons. They could hardly have chosen a better method of embarrassing the Prime Minister,[1] whose pledges to the Irish Catholics troubled the consciences of many of his friends; and the question of Catholic relief remained, for long after Pitt's death, the chief moral asset of the Whigs. But they paid dearly for their principle in 1807.

While the Whigs were occupied, in 1805, with organizing opposition, they were also active critics of the Government. As critics of war-policy they had the advantage of assistance from Windham, whose past experience had made him more conversant with military science than with Whig principles. Fox himself had views about the methods of meeting an army of invasion. Grenville (and to some extent Fox also) laughed at Pitt for believing that the Boulogne flotilla was a real menace, and took him to task (after the event) for having hurried Austria into the disastrous campaign of Ulm and Austerlitz. But the chief parliamentary *coup* of the Whigs in 1805 was the impeachment

---

[1] On 19 March 1805 the Marquis of Sligo wrote to an Irish official from London : ' I wrote to you yesterday that all had gone wrong on the Catholic question, which in fact has been sold to the Opposition, the Commissioners having agreed, at the instance of their friends the Opposition, to give up the restriction, which their instructions imposed on them, of not pushing it if the public good stood in the way of it ' (Irish State Paper Office, Carton 406).

of Lord Melville—a salutary example no doubt to office-holders
of all parties, but an example which would scarcely have excited
so much righteous fervour on the opposite benches if Melville
had not happened to be the right-hand man of Pitt.　Pitt at
least was doing his utmost to stay the progress of Napoleon ;
and, when he had failed, the Whigs were utterly at a loss to
think of remedies.　On hearing the news of Ulm Lord Grenville
wrote to Windham : 'One's mind is lost in astonishment and
apprehension when one looks at what has happened and is still
to be expected.'[1]　Fox's commentary is simply that of the party
leader.　'Pitt ought to be fallen on without any mercy for
having set on foot the ill-timed, rash, and ill-constructed attack
of the Austrians, without waiting either for Prussia or the
Russian armies.'[2]

Yet early in 1806, after Pitt's death, Grenville and Fox
were called upon to save the State by forming an administration.　They entered on their work with many misgivings.　Their parliamentary prospects were not good.　Pitt's
majority in the House of Commons, though diminished by
Addington's defection, had been substantial to the last.　The
King thought it quite possible that Lord Hawkesbury could
carry on Pitt's system, and Hawkesbury's refusal seems to have
been due to a feeling, on his own part and on that of his
colleagues, that they could not count on the support of the
country.　It was necessary for the Whigs to purchase the votes
of Sidmouth's [Addington's] following; and the price was high.
For Sidmouth claimed, besides two seats in the Cabinet—one
for himself and the other for Lord Ellenborough—the right of
continuing to resist the Catholic claims.　This was ominously
like the bargain which the Whigs had made with North in 1782.
Sidmouth, unlike North, was much inferior in voting strength
to his allies ; but still it would be difficult for them to raise the
Catholic question, so long as he insisted on his rights.　The
best apology that can be made for Fox and Grenville is that
any other party leaders at that moment would have been hard
put to it to secure a working majority without a similar sacrifice
of principles.

Another difficulty was that Fox and Grenville were for the

[1] *Windham Papers*, ii. 275.　　　　[2] *Correspondence*, iv. 122.

moment at variance about the grand question of the war. Fox
had hopes of making peace on reasonable terms, while Grenville
justly believed that Napoleon would never make peace in good
faith till he was conscious of defeat.   Months were wasted, after
the formation of the Cabinet, while Fox entered into negotiations
and laboriously satisfied himself by eight months of experiment
that Napoleon was untrustworthy.[1]   As Castlereagh remarked,
he would have been better engaged in overtures to Prussia and
to Russia, the only possible allies that we could gain.[2]   It is idle
to speculate how a military policy might have been conducted
by Fox at the Foreign Office, Windham as Secretary of War,
and Grey as First Lord of the Admiralty.   The one war
measure of any consequence for which the Ministry of All the
Talents stands responsible is the first of the Orders in Council
against French sea-borne trade, and this Order (based on the
Rule of 1756) was only important as offering a precedent for
the publication of later Orders, far more offensive to neutrals,
by the Portland Ministry.

The Ministry of All the Talents is remembered for two acts of
faith.   It abolished the slave-trade within the British Empire ;
and it went out of office, when forbidden by the King to
raise the Catholic question in any shape.   These were not
questions which a war ministry was constrained to raise in 1806.
But the Whigs were not content to employ themselves with the
small and indecisive measures of war policy which were open
to them in 1806 and 1807, a small expedition to the Dardanelles,
a small expedition to Egypt, a small expedition to Buenos Ayres.
They wished to prove that, notwithstanding the pact with Sidmouth, they were still a party of principle.

It was natural enough that they should accept the invitation
of Wilberforce, and assume responsibility for the Abolition Bill
which Pitt, at the height of his power, had been unable to carry.
It was natural because their Chancellor of the Exchequer,
Lord Henry Petty, was one of the most active supporters of
Wilberforce at the moment when the Whigs came into power ;

---

[1] Wilberforce, though not in their councils, was aware of the difference on
this point between Fox and Grenville. On 5 April he notes : ' Fox appears to
be rather yielding to Grenville's foreign policy against peace ' (*Life*, iii. 267).

[2] *Parl. Debates* (Cobbett's), viii. 78.

also because both Fox and Grenville had been among the earliest and the most stedfast advocates of Abolition. The case against slavery rested on a principle which was, or should be, dear to all Whigs; and the classical statement of it is to be found in Fox's celebrated speech of 18 April 1791 :

‘ Political freedom is undoubtedly as great a blessing as any people under heaven can pant after ; but political freedom, when it comes to be compared with personal freedom, sinks into nothing and becomes no blessing at all by comparison. It is personal freedom that is now the point in question. Personal freedom must be the first object of every human being. It is a right, and he who deprives a fellow creature of it is absolutely criminal ; and he who withholds it, when it is in his power to restore it, is no less criminal.’

It is true that in the near past some Whigs of note had shown themselves indifferent, or worse than indifferent, to Abolition. Charles Grey refused to vote with Wilberforce in 1789, because he feared that the whole slave trade might drop into the lap of France. In 1791 Lord John Russell, Grey's close friend, was a protagonist of the West Indian planters, and for some years afterwards this opposition confirmed Wilberforce in his un-favourable estimate of the Whigs, whom he described, in 1801, as ‘ able, vigilant, active, inveterate, powerful from their talents, formidable from their principles, not very scrupulous in their means ’, a party, in short, with which an independent patriot could not safely co-operate.[1] But it was his maxim always to work with the Government in power, and he saw no harm in suggesting to Grenville, early in 1806, that the Whigs should help him about Abolition. From a practical point of view the suggestion could not be lightly rejected. For behind Wilberforce stood the small but influential phalanx of the Saints, men like Henry Bankes, the two Thorntons, and Charles Grant, solid country gentlemen and financiers, who had consistently sup-ported Pitt, and who might be useful as regular, or even as occasional, allies of the Whigs. Wilberforce, with that worldly wisdom which marked his whole career, rejected the proposal of some among his followers that there should be a formal treaty with the Whigs, ‘ that we should befriend them as we did Pitt, i. e. give them the turn of the scale, &c., if they would promise

[1] *Life*, ii, pp. 35-6.

us to support Abolition as a government measure'. That, he said, would not be consonant with rectitude; nor would it be good business, for the Whigs might interpret the bargain more stringently than would be agreeable to the Saints. 'Yet', he added, 'I think we ought to contrive that the effect intended by it may be produced'.[1]

Fox and Grenville were more than willing to accept the unwritten alliance, and to do what Wilberforce required of them. It must have been a surprise to Wilberforce that Fox, whom he had long regarded as a reprobate, was the most enthusiastic of the Whig abolitionists; and that Grenville, for whom he felt a sincere respect, was anxious on more than one occasion to blunt the edge of the Abolition Bill[2] by making concessions to its critics. Yet Grenville was completely loyal in the end; and Grey (now Lord Howick), when he succeeded Fox as Foreign Secretary, turned out to be 'earnest and very pleasing' in spite of his past record. Grenville experienced difficulties within his Cabinet which fully account for his desire to make a compromise. He had against him Lord Sidmouth, an obstinate opponent of Abolition, and he was naturally afraid lest Lord Sidmouth might be exasperated to the point of withdrawing his support.[3] Wilberforce and the Whigs had both good cause to be satisfied with their alliance. There can seldom have been a parliamentary arrangement made for so honourable a purpose and so punctually fulfilled on both sides. It did not outlive the passing of the bill (23 March 1807). By that date the breach between the King and Grenville was complete; and Wilberforce decided that neither honour nor gratitude required him to follow his late allies into opposition for the sake of a plan which he thoroughly disliked, a plan 'of embarking on a Roman Catholic bottom (if I may so term it) the interest and well-being of our Protestant empire'.[4]

This description of the design of Grenville's relief measure is, of course, ludicrously wide of the mark. But there were others,

---

[1] *Life of Wilberforce*, iii. 257.   [2] *Ibid.*, iii. 271, 299, 304.
[3] See the *Life of Sidmouth*, ii. 427 (Grenville to Sidmouth, 1 June 1806), where we find Grenville suggesting a compromise which Wilberforce afterwards rejected.
[4] *Life of Wilberforce*, iii. 308–9.

besides Wilberforce, who thought that he was engaging on an ill-considered enterprise. Sheridan remarked that he had never heard before of a man who built a brick wall to run his head against it. The truth is that Grenville had intended a small, stop-gap concession which would indicate his good faith to the Irish Catholics, and would strengthen the influence of the ministry in Ireland. The starting-point of the whole business was a report from the Chief Secretary that the Irish Catholics were extremely restive. This was followed by a report, from the Lord-Lieutenant, of the terms which the Catholic body would demand. One of these was that military commissions should be tenable by Roman Catholics not only in Ireland, as the existing law permitted, but also in Great Britain. Grey fastened upon this demand; he thought it might be recommended to the King and Parliament on military grounds as calculated to improve the prospects of raising recruits in Ireland. Another consideration, which probably originated with Grey, was that something ought to be done for the Catholics before Napoleon should return from the campaign of Eylau and Friedland and revive his plans for invading the British Isles. The Cabinet agreed to ask the King's leave for inserting an amendment in the Mutiny Act which would throw open military commissions as the Catholics desired. With some difficulty they obtained their request, subject to the stipulation that nothing should be granted to the Catholics of Great Britain in this matter which had not been already granted to those of Ireland. To this they agreed, but through the carelessness of Grey, who was charged with the drafting of the amending bill, it was so worded as to open even the highest commissions in the army to Catholics in Great Britain, although in Ireland such commissions were only open to Protestants.[1] To this mistake the King's attention was drawn by Lord Sidmouth after the terms of the amendment had been announced to the Irish Catholics and also in the House of Commons. The King then insisted that the bill should be made conformable to his first instructions; and the Cabinet decided to withdraw the amendment altogether.

[1] See Grey's own explanations reported in Lord Colchester's *Diary*, i, pp. 111–12; also the *Life of Sidmouth*, ii, pp. 448–58. *Dropmore Papers*, ix, pp. 4, 101–2.

This was perhaps the best way of retreating from the false position in which they found themselves. But in announcing their decision to the King they presumed to state that they reserved their right to give his Majesty free and full advice on Irish questions. To this minute the King replied on 17 March by demanding a general pledge that they would never advise further concessions to the Catholics or offer him advice upon that subject. This demand was tantamount to a notice of dismissal. They refused to give the pledge required, and left to the King the responsibility of dismissing them, which he did not hesitate to assume.

It was perhaps the most high-handed action that George III had ever taken in dealing with any of his Cabinets. He himself declared that he consulted no one before dispatching his ultimatum. But, at the time when he wrote it, he had before him a secret offer from the Duke of Portland to form a new administration for the purpose of resisting the Catholic claims.[1] The Duke, who was old and enfeebled, was inspired to take this step by Lord Malmesbury, Lord Castlereagh, Lord Eldon, and Lord Hawkesbury. The latter had become, since the death of Pitt, the leader of the Tory Opposition. He had suggested to the King in 1806 that the position of the Whigs might be made untenable by a refusal, on the King's part, to permit a general election; and in 1807 he and Eldon cheerfully assumed at the King's request the duty of constructing a new Tory administration under the nominal leadership of the Duke of Portland.

The Whigs came out of office with diminished reputations. It was arguable that they had been detected in an attempt to deceive their royal master; for when Grey's blunder was detected they had endeavoured to conceal it from him, and to let the amendment go forward to Parliament. The position in Ireland was not so black as they had imagined, and therefore their conduct cannot be excused on the plea of political necessity. As to their conduct of foreign policy, it is true that Grey made a very able reply, on 19 December 1806, to the charge of inertia which the Opposition formulated in the debates

[1] On the history of this letter see the *Malmesbury Diaries*, iv. 357. Malmesbury helped Portland to draft it. On March 14 Eldon, Castlereagh, and Hawkesbury met at Portland's town house (*ibid.*, p. 371).

on the Address. But it was true, as Castlereagh said, that every month of hesitancy made our chances of forming a new coalition more remote.

The new Portland ministry was at least free from the vice of inactivity. In the first sixteen months of its existence the Danish fleet was seized (Sept. 1807); the Crown Prince of Portugal was induced by moral suasion to sail for Brazil with the Portuguese fleet, which was thus placed beyond Napoleon's reach (Nov.); three Orders in Council were issued to strangle the foreign trade of France and her allies (Nov.); an expeditionary force was sent to Portugal (July 1808); the Russian fleet was seized in the Tagus; Heligoland was occupied as a base for the smuggling trade with the Continent; and a British expeditionary force appeared in the Baltic. Some of these proceedings the Whigs, now in opposition, challenged on grounds of international law; and it was in the character of advocates of neutral rights that they appeared to the best advantage in the parliamentary debates of these years. Our conduct towards Denmark could only be excused on the plea of necessity, and there was much force in the contention that the dangers of our situation would not be greatly enhanced if Napoleon got control of the small Danish fleet. The new Orders in Council could only be defended on what a Whig critic called the damnable doctrine that it is lawful to take any step which your enemy has already taken, and it was probable that neutral trade with the enemy could be kept within bounds by a strict enforcement of the old law of nations.[1] But the Whigs were not fertile in positive suggestions; and they were too ready to assume that, so long as Tories managed the war, our victories would be fruitless and our reverses irretrievable. The convention of Cintra and Moore's retreat to Corunna filled them with gloom and dark suspicions; Grey even refused to believe that Talavera was a victory.

In September 1809, when the Portland administration fell to pieces in consequence of the quarrel between Castlereagh and Canning, the Whigs were invited by Lord Liverpool and Perceval to join 'an extended and combined administration'.

---

[1] Criticisms to this effect by Auckland and by Grenville will be found in the *Dropmore Papers*, vol. ix, pp. 146, 176-7.

Grey put the case for a refusal on grounds which do little credit to his patriotism or his judgement :

' After all that has passed in the last three years, standing chargeable as they do to the country for the series of crimes and follies by which we have been disgraced and nearly ruined, and exposed as they have been for their want of fair dealing and even of common decency in their conduct towards each other, it must be a sense of very strong necessity indeed which could induce me to hazard my personal security and honour in any connection with them.' [1]

The Walcheren expedition of that year, no doubt, had been culpably mismanaged. The behaviour of Canning to Castlereagh, whatever the motives which inspired it, was discreditable. Perceval had some of the faults of a special pleader, and Liverpool was a bland, dexterous, furtive party manager. But it so happened that a government could not be formed at all without these men or some of them. Was it permissible for the Whigs to stand aside when the country needed them? Was it probable that the government of the country would be more enlightened, or the management of the war more effective, if Perceval and Liverpool were obliged to eke out their administration with mediocre Tories instead of leading Whigs? The policy of allowing the Tories to blunder on without assistance, until they drowned themselves in ignominy, might be good party tactics, but it was not patriotism. If this was what Grey intended he was wofully disappointed, in 1810, when Perceval and his colleagues rode out the storm of criticism excited by the Walcheren failure, and when the House of Lords turned a deaf ear to Grenville's warning that any one who expected to hold Portugal against the French was unfit to take any part in the government of Great Britain. Lord Liverpool rose for once to the height of the occasion, and answered Grenville in language worthy of either of the Pitts :

' In Spain ', he said, ' our armies had the support of the whole armed population, which throughout two campaigns had fought under every circumstance of adversity and disadvantage, and were still as resolute not to yield to the foreign invader as at the beginning of the struggle. . . . The noble baron had spoken as if war had not its chances and reverses, as if the risks in military operations were not always pro-

---

[1] *Dropmore Papers*, ix. 330.

portioned to the magnitude of the contest, and had triumphantly asked, " What had we gained in the Peninsula ? " . . . We had gained the hearts of the whole population of Spain and Portugal. . . . Whatever might be the issue of the contest, to this country would always remain the proud consciousness of having done its duty.' [1]

The Whigs, with the honourable exception of Lord Holland, refused to put any trust in the Peninsular operations ; they were unmoved by the victories of Busaco, Albuera, Fuentes d'Onoro. As late as 10 March 1811 we find Ponsonby, their leader in the House of Commons, objecting to an increase of the Portuguese subsidy on the ground that ' neither in Spain nor in Portugal has anything happened to give us reason to believe that the war there will terminate to our advantage '.[2]

By 1812 Grey and Grenville were rather less confident than Ponsonby about the advisability of leaving the Peninsula to its fate. Ciudad Rodrigo and Badajoz, no doubt, gave a shock to preconceived ideas. But again they held back on being presented with a chance to labour in the vineyard at the eleventh hour. After Perceval's assassination the House of Commons petitioned the Regent to form a strong and efficient ministry, and the Marquess Wellesley accepted the duty of exploring the possibilities of coalition. Rebuffed by Lord Liverpool, Wellesley turned to Grey and Grenville, and suggested that a coalition might be formed for the two main purposes of giving satisfaction to the Roman Catholics and prosecuting the Peninsular War on an adequate scale. It was by no means certain that the Regent would accept the first of these two purposes as legitimate, or consent to the inclusion of Earl Grey, with whom, for personal reasons, he was then particularly incensed. It is also clear that the Whigs mistrusted Wellesley, who was on this occasion little more than the mouthpiece of George Canning. What kind of ministry was to be expected when both Canning and the Regent had a finger in the making of it ? But the first difficulty in these abortive negotiations was raised by a declaration from the two Whig leaders that they could not pledge themselves to support the war in Spain. They would give their dispassionate consideration to the subject ; but they doubted whether the finances

---

[1] Yonge, *Life of Liverpool*, i. 318.
[2] *Hansard*, xix. 397.

of Great Britain would permit any increase of expenditure.[1]
They were weary and they were lethargic, though they were
still middle-aged men. 'Such a court and such a Parliament',
Grenville wrote, 'in such a state of the country are too much
for any man to contend with. . . I believe things must prove
still worse (as they are rapidly doing) before either the Prince
Regent or the public will feel its real situation, and it may then
be too late'.[2] He wished to hand over to Grey the leadership of the party in the Lords; Grey would not hear of this
arrangement, which would pledge him to live half the year
in London.

Meanwhile the Whig party in the House of Commons was
changing its character, partly through the disappearance of the
men who had upheld Whig principles against North and Pitt,
partly through the rise of new men who were more susceptible
to new ideas. Grey was called to the House of Lords in
November 1807; and, although he was chafed by the decorous
atmosphere of the Painted Chamber, he was infected by it,
losing much of his energy and influence. Since the death of
Fox he had led the party in the Lower House, and there was
no obvious successor to step into his shoes. Grey and Grenville
selected for the post George Ponsonby, an Irish lawyer of good
family, who had earned a reputation for oratory in Grattan's
Parliament, and had sat at Westminster for Irish constituencies
since 1801. Ponsonby was Lord Chancellor of Ireland in the
Whig administration of 1806–7, and he was also the uncle of
Lady Grey. His critics alleged that he was selected in order
that the leadership might remain in the Grey family circle. He
remained leader until 1817, but without adding to his reputation,[3] and is unkindly commemorated by Lord John Russell as
a model of inefficiency and ignorance.[4]

The best orators of the party in 1807 were Sheridan and
Grattan, but the best days of both were over. Sheridan reached
his meridian in the impeachment of Warren Hastings; but in
1806, as in 1782 and 1783, he was not thought worthy of any

---

[1] *Wellesley Papers*, ii. 100; *Memoirs of the Regency*, i, pp. 313 ff.
[2] *Ibid.*, i. 380.
[3] *Dropmore Papers*, ix, pp. 147–8, 154.
[4] *Recollections and Suggestions*, pp. 30–1.

but a minor post in a Whig administration. He had not the talents of a practical politician, his private affairs were hopelessly entangled, and he had committed the mistake of adhering to the Prince of Wales through thick and thin. 'Old Sherry' was a rather forlorn figure in the House of Commons in these years. He lost his seat in Parliament in 1812, and with it not only his political importance but his immunity from arrest for debt. We have the word of an old friend for the statement that his death (in 1816) was hastened by his fear of arrest. 'His dread was a prison, and he felt it staring him in the face.'[1]

A more conventional representative of the older Whiggism was George Tierney, ten years younger than Sheridan, ready and sharp-witted, a complete master of the cut and parry of debate, a good business head, respectable and solvent. He succeeded Ponsonby as leader in 1817, and might reasonably have been preferred to Ponsonby in 1807. But he was a *novus homo*, undeniably the son of and nephew of merchants who dealt in oranges and sherry. Eton, Cambridge, an independent fortune could not obliterate the brand of trade. Also it was believed that in politics Tierney had his price. Men remembered how, during the Whig secession of 1797-1800, Tierney had attended the House of Commons more often than the orthodox thought fit and proper—trying, no doubt, to advertise his talents in the absence of better men. Then in 1803 he had ratted to Addington for the sake of a minor office; and in 1804 he had been all but persuaded to take office under Pitt. 'A self-interested, time-serving fellow' is the verdict of a great Whig lady in 1802, when Tierney was thought to be seducing Grey into the fold of Toryism.[2] After these vagaries were forgiven—though by no means forgotten—Tierney affected the character of the plain, honest man, 'speaking as an humble individual'; an affectation singularly out of keeping with his taste for small manœuvres and special pleading. He closed his career not unsuitably as Master of the Mint in Canning's administration of 1827. He had hopes of leading the House of

[1] Henry Bennet to Mr. Creevey, 12 July 1816 (*Creevey Papers*, ed. 1906, p. 257).
[2] Duchess of Devonshire to Lady Melbourne, February 1802 (Airlie, *In Whig Society*, p. 28).

Commons for Lord Goderich, after Canning's death. 'But ', says Lord Palmerston on this occasion, 'he would not do; people think him too sly '.[1]

Assuredly Samuel Whitbread (1758–1815) was a more genial character than Tierney. Many Whigs thought that he should have been made leader in 1807, and Grey was not unfavourable to Whitbread's claims, since Whitbread was his brother-in-law. But Whitbread was disappointed of the lead, as he had been disappointed of office in 1806, because the Grenville party complained that he was all for making peace with France.[2] Whitbread in truth was a very loyal Foxite, who had not outlived the ideals of his political youth.   He had other shortcomings, a bluff and rather vulgar address, habits too convivial for his health and worldly success; a desire to be all things to all men and to gain the reputation of a desperately good fellow; a sensitive esteem of his own merits and extreme irritability towards those who did not share his good opinion of himself. Yet not to be despised as an enemy or a supporter.   A terrible gladiator in debate, he was fitly chosen to lead the attack on Melville in 1805, and afterwards to manage the impeachment; again in 1809, when the venalities of Mrs. Clarke had been exposed, he constituted himself, in company with Lord Folkestone and Sir Francis Burdett, the political executioner of the Duke of York, who had the misfortune to be not only commander-in-chief, but also an inveterate enemy of Whig principles. Nor did his successes end here.   In 1810 his invectives drove Lord Chatham out of office for gross mismanagement of the Walcheren expedition.   In 1812 he carried the war into Carlton House by taking up the cause of the Princess of Wales and her daughter, Princess Charlotte, to remind the Prince Regent that Whigs were not altogether negligible, nor Tory ministers omnipotent to hush up scandals in high places.   Into the most justifiable of these raids upon the Government Whitbread never failed to impart a touch, or more, of grotesque violence.   His political chiefs held loftily aloof from any active share in his operations of this class; but behind the scenes they were discreetly sympathetic.

---

[1] Bulwer's *Life of Palmerston*, i. 196.
[2] *Dropmore Papers*, ix, pp. 147–8, 154, 157.

From the back benches Whitbread collected an enthusiastic body of supporters, known as the ' Mountain ', because of their supposed Jacobin principles. They were a heterogeneous group. Some of them followed Whitbread because they did not believe in opposing by halves, and desired a ' factious ' leader. Others, like Althorp, Milton, Western, Ord, Lyttelton and Dudley Ward, genuinely believed that, in attacking corruption and incompetence, Whitbread showed himself a true reformer.[1] He was genuinely concerned for the success of some necessary and overdue reforms. He had, as Wilberforce puts it, an Anglicism, or, as we might say, John Bullism, which made him a considerable and a wholesome influence in the House of Commons. Eminently humane in his private life, he took up philanthropic schemes which his contemporaries in general thought impracticable—a minimum wage for labourers, to be fixed by the justices in each county (1795 and 1800); a drastic reform of the Poor Law (1807);[2] free and compulsory education in elementary schools for the children of the poor (1807).[3] When we add that Whitbread was a firm supporter of the Emancipation movement and of Catholic relief, it must be allowed that he fully deserved the encomium, passed upon him by Romilly, that he was ' the promoter of every liberal scheme for improving the condition of mankind '.[4]

The two were kindred spirits, all due allowances being made for differences of temperament. Romilly (1757–1818), a generous humanitarian at heart, unwearied in the promotion of small definite measures for the reform of English law and particularly criminal law, seemed instinctively to shrink from large, comprehensive schemes, not because he shrank from labour but because he had weighed his own generation and found it wanting. He despaired of inducing the representatives of a corrupt and irrational system to reconsider their own principles, on the

---

[1] For Althorp's opinion of Whitbread see Marchant's *Life of Althorp*, pp. 116, 125-6, 178-9. The growth of the ' Mountain ', in 1809, is noticed in the *Dropmore Papers*.

[2] See for this scheme *Hansard*, viii. 865 ff.; ix. 794, 846; x. 1015. The Poor Law Bill was withdrawn for the session after it had passed the second reading in the Commons, and was never reintroduced.

[3] The Education Bill was thrown out by the House of Lords.

[4] Romilly, *Memoirs*, iii. 191.

strength of general arguments, or appeals to their humaner feelings. His was a lonely, austere, intolerant and rather scornful intellect, though, as he himself notes, he was sensitive to praise and admiration. Of Huguenot descent, by education almost half a Frenchman, he was enchanted by the earliest reforms of the French Revolution, and remained to the end of his life a democrat of 1789. But his democracy was tempered by a conviction that, when men are free, an aristocracy of intellect and virtue will come into its own, and he was completely confident of his own competence to govern and direct within the range of his own special subject.

Long before he entered Parliament, Romilly had set his heart on the Great Seal and had committed to paper the principles upon which he would act in that great office. Never would he submit to live from day to day, devoting the larger half of his energies to the meaner part of his official duties, the distribution of patronage, the discussion of Cabinet matters with his colleagues. His aim would be *condere leges*—to make England's jurisprudence the envy and model of the civilized world. This, he writes, no Chancellor since Bacon had ever dreamed of doing. In the meantime, while he waited for the great opportunity, he would patiently endeavour to collect all the knowledge and experience which might be useful to a Chancellor. His brief experience of legal office chastened his expectations for the future. At the end of 1807 he writes, with obvious reference to his efforts at legal reform in the Grenville administration, that the times are and will long remain unpropitious to a reforming Chancellor. As a result of the French Revolution, the higher classes of English society are averse to any kind of change, and the lower classes have a supreme contempt for moderate reforms. He scarcely dares to hope for another and better Whig Government, in which the first thought of every minister will be the public good, and no minister will be obstructed in well-doing by colleagues jealous of any action that looks like interference with their authority in their own departments. Still he is prepared to make the experiment of taking office ; and he notes for his own guidance that, if he is to achieve anything at all, he will need the co-operation of his colleagues and the support of Parliament. Therefore he persevered in the career of a public

man, meeting with a degree of recognition which suggests
that he judged contemporary politicians too severely. They
admired him all the more because they felt that he was a
puritan and a doctrinaire. Whoever else might trim his sails,
Romilly went on his way regardless of expediency. Not that
he was ever popular. He was precise, reserved, proud, independent; it can hardly have escaped any good observer
that, for all his unassuming deportment, he was terribly conscious, even of the men with whom he worked in office and in
Parliament.

Such was Romilly the politician—impressive and incorrup-
tible, but austere and intellectually arrogant. Romilly the
humanitarian was a different and more lovable being; still a
doctrinaire, but a doctrinaire kindled to white heat by his hatred
of cruelty in any shape. Romilly was a close and attentive
student of Beccaria's epoch-making essay on Crimes and Punishments, which had been translated into English as early as 1770.
From Beccaria he derived the principle, that offences against
property, unless accompanied with violence, should never be
punished with loss of life or limb, but only with fine or imprisonment; also the principle, that punishments will be more
effective in deterring men from crime when they are moderate
but certain, than when they are ferocious but easily evaded.
In 1808 Romilly also read with admiration a manuscript work,
by Bentham, on the Principles of the Penal Code [1] which was
eventually edited and translated by Dumont under the title
Théorie des Peines et des Récompenses (1811). Though Bentham and Romilly were intimate friends for thirty years (1788–
1818), [2] Romilly cannot properly be called a Benthamite. He
was indifferent to Bentham's ethical philosophy, a little scanda-
lized by the political alliance between Bentham and Major Cartwright, more than a little bewildered by the eccentricities of
Bentham's style. But the views of Bentham on the Penal Code
determined Romilly's course in politics. They confirmed him
in the resolution, which he had provisionally formed, of concen-
trating his energies upon the reform of English criminal law;

---

[1] Printed in its original form in vol. i of Bentham's *Collected Works*.
[2] See Bentham's letter to Place, 6 December 1818, in Bain's *James Mill*,
p. 451.

they also gave him a more precise conception of the lines upon which the reformer ought to proceed.[1]

The record of his long campaign (1808–18) is to be found in his collected speeches. His success is not to be measured by the scanty additions to statute law for which he is responsible, but by the revolution which he effected in the minds of hardened men of affairs, both statesmen and lawyers. His luminous speech of 9 February 1810,[2] on the principles of capital punishment, failed to secure the approval of Parliament for the three bills which he then brought forward, but it earned for them the support of Canning and of Wilberforce, and it deserves to rank as the classical statement of the case against the indiscriminate use of the death penalty. It was expanded by Romilly into a short treatise, *Observations on the Criminal Law*, which he published in the same year.

Romilly established for himself a parliamentary reputation similar to that of Wilberforce. This was partly due to the stern regard for principle which he showed whenever a moral or a constitutional issue was debated—as in 1810 when the privileges of the Commons were brought in question by the conduct of Burdett, and again in 1811 when the Duke of York was taxed with the misuse of his position as Commander-in-Chief.[3] As Creevey says, Romilly was thought to be ' no ordinary, artificial, skirmishing lawyer, speaking from briefs, but a sincere, honest man '. But greater still was the impression produced by his emotional sensibility. His friend Mackintosh writes of him : ' I never observed any man so deeply and violently affected by the recital of human cruelty.'[4] It is strange that a man so sensitive to human suffering should not have considered maturely the methods, other than punitive, which might be employed to diminish crime and to stop the growth of the class of habitual criminals. His views on this question were sound, but he did not translate them into action. He explains more than once that poverty and ignorance manufacture criminals, that material prosperity and education are prophylactics against crime. He

---

[1] Romilly's *Memoirs*, ii. 229, 239, 252, 385 ; Coleman Phillipson, *Three Criminal Law Reformers* (1923), pp. 286–7.

[2] *Speeches*, i. 106.   [3] See *Memoirs*, ii. 263–73, 305–13.

[4] *Life of Mackintosh*, ii. 349.

could be eloquent on the advantages of a penitentiary for juvenile offenders; but in 1807 he spoke briefly and slightly in support of Whitbread's education bill.[1] He had not the optimism or the courage of the man who is prepared to work for large and distant objects.

Romilly was at the time of his death regarded as the future leader of his party in the House of Commons. But the narrow limitation of his aims, his mistrust of his own powers, his melancholy conviction that he was and always would be fighting against an immovable mass of stupidity and prejudice, were drawbacks each in itself sufficient to secure his failure in a high and responsible position of command.

Romilly contributed materially to the education of the Whigs when he compelled them to take account of Bentham's work in jurisprudence. Sir James Mackintosh, who, like Romilly, had been in his youth an apologist of the French Revolution, and who, after Romilly's death, took upon himself the duty of completing the reform of the criminal law, was also in his way an intellectual influence. Five years after he attacked Burke in the *Vindiciae Gallicae* (1791) Mackintosh became a convert to Burke's political philosophy, and founded a new school of conservative whiggism which was sufficiently plausible to attract the intellectuals of the Whig party, and superseded for most purposes the creed of Charles James Fox. It is the creed which on the whole predominates in the *Edinburgh Review* of the Jeffrey period, the creed of Grey after 1807 and of the whole of his party except the Mountain. It is nowhere better expressed than in an article on parliamentary reform which appeared in the *Edinburgh Review* for July 1809. Here we have a defence of what Burke called a virtual representation of the people in Parliament; a sharp challenge to the usual assumption that a popularly elected House of Commons will be more intelligent or efficient than the existing assembly; and finally a spirited defence of the aristocratic principle. All Governments are aristocracies of one kind or another. In new states an aristocracy of talent is the general rule; in old states hereditary wealth and rank are the credentials most considered. Under the

---

[1] *Speeches*, i. 248; ii. 180; *Observations on a Late Publication* (1785), quoted by Phillipson, *op. cit.*; *Memoirs*, ii. 207.

second system there is some loss of vigour and ability in government ; but in compensation there is more stability. The ideal system would be founded upon an alliance between these two aristocracies. But no one is to blame for the habitual eclipse of the aristocracy of talent in old societies. It is a natural tendency, since wealth can be inherited and accumulated in augmenting masses, while virtue and talents die with the individual. There is after all something dignified and pleasing to the imagination in the consolidation of those great estates which are in effect patriarchal chieftainships :

'An old government is a mass made up of a congeries of little circles, each of which has its own fixed centre and point of radiation. Every county and district and parish and village has its settled heads and leaders through whom, as their natural organ, their sentiments and wishes are made known. . . . All the little springs and fountains of political power have worn themselves deep and permanent channels, and are reunited into certain great currents which hold their course with undeviating regularity and maintain the freshness and fertility of the land without danger or disturbance.'

The writer concludes by expressing his opinion that although a reform of the House of Commons would not materially change its character, it would stimulate in the newly enfranchised the feelings of citizenship and of political duty which are apt to languish in commercial countries. And the mere granting of a concession to which so much importance has been, perhaps foolishly, ascribed would be a pledge of the confidence and good-will with which the lower classes are regarded by their superiors.

Mackintosh was in India when this article appeared and it is unlikely that he wrote it. But it is very similar in argument to an article which he wrote, some years later, for the *Edinburgh Review* of November 1820, to explain and recommend the first of Russell's motions for parliamentary reform, which had been brought forward in the Commons on 14 December 1819. It was with good reason that he was put forward in 1831 to make an elaborate defence, on philosophic principles, of the Reform Bill for which Russell was responsible. He had been one of the few elder whigs who welcomed and promoted new movements in the party. His parliamentary career only began in 1813 and lasted only ten years, during which his attendance was often prevented by ill health and literary occupations. But in that period he enriched the meagre stock of Whig ideas on the science of politics. No one who has read his speech of 1831 or that of 1815 on the Vienna settlement, or his plea in 1819 for the amendment of the criminal code, will deny his title to rank among the great Whig orators. But in the opinion of his friends his main service was of a higher kind. ' He was ', wrote Lord Abinger, 'by disposition and nature the advocate of truth.' And Sydney Smith wrote: ' it was worth while to listen to a master whom not himself but nature had appointed to the office, and who taught what it was not easy to forget by methods which it was not easy to resist.' [1]

So far we have spoken of the older members of the party. The young men of promise were not too numerous. In 1807 Lord Henry Petty, younger son of Lord Lansdowne (Shelburne) was the Whig Marcellus. He became Chancellor of the Exchequer at the age of twenty-seven, having attached himself to Fox from his first entry into Parliament, and was regarded as the future leader in the House of Commons until he was called unexpectedly to the House of Lords as the heir of his half-brother. No other representative of a great Whig house gave promise of distinguished parliamentary talent until Lord John Russell entered the House in 1813 as a member for his father's borough of Tavistock. Born and bred in one of the inner shrines of Whig orthodoxy, we find him, while still a student at Edinburgh, expressing fears that Lord Grey is too warlike, and also too Laodicean about parliamentary reform, to be a suitable leader of the party.[2] A year or two after his entry into Parliament we hear a sad complaint from a lady whom he had favoured with particular attention. ' He is so hurried that he has never wrote me anything but the affairs of the nation.' [3] In 1821, when he was already launched on his reform campaign, an observant foreigner remarks upon ' his apparent coldness and indifference to what was said by others '.[4]

In that same year Russell's thoughts were busy with the English constitution and he published a treatise on the subject,

---

[1] *Life of Mackintosh*, ii. 294, 501.
[2] *Early Correspondence of Lord John Russell*, i. 132–6.
[3] *Op. cit.*, i, p. 183.　　　　[4] Walpole's *Life of Russell*, i. 131.

which contains, in addition to much good sense, some characteristic assumptions.   The following is his explanation of the way
in which county members are elected.

'The qualities which they (the electors of the dominant party) seek
for in a candidate are generally not eloquence or even abilities, but
sense, integrity, and property.   Property itself is supposed in some
manner to be a guarantee of character.   It therefore happens that
the person among them who has most land, if he has other common
requisites, is the member ; and if that person happens to be a peer,
then his brother or his son.'

This curious habit results, in his opinion, from the English
character, or some deep-seated trait of human nature.   It is
a habit which prevailed in the most glorious days of English
freedom.   'We will therefore rest contented with things as they
are '—at all events in the counties.   They have always returned,
they ought always to return, representatives of landed property.
A hostile critic of those days would naturally ask whether it was
right that landed property should also control such parliamentary
boroughs as Tavistock.   But Russell is forearmed with a defence :

'Their remains the aristocracy of talent, who arrive at the House of
Commons by means of the close boroughs, where they are nominated
by peers or commoners who have the property of those boroughs
in their hands.   In this manner the greater part of our distinguished
statesmen have entered Parliament.'

On further consideration, however, he remarks that boroughs
in which the seats are sold by the patron ought to be disfran-
chised.   For it usually happens that such seats are secured for
the ministerial party, and so are very far indeed from serving
to ensure a representation of the people.   One may infer from
such passages that a good deal of the old leaven of class-spirit
and party-spirit still subsisted among the Whig reformers of the
age of Lord John Russell.[1]

Two other recruits of unusual qualities were Francis Horner
(d. 1817), the first economist whom the Whigs brought into
Parliament, and Henry Brougham, who made his political début
as a pamphleteer and an organizer of Whig electioneering
literature.

---

[1] *The English Government and Constitution* (ed. 1865), pp. 248–50, 257,
260.

Horner was a native of Edinburgh, and Brougham, whose mother was a niece of Principal Robertson, may be called an adopted son of Scotland. Both were educated at the High School and the University of Edinburgh ; both became advocates and came south to try their fortunes at the English bar ; both were original contributors to the *Edinburgh Review.* Horner was brought into Parliament by his Whig friends as member for St. Ives in 1806, and so rapidly established his position as an authority on financial questions that he was chosen as Chairman of the Bullion Committee of 1810, which paved the way for a return to sound principles of currency. In 1813 and 1815, in debates upon the corn laws, he defended the principles of free trade which he had consistently advocated in the *Edinburgh Review.* His untimely death was a disaster to his party, which was singularly deficient in economic ability. Horner was far inferior in originality to David Ricardo, who sat from 1819 to 1823 in the House of Commons. But Ricardo was an independent radical. After 1817 the Whigs had no better financial guides than Sir Henry Parnell, Lord Althorp, and Poulett Thomson, until in 1847 they discovered James Wilson.[1]

Brougham's services to the Whigs were of a more varied character. He only attached himself to them after an unsuccessful effort to obtain a seat, through the influence of William Wilberforce, on the Tory side of the House. At no time in his career could he be described as an orthodox Whig. Still less was he distinguished for loyalty to his political allies. The keynote of his career is a naively egoistical ambition, which would have been completely odious if it had been united with ordinary prudence and a placid temperament. Every one who attempted to work with Brougham came sooner or later to the conclusion that he ' would not do '. Yet many of those who refused point blank to accept him as a colleague continued to treat him as a friend.[2] It was never wise to quarrel with an orator whose control of invective and sarcasm was unrivalled, and who, even

---

[1] The founder of the *Economist,* and Financial Secretary to the Treasury 1852–7. See his biography, *The Servant of All,* by his daughter, Mrs. Barrington (1927).

[2] Thus Brougham was Melbourne's executor, although it was Melbourne who turned him out of office.

after innumerable exposures, had still a following in the country
as a pioneer of educational reform,

> The statesmen who, in a less happy hour
> Than this, maintained men's right to read and know.

But, apart from all considerations of expediency, Brougham's
friendship was worth cultivating.   High spirited, full of sincere
though volatile enthusiasms for ideas and causes, recklessly
brilliant as a conversationalist, he was the life and soul of a congenial company.

Brougham entered Parliament in 1809 as the protégé of
Lord Grey, Lord Holland, and Lord Lansdowne.   Two years
later he introduced and carried a bill which, by making participation in the slave-trade a felony punishable by transportation,
completed the good work of Wilberforce.[1]   In 1812 he came
forward as the spokesman of the commercial classes to demand
the withdrawal of the Orders in Council, to which were ascribed,
rather too rashly, all the misfortunes of the British exporter and
all our differences with the United States.   Government yielded
to the outcry; and although none of the advantages which
Brougham had predicted were in fact secured, his triumph increased the respect of business men for the Whig party.
Brougham, already at this time, was regarded as indispensable
to the next Whig administration.   But he was out of favour
with Whig borough-owners, probably owing to his close connexion with Whitbread and the Mountain; and he was out of
Parliament from the dissolution of 1812 until the session of 1816.
During that period he employed himself in finding ways and
means to conciliate the popular reformers and the Benthamites,
with the intention of supplanting Burdett as the parliamentary
spokesman of the people ; and Francis Place and James Mill
appear to have been prepared to employ him in that capacity.
He had not the courage to take the necessary plunge when he
returned to Parliament, and failed to promote any one of the
reforms which were nearest to the hearts of his new friends.
He endeavoured to keep them in good humour by denouncing
the Holy Alliance, the profuseness of Government, the policy of
coercion in Ireland, and the profligacy of the Prince Regent.   It

---

[1] Slave Trade Act, 51 George III, c. 33.

would not do. He improved his influence with the commercial classes by leading the victorious onslaught on the property-tax, which was abandoned by the ministry in March 1816. But he was repudiated by Place in October 1816. This disappointment shook him out of any radical opinions which he had imbibed during his flirtation with the Westminster Committee.

Henceforth he accepted loyally the reserved and uneasy attitude of Lord Grey towards parliamentary reform. But he proposed to adopt on a larger scale Whitbread's policy of appealing to the country, over the heads of the Radicals, by offers of large measures of social reform ; and one such measure he persuaded Parliament to adopt in 1818—the Charities Inquiry Act for investigating the administration of educational charities in England. The measure was not allowed to pass in the form originally proposed ; the public schools, for example, and the universities were specially exempted from the inquiry. But the commission appointed under the Act rendered a great service to education, and was the seed out of which grew the Charity Commissions of later years. In 1820 he followed up this success by reviving in a modified form Whitbread's scheme of elementary education for all—the schools to be built at the public expense, but the teachers to be paid out of a local rate specially levied for that purpose. This bill was shelved by ministers after the first reading, and apparently not regretted by the Whigs. But it suffices to prove that Brougham was wiser than they. The times were ripe and overripe for reforms which had so far been omitted from the programmes of both parties. The Whigs were slow to learn this lesson ; they did not put it into practice until 1833, when the pressure of Radical opinion became irresistible, owing to the dependence of the Whig ministry on Radical support.[1]

But, while the party was rich in men of personality and talent, the record of the party is too much one of individual and disconnected efforts. The leaders were in hearty agreement on very few questions of importance. In the years 1812–25 Grey and Grenville were agreed on Catholic Relief and the question of the currency. But difficulties arose at once when Grey looked

[1] For Brougham's political activities 1809–20 see A. Aspinall, *Lord Brougham and the Whig Party* (1927), cc. ii–v and xii, pp. 235–7.

about for more attractive subjects. He suggested economic reform, a time-honoured cry, which had the merit of being specially appropriate in these war years and specially acceptable to the Radical party. But Grenville at once objected. He was nervous about the sense in which Cartwright and Cobbett interpreted the word economy. ' What the public mean is something about places and placemen, on which head they will never be satisfied, so long as there are persons in place and persons out of place.' His own theory was that sinecures constituted an abuse when in the disposal of the Crown; but that patronage of this kind was essential to the King's ministers; the sinecures which ministers disposed ought never to be diminished.[1]

About the war Grey and Grenville began to differ as early as 1813. Grey thought, as Whitbread did, that Napoleon, even after Leipzig, was still the idol of France, and that we ought to come to terms with him,[2] on the sole condition that Russia, Austria, and Prussia should receive back all that had been taken from them. Grenville held that the war must continue until the old balance of power was restored—that is until Holland and other small powers were emancipated from France. These differences were settled by the progress of military events. But a sharper dispute was occasioned by the return of Napoleon from Elba. Grey agreed with Whitbread that the Emperor was palpably more acceptable to the French nation than the Bourbons. To depose him a second time, now that his popularity was demonstrated, would be a breach of the law of nations.[3] Grenville, his patience exhausted by several speeches on this theme, replied to Grey on two occasions, on the text that Napoleon could never be trusted to observe a peace. There was no open quarrel; all the decencies were observed ; but in effect the Grey–Grenville coalition was dissolved. The parties of Grey and Grenville in the House of Commons took up the quarrel, which was barely quenched by Waterloo. At the end of 1815 Grey was still complaining that all we had got in compensation for a ruinous war was a ruinous peace settlement; for we had pledged ourselves to maintain the Bourbons in France,

---

[1] *Dropmore Papers*, x. 199.   [2] *Ibid.*, x. 345, 351.
[3] See Grey's speeches of 12 April, 27 April, and 23 May 1815 (*Hansard*, xxx. 372, 890; xxxi. 333).

and to honour that pledge we should need to keep on foot an
immense army for an indefinite period of time.[1]

The breach seems to have grown wider and deeper by imperceptible degrees in 1816 and 1817. The followers of Grey
insisted, against the wishes of their leader, that economy and
retrenchment, those bugbears of Lord Grenville, ought to receive
at least as much attention as the terms of the peace treaties.
The Grenvilles disliked, not without reason, the violence of
Brougham and Burdett, who seemed at times to be attacking
not so much the Government of the day as the fundamental
principles on which all Governments must stand. Grey in the
House of Lords and Tierney in the House of Commons worked
hard to keep the peace. They made it clear that they had no
sympathy for the demands of the Hampden Clubs, and that
they would not for the present introduce even the most moderate
measures of parliamentary reform. Grey further declared that,
when the time for such measures should arrive, his own proposals would be more moderate than those which he had supported in his youth. He rebuked the clubs for their indiscriminate abuse of the House of Commons, which was, he said, even
in its present state ' of all other institutions in all other countries
of the world the institution best calculated for the protection of
the subject '.[2]

But Grenville was not to be appeased. Early in 1817 he
wrote to Grey to intimate that their alliance was dissolved. In
February he took the decisive step of supporting the Government's proposal to suspend the Habeas Corpus Act. For Grey
and his friends the Habeas Corpus Act was the very ark of the
covenant, without which the liberty of the subject could have no
meaning ; for Grenville its suspension was a well-tried expedient,
which had proved most useful to his first leader, Pitt, under
circumstances very similar to those of 1817. For his own part
he desired nothing better than a final emancipation from politics.
He advised his followers not to come to terms with Lord Liverpool but to preserve their independence. They took the advice,
and for the next four years acted as a Third Party in the lower
House, their hope being that the moderate followers of Grey
would part company with the hotheads of the Mountain, and set

---

[1] Brougham's *Memoirs*, ii. 301.   [2] *Hansard*, xxxv. 424–8.

about the reconstruction of the old Whig interest. But this hope was not fulfilled, and insensibly the Third Party began to contemplate alliance with Lord Liverpool. The signing of the treaty was postponed till the end of 1821. It would have been concluded twelve months earlier but for the impression, which was not peculiar to the Grenvilles, that the Liverpool ministry was *in extremis* at the end of 1820.[1]

The secession of the Grenvilles appreciably impaired the voting strength of the Whigs, but it was a blessing in disguise. Grenville himself was a spent force ; among his followers only Charles Wynn could boast of a parliamentary reputation, and Wynn's chief asset was a considerable knowledge of the procedure of the House of Commons, acquired in the hope that he might one day be elected Speaker. The loss of Grenville and of Wynn was as nothing compared with the freedom which Grey and his followers now gained to shape their own policy without reference to unsympathetic allies.

[1] *Memoirs of the Court of George IV*, i. 96. For the beginnings of the Third Party see *Memoirs of the Regency*, ii. 208-80.

VII

IDEALS OF THE TORY PARTY 1784–1830

BETWEEN 1784 and 1830 the growth of a new and
enlightened Toryism was more apparent in literature and
in the views of educated men who held aloof from politics than
it was in either House of Parliament, where the 'pig-tail school'
seemed always to predominate except when it was paralysed by
the dissensions of its members. The views of that school are
nowhere better illustrated than in the official biography of Lord
Eldon, and in Wellington's political correspondence, which
presents us with Eldon's political philosophy minus Eldon's
cant and sycophancy. To study in detail these classics of older
Tory thought would take us far afield. But we may illustrate
the blind complacency of the 'pig-tails' by reference to the controversy which raged in 1807 round Whitbread's bills for the
reform of the Poor Law and for establishing a system of elementary education. These measures were not carefully thought
out in detail, and were justly criticized on that account. But it
is surprising to find that Whitbread's benevolent objects are
ridiculed as much as the details of his scheme of social reform.
John Weyland, an educated country gentleman, who had
a practical acquaintance with the Poor Law and the conditions
of life among the agricultural poor, summed up the leading
arguments of his party in an outspoken pamphlet entitled
A Short Enquiry into the Poor Laws (1807). He maintains
that the granting of lavish outdoor relief has rendered an in-
estimable service to English manufacturers by supplying them
with the cheap labour that they must command if they are to
conquer foreign markets. The poor rates, he holds, ought to
be regarded as a judicious bounty to the staple industries.
Again he asks his readers to reflect that, but for the existence
of this superabundant population which the Poor Laws foster,
England could never have sustained the long and still unfinished
war with France. That education was a cure for pauperism and
vice he could not believe. The poor, of course, should be

taught to read ' the fundamental books of religion and morality ', the Bible and the Prayer Book. But ' a reasonable doubt may be entertained how far an universal knowledge of writing and arithmetic, among those who must subsist by the coarsest manual labour, is calculated to render them more contented and happy in that lot '. Mr. Whitbread desired, on his own showing, to reduce the sum of human vice and misery, to augment the sum of human happiness and virtue. But, asks Weyland, does Whitbread expect to bring about this result by lifting the poor out of the state of want in which an all-wise Providence has placed them? Would they not cease to be industrious when they cease to be poor? And if no paupers remained to be relieved what opportunity would then be left to the rich of developing their humane and charitable impulses?

The rank and file of the Tory party did not always or often talk in this unctuous fashion. But Weyland expressed some of their most obstinate convictions. In resisting changes of a purely constitutional character they had recourse to those parts of Burke's teaching which showed that great genius at his worst and weakest. Either they would defend anomalies as the fruit of the unconscious wisdom of the past; or they would take it for granted that the wit of man was incapable of patching and repairing the old constitution without destroying it altogether; or, finally, they would talk in the style which ' Noodle's Oration ' has immortalized:

' I am an enemy to the corruption of Government, but I defend its influence. . . . I dread reform, but I dread it only when it is intemperate. . . . Nobody is more conscious than I am of the splendid abilities of the honourable mover, but I tell him at once, his scheme is too good to be practicable. It savours of Utopia. It looks well in theory, but it won't do in practice.' [1]

It is good to turn back from these parodies of Burke to Burke's own stately encomium upon the British constitution, to recapture the vision which floated before his eyes, and to forget the strange and harsh corollaries with which Burke's disciples deformed his theory. Burke inspired the wise as well as the foolish, and every Tory thinker of distinction since his time has

[1] Sydney Smith published this in 1825, in a review of Bentham's *Book of Fallacies*. It is reprinted in Smith's *Works* (ed. 1851), pp. 425–7.

been his pupil in a greater or less degree. What can be more inspiring than Burke's account of the British polity, addressed to 'a gentleman in Paris'?

'Our political system is placed in a just correspondence and symmetry with the order of the world, and with the mode of existence decreed to a permanent body composed of transitory parts ; wherein, by the disposition of a stupendous wisdom, moulding together the great mysterious incorporation of the human race, the whole at one time is never old, or middle-aged or young, but in a condition of unchangeable constancy moves on through the varied tenor of perpetual decay, fall, renovation and progression. Thus by preserving the method of nature in the conduct of the state, in what we improve, we are never wholly new ; in what we retain we are never wholly obsolete. . . . *Through the same plan of a conformity to nature in our artificial institutions, and by calling in the aid of her unerring and powerful instincts, to fortify the fallible and feeble contrivances of our reason*, we have derived other, and those no small benefits from considering our liberties in the light of an inheritance. . . . All your sophisters cannot produce anything better adapted to preserve a rational and manly freedom than the course that we have pursued, who have chosen our nature rather than our speculations, our breasts rather than our inventions, for the great conservatories and magazines of our rights and privileges.'[1]

This adoration of things as they are showed itself in unexpected quarters after 1806. The Methodist connexions, notwithstanding their resentment of the religious tests, were driven to support a Tory Government by the extravagances of the Radical reformers. In November 1819 the central committee of the Wesleyans issued a circular to warn their congregations against Radical theories, and expressed their disapproval of the reformist agitation which had recently culminated in the massacre of Peterloo. The committee were influenced by very natural prejudices against the writings of Paine and Cobbett, whom they regarded as enemies of religion. But the second reason which moved the committee to condemn the agitation was that it called in question the laws, the authorities, and the constitution of the country.

The contributors of the *Edinburgh Review* who wrote on politics are hardly to be suspected of Tory sympathies in

---

[1] *Reflections on the Revolution in France* (1790).

politics. Yet the early numbers of that periodical contain some articles which, twenty years later, would have been cheerfully printed by Mr. Croker in the *Quarterly*. In 1807 an Edinburgh reviewer gravely states that the balance of the constitution can only be maintained by the exercise both of royal and of aristocratical influence in the House of Commons. It is essential, he maintains, that there should be some members in that House who owe their seats to the help of the Treasury, or to the patronage of noble lords. The sale of seats for money had not yet been made illegal;[1] and the reviewer thinks the practice not wholly indefensible. The seats which are advertised for sale are open to competition, in a sense. ' The independent and well-affected part of the nation is far richer than the Government or the peerage; and if all seats in Parliament could be honestly and openly sold for ready money, we have no sort of doubt that a very great majority would be purchased by persons unconnected with the Treasury or the House of Lords.' The reviewer protests that he has no great affection for rotten boroughs, since the sale of seats cannot fail to demoralize the electorate. But he does not believe that the efficiency of the lower House would be destroyed by the extension of the system or much improved by its suppression.[2] This opinion is Toryism with a vengeance, though it carries a certificate of Whig origin. The voice is Jacob's, though the hands be the hands of Esau. At other times the *Edinburgh* accentuates the most conservative features of Whig doctrine. In July 1809, in an article on parliamentary reform, we find the social fabric described in the spirit of Burke, though with vastly inferior imagination :

' An old government is a mass, made up of a congeries of little circles, each of which has its own fixed centre and point of radiation. Every county and district and parish and village has its settled heads and leaders, through whom, as their natural organs, their sentiments and wishes are made known, and by whose influence they may generally be reconciled with the wishes and sentiments of others. All the little springs and fountains of political power have worn themselves deep and permanent channels, and are reunited with certain great currents which hold their course with undeviating regularity, and maintain the freshness and fertility of the land without danger or disturbance.'

[1] It was prohibited in 1809 by Curwen's Act (49 George III, c. 118).
[2] *Ed. Review*, July 1807 (Article No. 9, on Cobbett's *Political Register*).

This passage comes very near to a defence of the House of Lords as a guarantee of sanity and continuity in the political life of Great Britain. It is undisguisedly a defence of government by an hereditary landed interest. The reviewer admits that the ideal aristocracy would found its claim to rule upon superior character and talents. But the ideal aristocracy, he thinks, only comes to its own in times of revolution, and its rule will not endure:

'Wealth can be transmitted to a successor and can be accumulated, while virtue and talents can not . . . and thus the aristocracy of personal merit is gradually supplanted, or at least overtopped by the aristocracy of hereditary wealth.'

It is useless to fight against the course of nature. But the hereditary rulers of society should recollect that their position can never be secure unless they strike an alliance with the aristocracy of merit, and admit the latter to some share of political influence. It may be also advisable—and here we note a deviation from the attitude of the *Review* in 1807, just two years earlier—that some measure of parliamentary reform should be conceded by the aristocracy. Not because a moderate reform will alter the composition or character of the House; but because it will have the effect of rooting the authority of the House in the affections of the people. The writer is, in fact, a Tory in the sense that he deprecates any substantial change in the existing constitution; only a Whig in the sense that he desires to maintain stability and order by the influence of an aristocracy, not by means of strong government.

These utterances of the *Edinburgh Review* reveal the common platform upon which the two great political parties stood at the beginning of the nineteenth century. Both desired that political power should go with property and should be proportionate to property. As property was heritable, so too should be power. 'The hereditary principle' was sacred in the eyes of both, and the man who denied it was held to be the worst kind of revolutionary. Property of every kind was also sacred; and we have seen the *Edinburgh Review*, in 1807, contemplating the rule of a plutocracy as a rational and desirable system. But the old prejudice in favour of the men with 'a stake in the country' still survived, for the old reasons, which still seemed unanswerable. The landowner cannot pull up his stakes and desert his country, even if he would. The wealth of the landowner is more solid, more enduring, than that of the manufacturer, the merchant, or the mere speculator.

Still, Whigs and Tories remained at variance on questions which cannot be described as trifling. Two subjects of dissension are indicated in the catch phrase 'Church and King', which became the motto of the Loyal Associations in the epoch of the French Revolution. The extreme Whigs of Walpole's time had been theoretical and speculative republicans, but by 1793 the republican ideal, at least as a panacea for the defects of the British constitution, had been entirely renounced, even in Fox's circle, and Major Cartwright cheerfully admitted that monarchy was an essential feature of the Anglo-Saxon constitution. Most Whigs were also staunch supporters of the Established Churches. But they could not accept the Tory catchword in the Tory sense.

The respect of Tories for the King, and their desire that he should not only reign but rule, had been rudely shaken during the administrations of Lord Bute and Lord North. It had been shaken, but it had not been destroyed. However faulty the methods and the instruments of George III had been, his general views on policy had been those of the great majority of his subjects. We may fairly say that he remained personally popular, not in spite of, but by reason of his most mistaken and calamitous decisions—the decision to reduce the American colonies by force of arms, the decision to annul Pitt's bargain with the Irish Roman Catholics. While the Tories hated a coalition of parties, as an immoral compact between immoral factions, they still believed that it was the right and duty of the sovereign to form a 'broad administration' in any grave conjuncture, to select for himself the 'honest men' who could best serve the country, and to insist that his own views on policy should have their respectful consideration. This theory slumbered during Pitt's administration, when 'honest men' appeared to be primly in the saddle and the King was constantly incapacitated. But in 1801, 1804, and 1807 the King was again, to all outward appearance, selecting ministers as Tories wished

them to be selected, and the Prince Regent, after 1810, seemed
to be capable, despite his past connexion with the Whigs, of
making administrations which were broad enough to be efficient
and Tory enough to satisfy the natural supporters of the royal
prerogative.

Royalism, in its more indiscreet ebullitions, was sometimes
embarrassing to a Tory minister. In 1795 John Reeves, the
founder of the Loyal Associations, incensed the House of Commons by alleging, in his *Thoughts on the English Government*
(1795), that the two Houses of Parliament were no more than
branches of the tree of monarchy; 'without the King his Parliament is no more'. John Reeves was duly prosecuted for
seditious libel by Pitt's attorney-general. But he was acquitted,
and five years later he received from Pitt the remunerative office
of King's printer; and this in spite of the fact that the discreditable methods of his Associations had been fully exposed
in the trial of Thomas Walker of Manchester (1794). For the
sentiment of royalism, discreetly used, was not to be despised
by any Tory minister. It was invoked, for example, in 1799 to
justify the suppression of the so-called seditious societies;[1] and
in 1819 it was the chief argument for the suspension of the
Habeas Corpus Act. The plea of personal devotion to the
sovereign was used, and used with complete success, to justify
deviations from the current code of political morality. It was
so used by Pitt (in 1801) to justify his repudiation of his understanding with the Irish Catholics. Lord Eldon was accustomed
to boast that he held the great seal as the King's servant, and
not as a minister in the ordinary sense. In 1804 he told the
House of Lords that 'to do my duty to His Majesty is to do my
duty to the country', by way of explaining why he, a member
of Addington's administration, had used his influence to get
Addington turned out of office.[2] In 1807, when the Whigs
were evicted by yet more dubious measures, Eldon rallied to
the King's side, with the declaration that 'this great and
excellent man shall not want the aid of every effort that I can
exert'.[3]

A greater man than Eldon, but bred in the same school of

---

[1] Twiss, *Life of Eldon*, i. 312.   [2] *Op. cit.*, i. 443.

[3] *Op. cit.*, ii. 34.

thought, the Duke of Wellington, maintained that he could not, in honour or loyalty, refuse office when he was pressed by the King to undertake it, even though the policy to be pursued was repugnant to his own convictions.[1] It is permissible to doubt whether these statesmen were actually convinced by their own arguments. But they were much too shrewd to use arguments which would fail to convince their followers. Even Sir Robert Peel used a modified form of the same pleas to justify his acceptance of office in 1834:

'I could not reconcile it to my feelings, or indeed to my sense of duty, to subject the King and the monarchy to the humiliation, through my refusal of office, of inviting his dismissed servants to resume their appointments. My refusal could only have been founded on avowed disapprobation of the course taken by the King.'[2]

It is hardly fair to say that Melbourne and his friends acted on the same principle in 1839 when they supported the youthful Queen Victoria on the great Bedchamber question, in spite of their grave doubts as to the propriety of the line which she had taken. But in the Whig party there were searchings of heart; their leaders seemed, as Charles Greville remarks, to be endorsing 'the highest Tory principle'.

One result of excessive deference to the personal wishes, and even the caprices, of the sovereigns, was to perpetuate a court theory of the royal prerogative, much more embarrassing to the Tories than to their opponents, who were not hampered to the same extent by exuberant professions of loyalty to the sovereign. The fitful and capricious attempts of George IV to tie the hands of his ministers on the Catholic question and to assert his right of interfering with foreign policy were extremely troublesome to Lord Liverpool and Canning, to Peel and Wellington. Even William IV intermittently claimed powers which the Whigs regarded, usually with justice, as quite inadmissible. He asserted that the Duchy of Lancaster was 'his private and independent estate', with which Parliament had no right to meddle. He

---

[1] In 1832. See his defence of his conduct in the House of Lords (*Speeches*, i. 546).

[2] *Peel's Memoirs*, ii. 31-2. He had refused the King's invitation in 1832; but, as he told the House of Commons on 7 May 1832, this was because he could not conscientiously take office to pass a Reform Bill.

argued that the great household officials were his personal
servants, whom ministers had no right to dismiss for opposing
ministerial measures in the House of Lords. He held that the
Commander-in-Chief was personally responsible to himself, and
not to ministers, in whatever concerned the army and more
especially in questions of military patronage. He once (1832)
demanded that no instructions should be sent to any embassy
abroad without his approval and concurrence. It is interesting to observe that Lord Palmerston was the minister whose
conduct occasioned this protest ; and that the pretensions of
William IV in 1832 were exactly reproduced by Queen Victoria
in 1851.[1] It was no doubt one of the unwritten rules of Tory
statecraft that the boundaries of the royal prerogative should
not be too closely defined. But the consequences of this rule
must have caused serious misgivings to all thoughtful Tories
between 1760 and 1837.

When we turn from the King to the Church we approach
a subject which was more feelingly and profoundly investigated
by Tory men of letters than by Tory statesmen, but still a subject on which many Tory statesmen held strong views. In the
highest and most unexpected quarters we find, in this period,
a revival of religious feeling. Even Lord Eldon, in his maturer
years the least spiritual of men, had thought of taking orders in
his youth, and to the end delighted in theological studies. Lord
Liverpool, whom no one would suspect of enthusiasm, was
a devoted Evangelical; Chateaubriand in 1822 observed that ' he
had almost reached the stage of puritanical illumination '. Lord
Sidmouth was the leader of a movement for building new
churches in the great industrial centres, and in 1818 Lord
Liverpool agreed to allocate a million of public money for this
purpose.

Wilberforce's parliamentary group—the Saints as they were
called—were an important factor in many political crises. They
could not be ignored by the most case-hardened Whips. Nearly
all the Saints were men of affluence and good connexions—

---

[1] See the *Correspondence of William IV and Earl Grey*, i, p. 9, 13
(Duchy of Lancaster) ; i. 206, 208 (household officers) ; ii. 280 (military
patronage) ; ii. 364 (foreign relations).

country squires, lawyers, bankers, men of business. They had
fallen under the spell of the Evangelical movement; they had
sat at the feet of Isaac Milner, John Newton, the Venns, Charles
Simeon. None of them but Charles Grant the younger held
high office; none except Henry Thornton the economist was
intellectually eminent; Wilberforce and Ashley (the latter from
1826) were their only considerable debaters. But the collective
influence of the Saints was great when they decided to join
battle on a moral or religious issue; and Wilberforce, from 1790
to 1825, held a unique position in the House. He was the
friend and mentor of Pitt and Perceval, the gadfly of Addington,
Liverpool, Castlereagh, and Canning. What he could do by
force of oratory, party management, and personal character he
showed in 1792 and 1806. On the first of these occasions he
measured swords with Henry Dundas, that prince of wire-
pullers; he converted Pitt to his view of the question; and he
persuaded the House of Commons to fly in the face of the great
West India interest, by resolving the abolition of the Slave
Trade. In 1806 he offered to Fox and Grenville the support of
the Saints in return for a bill prohibiting the slave-trade; and
although his allies would not make the bill a ministerial measure,
it was triumphantly carried by his influence. In 1820 we find
Wilberforce again taking advantage of a critical situation in
Parliament to put pressure on a minister. He rebuked Lord
Liverpool for neglecting the Church of England, and promoting
to the episcopal bench only those who represented 'a low and
depraved system of practical religion', and told him that the
moral disease of the age could only be cured by making better
use of that party among its ministers 'which is stigmatized by
the general name of Calvinistic or Evangelical'. To this letter
Liverpool replied frankly and apologetically, as though aware
of the fact that Wilberforce was seriously considering the
transfer of his influence to the Whig side.[1]

Wilberforce belonged to that party in the Church of England
which attached least value to organization and to continuity,
a party for which the religious life meant, above everything,
a personal relation between God and the individual. But even

---

[1] Add. MS. (B.M.) 38191, fos. 274 ff. (Wilberforce to Liverpool, 16
Sept. and 30 Sept. 1820). See also *Life of Wilberforce*, v. 79.

Wilberforce could not refrain from thinking in political terms of
Christianity.   It was, or it ought to be, the great bond of union
in the state, the nurse of civilization, the great bulwark of law
and order.   It could not fulfil this function properly unless embodied in the form of an establishment which was so closely
connected with the State that State and Church should be
practically inseparable. As Croker put it : ' Westminster Abbey
is part of the British constitution.' Up to a point, the Whigs
could sympathize with this ideal. They too believed that
religion was essential to the well-being of the State.   But
historical traditions compelled them to deny in the most emphatic fashion the Tory doctrine that a dissenter or a Roman
Catholic could not properly be a full citizen of the British
State,[1] because he had no lot or part in the Established Church.
' I am as satisfied ', writes Croker, ' that no political state can
exist without some connexion with religion as I am that the
body cannot be kept in heat and motion without the *soul*.' [2]

But how could the Churches be made more efficient ?   This
was a problem to which earnest attention was devoted both in
England and in Scotland.   The most striking results were undoubtedly achieved by those very practical reformers who were
busy in the eighteenth and nineteenth centuries extending and
improving the parochial system.   In this kind of work there
was an honourable rivalry between the Anglicans and the dissenters.   Of this rivalry a convenient example is afforded by
the district which is included in the modern cities of Manchester
and Salford.   Here, in the period of 1741-1830, were built
eighteen new Anglican churches (three of these at the expense
of the nation) and forty-one other places of worship (mainly by
protestant dissenters).   In almost every case the building of
a church or chapel meant the establishment of a new social unit,
a parish or a congregation, which undertook the relief of distress
and a moral supervision over its members ; from 1784 onwards
the Anglicans and dissenters of this district were organizing
Sunday schools ; from 1810 the dissenters were founding day
schools, on the model devised by Joseph Lancaster, and the
Anglicans responded by founding National Schools, on the plan

---

[1] *Croker Papers*, i. 277 (Croker to Southey, 3 Jan. 1825).
[2] So Gladstone in *The State in its Relations with the Church* (1838).

of Dr. Andrew Bell. Judged by modern standards these schools were miserably equipped and staffed; but they provided places for a larger number of children than could be spared from the factory and the shop.[1] In this race of improvement some of the smallest and poorest of religious denominations were distinguished for their practical enthusiasm. The Methodist Unitarians, whose ministers lived of necessity by the labour of their hands, could not afford the luxury of day schools; but to each of their chapels was attached a Sunday school in which their children were instructed in reading, writing, and arithmetic.[2] These matter-of-fact experiments in social reform, these unambitious communities founded on a sectarian basis, were either ignored or derided by the Radicals, who believed in short cuts towards social progress. But they interested Tory thinkers; and in 1821 Dr. Thomas Chalmers published the first part of his massive work on *The Christian and Civic Economy of Large Towns* to demonstrate how large a service the well-organized parish could render to the State. What he had to say carried weight, for he spoke of his own experiences as a minister in Glasgow, where in the years 1815 and 1823 he reorganized successively two large and poverty-stricken parishes. As minister of St. John's (1819–23) he undertook by agreement with the city council the whole business of relieving pauperism, and made the system of relief more effective and far cheaper than it had ever been before. He argued that every minister of an urban parish in Scotland was to some extent a trained administrator and an unpaid official of the central Government. What he had done any intelligent minister could do, with the help of a body of elders and of deacons. Who could be better qualified than a minister to supervise the education of the young? Or to mediate as Chalmers himself had mediated in the disputes between workmen and employers, which were so dangerous to the peace of industrial communities? Or to bring the classes together by inducing them to co-operate in good works? And the minister who could do so much as this would be not only serving the interests of social

---

[1] Axon, *Annals of Manchester*; S. E. Maltby, *Manchester and the Movement for National Elementary Education* (1918).

[2] H. McLachan, *Methodist Unitarian Movement* (1919).

order. He would be engaged in forming a model Christian community in which class differences were for all essential purposes obliterated. Still Chalmers, in his desire to convince practical men of the utility of this new parochial system, laid special emphasis upon the political consequences that it might produce:

'In a great town, where the parishes are little better than nominal, and there is no affecting relation between administrators and subjects, all the public and political tendencies of the popular mind run towards one point, and may form into one impetuous and overwhelming surge against the reigning authority of the place. The more that this else unmanageable mass is penetrated and split up into fragments, and that the effervescence which is in each is made to play round a separate machinery of its own, the more safe will be the leading corporation from any of those passing tempests by which the multitude is often thrown into fierce and fitful agitation. A parochial economy is not the less effectual for this purpose that the jurisdictions which it institutes, instead of being of a legal are rather of a moral and charitable nature. The kindly intercourse that is promoted between the various classes under such an arrangement is the best of all possible emollients in every season of political restlessness. . . . They are the towns of an empire which form the mighty organs of every great political overthrow; and if a right parochial system in towns would serve to check or rather to soften the turbulence that is in them, then ought the establishment of such a system to be regarded by our rulers as one of the best objects of patriotism.'[1]

Chalmers was thinking principally of the territorial parishes with which an Established Church had to deal. But he argued that the methodist congregations, though less compact, could be, just as much as the parish, a useful ally of the civil power.[2] He pointed out that the Wesleyan body had enforced its circular of 1819, against the Radical agitations, by threatening to exclude from membership any Wesleyan who attended a seditious meeting.[3]

Chalmers was obliged to admit that his proposals were not altogether easy to put into practice. Both in England and in Scotland town parishes were frequently so large that the minister could not establish personal relations with more than a small

---

[1] *Op. cit.*, ii. 40-1.   [2] *Op. cit.*, i. 355.
[3] *Op. cit.*, i. 342-3.

minority of his parishioners. In most parishes there was a dearth of lay helpers and of benevolent institutions. He admitted that a large increase in the number of endowed parishes would be required, and that no parish ought to have the care of more than 4,000 souls. In every parish of this size, he estimated, there should be Sunday schools and day schools to accommodate 450 children, and a corresponding staff of salaried teachers. Each parish, furthermore, would be required to raise by voluntary contributions a revenue sufficient to provide for its own poor; and in his view it was essential that the parish should assume this responsibility, if it was to have real influence over the poorer classes. He made great efforts to secure a fair trial for his scheme in Scotland. But in 1845, two years before his death, Scotland was converted, despite his protests, to the principles of the English Poor Law.

In England Chalmers's scheme was seriously and sympathetically considered. Wilberforce recommended it to the attention of Lord Liverpool.[1] Ashley took up with enthusiasm so much of the scheme as related to elementary education. In 1842 he wrote:

‘ I would recast the whole arrangement of parishes, especially in towns. I would assign to every 3,000 souls a resident pastor with a decent income and comfortable house ; and I would then leave education to take care of itself, forbidding to the State any meddling, suggesting, directing, planning, in matters wherein it can have no knowledge. The State should insist and enforce that the duty be done, but not presume to interfere with its own theories and doctrines.’ [2]

Ashley was soon forced to realize that the dissenting bodies would not tolerate this solution of the educational problem. It was left for the Whigs to suggest a system of concurrent endowment of dissenting congregations and their schools,[3] but such a system did not commend itself to Anglicans.

From Chalmers we may turn to two English thinkers, Southey and Coleridge, whose views on the mission of the Church were not suggested by practical experience, but nevertheless carried

[1] Add. MS. 38191, fos. 274 ff.

[2] Hodder's *Life of Shaftesbury* (popular edition), p. 237.

[3] Stanmore, *Life of Sidney Herbert*, i. 60 (a proposal of the third Earl Grey); *Early Correspondence of Lord John Russell*, ii. 43.

considerable weight with Tory members of the Church of England. Coleridge was and Southey was not a philosopher. But both started from the same general principle. Both held that since man's reason is fallible and weak, while his passions are strong and insistent, it was good for man to be ruled by a moral law which he could never have devised for himself, and by an intelligence higher than his own.[1]

Southey devoted a large part of his thoughts to social problems. On these, as on other subjects, he wrote for money because his pen was, for the greater part of his life, his sole means of support. But to treat him as a hireling scribbler is absurdly unjust. He was independent both in his choice of subjects and in his treatment of them. He had an honourable ambition to educate his party and to turn its energies into useful channels. He did not pretend to originate proposals for social reform. But he made it his business to study and to describe all social experiments or projects which seemed likely to be fruitful. The width of his sympathies is attested by his generous tributes to Robert Owen and to the pioneers of the co-operative movement. It was no sectarian, no party hack, who in 1829, when Owen had been thrown over by the bishops and the royal dukes, acknowledged him as one of the two or three great moral reformers of the age. Southey was too sanguine, too easily persuaded of the practical value of any large-hearted scheme. But his party was not suffering from any excess of idealism, and the shocks which he administered to its complacency were a much-needed tonic. His ignorance of political economy, his want of experience in practical affairs, led him into some mistakes. But he was sometimes in the right when he challenged the fashionable but unverified assumptions of economists and statesmen. His moral sense revolted against the shibboleth of *laisser-faire*. He could not bring himself to think of the State as a joint-stock company working for profit and kept in being by the enlightened self-interest of the shareholders. Great examples of patriotism and virtue, venerable traditions, an unchanging and immemorial creed—these things seemed to him at least as essential as a well-ordered admini-

[1] See Mill's remarks to Sterling in H. Elliott, *Letters of J. S. Mill* (1910), i, p. 15.

stration, a general diffusion of useful knowledge or a competent acquaintance with Bentham's calculus of pains and pleasures. And since he refused to think of the State as a mere mechanism he was finely sceptical of the worth of any schemes which proposed to reform the State by some simple and mechanical alteration in its government.

Southey held that social reform, to be effective, must be carried through by the voluntary efforts of private citizens, co-operating under the influence of altruistic motives. And how, he asked, could altruism be kindled and sustained, except by organized Christianity? It was idle to expect that irreligious men would persevere in the long and difficult struggle which must be waged before pauperism and disease could be reduced to tolerable proportions, before humane relations could be established between employers and employed, before a higher standard of morality could be taught to those who were brutalized by the hard conditions of their daily life. Religion alone could supply the antidote to the moral poison which had penetrated every limb and sinew of the body politic.

He was a devoted adherent of the Church of England, 'the best ecclesiastical establishment which exists at present or has yet existed '.[1] But he freely admitted that, as an instrument of social reform, that Church left much to be desired. He surprised and sometimes irritated his fellow Anglicans by inviting them to study and to imitate the practical expedients of the Methodist congregations and even of the Roman Catholic Church. But, like Sismondi[2] and most other contemporary critics of orthodox political economy and the utilitarian ideal, Southey derived his main inspiration from a study of the Middle Ages. Here he found the record of an experiment after his own heart—of a deliberate attempt to make religion supreme over society and inspire the State with a religious purpose. He confessed that the experiment had failed through the over-readiness of those who made it to put constraint upon the conscience of the individual. But in the world around him he saw the opposite fault—a want of conscious purpose in the State, leading to an

[1] *Life*, v. 308.

[2] Sismondi, *Nouveaux Principes d'Economie Politique* (1819-24), and *Etudes sur L'Economie Politique* (1837-8).

excess of individual liberty.[1] It was this criticism of modern
society which drew down the vials of Macaulay's indignation.   The idea that the magistrate, the representative of
the State's authority, should be a paternal meddler, a schoolmaster, a theologian, 'a Lady Bountiful in every parish, a
Paul Pry in every house', was abhorrent to that secular
intelligence.   It is true that, in the book which Macaulay
criticized, Southey has too much to say about the sovereign
State, too little about the community of men of goodwill
and high convictions.   But Southey was not enamoured of
medieval institutions.   What he desired was more of medieval
charity and medieval respect for authority.   He failed to convert Macaulay ; but in Ashley he found a disciple after his
own heart.[2]

Coleridge, in his time, wrote on the nature both of Church
and State.   In 1818, in his *Principles of Political Knowledge*,
he had contended that the sufficient and only justification of any
national institution is that it leads to good results.   He rejected the
supposition that a system of government, to be defensible, must
be founded upon principles of pure reason.   He condemned the
' police theory ' of the State, and demanded of the civil government
that it should not only protect life and property and individual
liberty, but should also do whatever could be done to improve
the material conditions of existence.   The State should arrange
such a division of labour as will assure to every individual
a share in the comforts and conveniences which will humanize
and refine his nature.   And he insisted that, even when the
State had been organized so as to fulfil these purposes, there
would still remain a need for sustained and intelligent effort, on
the part of its citizens, to preserve and to improve the new social
order.   The fault of the Radicals, he remarked, lay in supposing
that the world could be mechanized and left to run of itself.
We have in this little work, more definitely than in Southey's

---

[1] *Sir Thomas More* (1829), i. 93.

[2] In 1830, before he had made Southey's acquaintance, Ashley wrote :
'I have derived the greatest benefit from the study of your works ' (Hodder,
p. 63).   In 1841 we find Ashley sighing for '*paternal* and constitutional
government' (*op. cit.*, p. 63).   In 1839 he writes that he owes much to
Southey's books, especially to the *Book of the Church*, *Sir Thomas
More*, and the *Moral Essays* (*op. cit.*, p. 137).

Sir Thomas More, a programme for the secular activity of the State when reorganized on Tory lines.

In his later work on the *Constitution of Church and State* (1830) Coleridge is mainly concerned with the moral responsibilities of the State. Since the State has the fundamental duty of protecting religion, it maintains, or should maintain if it does not already do so, a National Clerisy, or spiritual estate, which for the sake of convenience may be called a National Church, although it has other duties besides the exposition of theology. In this Clerisy there should be two classes—first, the pastors and sub-pastors who are in charge of parishes, secondly men learned in the physical and moral sciences. The second of these classes is to be charged with the higher education of the citizens, and more especially of the pastors. Elementary education is to be managed in every parish by a sub-pastor ; but the pastor himself is to be responsible to the State for imparting to the youth ' a civic education ', that is to say, instruction concerning the rights and responsibilities of citizenship. In this way, says Coleridge, it is possible to produce a nation of ' obedient, free, useful, organisable subjects, citizens and patriots who will devote their lives to the benefit of the State '.

Coleridge thus proposed to place all education under the control of the State, to entrust the parochial clergy with the work of primary education, and to give a semi-clerical character to the teachers of higher studies. Obviously he was influenced by medieval theory and practice in making these suggestions. Medieval also was his conception of the invisible Church, the community of Christian believers, which transcends the State and is subject to no earthly jurisdiction, which, however, supplies to the State a conscience and a soul, which corrects and supplements the hard and imperfect ethics of secular society. None the less the book was welcomed by John Stuart Mill as evidence that Coleridge had broken away from sectarian traditions to become a true reformer. Maurice accepted with entire approval Coleridge's theory of the right relations between Church and State and the plea for a National Clerisy.[1] Mr. Gladstone found

---

[1] *Kingdom of Christ*, iii, p. 2. ' The portion which refers to the State seems to me entirely satisfactory.' See also his lectures, *Has the State or the Church the Power to educate the Nation ?* (1839).

in the book 'the clear, definite and strong conception of the
Church which . . . has proved for me entirely adequate, and
saved me from all vacillation'.[1]   It came at a time when many
minds were preoccupied with the question how the Church could
be restored to her old position in the world; and already Tractarian views were developing in Oxford.   But on one essential
point of policy Coleridge stood opposed to the Tractarians. He
said to a friend in 1834:

'The National Church requires and is required by the Christian
Church for the perfection of each. For, if there were no National
Church, the mere Spiritual Church would either become, like the
Papacy, a dreadful tyranny over mind and body, or else would fall
abroad into a multitude of enthusiastic sects as in England in the
seventeenth century.   In a country of any religion at all, liberty of
conscience can only be permanently preserved by means of and under
a National Church.'[2]

So far we have been considering the ideal of 'Church and
King' as it was presented by Tory theorists. For the theorists
it was axiomatic that under one King there should be one
Church. But by the end of the eighteenth century this principle
was already undermined. In Ireland the Presbyterian clergy
were in receipt of the *Regium donum*, first granted by
Charles II, revived and increased by William III. The Act of
Union with Scotland recognized the existence of two distinct
establishments, with distinct constitutions and distinct theologies
within the Kingdom of Great Britain. In the province of
Quebec the Catholic clergy were permitted, by an act of 1774,
to collect their accustomed dues and rights from their Catholic
parishioners. In 1795 Pitt agreed to endow Maynooth College
for the education of the Catholic clergy of Ireland. Even some
Tories of the type of Sidmouth were willing soon after the
union with Ireland to provide some form of endowment for the
Irish Catholic clergy;[3] and in 1825 the House of Commons
passed a resolution in favour of this arrangement. Peel thought
at that time, and for a long time afterwards, that to put the
resolution into practice would be 'a fearful experiment'. But

---

[1] *Life of Gladstone*, i. 462.   [2] *Table Talk*, 31 May 1834.
[3] Speech in the House of Lords, 27 May 1808 (*Life of Sidmouth*, ii. 502).

his objections were political rather than religious. He admitted that the endowment of Irish Presbyterianism had produced most salutary results. He admitted that it might be dangerous to leave the Irish Catholic clergy totally disunited from the State. But would not a measure of endowment encourage them in the hope of restoring the former state of things when Catholicism had been the religion of the State in Ireland, and had been endowed with temporalities now belonging to another Church.[1] He was still of the same mind in 1843, when he was earnestly discussing the Irish situation with his chief lieutenant, Sir James Graham. The latter felt no conscientious objection to a policy of concurrent endowment, and was firmly convinced that, without such a policy, no measures of conciliation would succeed in Ireland. But he admitted that the ' British public ', or in other words Peel's majority, could not be induced to agree to concurrent endowment.[2] They still thought, as Mr. Gladstone thought in 1838, that it was a moral duty to maintain the Established Church in Ireland solely and exclusively. ' It appears not too much to assume ', Gladstone wrote, ' that our Imperial legislature has been qualified to take and has taken in point of fact a sounder view of religious truth than the majority of the people of Ireland in their destitute and uninstructed state.'[3]

Hence Peel's utmost concessions to the Irish Catholic clergy were the Charitable Donations and Bequests Act of 1844, which enabled Catholics to endow their own priests and institutions, the Maynooth Act of 1845, which increased the annual grant from £9,000 to £26,000. Even these measures excited some discontent among his followers ; and Macaulay taunted Peel with giving up the cherished principles of Toryism at his own arbitrary will and pleasure.[4]

But to touch the rights, real or imaginary, of an Established Church was even more repugnant to Tory principles. The first symptoms of a split in Lord Grey's Cabinet were produced by the eagerness of Russell, Grey, and Althorp to devote the

[1] Parker's *Peel*, i. 369-70.   [2] *Op. cit.*, iii. 65.
[3] *State in its Relations with the Church* (p. 80).
[4] See the concluding paragraphs of Macaulay's speech of 14 April 1845 (*Misc. Writings*, pp. 686-7).

revenues of superfluous Irish bishoprics to secular education.
The speech with which Russell upset the coach in 1834 was a
speech asserting the propriety of this scheme. The Melbourne
ministry in 1837 received a less severe, but still a sensible rebuff,
when it endeavoured to abolish Church rates in England without
giving compensation to the Church. The bill was dropped, and
this reform was postponed until 1868. In 1839 Russell had the
greatest difficulty in appeasing the opposition felt in both
Houses to a system of inspection of State-aided schools. His chief
opponents were the bishops, and the object which some of them
had in view was to leave the Church entirely free and unsuper-
vised in her teaching of secular no less than of religious knowledge. One unexpected result of the Reform Act of 1832 was
that the new electorate showed itself even more violently interested than the old in questions which appeared to involve religious principles; and the Tories reaped the chief advantage of
this circumstance.

Macaulay believed that Peel, so long as he remained in opposition, was personally responsible for whipping up Anglican
fanaticism. This theory, however, is not supported by Sir
Robert's printed correspondence, which shows that from time
to time he deprecated the selection. of ecclesiastical issues as
subjects of party warfare.[1] He was not anxious to engage himself in an unlimited partnership with any religious body. 'The
recourse to faction, or temporary alliances with extreme opinions
for the purposes of faction, is not reconcilable with a *Conservative* opposition.'[2] Rather was he anxious to give the Whigs an
honourable opportunity of abandoning the onslaught on Irish
Church endowments, and to leave his own hands free for the
future. When he himself assumed office, it would be his first
concern to deal with questions of finance and tariffs and the
mitigation of industrial distress.

Nevertheless Peel was responsible for one substantial though
unobtrusive measure of ecclesiastical reform. The Tamworth

---

[1] See e. g. his letters of 3 January 1836 to Mr. Goulburn (*Parker*, ii. 318)
of 10 February 1836 to Wellington (*op. cit.*, ii. 322) ; his rejection of Ashley's
proposal, in December 1839, 'to get the government out on the Protestant
point' (*op. cit.*, ii. 414–16).

[2] *Parker*, ii. 338.

Manifesto promised that his first ministry would improve the distribution of ecclesiastical revenues, while reserving them entirely for ecclesiastical purposes. This promise he honoured by appointing a Royal Commission (1835) to review the whole of the patronage vested in the Crown, the Lord Chancellor, and the bishops, ' with a view of attaching spiritual functions to all offices that are at present sinecures '. The larger scheme which lay behind this unassuming proposal is explained in a letter which he wrote to Bishop Phillpotts, the most efficient of his ecclesiastical supporters. He intended to abolish all lucrative sinecures, and to appropriate the revenues thus saved to the extension and improvement of the parochial system ; that is, to the religious and moral education of large working-class communities which would otherwise be left entirely to the ministrations of dissenters. The larger scheme could not be taken in hand without legislation ; and Peel knew well that he could not expect to pass a Church bill until his party in the House of Commons should be greatly reinforced. But his Commission could undertake a preliminary survey, and did so, not suspending its labours when Peel's brief administration ended. The Melbourne Government took action on the first reports by passing Acts in 1838 and 1840 to deal with the abuses of pluralism, sinecurism, and non-residence of incumbents.[1] The second of these Acts redeemed the pledge that Peel had given to the Church through Phillpotts; for it applied to the augmentation of poor benefices a part of the revenues of cathedral chapters. When Peel returned to office he desired to go still farther in appropriating surplus funds to the parochial system. But unforeseen difficulties emerged, and all that he could do was to pass, in 1843, an Act which empowered Queen Anne's Bounty and the Ecclesiastical Commission to use surplus funds for endowing new parishes and augmenting poor livings.[2]

This was much less than he had hoped ; for in his opinion an efficient parochial system should have provided elementary education. He had proposed to use the funds of the Church for this object, and intended to clear the way by setting up a Commission to investigate both the religious and the educational needs of the manufacturing classes. But the Home Secretary,

---

[1] 1 & 2 Vict. c. 106 ; 3 & 4 Vict. c. 114.   [2] 6 & 7 Vict. c. 77.

Sir James Graham, was afraid that such an inquiry would disclose wants and would raise expectations which could only be met by large subsidies from the Exchequer. But any proposal to spend public money on churches, or on schools which would be controlled by the Anglican clergy, would excite bitter opposition from the Presbyterians, the Roman Catholics, and the Protestant dissenters of England and Wales. On the other hand, the Church of England would never agree to any scheme of elementary education which took out of her hands the control over religious education. Some of Peel's advisers—Lord Brougham was one of them—desired that elementary schools should be entirely financed and managed by the State, and that all religious teaching in such schools should be undenominational.[1] But this plan had already proved a failure in Ireland ; and in England it was more than likely to be wrecked by the same critics who had resisted Russell's scheme of State inspection. Peel's inclination was to rest content with two modest steps—a gradual increase of the annual grant for education, and a gradual extension of the supervisory powers vested in the Education Committee of the Privy Council.[2] In 1843 the difficulties which Graham had foreseen were raised by the education clauses in the factory bill which Graham had prepared. These clauses provided that in factory schools there should be compulsory lessons in scripture for all the pupils, and supplementary instruction in the catechism and the Book of Common Prayer for all children whose parents were Anglican. In order to conciliate the Church of England, the Home Secretary proposed that the teachers and the text-books in these schools should be selected by the bishop of the diocese. But this concession raised such a storm of protests from dissenters and Roman Catholics that Graham was obliged to withdraw the educational clauses. Even Lord Ashley, whose pressure had caused the Government to draft these clauses, showed plainly that he would prefer to see the factory children uneducated than to tolerate ' united education '.[3]

---

[1] Parker's *Peel*, ii. 547–51. The claim of the Church to control all schools endowed by the State was formulated as early as 1807 by Lord Eldon, in a debate on Whitbread's educational scheme (*Hansard*, ix. 1174 ff.).
[2] See Brougham's proposals and the criticisms of Graham and Peel in the *Life of Sir J. Graham*, i. 337–40.   [3] *Op. cit.*, i. 345.

In regard to the Church of Scotland Peel would certainly have remained neutral, had such a course been possible for a Prime Minister. But he could not accept all the claims of the Non-Intrusionists. He admitted that in purely spiritual matters a free hand ought to be given to the Church of Scotland. He promised that if the law courts should attempt to control her in such matters, Parliament would at once intervene to control the courts. But where the boundaries between spiritual and civil matters were imperfectly defined by the statute law, there the definition must rest with the courts. To allow the Church of Scotland to define her own sphere of action, as she had attempted to define it in the Veto Act, would be to endanger the religious liberties and civil rights of the people.[1]

It is idle to discuss the large general claims raised by the Church of Scotland at this time. In the form in which they were raised, they could hardly be accepted by any Government which was strong and self-respecting. But we may well ask whether these claims would have been raised, or having been raised would have been maintained, if Government would have consented to abolish the rights of patronage. This was actually done in 1874 by a Conservative Government. Why could it not be done in 1843? There was no difficulty so far as Crown patronage was concerned. The practice of the Home Office under Peel, under Russell and Sir James Graham was to make Crown presentations in accordance with the wishes of the parishioners. The only difference between Whig and Tory practice was that Russell practically acknowledged the exclusive right of the parishioners to elect, while Peel and Graham reserved the right to nominate when the parishioners did not agree among themselves.[2] The private patron was a real stumbling-block. His rights were always present in the mind of Graham.[3] But he and Peel were influenced by another con-

[1] Peel's speech of March 1843 (quoted *Parker*, iii. 91–3).

[2] Parker's *Peel*, iii. 415.

[3] Graham to Stanley, 21 October 1838: ' Here is the General Assembly labouring to establish the voluntary principal and the free election of pastors by the congregation, in opposition to the claims of the patrons ' (Parker's *Graham*, i. 273). See also his official reply of 30 December 1842 to the Moderator of the General Assembly (*op. cit.*, i. 387), which in effect refuses to abolish patronage.

sideration, which perhaps weighed with them even more than the rights of property. 'You must be aware', writes Graham to a Scottish member, 'of my reluctance to give the popular will the commanding influence over clerical appointments which you are disposed to concede'; and he informs another correspondent that 'the admission of popular election in the choice of ministers appears to me dangerous and derogatory to the dignity and independence of the sacred calling'. The Prime Minister expressed the same view in much blunter language. 'Popular election leads directly to every evil and abuse of canvassing and all the low artifices by which popular election can be influenced.'[1] Lord Aberdeen, to whom Peel and Graham looked for the outline of an amicable arrangement, was averse to allowing the presentation of a patron to be annulled by a popular veto; and he appears never to have contemplated the more drastic concession of introducing popular election and abolishing patronage. The best defence of the line which was taken by the Tory Government is that they expressed the views, not only of English lawyers, but also of a large party in the Church of Scotland, and that they could not have thrown the patrons overboard without provoking a revolt of the Moderates. This aspect of the case is well put by Hume Brown:

'For upwards of a century the spectacle had been seen of two sections of the Church [of Scotland] in chronic antagonism, and engaged in never-ending strife for the direction of its councils. A common policy in the religious interests of the people had hitherto proved impossible; and so long as the two parties existed within the Church it could not be possible. . . . Such being the relations of Moderates and Evangelicals it was necessary and desirable that they should part company in the interests of the religion they both professed.'[2]

The Disruption was an omen and a portent of similar troubles in the Church of England. Graham foresaw that Dr. Chalmers would find Anglican imitators of his policy. And in fact the leaders of Tractarianism, widely as they differed from Chalmers in theology and in their interpretation of Church history, thought as he did about the relations of Church and State. In the Gorham case (1847–50) the Tractarians were practically

---

[1] *Op. cit.*, i. 376, 385.
[2] Hume Brown, *History of Scotland*, iii. 432.

contending that the Church of England should define the limits of
her own spiritual authority, and the judgement in that case led to
a secession which was headed by Archdeacon Manning. Bishop
Phillpotts of Exeter, who raised this storm by refusing to insti-
tute Mr. Gorham, was no Tractarian, but a high churchman of
the old Tory type, and an outspoken critic of Tract 90. For
many years he had been the leader of that party in the Church
whose views Peel had always felt himself bound to respect. He,
however, unlike his Tractarian allies, felt himself under no obligation to secede ; he merely satisfied his conscience by renouncing
communion with his archbishop. With such men as Phillpotts a
Tory Government knew how to deal. But they regarded the
Oxford school with serious misgivings. Sir Robert Peel was
prepared to excuse a taint of Puseyism in young and inexperi-
enced clergymen who had not yet found their theological sea-
legs; but he had not been long at the head of his second ministry
before he decided that a confirmed Puseyite was quite unsuitable
for the responsible position of a dean or bishop.[1]

[1] Parker's *Peel*, iii. 416.

VIII

HAMPDEN CLUBS (1816–1817) AND COBBETT

HOW far were the rights of public meeting and association curtailed in the years 1799–1819? We have first to notice that after 1802 Government ceased to suspend the Habeas Corpus Act, so that arbitrary detention of political suspects without a trial became a thing of the past. The Act was again suspended in 1817, and the suspension was continued for ten months; but this was the last occasion this method of checking political agitation was utilized in Great Britain. Secondly, the Seditious Meetings Act of 1796 expired in 1799, and was only renewed for a short period in 1800. Under this Act it had been illegal to hold a political meeting except in the presence of a magistrate, who could, when he thought fit, arrest any speaker or disperse the meeting. Under the same Act no hall could be used for political lectures unless it was licensed by two magistrates, and no money might be taken at the door. In 1799 the Seditious Societies Act introduced a tighter control of lecture halls. Whatever the subject of the lectures, the hall required a licence, if there was any money taken at the door—a rule which was no doubt aimed at Thelwall and other itinerant agitators whose harangues were transparently disguised as lectures on improving subjects. The same Act elaborately defined the characteristics which made a society seditious. To take from the members any oath which was not authorized or required by the law; to conceal from the society at large the list of members, or the names of the officials and committee men; to organize branches or divisions; to appoint delegates to represent the society—any one of these acts was sufficient to bring a popular society within the meshes of the law. It was the prohibition of branches which especially hampered agitators between 1815 and 1820.

The exact state of the law was by no means easy for the layman to ascertain. It seems to have been made clear for the first time by the efforts of the Hampden Club, a society which was founded in 1811 and which held its first public meeting on 20 April 1812. It was formed, probably, in imitation of the defunct Society of the Friends of the People, and its constitution was distinctly aristocratic. No one was eligible for election unless he had an income of £300 a year derived from land. Sir Francis Burdett was its chairman. He was a Whig Member of Parliament who had made himself notorious by defending the freedom of the Press against the House of Commons, by incurring commitment for a breach of the privileges of the House, and by suing Speaker Abbot for unlawful imprisonment (1810). He was one of the members for Westminster, and was pledged to parliamentary reform. His views on that subject were undeterminate; but the policy of the Hampden Club was settled by Major Cartwright, who was an original member, and hoped by means of the Club to carry a measure of reform resembling that which Grey had produced in 1797. In the autumn of 1812 Cartwright made a tour through the North of England and the Lowlands of Scotland to encourage the foundation of popular societies which would agitate for reform.[1] They were not to be branches of the London Hampden Club, or in regular correspondence with it; but they were to stand towards that club in the same relation in which the provincial societies of 1792 and 1793 had stood to the Society for Constitutional Information. Cartwright was arrested in 1813 on account of his missionary activities, but was soon released, as no illegal action could be proved against him. He made another tour in 1815; but this produced no visible effect at the time.[2]

M. Halévy is of opinion that from 1810 to 1815 there was a perpetual ferment both in London and in the country.[3] This

---

[1] Henry Cockburn, *Memorials* (p. 309), states that on this tour Cartwright drew large audiences in Edinburgh, but not one of the local newspapers would report his meetings or insert his advertisements.

[2] A Glasgow divinity student writes in November 1815 that 'there are now in the house of Major Cartwright . . . no less than 600 petitions for Parliamentary Reform from Scotland. These will be thrown into Parliament in the spring of next year ' (H. McLachlan, *A Nonconformist Library* (1923), p. 125). Bamford (*Recollections*, i. 7) states that many Hampden Clubs were founded in Lancashire as the result of Cartwright's visit in 1812.

[3] *Hist. du Peuple Anglais*, i. 142.

statement appears to be an exaggeration. The textile districts were indeed restless and turbulent in the years 1811–12. But early in 1813 the Home Office withdrew the troops which had been quartered in the West Riding for the preservation of the peace; on March 11 Sidmouth, the Home Secretary, wrote to Pellew: 'the people are sound and firm. A most material and happy change has taken place in their temper and disposition in the last few months'; and nothing occurred in 1813 or 1814 to shake this optimism.[1] The Corn Law riots of 1815 in London were perhaps exaggerated by the newspapers,[2] but in any case they soon died down, when the return of Napoleon from Elba distracted public attention from the Corn Law to the events of the Hundred Days.

But before peace was thoroughly restored an economic crisis burst upon the country. There was a recrudescence of Luddism in Nottingham, and there were riots at Newcastle-on-Tyne in 1815. In the winter of 1815–16 the farmers of the eastern counties, hard hit by the low price of wheat, began to discharge their labourers and to abandon the cultivation of their poorer lands. In Norfolk, Suffolk, Cambridgeshire, Huntingdonshire, and the Isle of Ely there were nocturnal meetings of farm labourers; threatening letters and incendiary hand-bills were in circulation; houses, barns, stacks, and threshing-machines were fired, and cattle were mutilated. The Lord-Lieutenant of Suffolk raised a force of mounted special constables; the magistrates of North Essex called out a troop of yeomanry, and so did those of Cambridgeshire; the magistrates of Ely raised a mixed force of gentlemen and special constables. At Littleport, in the Isle of Ely, some local magistrates promised, to the indignation of the Home Office, that wages should be raised to two shillings a day, and that flour should be sold below cost price if the rioters would disperse. But these promises failed to restore the peace, and the magistrates of Ely and Cambridgeshire concentrated their forces at Littleport. Seventy of the rioters were captured, of whom thirty-four were convicted on capital

---

[1] *Life of Sidmouth*, iii. 95–7.
[2] So Peel asserts (*Parker*, i. 168–9). But the biographer of Sidmouth states that he 'environed' London with troops and called upon the metropolitan parishes to raise special constables' (*Life*, iii. 126).

charges and five were actually hanged at a special assize held at Ely in June 1816.[1] 'I think it my duty', wrote Lord Sidmouth, 'to take the earliest opportunity of reprobating in the strongest terms any attempt to restore tranquillity by entering into terms of compromise with a lawless assembly of rioters, however desperate.'[2] Major-General Sir John Byng was sent from Colchester to Ely with a body of regulars, for the purpose of restoring order; but on the 28th of June he reported that the presence of his troops was no longer necessary in the eastern district.[3]

Meanwhile the industrial districts had begun to cause trouble. On 1 January 1816 the Duke of Rutland drew the attention of the Home Secretary to Birmingham. Here the hardware trades were depressed, wages had been reduced, and in consequence some of those for whom work was available were out on strike; disturbances had only been prevented by the quartering of a considerable military force in the district.[4] In Worcestershire and Staffordshire a large number of colliers, forgemen, nailers, and labourers were roaming over the country-side in small parties, some begging and others demanding money and provisions. A party of the unemployed from Staffordshire appeared at Uppingham in July, 'drawing a waggon, with the avowed intention of proceeding to London and collecting money as they proceed.' To this report the Home Office replied by ordering that the party in question should be reasoned with, and persuaded to go home. If obstinate, they should be warned that they were rendering themselves liable to be arrested and committed.[5] When other magistrates inquired what was to be done to relieve such vagrants, the Home Office answered that local authorities must take their own measures. 'The great desideratum is to find work for those who are thrown out of

---

[1] For these disorders see Mr. Western's speech of 7 March 1816 (*Hansard*, xxxiii. 31); also the proclamation of 25 May 1816 (H.O. *Papers*, 41. 1, p. 37).

[2] H.O. *Papers*, 41. 1, p. 51 (Lord Sidmouth to Sir Bate Dudley, Bart., of Ely, 25 May 1816).

[3] H.O. *Papers*, 41. 1, p. 179 (Mr. Beckitt to Sir J. Byng, 2 July 1816).

[4] *Life of Sidmouth*, iii. 144.

[5] H.O. 41. 1, pp. 56, 213. Similarly a party of colliers found at Leicester was turned back about the same time (H.O. 41. 1, p. 215).

any particular course of work; but the accomplishment of such an object must necessarily depend very much, if not entirely, on the higher orders and persons having authority in the districts where the distress is felt.'[1]

This indeed was the essential principle of the existing system, if system it can be called, for dealing with distress. But in 1816 the unemployed were numerous and some of them were desperate; they would not all sit at home with folded hands awaiting charity. Some who were turned back, on the roads which led to London from the Midlands, made for Liverpool, or Chester or Worcester; some went to their homes with the intention to advertise their needs by rioting.[2] In Lancashire the cotton operatives and hand-weavers were less vagrant than the unemployed of the Midlands; but Lancashire was not the quieter on that account. From Preston it was reported that a great number of persons, who had struck against a reduction of wages, 'have been parading the streets and assembling in groups, using the most threatening language'. Part of the regular troops stationed at Manchester were ordered to march without delay to Preston. The magistrates of Bolton asked for troops. Those of Stockport announced that the discontented and disaffected were taking advantage of the distress in that town; and a similar report came from the Mayor of Wigan. From Manchester came news that the hand-loom weavers were left destitute, and that application had been made on their behalf to the 'Association for the Relief of the Manufacturing Poor', which Wilberforce and his friends had founded in 1812. Early in 1817 the Manchester authorities reported that the cotton trade was taking a turn for the better; but there are many facts to suggest that this optimism was premature.[3]

In South Wales the trade depression was embittered by disputes of long standing between the ironmasters and their men.[4] When therefore wages were suddenly reduced in the

[1] H.O. 41. 1, p. 199 (Mr. Beckitt to Mr. W. Chedde of Orleton, Shifnal, 7 July 1816).

[2] H.O. 41. 1, pp. 215, 227.

[3] For the state of things in Lancashire see H.O. 41. 1, pp. 263 (Preston), 267 (Bolton), 298 (Stockport), 312, 315 (Wigan), 450 and H.O. 42. 1, p. 174 (Manchester).

[4] For which see the Hammonds' *Town Labourer*, pp. 65, 67, 70–1.

ironworks, owing to a fall of sixty per cent. in the price of iron, the ironworkers of Brecon, Monmouthshire, and Glamorgan came out on strike (Oct. 1816). They assembled in great force near Merthyr Tydfil, apparently ripe for any mischief. Troops were hurried to the spot at the request of the High Sheriff of Glamorgan, two companies of regulars from Bristol, yeomanry from Swansea and Cardiff, and the regimental staff of the Glamorgan militia. The Duke of Beaufort, who was Lord-Lieutenant of Monmouthshire, called out two troops of the county yeomanry to keep the peace in his own jurisdiction. No serious trouble occurred in South Wales; but still, in the spring of 1817, this unquiet region was watched by a cordon of military detachments, stationed at Carmarthen, Brecknock, Merthyr, Pontypool, Abergavenny, and Gloucester.[1]

In the cases that we have so far noticed there was no hint of any organization more political or more criminal in character than the ordinary trade union. But in the counties of Leicester and Nottingham there were machine-breaking societies at work. In June 1816 there was an organized attack on the mill of Messrs. Heathcoats at Loughborough, a mill where bobbin lace was made by machinery. The magistrates expected to obtain, from the trials and confessions of the ringleaders, some evidence of a far-reaching conspiracy. But they were disappointed, as is clear from the following report of the confession made by James Towle on the morning of his execution[2]:—

'Towle never took an oath of secrecy, or indeed of any kind, nor ever heard of any being made use of among the gang. They have no particular fund of money, but when any job is intended, or money wanted for any purpose, it is collected among the stockingers or lace-hands who happen to be in work at the time. The sum required of each is so small that it is never refused; the Frames would be sure to be broken if it were refused. They have no depôt of arms. Many of the gang have a pistol or two concealed in their houses, and when a job is intended they borrow them of each other. He believes Savage bought a brace of pistols at Derby on purpose for the Loughboro job. He knows of no persons in the higher ranks of life that are connected with them. When any job is intended, three or four of the principal people

---

[1] For the situation in South Wales see H. O. 41. 1, pp. 134, 143, 347, 360, 368, 389; also H. O. 41. 2, pp. 88, 373-91.

[2] The charge on which he was sentenced was one of homicide.

go about to collect hands for it among those whom they know to be well inclined to Ludding.'[1]

The execution of Towle did not end the frame-breakings ; and in the autumn the Leicestershire magistrates enrolled special constables, at the suggestion of the Home Office, to repress this particular form of crime. The Home Office clung to the theory that the frame-breakers were directed by a secret committee which they believed to be in correspondence with London agitators. Under this impression Lord Sidmouth offered to the magistrates the help of London police officers and of a body of troops.[2]

We have here one of the many indications that the Home Office were bewildered and alarmed by the well-staged demonstrations of the London Radicals, whose game, in 1816, was to create the illusion that all the distressed and discontented classes in the country were linked together in the closest correspondence for a common purpose. In sober truth the London Radicals themselves were thoroughly disunited. Burdett and Lord Cochrane, who, like Burdett, sat for Westminster, were simply the figureheads of a movement about which they knew very little. Cartwright, Henry Hunt, and Cobbett were rivals for the favour of the mob, and were thoroughly despised by James Mill and Francis Place, the one the philosopher, the other the party manager of the Westminster group of Radicals. As to the plan of campaign there was little difference between them. All advocated the plan of simultaneous petitions, and thought that to organize petitions was enough. The walls of Jericho were to be overthrown by shouting.

Simultaneous petitions were the only way in which, at that particular date, great publicity could be given to a drastic plan of reform without any serious risk of prosecution. The freedom of the political press had been seriously restricted by the use of special juries in press trials ; also by two Acts of 1798 and 1799 which required the disclosure of the names of the proprietors, publishers, printers, and editors of every newspaper. The severity of the courts terrified all journalists whose sympathies were on the Radical side. Even Cobbett had been much chastened by the sentence of two years' imprisonment which

[1]. H.O. 40. 3.   [2] H.O. 41. 1, pp. 255, 330, 345, 382, 414, 432.

he incurred in 1810. The spell of fear held good until 1817, that *annus mirabilis* of the gutter press, when the new demand of the working-classes for political literature encouraged Wooler, Carlile, and Howe to take the risks and the profits of denouncing persons in authority with the most unmeasured violence.

But the right of petitioning remained. Neither Pitt nor Eldon had cared to lay impious hands on this palladium of the constitution. The only serious restriction on the right was that imposed by the Act of 1661 against Tumultuous Petitioning, which is still upon the Statute Book. This makes it unlawful to solicit more than twenty signatures to a petition which craves alteration of the laws concerning Church and State, unless the petition be agreed to by three magistrates or the major part of a grand jury. It also forbids the presenting of a petition by a company of more than ten persons. The authors of the plan of simultaneous petitions recommended that as many reform clubs as possible should be formed; that each club should be provided with printed copies of a petition drafted in London, and that as many copies as possible should, through the efforts of the clubs, be signed with twenty signatures. Arrangements should then be made for sending the 'Score Petitions' up to London with a numerous escort for each consignment; and the petitions should be presented to Parliament through members who were favourable to the popular cause.

Early in 1816 the London Hampden Club published a pamphlet to explain its aims.[1] These were the 'free election' of members of the House of Commons; and the extension of the franchise to all who paid direct taxation. Major Cartwright and his assistant Cleary began to circulate a form of petition, and two batches of signed petitions were presented through Burdett to the House of Commons on April 30 and May 8. At the end of August an open-air meeting, held in Westminster, which was addressed both by Burdett and by Cochrane, resolved that the collecting of petitions should be organized throughout the country, and that the petitions should be brought to London by two delegates from each district; and very shortly afterwards we hear of the organization, in the Midlands and the North, of reform societies of working-men.

[1] *Proceedings of the Hampden Club*, 23 March, 1816.

On 7 October 1816 Cobbett opened a reform campaign in his *Political Register*, taking as his text the proposals of the London Hampden Club; although Cobbett was a free lance it was his case for parliamentary reform which the provincial societies studied and which the Government press attacked. He did good service to the movement by his outspoken condemnation of the Luddites, who were generally imagined by conservatives to be the left wing of the Reform party,[1] and also by his sensible and mediating attitude towards the differences which arose between the contending supporters of household suffrage and universal suffrage. But the picture which he drew of the consequences that might be expected from parliamentary reform, however grateful it might be to his readers, was calculated to arouse the fiercest hostility in the minds of quiet men. To the question, What good would a reformed Parliament do? he replies with a catalogue of probable advantages. One would be an immediate reduction of such pensions as those of Mr. George Rose and Mr. Huskisson, of Mr. Ponsonby and Lord Erskine. Another would be an immediate reduction of official salaries, among which Cobbett particularly instances the salaries of the judges, and of the police magistrates. The Civil List ought to be reduced; junior members of the Royal Family ought to be allowed no more than £6,000 a year apiece, and £60,000 would be a handsome revenue to allow to His Majesty, if indeed it is reasonable to allow him anything on the Civil List when he is notoriously the owner of great private wealth. It would be no robbery, considering the appreciation of the currency in recent times, to diminish the interest on the public debt by half.[2] It was useless to tell the critics of the London Hampden Club that these measures were not part and parcel of the reformers' programme, when they were advocated in the one newspaper to which the rank and file of the reform movement looked for guidance. Had Cobbett never existed or never written, the movement would still have been doomed to failure, but there might have been considerably less rancour between

[1] See his Letter to the Luddites in the *Political Register* for November 1816 (*Political Works*, v. 18 ff.).

[2] Letter to Sir Francis Burdett, 7 October 1816; Address to the Country Gentlemen, 20 December 1816 (both in the *Political Register*).

the majority and minority ; and it would have been possible for the Whigs to stand by their pledges of 1797. As it was, the programme of the London Hampden Club, which was at first regarded by the Whig ' Mountain ' as a practicable policy, or at all events a foundation on which a policy might be constructed, was rejected in 1817 by Brougham and his friends.[1]

The reputation of the reformers was further injured by the indiscretions of Henry Hunt—the very type and pattern of that new class of gentlemen farmers which Cobbett so cordially detested. Hunt began his career as an agitator in his native county of Wiltshire, whence he extended his activities into Somerset. In 1812 he stood for Bristol as a reformer against a Whig (Samuel Romilly) and a Tory, and in that city he organized a reform association. In 1816 he appeared in London as one of the competitors for the leadership of London radicalism. He stood alone in demanding universal suffrage till Cobbett came down on his side ; and this extremism helped his reputation materially in Lancashire, where the ultra-toryism of the propertied classes had for many years exasperated labour into accepting ultra-democratic views. Hunt was the only Radical of note who gave his countenance to the celebrated and still rather mysterious Spa Fields meetings of 15 November and 2 December 1816, the first mass meetings which the Radicals ventured to hold in London after the return of peace. Hunt was well equipped for the work of a mob orator. He had a fine presence, great vitality, and a clear bell-like voice which enabled him to hold the attention of the largest and most restless crowds. He had not organized these meetings ; he had nothing new to tell them ; he was *vox et praeterea nihil*. But to the country clubs, regarding him from a distance, he seemed to be a lion-hearted philanthropist, and the one militant leader that the popular cause had yet produced. In Great Britain and in Ireland the wildest expectations were excited by the Spa

---

[1] The Whigs who were reputed favourable to reform were Brougham, Whitbread, Brand, Creevey, Benet, Grattan, Lord Ossulston, Lord Archibald Hamilton, at the time when Brougham offered himself as a candidate for Westminster (June 1814) and on behalf of himself and his friends accepted the principles of annual parliaments and household suffrage. (See Cobbett's Letter to Earl Grosvenor in the *Political Register* for Feb. 1817).

Fields meetings.[1] Even after the ignominious end of the second meeting (Dec. 2) it was supposed that something extraordinary would occur on 2 February, the date to which the meeting stood adjourned. Sir Francis Burdett, Lord Cochrane, the Hampden Club, the Westminster Committee, were all supposed to be behind Hunt and at his command.

Meanwhile clubs were forming at different centres outside London, especially in those where the cult of Equality and of Tom Paine had flourished in 1793. Lancashire led the way ; other foci of the movement were Sheffield, Birmingham, Leicester, Nottingham. The first club to be formed was apparently the Oldham Union Society, which was founded on 23 September 1816 at an orderly public meeting, at which the chair was taken by William Browe, a journeyman machine maker who was also a trustee and preacher of a Methodist Unitarian chapel. Other original members of the society were Wilson, another trustee of the chapel, a silk-weaver named Haigh, a hatter named Joseph Taylor, and another Taylor who was a surgeon. The other societies were recruited, in like manner, chiefly from the class of skilled labourers, who appear to have suffered more severely than the factory hands in this period of depression. The Oldham reformers seem to have been regarded as exceptionally dangerous, to judge from the care with which they were watched by the spies of the Manchester magistrates and of the Home Office.

Another Lancashire club which achieved some notoriety was the Middleton Union Society, founded on 19 October 1816.[2] Its first secretary was Samuel Bamford, the weaver-poet, and several of its members became notorious in the later and more violent stages of the movement. The Middleton men desired to agitate against the new Corn Law as well as in favour of parliamentary reform. The Manchester Union Society was founded in like manner, at a public meeting held on 28 October, which was attended by reformers from Oldham, Middleton, and other neighbouring places.[3] The proceedings were orderly,

[1] On 2 December or 3 December 1816 Peel wrote from Dublin of current rumours ' that the Royal family were flying for protection to Ireland —that the populace had possession of London—that the soldiers were in league with them ' (*Croker Papers*, i. 100). Similar rumours were rife in Manchester and Sheffield.

[2] See the pamphlet *Foundation of the Middleton Union Society* (1816).

[3] *Report of a Public Meeting near the Quaker Chapel* (Oct. 1816).

and although a resolution against the Corn Law was adopted, the main object of the society was declared to be the political education of the people. The funds of the society, raised by a modest subscription of one penny a week from every member, were to be spent in disseminating political literature, to the end that every man might become acquainted with 'the science of general politics'. John Knight, who took the chair on this occasion, and became the secretary of the society, was a veteran reformer, who had been prosecuted as a Luddite in 1812 but was triumphantly acquitted; it is possible that he was, even at that time, in the counsels of Major Cartwright. He acted as an intermediary between the Lancashire reformers and the London Hampden Club in the winter of 1816-17. His record shows that he cannot have been timid; his advice to his fellow reformers was, however, generally remarkable for its moderation. In his official capacity he convened a delegate convention which sat at Middleton on 11 December 1816 and 15 January 1817 to organize a campaign of propaganda and to send deputies to London; but this appears to be the only instance in which he overstepped the law. He hired a disused factory as a debating hall for his society, and at the end of 1816 arranged a series of debates which were nominally concerned with abstract questions; as, for instance, 'Whether Englishmen answer the end of their creation'. Admission was free and the debates were sometimes well attended.

All the reform clubs in Lancashire except those at Manchester, Oldham, and Ashton-under-Lyne appear to have been small and ill supplied with funds; they corresponded with the Manchester Union Society, but did not look to it for orders. The theory was that they should arrange a common policy through conventions in which all the societies of Lancashire were represented, and should as far as possible follow the advice of the London Hampden Club. At first this advice was simply to obtain signatures for the reform petitions. In December they received a circular signed by Sir Francis Burdett which suggested that the petitions should be escorted to London by ten out of every hundred of the members of the clubs. Early in January the London club wrote again to announce that the draft of a Reform Bill had been prepared, and to request that deputies should be sent to a convention which would meet in London on the 22nd. The Lancashire clubs responded to this invitation and arranged to elect fifteen deputies for this purpose. One of those elected was the weaver-poet Samuel Bamford, to whom we owe an exceedingly curious account of the proceedings in London.[1]

Much less is known about the Hampden Clubs in other counties. That in Sheffield was probably founded at or shortly after a reform meeting which was held there on 9 October 1816. It was believed by the Manchester informers to be closely connected with the Manchester Union Society; and it was apparently represented in the second session of the Middleton convention, which voted that Sheffield should send two deputies to London; but the first public meeting which the Sheffield society organized was held on 18 January 1817. There was another club at Barnsley; and a third was formed at Leeds at the end of 1816, which, however, disbanded itself after an existence of ten weeks.[2] In Birmingham an important club was organized by George Edmonds, formerly a school teacher; this was in existence by 8 November 1816, when the Home Office acknowledged the receipt of one of its hand-bills. It was at first a middle-class association; but it began to hold open debates after the Manchester Union Society had set the example.[3] The main object of Edmonds was to turn the thoughts of Birmingham reformers to constitutional courses, and so prevent a recurrence of the riots which had disgraced the town in 1816. But in the early part of 1817 his society leaped into fame by holding a mass meeting on Newhall Hill, and by recommending to other societies of the same character a policy of simultaneous mass meetings at frequent intervals.

Our information as to Norwich comes from a letter written

---

[1] For the documents relating to the Lancashire clubs see my *Lancashire Reformers, 1816–17* (Manchester Univ. Press, 1926).

[2] For the Sheffield Reform Meeting see the *Sheffield Iris*, 15 October 1816; for the Sheffield Club, the same paper, issue of 25 January 1817; for the Barnsley Club, the *Leeds Intelligencer*, 6 January 1817. For the Leeds Club see H.O. 41. 1, p. 60. The newspaper references I owe to the kindness of my pupil, the Rev. D. O. Parker.

[3] H.O. 40. 3 (Hampden Clubs, No. 34, an undated letter from Edmonds to a friend) Buckley, *Joseph Parker*, p. 16.

by Lord Orford to the Home Secretary (29 Dec. 1816). This states that a number of Hampden Clubs exist in Norwich. 'They never consist of more than sixty members, and when more candidates offer a new club is formed. A short time ago there were five of these. A working tailor is the chief director, who is not a native of Norwich.'[1] Perhaps we have here a reference to Francis Place, who is known to have interested himself in organizing the collection of signatures for the reform petition.[2] Finally, at Leicester a Hampden Club was founded before 19 October 1816, when the Home Office received a copy of its rules.[3] Of this club's activities we have many interesting particulars in the Home Office papers; and, although its history was on the whole uneventful, these records supply an unusually vivid account of a local agitation as it was observed by com-petent witnesses. Whatever may have been the villainy of informers elsewhere—and I do not think that they were all so villainous as Mr. and Mrs. Hammond ask us to believe—those who served the Leicester magistrates were not anxious to make out a hanging case. They are such reports as might be supplied to-day by an honest and unimaginative sergeant of police.

Here, for example, is a portion of a report on what appears to have been the first general meeting of the Leicester Hampden Club (25 Nov. 1816):

'I attended last night at the Bowling Green Inn to hear what passed at the Hampden Club. I was concealed. They assembled at 7 o'clock. There were more than 200. They were occupied till half-past eight in collecting subscriptions and drinking and smoking and talking. Then silence was called, and Mr. Scott was appointed chair-man, and Bailey (political cobbler) Vice-president. Mr. Scott addressed the company upon the destructive system of taxation.'

Mr. Scott afterwards illustrated the extravagance of the Government by reading, from a copy of the Court Calendar, a list of pensioners with the amounts of their respective pen-sions. This recital elicited some hisses and running comments:

'Some one said, We are met to get shut of some of these fellows. ...
Another said, Wait only two years. . . . One said, Political revolutions

---

[1] H.O. 40. 3 (Hampden Clubs, No. 24).   [2] Halévy, ii, p. 11.
[3] H.O. 40. 1, p. 340.

in constitutions are as necessary as revolutions in nature. Standing armies loudly condemned. . . . A man named Riley made a motion that 100 copies of Cobbett's *Register* be purchased every week, and sold at twopence each, to further the cause. It was carried by a show of hands. Silence called, and William Goodrich appointed Secretary to the Society.'

Cheers were then given for the editor of the *Leicester Chronicle*, and hisses for the editor of the *Journal*. On a vote of thanks to the chairman being moved, that gentleman responded by offering to give a song:

'He said it was the same that he was singing when the ruffians broke in at the Three Crowns about eighteen years ago; *Millions be free!* Loud applause. He sung a revolutionary song.'[1]

Evidently Mr. Scott was not the man to lead a formidable conspiracy. But the Leicester magistrates, encouraged by the Home Office, took pains to investigate the proceedings of the elected committee in which the real business of the club was handled. Their agent, when attending another general meeting on 6 January 1817, obtained proofs that there was correspondence with Lancashire and London:

'A deputation had been sent to Manchester. Graham and Warburton went. Graham stated what great distress they were in, in Lancashire. That the greater part of the poor people could only get a little water and salt and oatmeal—some had one meal a day, and some had one meal in three days. Then he read a letter from Derby, saying that a person from Manchester would call upon the Leicester club on his way to Birmingham and Bristol.[2] Then reads a letter from Major Cartwright, saying he had received information of fourteen different societies that intend to send Delegates to a Committee in London on 22 January.[3] Graham gets up and exhorts the people to stick to each other, as it has become a party concern, and he finds the other party sticks to each other.'

A new committee having then been elected to serve for one month (the usual term) Graham announced:

'We shall have some of our country friends in to-morrow, and I beg

---

[1] H.O. 40. 3 (Hampden Clubs, No. 8).

[2] Two Lancashire 'missionaries', appointed by the first Middleton Convention were at this time on the way to Birmingham. Their names were Mitchell and Benbow.

[3] i.e. the Convention to discuss the Reform Bill.

some will volunteer their services to meet them as they come, and exhort them to be cheerful.   But be sure to be peaceable.'[1]

What was the business of these country friends?   Probably to sign reform petitions or to make arrangements for having them signed in the surrounding country.   At the general meeting of 13 January the agent found that the main business was to appoint delegates who would carry these petitions to London, in time for the opening of the parliamentary session.   On the 14th the club committee conferred with the delegates from the country.   The agent contrived to be there—possibly in concealment:

'There were present two Delegates from each of twenty-eight villages. The numbers at each village upon an average were one hundred.[2] The resolutions were read over. They were desired to get as many as possible to sign the petitions and to get as many more in the clubs as possible. Pares stated that the number in the Hampden Clubs now amounted to 459,000 in England, Scotland and Wales.'[3]

The resolutions mentioned above are those which had been adopted by the London Hampden Club on 2 November 1816. They provided that a draft Reform Bill should be prepared by a committee of that club, considered at a general meeting in the spring of 1817 and submitted to a convention of delegates, or, as the resolutions put it, of 'Persons who may be deputed from petitioning cities, towns, or other communities to confer together in the Metropolis on the best means of effecting a constitutional reform.'

Whoever managed the tactics of the Leicester Club had thoroughly grasped the plan which the London Club had in view for frustrating the Seditious Societies Act of 1799.   A village could of course petition Parliament.   There was no law which forbade one village to correspond with other villages or with the town of Leicester; nor was it illegal for villages and towns to elect delegates to represent them.   By the simple expedient of using the village as a branch of the Leicester Club the local reformers kept on the safe side of the law.

[1] H.O. 40. 3 (Hampden Clubs, No. 29).
[2] Presumably the numbers of those who had expressed reforming sympathies.
[3] H.O. 40. 3 (Hampden Clubs, No. 34).

But the Town Clerk of Leicester believed that the village clubs, though strictly legal, were much more dangerous than the Hampden Club in the town. According to one of his agents these village patriots 'were solely impressed with the belief that Revolution was the object, and were no further interested than to hold themselves in readiness to fight when necessary'.[1] Happily this diagnosis was false. There had been grave symptoms of unrest round Leicester in 1816. 'The poor starved inhabitants', writes George Edmonds of Birmingham, 'were in the habit of meeting in the fields in considerable numbers and for purposes of a dangerous nature.'[2] Whether, as Edmonds thought, the Hampden Club had exercised a soothing influence, or whether, as seems more probable, hard times were becoming less hard in 1817, certain it is that the villages round Leicester remained quiet, except when the magistrates attempted to swear in special constables. The villages did not mean to be at the mercy of special constables. On 20 January 1817 the inhabitants of Oadby raised a riot because two magistrates had arrived there for the purpose of swearing in. 'Having entered upon this business they were unfortunately prevented from completing it by the outrageous and insolent conduct of the lower classes of the parish, who, being assembled in large numbers, unfortunately succeeded in intimidating the persons intended as constables from coming up.' The magistrates withdrew from Oadby, and that night some of the villagers did a little rick-burning. Next day, however, the magistrates returned with an escort of yeomanry and three of the leaders of the riot were sent to prison. The yeomanry were drawn from the farmer class, and no love was lost between them and the cottagers. A Leicester magistrate complains that Oadby people were subsequently most insulting to members of the yeomanry who resided in the village 'and have in alehouses openly boasted that in two months they should take their arms from them'.[3] This gentleman thought that the Hampden Clubs were likely to be productive of more mischief than Luddism had ever caused.

[1] Town Clerk to Mr. Hiley Addington, 22 January 1817 (H.O. 40. 3, Hampden Clubs, No. 37).
[2] H.O. 40. 3 (Hampden Clubs, No. 41).
[3] H.O. 40. 3 (Hampden Clubs, No. 40).

In Manchester there was more cause for anxiety. The population was four times that of Leicester, and was largely composed of recent immigrants. There was a considerable element of blackguardism in the town, and rumours of the most exciting kind were spread by the strangers who came thither on business, legitimate or otherwise, from every part of the British islands. There was a minute and unpopular police force. There were no resident magistrates of considerable influence or character. The city was full of ill-protected wealth. It was also full of sordid poverty and veiled trade unionism. An unpaid and voluntary observer gives, in 1816, a most gloomy account of the state of feeling in the numerous public houses of the city to which, he says, he was bound to go in the ordinary course of business. The talk in these houses was all 'irreverent expressions of government and revolutionary ideas'. The blame for low wages and unemployment was imputed to the Prince Regent and his ministers. 'Their oracles are the *Statesman* newspaper, *Independent Whig* and Cobbett's *Register*'.[1]

At the end of 1816 some of the more restless of the Lancashire reformers seem to have been in communication with the Spencean Club or similar fanatics. One or two of them went to London to attend the second Spa Fields meeting, and left behind them in Manchester hints and perhaps hopes of impending revolution. Henry Hunt, and the furtive mischief makers in London who made use of Henry Hunt, loomed larger in the minds of sanguine and irresponsible reformers than the Hampden Club with its firm insistence upon respect for the law. On 4 December, two days after the Spa Fields meeting, the wildest rumours were afloat in Manchester: the Tower had surrendered to the people of London; the Bank of England had been destroyed; five-pound notes were not worth twopence in the capital. 'The people assembled on all sides and listened with the greatest avidity.' Mr. Chippendale of Oldham, the intelligence officer of the county magistrates, sent out his agents that night to learn what was the state of feeling:

'The Person who was sent in the direction of Manchester found the road crowded with groups of people all the way. About midnight they

[1] H.O. 40. 4, Suppl. Papers, No. 20.

began to draw towards Manchester for the purpose of learning the news brought by the Mail. My informant saw 300 in one group in a street adjoining the Bridgewater Arms where the Mail stops, all delegates from the country. When the news was not confirmed, their disappointment was extreme. My informant attended a committee meeting of the Unions the same evening. They were engaged in drawing up short instructions intended to distribute among the people, for converting various kinds of implements into pikes, in case their friends had met with success.'[1]

The last tit-bit of information in this report may be a flight of the agent's fancy; but Sir John Byng reported from Yorkshire that there also there had been some excitement aroused by the Spa Fields meeting, and some hopes or plans for sympathetic demonstrations; and in Sheffield there was a political procession on 3 December, followed, three days later, by an abortive riot.[2] The denunciations of the ruling classes with which the London agitators had deluged the country were producing their natural effect on the minds of men who were uneducated, unemployed, and half-starving. These men saw threats of tyranny and revenge in every movement of the regular troops which the Home Office was moving from one point of danger to another. Thus on the 15th and 16th of November the arrival of two infantry companies in Manchester 'made the old Jacks look with long faces, and some of them swore it would be an 1812 job, and that the point of the bayonet was the ruling law of England at present'.[3] The fears and tremors of many law-abiding reformers are voiced in the proceedings of the committee of the Bolton Club, which met on 18 November 1816 to arrange for the hiring of a lecture room:

'John Kay began the business by asking us if we had deliberately weighed the consequences in our own minds. He said, are you prepared to suffer persecution, separately and in your own persons, for the sake of that great and good cause of reform? ... We may expect to

[1] Mr. Chippendale to Major Gen. Sir John Byng, 7 December 1816 (H.O. 40. 3).

[2] See Sir John Byng's report (from Pontefract) to the Home Office, 7 December 1816 (printed in *Lancashire Reformers*, p. 26). Also Earl Fitzwilliam's report of the same date to Lord Sidmouth (H.O. 40. 4, Cheshire, Lancashire, Miscellaneous).

[3] H.O. 40. 3 (Mr. Chippendale: report of agent *B* (Mr. Bent) to Col. Fletcher of Bolton).

feel the weight of the displeasure of the corrupt faction, placemen, pensioners, sinecurists, not only their displeasure, but their vengeance. Therefore our task is an arduous task and a dangerous one. Are you who are here willing to engage in it such as it is ? Robeson Bradly said, I know we shall be sufferers as it is, I am afraid before the Winter is over. He said we are all brought into such a situation by our oppressors that both life and liberty is scarce worth preserving. They all said they were willing to risk all for the sake of their posterity seeing better days.' [1]

The main anxiety of the Home Office in this winter was to discover the future plans of the clubs. The general tenor of the evidence from Leicester, from Sheffield, and from Lancashire was that the country clubs were following the comparatively harmless plan of the London Hampden Club ; and it seems to have been at length assumed by the Office that nothing serious would occur until the London Convention hàd prepared its Reform Bill. The London Convention was allowed to hold its meeting without interruption ; and indeed, as we have seen already, its legality could not well be impugned. On 23 January, after an animated debate, the majority decided that their Reform Bill should provide for universal suffrage, and requested Sir Francis Burdett to draft the bill on this basis, and to bring it before Parliament. But Burdett was not at the Convention ; he was hunting in Leicestershire while the Convention sat ; he evaded the duty of presenting the petitions ; and when Parliament assembled he ignored the bill altogether and merely gave notice of a motion for a Reform Committee. The deputies were driven at the last moment to accept the good offices of Lord Cochrane, whom they carried shoulder high across Palace Yard to the door of Westminster Hall, with the petition of the city of Bristol in his arms. For Burdett could not swallow universal suffrage— the negation of the old Whig theory that power and property must go together.

Meanwhile the ministry launched their attack upon the Hampden Clubs, laid before Secret Committees of both Houses the evidence of criminal designs, real or supposed, which the Home Office had been collecting for the past three or four months, and carried the suspension of the Habeas Corpus Act,

---

[1] *Lancashire Reformers*, p. 21.

which hung the threat of arbitrary imprisonment over the head of every agitator.

The case against the Hampden Clubs was put at its highest in the reports of the Secret Committees of February 1817. The Lord's Committee pointed out that the proceedings of the clubs (i.e. of their committees) were secret; that subscriptions were collected from the members; that many of the members had procured arms;[1] that the clubs issued inflammatory publications — probably a reference to their practice of distributing Cobbett's *Register*; that their meetings were frequently terminated by profane and seditious songs. The Commons Committee referred severely to the reform petitions of the Hampden Clubs as a new method of intimidating Government, and spoke of the recent Convention as a proof of dangerous designs. But in fact both Committees appear to have been chiefly impressed by the riot in London which had coincided with the second Spa Fields meeting, and by the information which they had received concerning the revolutionary activities of the Spencean Society, which was in no way connected with the reformist agitation.[2] They assumed, but they did not give any plausible grounds for believing, that behind the Spencean and the Hampden Clubs there lurked, somewhere in London, a central committee of revolutionaries. The only serious charge against any of the provincial clubs came from the Lord Advocate of Scotland, who assured the House of Commons that some of the Glasgow reformers had been revolutionaries in 1795. There had been, it appears, a Central Union Committee in Glasgow, which caused anxiety to the Home Office in the winter of 1816-17. But, as one of the critics of the Lord Advocate remarked, there had been no difficulty in arresting all the members of this redoubtable body under the existing law.[3]

The suspension of the Habeas Corpus Act need not be

---

[1] The evidence for this was doubtful.

[2] The reports of both Committees are printed in *Hansard*, vol. xxxv.

[3] References to Glasgow in the correspondence of the Home Secretary are infrequent. But there was a great reform meeting at Glasgow in the autumn of 1816, and on November 1 the Provost asked for a detachment of cavalry (H.O. 41. 1, pp. 422, 480), and in December a portion of the Lanarkshire militia was sent to Glasgow (H.O. 41. 2, p. 134).

explained by any of the sinister designs which the Hampden Clubs and the Whig members of the House of Commons imputed to the Government. But this measure, and the permanent Seditious Meetings Act which was passed in the same session, drove the reform movement underground. The law-abiding were frightened out of it, the reckless were tempted to meet official terrorism with their own methods of intimidation.

The march of the Lancashire Blanketeers (10 March 1817), organized by the extremists of the Manchester Union Society, was an ingenious combination of two well-tried forms of protest: of the hunger-march which had been used by the unemployed in 1816; and of the petition-march which the London Hampden Club had recommended and which the London Convention had adopted. Each Blanketeer carried a petition asking the Prince Regent to dismiss his Tory ministers and to choose others who would promote a reform of Parliament and a retrenchment in national expenditure. But one of the leaders announced, before the procession started: 'It is bread we want, and we will apply to our noble Prince, as a child would to its Father for bread.' The hope was that the Blanketeers would pick up recruits on the road to London, and arrive there in irresistible numbers. They had also been assured that similar processions would be organized in the West Riding. It is therefore not surprising that regulars, yeomanry, and special constables were employed to disperse them at the beginning of their march.[1] A large number of the marchers were detained for a short while in gaol, though only thirteen persons, considered to be ringleaders, were eventually reserved for trial.

The abortive Ardwick conspiracy, which was denounced by the Manchester magistrates on 28 March as a 'traitorous conspiracy' for 'open insurrection and rebellion', was provoked by the failure of the Blanketeer march, and was intended to spread terror among the Manchester Tories; it is possible that the main purpose was to release the two hundred Blanketeers who were lodged in the town prison. Rumours of the plot were abroad some days before any arrests were made, and Samuel Bamford, who was an official of the Middleton Club, firmly believed that there was a plan to make 'a Moscow of

[1] *Lancashire Reformers*, pp. 14-16, 31-3.

Manchester'; he attributed it to the organizers of the Blanketeer march, but these were for the most part already in gaol. The final arrangements were made in a secret convention of delegates from the Lancashire clubs, which met at Middleton and Chadderton. It included no prominent reformers; and the members of it who were detained under the Habeas Corpus Suspension Act were a cooper (Roberts), a knife-grinder (Sellers), a bleacher (Hulton), and a barber-surgeon (Healey). There was something in the plot no doubt; but the Manchester magistrates were unable to collect evidence other than that of informers. Consequently no one was sent to trial and the riddle of the conspiracy was never unravelled.[1]

The Government treated the matter seriously because they had information that the Ardwick plotters were in correspondence with the reformers of Sheffield, Nottingham, Leicester, and Birmingham. At Sheffield there was certainly unrest. It was possibly fomented by Oliver, the Government spy, who appeared there in the months of April and May in the character of a reformist missionary. Oliver dealt in sensational reports, and also acted as *agent provocateur*, but he undoubtedly came across inflammable material at Sheffield, at Huddersfield, and in Derbyshire. That it was not really formidable is shown by the ignominious fate of the attack on Huddersfield (June 8) and of Brandreth's attempt to seize Nottingham on 10 June. But to assert that no outbreaks would have occurred if Oliver had not been busy in these districts is to accept uncritically the line of defence which was adopted by some of the accused and by some of the Whig Opposition. The suggestion has been made, in a brilliant reconstruction of Oliver's career, that the Home Secretary and his assistants deliberately sacrificed the lives of innocent men, in order to save their own credit. Such a guess is not lightly to be accepted. Sidmouth was weak and timid, but he was no criminal, nor was he incapable of weighing evidence. It would have been better for him and for the country if he had enjoyed the assistance of other Lords-Lieutenant as courageous and as statesmanlike as Earl Fitzwilliam

---

[1] *Lancashire Reformers*, pp. 16-20, 33-5. Bamford in his *Recollections* admits that there was a good deal known to his fellow prisoners and himself which they carefully concealed.

proved himself. But Sidmouth was not wrong in believing that the position in the industrial districts might easily become critical. On later occasions it did become critical, in Lancashire and the West Riding, in Nottingham and Birmingham, and many other places ; it was critical in 1819 and 1820 ; it was critical in 1830. At those dates no Oliver was in the field.

The Government of this country, a hundred years ago, was very ill equipped for the maintenance of order. The justices of the peace were often quite unequal to their duty of watching and forestalling dangerous movements. There was no efficient system of police even in the metropolitan area until Peel's Act of 1829 came into force ; the yeomanry and the regular forces, even if they had been suited for police work, were not nearly numerous enough to police all dangerous centres in times of discontent. Hence the use of spies ; hence such savage laws as the Seditious Meetings Act of 1817 ; hence too the reluctance of the Government to show mercy in cases where mitigating circumstances could be adduced in favour of a defendant convicted on a political charge.

The grand fault of the Government in 1817 was that it simply endeavoured to scotch the agitation without inquiring into the causes that had produced it. The main cause, unemployment, could not be cured by any action of Government. But among the contributory causes there was the impression that Government had no desire to cut down public expenditure, for the relief of the taxpayers in general, or to shift a part of the poor man's burden of taxation to the shoulders of the property owner. It was quite true, as defenders of the existing system pointed out, that the abolition of all so-called sinecures would do very little to help the taxpayer ; at the utmost a saving of three or four hundred thousands would have been effected. It was also true that some of the so-called sinecures were used to augment official salaries which would otherwise have been inadequate. But any reform of this branch of expenditure would have been welcome as a token of goodwill. Much more relief would have resulted to the poor from the continuance of the property tax, which in 1815, at the standard rate of 2s. in the £, had yielded over fourteen millions. If the property-tax had been retained, it would have been possible to remit, for example, all taxes on articles of food (which amounted in 1815 to five millions) and at the same time to provide a substantial sinking fund for the debt. Unhappily Lord Liverpool and Castlereagh chose to abandon the property-tax, against their better judgement, because it was attacked by the trading classes and by the Opposition. The Whigs must in this case bear a considerable proportion of the responsibility for the policy pursued by Government. But if Liverpool had defended the property-tax as resolutely as he had been accustomed to defend his war policy, the votes of the country gentlemen and the moral support of the unrepresented might very well have enabled him to defy the Whigs and the City of London.

As, however, Government remained inert, and the economic situation remained unsatisfactory, the parliamentary reformers were emboldened to revive in 1819 the plan of campaign which had failed two years before. In 1819 their demands were crystallized in the six points which afterwards became the People's Charter, and at the time of Peterloo the reformers still believed, as their fathers had believed in 1780, that these simple demands should suffice to bring about the millennium. But after 1819 other schools of thought begin to influence the working-man, with the result that the Chartists of the 'forties found themselves distracted between several conflicting programmes of economic reform, which were not indeed inconsistent with the Six Points, but which claimed superior importance and practicality. To some of these we shall devote attention in another chapter.

Radicalism of the old kind, radicalism which derived its simple tenets from Horne Tooke, Major Cartwright, and Tom Paine, survived in a fashion until 1830 or even later. Its literary exponents were principally journalist booksellers who some-times succeeded in evading the stamp duty of 1817 for consider-able periods of time [1]—Thomas Wooler, the editor of the *Black Dwarf* (1817-24), Richard Carlile, the editor of the *Republican* (1819-26), and William Hone. Hone, the eldest of the three, learned his radicalism in the school of the London Corre-sponding Society; Wooler graduated in the Radical debating

[1] J. Holland Rose, 'The Unstamped Press, 1815-1836', *E.H.R.*, xii, pp. 711 ff.

societies which flourished in London after and in spite of Pitt's repressive legislation; Carlile was a self-taught Radical who found his political creed when, as a journeyman printer, he lighted upon Paine's *Rights of Man*. Wooler, during the brief existence of the *Black Dwarf*, was Cobbett's chief rival, and in 1817 shared with Hone the honour of escaping conviction when prosecuted by the ministry for libel. As a political writer he was far superior to Hone, whose notoriety was earned by feeble imitations of the parodies of Wilkes.[1]

For sheer audacity both Hone and Wooler must yield the palm to Carlile, who gloried in defying the authorities on every possible occasion, and fought for what he considered to be the freedom of the Press from 1817 to 1825. In consequence of his offences against the law of libel, he himself was imprisoned for six years, his wife for two years, and his sister for one year; and in 1821 a society which styled itself the Constitutional Association, but was popularly known as the Bridge Street Gang, raised a fund of £6,000 for the purpose of prosecuting the assistants who carried on his publishing business while he was in gaol. Most of his troubles were due to his reprints of literature which had been already decided to be seditious, such as the writings of Tom Paine. But his own *Republican*, which he edited from his prison, was as violent as any work that he reprinted. The number for printing which his wife was sentenced to imprisonment contained an apology for tyrannicide; and, if the Government had been wise enough to leave Mrs. Carlile untouched, and if the Bridge Street Gang had not rushed into the fray, it is probable that little more would have been heard of her husband. Through the blundering malevolence of his opponents he became a popular hero; the sale of his publications increased by leaps and bounds; and a fund was raised to assist him in his business after his release, which occurred in 1825. But the interest of the public in Radical propaganda was waning rapidly, and Carlile's fortunes declined after his release. Wooler and he remained true to their original tenets, and Wooler's last journalistic venture was the editing of a Chartist organ, the *Plain Speaker*, in 1849. But Hone gradually aban-

---

[1] The three parodies for which Hone was prosecuted were *John Wilkes' Catechism*, the *Sinecurists' Creed*, and the *Political Litany*.

doned politics after 1820, and betook himself to the compilation of miscellanies of a popular character. He was a better tradesman than Wooler and Carlile; he saw that the Radical tide was ebbing and would not return. The same reflection occurred to his friend and colleague George Cruickshank, who was indefatigable as a political caricaturist in the years 1818–22, but thenceforward turned to other fields of illustration.

It may seem strange to omit the name of Cobbett from the list of those who kept alive the ideal of the Hampden Clubs. For he advocated parliamentary reform in 1816 and in 1830. Nor should we consider him a lukewarm reformer. In 1816 he stood by the moderates who advocated a householder franchise in preference to universal suffrage; but he did so for a tactical reason, because it was certain that Sir Francis Burdett, the nominal leader of the Hampden Clubs, would not support a petition which demanded that the right to vote should be independent of any property qualification. But in 1830, when he had ceased to rely on the help of such men as Burdett, he pronounced for universal suffrage. He accepted something considerably smaller as a first instalment of reform, but with the statement that he considered the case for universal suffrage to be quite unanswerable. So far he acted in unison with many Radicals of the purest water. Still he was something less or something more than a true Radical. For, in the first place, he disliked the organization of the clubs.

'I have always most earnestly endeavoured to persuade the public that clubs of all sorts were of mischievous tendency in general, and in no possible case could be productive of good. . . . Since the question of reform has been so much agitated, I have taken particular pains to endeavour to discourage all sorts of combinations, associations, affiliations and correspondencies of societies having that object in view; and I have said upon these occasions that, if the object were not to be obtained by the general, free, unpacked, unbiassed impression and expression of the public mind, it never could be, and never ought to be obtained at all.'[1]

Secondly, he refused to believe that a change in the constitution was the one thing needful. As early as 1806 he believed that the country could only be saved from ruin by total repudia-

[1] *Political Works*, v. 155.

tion of the funded debt; after the conclusion of peace he proposed that the interest on the debt should be reduced by half;[1] and from 1817 to 1830 the debt and the paper currency were evils which occupied his mind much more than parliamentary reform. He was no economist; but he had a shrewd and obstinate conviction that many, if not most, of the evils of his time were the consequences of mistakes in economic policy. Thirdly, he was in his heart of hearts a Tory, cherishing the dream of a golden age, when the country had been ruled by a benevolent aristocracy of fair and sympathetic landlords; when the farmer did not ape the gentleman, or add farm to farm in an unthinking race for wealth and consideration; when the basis of English society had been ' the little, industrious, decent, rural hives ' in which the highest classes merged into those beneath them by almost imperceptible gradations.[2]

Cobbett could write fiercely enough of the mistakes in national policy, and of the injustice to social inferiors, of which the landed interest had been guilty in the past, without surrendering the belief that in the old order at its best, before the evil effects of the Reformation had made themselves felt, there was at least the promise and the possibility of humaner relations between gentle and simple, master and employed, than he discerned in the England of his own time. Lastly and most inconsistently he was allured by the doctrines of contemporary socialists, particularly when he reflected on the treatment of the parish pauper. He quotes with approval the statement of Charles Hall that the labouring man produces six or eight times as much as his family requires; that he is in justice entitled to all that his hands have made or produced ; but that the greater part of it is taken from him by those who produce nothing.[3] Cobbett believes that every man is entitled by nature to the means of subsistence. Addressing himself to the landowners of England he says that without the labourer they would be nothing, and that their estate must decline in proportion as

---

[1] See his letter of 6 March 1806 to Windham (*Pol. Works,* v. 388) ; for his later views *Pol. Works,* v. 188 ; vi. 124-6.

[2] *Ibid.,* vi. 83, 120.

[3] C. Hall, *Effects of Civilization on the People in European States* (1805); quoted in Cobbett's *Pol. Works,* v. 86.

the labourer becomes wretched. ' After all the talk about independence we must still be dependent on one another. You do not call the labourers of your parishes members of your family; but in fact, from the very nature of things, the connexion between you is little less strict than if they were related to you by the ties of kindred.'[1] A man who taught such doctrines weekly to an enormous circle of readers was bound to cause considerable searchings of heart to those who believed in the existing laws and usages of England. And therefore Cobbett must be classed as a Radical of a kind. But on many questions he had more in common with the old-school Tory than with Hunt or Cartwright or Francis Place.

[1] *Pol. Works*, vi. 441.

IX

LORD GREY AND THE WHIG PARTY, 1819–1830

SOME apology is needed for trespassing on ground which Mr. George Trevelyan has made peculiarly his own. *Lord Grey of the Reform Bill* is one of the most delightful books in the literature of Whiggism. It is impossible, in reading it, to shake off the spell created by Mr. Trevelyan's persuasive style. Only when we close the book and ask ourselves how such a character came to be so maligned by so many independent critics among his own contemporaries, only then do misgivings begin to arise. Mr. Trevelyan sees this great Whig through a golden haze which softens all asperities, and disguises whatever is inconsistent and irrational in a very complex, rather petulant, and too fastidious personality. Indeed the haze becomes a halo. In one sense Mr. Trevelyan gives us a scientific study. He has studied as a whole the Howick Papers—material which hitherto had only been utilized unskilfully and superficially, in the unfinished biography by General Grey. From these papers Mr. Trevelyan has extracted much valuable information which General Grey either overlooked or deliberately withheld. But the truth is that both the new biographer and the old have the same tendency to idealize and magnify their subject. General Grey writes as an affectionate son, and Mr. Trevelyan has looked too long at Lord Grey through the glasses of a devoted family circle. Lord Grey was never more happy, never seen to better advantage than when he was at Howick, untroubled by public business or important visitors. Such as he was then, such or nearly such he must have been in public life ; that appears to be Mr. Trevelyan's habitual assumption. But public men must be judged by their public conduct. We are inevitably reminded of Macaulay's rejoinder to the eulogists of Charles I : ' He had so many virtues ! And what, after all, are the virtues ascribed to Charles ? A few of the ordinary household decencies which half the tombstones in England claim for those who lie beneath them.'

No account of Grey's public life would be complete if it
ignored his family circle and his private friendships. Mr. Trevelyan admits that Grey became a Whig, at the outset of his
political career, not through intellectual conviction, not from
deference to any traditions of his family, but by personal friendships. Before his marriage, which took place in 1794, the
beautiful Duchess of Devonshire was his chief confidante ; it was
Lady Holland's opinion that the Duchess had much to do with
his conversion, although the good work was completed by
Charles James Fox and by the Prince of Wales ; and this view
is to some extent corroborated by recently published evidence.[1]
Lady Grey was no politician, but her uncle George Ponsonby
can hardly have been chosen to succeed Grey as leader of the
Opposition in the Commons on any other grounds but those of
family ties ; and it is probable that Ponsonby influence accounts
for Grey's decision, in 1807, to make Catholic Emancipation the
main article of the Whig party programme. It is even probable
that Grey was swept into the camp of the parliamentary reformers by friends more doctrinaire or more reckless than himself. That is the opinion of Lord Holland, who states that Grey,
in 1792, 'was wrought upon by the restless activity of Lord
Lauderdale and the ambition of some of his younger friends,
viz. Mr. Whitbread, Mr. Lambton, and Mr. Tierney'.[2] Grey
was impetuous and headstrong when once he had embraced an
opinion. But in his younger days, before his principles had
been moulded and fixed by long co-operation first with Fox and
afterwards with Grenville, he was extremely susceptible to the
advice of those whom he accounted his friends. In his old
age he said that one word from Fox would have kept him out
of 'all that mess of the Friends of the People' ;[3] but as Fox's
advice was not given, he fell back on the advice of smaller men.
Even after his opinions had solidified, and when he had established that reputation for political constancy which was his
chief asset in later life, Grey was always strongly influenced by
the sympathies and prejudices of those with whom he lived on

---

[1] See Mabel, Countess of Airlie, *In Whig Society* (1921), pp. 13-14, 27-8,
31. The friendship survived Grey's marriage.

[2] *Memoirs of the Whig Party*, i, p. 13.

[3] *Life and Opinions*, p. 11.

intimate terms; and he habitually overrated the abilities and the services of his friends and his relations.[1] Living as far as possible in Olympian seclusion, he formed his views of men and situations at second hand, relying too often and too implicitly on the facts and the impressions supplied by confidants who were much inferior to himself.[2]

It is a singular fact that the opinions which made Grey popular were formed in the days when he was sowing his wild oats. Up to 1806, when he first took office, his reputation was ambiguous amongst the well informed. He belonged to that little group of Fox's intimates whom Mr. Creevey describes, no doubt with some exaggeration, as 'having all the air of shattered debauchees, of passing gaming, drinking, sleepless nights'.[3] Grey was no debauchee or gamester; but in his youth he could drink more heavily even than Sheridan, and he lived in an atmosphere of feverish excitement which made calm reflection difficult, if not impossible. Like Fox, he staked heavily upon the friendship of the Prince of Wales at least as late as 1789, when Grey in the House of Commons twice denied the fact of the Prince's marriage, of which Grey had been aware, through the Prince's own confession, for nearly two years. It may be, as Mr. Trevelyan argues, that Grey was more concerned on this occasion to shield Fox, who had already denied the marriage, than to shield the Prince. But the fact remains that Grey, like Fox, did not scruple to resume and to maintain friendly relations with the Prince. Creevey reports an anecdote, told to him by Lady Grey, which shows that in or after 1794 Grey and the Prince were on dining terms:

'I well remember that on the only day he (Lord Grey) ever was tipsy in my presence, when he returned from dining with the Prince of Wales, nothing would satisfy him but dressing himself up in a red turban, and trying to dance like Paripol.'[4]

In tolerating the Prince Grey had the whole of his party to

---

[1] See *Greville Memoirs*, 1 December 1830, for comments on the distribution of minor offices in the Grey Government.

[2] e.g. Sir Robert Wilson, for whose letters to Grey see Add. MSS. 30123-4. Mr. Trevelyan's contention, that the Princess de Lieven had no political influence over Grey, seems to be sound.

[3] *Creevey Papers*, p. 13.   [4] *Op. cit.*, p. 265.

keep him in countenance. But he committed himself, in other connexions, to steps which caused his party much misgiving. He was, according to Holland, principally responsible for the secession of 1797, which Fox at first resisted. Late in 1801 he allowed himself to be entangled in a personal negotiation with the Addington ministry. It came to nothing because Grey insisted on parliamentary reform as one of the essential terms of a coalition. When the facts leaked out, Fox generously took the part of his lieutenant and maintained that he had done nothing improper. There had been no attempt to conclude a treaty, only a conversation which revealed the absence of any ground on which a treaty could be based. From the fact that Grey speaks of his 'escape' we may infer that he had been mis-informed at the outset and found himself in a false position. No doubt the Duchess of Devonshire gives his own case when she writes in his defence :

'That Mr. Grey, pleased with peace, beset by Relations and dazzled by the overtures Addington might make of repealing odious Acts, might examine if there was not a chance of arrangement, I cannot blame or wonder at, especially as he was soon convinced there was not and went into the Country for an intention of staying perhaps the whole year.'[1]

But there were mischief-makers at work. The secret leaked out, perhaps through the indiscretion of Tierney and Erskine, who were involved in the business, and who actually put their services at the disposal of the ministry. Sheridan chose to attack them comprehensively at the Whig Club in an after-dinner speech which stung Grey to the quick. He described them as 'persons who, thrown by accident in the outset of life into situations for which they are not fitted, become Friends of the People for a time and afterwards, finding their mistake, desert the popular cause'.[2] The sarcasm was at the moment peculiarly unjust, so far as it applied to Grey. In his case, at all events, the negotiations had foundered on the rock of parlia-mentary reform. But the mud stuck. The popular party watched Grey's conduct with a censorious eye ; and it did not

[1] Fox, *Correspondence*, i. 351-9. *In Whig Society*, pp. 26-7.
[2] Quoted by Trevelyan, p. 126.

escape their notice that as a member of the Ministry of All the
Talents he avoided the subject of reform. They did not know
that Grenville was inflexibly opposed to his Foxite colleagues
on this subject. Had they known it, they would probably have
thought all the worse of Grey for serving under such a chief.
As it was they welcomed the King's *coup d'état* with a certain
gloomy satisfaction.

Cobbett, himself a very new convert to radicalism, taunted the
Foxite Whigs with 'their great and forfeited pledge'.[1] In a
sense the charge was easy to rebut. Great constitutional
changes could not safely be attempted in the middle of a war.
But it was true that a short experience of office had changed
Grey's interests. Before 1806 he had no special knowledge of
European affairs. Indeed he does not appear to have visited the
Continent after his grand tour in the years 1784–7. But as First
Lord of the Admiralty and as Foreign Secretary he was privileged to study *la haute politique* at first hand. He was an apt
pupil, though it may be doubted whether his mind was flexible
enough to adapt itself readily to the kaleidoscopic changes of
the international situation. Henceforth it was his intention to
lay the ground-plan of a foreign policy which should be both
efficient and true to the leading ideas of Charles James Fox.
Constitutional reform receded into the background of his
thought. It became a possibility which he would not avoid,
instead of an object for which he would work heart and soul.
So long as Napoleon remained a menace this attitude was
practical and right. But Grey, like his Tory opponents,
emerged from the war with a certain distaste for the less
dramatic and more solid work of constructive reform.[2] In the
years 1807–12 Grey convinced his parliamentary followers—not
always to their satisfaction—that he was a staunch defender of
such principles as were common to himself and Grenville. For
he was even stiffer than Grenville in resisting insidious plans of
coalition with Tories or with Canningites or with Whigs of the
Prince Regent's school. But even in those years there were
puritanic Whigs, like the youthful Lord John Russell, who

[1] In the *Political Register*, April 1807 (*Political Works*, ii. 161).
[2] *Early Correspondence of Lord J. Russell*, i. 147 (Duke of Bedford to
Lord John, 8 Feb. 1811).

thought him too warlike, too Grenvillian, to be called orthodox.[1]
The popular party thought him a lost soul. In 1819 James Mill
alleged that Canning himself would be more easily converted to
sound principles of government than Earl Grey.

It was all the more natural to suspect him of insincerity
because he showed at all times a complete indifference to the
routine duties which make up three parts of the life of an
industrious statesman. Except for the few months when he led
the House of Commons, Grey was accustomed to reserve his
voice and vote for great occasions. He liked to come up to
London after the session had begun and to vanish before it was
concluded. During his long absences at Howick he maintained
only an intermittent correspondence with the men who in his
absence steered the party ship. Even Fox, who was never too
conspicuous for regular attendance in the House, was moved to
lecture Grey for indolence. From April 1803 to April 1804—
to take only one instance—Fox's letters to Grey hardly ever
conclude without a cry for help. ' Without your being on the
spot as well as me, to take advantage of such occurrences as
may arise, I am sure nothing can be done.' ' I must still maintain that Mrs. Grey being to be confined in March was no reason
why the family could not come up in November or December.'
' You will perceive by all this how very desirable every possible
attendance is, and that for weeks at the very least.' ' You must
brave the expense and inconvenience and bring Mrs. Grey for
a month or two.'[2] These were months when the Whigs had
reasonable hope of coming into power, and Grey behaved much
as Rockingham and Richmond had been accustomed to behave
when Burke was straining every nerve to keep the flag of
opposition flying. After Fox's death there was no one to
exercise this steady pressure on Grey's indolence. For indolence it was that kept him at Howick. He could not plead, like
a Whig peer of the old school, either the pressure of county
business or the cares of a great estate. He loved seclusion for
its own sake. ' How I long ', he wrote as a young man, ' to
return to Tacitus and our own comfortable fire.'[3] To his col-

---

[1] See Holland's reply to these charges in *Early Correspondence of Lord
J. Russell*, i, pp. 135-7.

[2] Fox, *Correspondence*, iii. 431, 444, 457.   [3] *Life and Opinions*, p. 396.

leagues he usually pleaded the bad health of Lady Grey as an excuse for all defaults; and they acknowledged gracefully that he was indeed a forlorn and fretful creature when he ventured to come alone to London. But Lady Grey herself lamented that Charles insisted upon treating her as an invalid when she was in the best of health.

Charles in fact was by temperament .unfitted for the daily round. He hated the business of pelting ministers with small charges and small innuendoes wrapped up in small questions. He hated still more the sepulchral atmosphere of the House of Lords. When he was in the Commons he loved to sally forth from Howick, like another Chatham, for an operation of war; to deliver a rousing speech on a subject of first-rate importance; to defend the liberties of British subjects, or the rights of oppressed peoples; to expatiate on the first principles of the constitution or of international law. On such a subject he was graceful, incisive, even eloquent, his gestures and his delivery were consummate. His mental equipment was considerable. He knew the British constitution better than Fox, almost as well as Lord John Russell. Romilly, the best of the Whig lawyers, did not disdain to borrow without alteration one of Grey's legal arguments.[1] In mere debating power he was inferior to Fox, who never seemed to let a single argument upon the other side remain unanswered. In set speeches he fell below the highest level because he was as unimaginative as it is possible for a man of literary tastes to be, and because he appealed almost exclusively to the reasoning. faculties of his audience. But his language was felicitous, his arguments were admirably marshalled. His sarcasm provoked almost to madness such thin-skinned adversaries as George IV and Canning. The opinion of his Whig admirers was tersely summarized in 1820 by Mr. Creevey. ' There is nothing approaching this damned fellow in the kingdom when he mounts his best horse.' Creevey, to be sure, would not have appreciated the higher flights of Chatham or of Burke; and party principle forbade him to see any excellence in Canning's oratory. Grey was not a philosopher statesman, nor had nature endowed him with an

---

[1] Romilly, *Speeches*, ii. 249.

Irish wit. But, to use the cant of his own time, he was a 'factious speaker' of the highest class.

Was he more than this? Some of his contemporaries denied it. 'A more overrated man', writes Greville, 'never lived or one whose speaking was so far above his general abilities, or who owed so much to his oratorical plausibility.'[1] Burdett, though a dull man, put his finger on a more deep-seated defect. 'Lord Grey is always thinking of himself and of his failures in life.'[2] And Burdett is unexpectedly corroborated by Lady Grey in a letter which we owe to Mr. Trevelyan :

'You were quite right in supposing that I should be very anxious about your father's speech, and your account of it delights me. . . . If he is not bouncing about the room and making exclamations and groans, I may be certain that he said nothing of which the recollection makes him hot.'[3]

After we have quoted these opinions it is perhaps not amiss to observe how Grey was judged by the Benthamite Radicals when he had accomplished all, and more than all, that they had ever expected of a Whig Prime Minister. J. A. Roebuck suggests that Lord Grey had thought little and cared little about parliamentary reform between 1807 and 1830. He had, of course, spoken on the subject from time to time, expressing a favourable opinion 'with a certain grave earnestness which made men believe it to be actually entertained by the noble lord'; but, adds Roebuck, he could speak with decorous gravity on any subject whatsoever. Roebuck found it hard to distinguish between Lord Grey and any other Whig peer of the school of Fox; in his opinion they were all on the same level in point of public spirit. 'Every man in the party had always shaped his political course with reference to office.' This charge is of course ridiculous, so far as Grey is concerned. There is more truth in the charge which follows that the Whigs despised and feared the people, desiring that the country should be ruled, reform or no reform, by a ring of aristocratic families, supported if possible by the favour of the sovereign. Broughton, a much better informed politician than Roebuck, was of much

[1] *Greville Memoirs*, ii. 90.
[2] Broughton, *Recollections*, under date 15 March 1828.
[3] Trevelyan, p. 186.

the same opinion.[1] It was the *mot d'ordre* in Radical circles to
speak of the Whigs as selfish aristocrats and courtiers, and Grey
was involved in the general condemnation which these purists
passed upon his party.   The memory of the Radical party did
not go back very far, and their verdict was founded on the
events of the period 1807-1827.   What then were the relations
of Grey in these years with the Court and with the popular
party?

Grey and Grenville were approached by Spencer Perceval
in 1809 with the King's approval and consent; they were
approached by the Regent himself in 1811 and in 1812.   In
1809 it appears that Grenville was ready to negotiate and Grey
was not.   Grenville wished at all events to learn what terms
the King would allow his ministers to offer.   Grey felt convinced
that the terms would be impossible; and Grenville soon discovered that Grey was right.   The King proposed to demand
in 1809 the same pledge with regard to Catholic Relief which
the Whigs had refused in 1807.   Grey's policy, in which Grenville acquiesced, was to wait until the King should be forced
to accept a Whig ministry without conditions.[2]   In January
1811 the case was altered.   It was expected that the King's
health would necessitate a Regency, and that the Regent
would call upon the Whigs to form an administration.   Grey
and Grenville made their plans accordingly.   It was arranged
that Grey should be Foreign Secretary and Grenville First Lord
of the Treasury if the Regent's offer was acceptable, and the
disposal of some minor offices was settled.[3]   But Grey was a
most unwilling and sceptical participant in these proceedings.
He came up to London under protest, and he insisted that, as
a preliminary to arrangements with the Regent, the Whigs
must demand that he would consult no one but his ministers;
there was to be no *camarilla* of such advisers as Sheridan and
Moira.   The two Whig leaders addressed the Regent so
emphatically on this point that he broke off the negotiations;

[1] See e. g. the entry in Broughton's diary, 9 February 1832 (*Recollections*,
iv, p. 174).

[2] *Dropmore Papers*, ix. 333; *Life of S. Perceval*, ii. 21-32.

[3] *Memoirs of Sir S. Romilly*, ii. 365; *Early Correspondence of Lord
J. Russell*, i. 147; *Creevey Papers*, pp. 137, 139, 141-3.

his original determination having been to impose upon them
as a colleague Lord Moira, who would have represented the
Regent's personal views and interests [1]—as Bute and Cumberland had in the past represented those of George III.   Thus
the discussions broke down because the Whigs would not make
a concession to the Crown which Newcastle and Rockingham
had granted quietly enough.

   Finally, in 1812, the Regent's proposal was that the Whigs
should take part in a coalition, and was at first so worded as to
indicate a coalition with Spencer Perceval.   The reply of Grey
and Grenville was that they could not unite with a minister from
whom they differed on so many fundamental points.   The
alternative proposal which was then made to them was coalition
with the party of Lord Wellesley and Canning; and this was
declined ostensibly on the plea of differences of opinion regarding military policy, but in fact for the reason that Grey and
Grenville suspected a trap and were not willing to consider any
coalition which the Regent had any share in forming.   Grey
expressed a part of these suspicions in the House of Lords on
19 March 1812.   He stated that

' There existed an unseen and pestilent influence behind the throne
which it would be the duty of Parliament to brand with some signal
mark of condemnation.   It was the determination of himself and his
friends not to accept office without coming to an understanding with
Parliament for the abolition of this secret influence.'

After this outbreak there was very little prospect of an arrangement between the Whigs and the Prince.   Indeed the Prince
instructed Lord Moira to inform Lord Wellesley that Grey
could not be brought into office until he had explained away
the objectionable speech.

   From this time we may date the fierce vendetta between the
Whigs and the Prince, which Brougham, Whitbread, Denman,
and other free lances prosecuted by very questionable means in
1812-14, when they took up the cause of Princess Charlotte, and
again in 1820-1, when they seemed more anxious to blacken
the character of the King than to vindicate his injured wife.
The motives of these gladiators are quite frankly explained in

[1] *Memoirs of the Regency*, i, pp. 20 ff.

a letter of 1813, from Brougham to his friend Creevey. The subject is the grievances of the Princess. Brougham writes:

'My principle is—take her along with you as far as you both go in the same road. It is one of the constitutional means of making head against a revenue of 105 millions, an army of ½ million and 800 millions of debt.' [1]

Grey was not behind the men who reasoned thus. He had no illusions about the Queen, whose conduct had been condemned as indiscreet or worse by a secret commission over which Lord Grenville had presided (1806). He came up to London for the debates on the Bill of Pains and Penalties with a determination to vote according to the evidence, and not to make party capital out of judicial proceedings; and he gave great offence to some of his followers by adhering to this line.[2] But, having decided that ministers had failed to prove their case, he could not refrain from taking advantage of the odium which their conduct and that of the King had brought upon them. He made a public speech at Durham to announce his belief in the Queen's innocence. He called on her, and he dined with her,[3] and accepted complacently enough the credit for the failure of the bill, which properly belonged to Brougham and to Denman. This was not conduct that a strict moralist would approve. Grey thought that the ministry was doomed and that, when they went out, the King could not help sending for the Whigs. He was so confident of success that he began to make out the list of a Whig administration. But his conduct was the reverse of courtier-like. He proposed to carry the citadel by storm. It is small wonder that the King's private language about Grey's conduct was quite unprintable.[4]

Yet, curiously enough, the Queen's trial led to the last serious efforts for a reconciliation between the King and Grey. They were not made by Grey, nor by the King, but by the reigning favourite, Lady Conyngham, who must have diagnosed the

---

[1] *Creevey Papers*, p. 179. Cf. Russell's comment on the Queen's trial; it 'has done a great deal of good, in renewing the old and natural alliance of the Whigs and the people'. S. Walpole's *Life of Russell*, i, p. 122.

[2] *Creevey Papers*, pp. 313, 325, 331, 332.

[3] *Op. cit.*, pp. 349, 357.

[4] *Memoirs of the Court of George IV*, i, p. 98.

political situation in the same sense as Grey. Thanks to her efforts Grey, Lansdowne, the Duke of Bedford, and some Opposition ladies were brought together at Carlton House on the occasion of a children's ball; and the King dined next night with the Duke of Devonshire to meet the leaders of the Whig Opposition. Liverpool thought that Lady Conyngham would succeed; perhaps the wish was father to the thought, for he was sick of office and disheartened by Canning's resignation.[1] But Lady Conyngham failed. The King took no trouble to speak to Grey or to show the commonest civility to the other Whigs. There is no reason to suppose that Grey was disappointed or surprised. It was not by these means that he hoped to become Prime Minister. Some of his younger friends continued to hope for royal favour, even after the Liverpool ministry had recovered its equilibrium and had brought in Canning to lead the House of Commons.[2] They were disappointed. Eight years later we find Grey announcing to his friends that he will never again attend the levee because he is invariably ignored by the King when he does so;[3] and this at the very moment when Lambton and others of the younger Whigs were hoping that the Duke of Wellington would ask the King's leave to negotiate with Grey for a coalition.

Grey's relations with William IV must be discussed hereafter. Here it is sufficient to point out that, even in dealing with a sovereign for whom he felt so genuine a regard as he did for William, Grey jealously maintained his independence. We must now turn to his relations with the popular reformers.

Grey was justifiably annoyed by the tactics of the parliamentary Radicals, Wardle, Burdett, Cochrane, Hobhouse, who to tell the truth were completely carried away in the years 1809-16 by their desire to win the favour of the Radical middle classes in London and Westminster. He thought that these members were attacking not so much the abuses of the constitution as its fundamental features, and were diverting the attention of Parliament from the real and crying sins of Tory administration. 'They aim at nothing but the degradation of all public character, their cry being that all Ministers are alike, and that

---

[1] *Bathurst Papers*, pp. 512–13; *Croker*, i. 210.
[2] *E. H. R.*, xxxviii, p. 541.   [3] *Creevey Papers*, p. 543 (June 1, 1829).

no advantage is to be derived from any change.'[1] In 1810 he held that these politicians had no effective support in the country for their cry of parliamentary reform,[2] and stated that he himself would not move until he saw evidence of a serious popular interest in the question. He found no such evidence in the disturbances of 1816–17. He had no opportunity of watching the ferment in the centres where Hampden Clubs abounded and Cartwright's proposals were all the vogue; for the disturbances of that time at Sunderland and North Shields were insignificant, and apparently devoid of political significance.[3] Such information as Grey possessed probably came from his friend Lord Fitzwilliam, who kept a watch upon events at Sheffield. Fitzwilliam found that the gaze of the Sheffield Radicals was fixed on London; that they had been agog to hear the result of the second Spa Fields meeting (2 Dec. 1816), and to follow whatever line the London Radicals might take; but that all danger was at an end when it was discovered that the Sheffield magistrates were forearmed, and that the Spa Fields meeting had led to no results. Fitzwilliam deduced from these facts the conclusion that the London agitators were dangerous, but that the movement in the West Riding was not due to any substantial grievance, such as the want of employment or the scarcity of provisions. The object in view was a complete change of the constitution, and the driving force was a revolutionary spirit excited by the Radical proceedings in London.[4] Fitzwilliam was alarmed; but he was confident that the West Riding could be trusted if the London agitators could be kept at arm's length. Six months later Fitzwilliam reported that 'all the mischievous in the country have considered themselves as subordinate members of a great leading body of Revolutionists in London', and argued that the continuance of this illusion into the year 1817 was chiefly due to the activities of Oliver, the *agent provocateur* of the Home Office.[5]

[1] Grey to Holland, January 1810 (quoted by Trevelyan, 169).
[2] Trevelyan, p. 169.
[3] H.O. 41. 1, pp. 238, 282, 284, 317, 491.
[4] See Fitzwilliam's report of 7 December 1816 to Lord Sidmouth (H.O. 40. 4, No. 13). In the same bundle there is a report of much the same tenor from Lord Talbot on the state of feeling in the Potteries (No. 21).
[5] Quoted by the Hammonds, *Skilled Labourer*, p. 364.

Grey appears to have accepted Fitzwilliam's diagnosis of the situation. He assumed that there was a conspiracy, organized in London; but he also assumed that it was not dangerous enough to call for coercive legislation. Twice in the session of 1817 he protested against the measures which Government thought necessary. On 4 February he developed the old Whig theme that it is always dangerous to invest the executive with new powers. On 24 February, being confronted with the proposal to suspend the Habeas Corpus Act, he explained the situation as he saw it. Large parts of the country had no doubt been raised in an uproar by the Spa Fields meeting. The promoters of that meeting had formed a design of promoting insurrection under cover of an agitation for constitutional changes. But how could it be plausibly contended that these 'miserable wretches, reduced to the lowest poverty and distress', who had trusted wholly to chance for the realization of their design, could only be defeated by suspending the liberty of the person. The utmost precaution that was called for was a measure to restrict the holding of meetings in the open air for the purpose of intimidating Parliament. But the remedy which he himself preferred was the remedy proposed by the Friends of the People. He desired to cut the ground from under the feet of the agitators by carrying a reform of the representation which would satisfy all reasonable complaints. In a speech of 18 February 1817, with reference to a reform petition from the City of London, he called for the abolition of 'admitted abuses and flagrant anomalies'. At the same time he explained that he was not personally prepared to go so far as he had gone in 1797. He had come to realize that the enfranchisement of all rate-paying householders would be too sudden a change. Neither would he now acknowledge that constitutional reform was the indispensable preliminary without which it would be hopeless to lay plans for improving the condition of the people. The House of Commons was not so imperfect as to be powerless for good. Even in its present shape it was 'of all other institutions in all the other countries of the world the institution best calculated for the protection of the subject'.[1]

He did not allow himself to be shaken in his policy by that

---

[1] For these speeches see *Hansard*, xxxv. 200, 424, 573.

curious series of riots, in the early summer of 1817, which began at Huddersfield and culminated in Brandreth's march on Nottingham.   He accepted Fitzwilliam's explanation and improved upon it.   The whole story, he wrote to Lord Wellesley, had been got up to justify the renewal of the Habeas Corpus Suspension Act.   A force of 250 men at the utmost, led in part by parish paupers,[1] was credited with a design to seize London and half a dozen other of the principal cities of the kingdom! Truly Lord Sidmouth was like Tom Thumb: ' He made the giants first and then he killed them.'[2]   He and his party were not able to prevent the second suspension.   But in the session of 1818 they had the honour of exposing Oliver to execration, and there was no further risk that the Habeas Corpus Act would be suspended as a measure of police whenever the magistrates of England were in a nervous frame of mind.

The General Election of 1818 brought to the Whigs a gain of 33 seats in the House of Commons, with the result that their strength on a division rose to 173.   For this result the party was much indebted to Grey's exertions in the last two years.   But the Radical tide was rising again, for the same reason as in 1816.   After a short period of prosperity the staple trades began to contract in the spring of 1819, and the general impoverishment of labour was painfully reflected in the rise of poor rates and an increasing tide of emigrants. The textile districts were particularly distressed, and the agitators took advantage of this circumstance to bring forward in Lancashire and Yorkshire the old panacea together with the new expedients of mass meetings held by professional orators and of the election of ' legislatorial attornies ' in these meetings, and of ' military trainings ' preparatory to the meetings.   Apart from the avowed hostility of the Radical leaders to Lord Grey—he was very grossly attacked by the Westminster Radical committee at the by-election of this year—it was out of the question that he or any other responsible statesman should sympathize either with the objects or with the methods of the campaign. But he kept his head when many of his old associates, and

---

[1] This is a reference to Brandreth.

[2] *Wellesley Papers*, ii. 135-7.   See also Grey's speech in the House of Lords, *Hansard*, xxxvi. 996-1005.

especially Lord Grenville, raised the cry of a Jacobin peril. In
1819 as in 1817 he desired to draw a sharp distinction between
the agitators and their misguided adherents, and set his face
against the Government's demand for emergency legislation.

After Peterloo it would have been easy and popular for
Grey to join with Burdett[1] in prejudging the behaviour of the
Manchester magistrates and the precipitate decision of ministers
to support the magistrates without reserve. Some of Grey's
friends, among them Lord Fitzwilliam, helped to arrange county
meetings for the purpose of criticizing the magistrates. Others
subscribed to a fund which was organized by Hunt for the
purpose of investigating the so-called massacre. Grey held
aloof from these manœuvres, and reserved his views until the
opening of Parliament. On the first day of the session he
delivered one of his weightiest and most judicial speeches. He
denounced the agitators as men who were all equally mischievous
though they might not all be equally criminal. He dissociated
himself from the Radical programme, but he urged his hearers
not to countenance remedies which would be worse than the
evil that it was proposed to cure. The first duty of Parliament
was to discover, if possible, the causes of the prevailing discontents and to consider how they could be appeased. Undoubtedly it was the distress of the manufacturing districts
which had given the agitators their opportunity. He was not
prepared to presume that the Manchester magistrates had been
guilty of illegal action. But ministers were wholly unjustified
in presuming the contrary. There was prima facie a strong
case for an investigation, not only of the objects of the Peterloo
meeting, but also of the methods by which it had been dispersed.
He understood that extraordinary measures of repression were
proposed, and he pointed out that the measures of 1817 had
only increased the discontent which they were expected to cure.
It was ridiculous to suppose that a reign of terror could restore
commerce and manufactures and credit to their former level.
Liberty has been the source of our prosperity in the past. He
asked the House to give assurances, in its address to the Prince

---

[1] Burdett on August 22 published a letter to the Electors of Westminster
in which the Manchester magistrates were denounced as 'bloody Neros',
for which he was sentenced in 1820 to imprisonment for three months.

Regent, that the complaints of the people would receive attention and that their rights would be protected.[1]

In this otherwise admirable speech there was a noticeable avoidance of the main question which Grey himself had raised. What concession could the Government promise which was likely to kill the Radical campaign? He indicated that public economy and a reduction of the taxes were expected; he also made, in passing, a remark that some kind of parliamentary reform was needed. But on both these topics he was studiously indefinite. The same indefiniteness appeared in his speech of 29 November, when he criticized Sidmouth for declaring that it was a most dangerous policy to make concessions before the safety of the State had been secured. He said that there were concessions which the people had a right to expect. There were abuses in the government and defects in the constitution of Parliament which ought to be taken into consideration by Parliament itself.[2] And here he stopped. He pointedly refrained from explaining how far he was prepared to go along this line of conciliation. And yet there were men in his own party who urged him to commit himself.[3]

The situation in which Grey stood was difficult. He found himself opposed by Lord Grenville on some of the main issues which were under discussion. Grenville believed in the existence of a great conspiracy—against the constitution. Grenville lamented the insufficiency of the existing Press laws, and not content with asking in the House of Lords for more effective legislation he had been advising Lord Liverpool as to the ways and means in which that law might be stiffened.[4] On 30 November 1819 the two Whig leaders crossed swords in debate for the first time since their original alliance of 1806. Grey had not shirked the encounter, and there was a certain undercurrent of asperity in his criticisms of Grenville's plan for dealing with popular discontents. Had it not been tried during the war against the French Revolution, when Grenville was in

---

[1] *Hansard*, xli. 4–21 (23 Nov. 1819).   [2] *Hansard*, xli. 349–53.
[3] See Sir Robert Wilson's letter (of 5 Oct. 1819) to Grey in *E. H. R.*, xxxviii, pp. 535–6.
[4] See Grenville's memorandum of 12 November in Yonge's *Liverpool*, i, pp. 419–26.

Pitt's cabinet? Was there any reason to suppose that it would be more successful now?[1] Still there was not yet an open breach between the Grenvilles and the main Whig body; and it was not for Grey to make the breach inevitable by proposing a measure of reform which would amount to a formal repudiation of the compact of 1806. For the present the Grenvilles were a Third Party united with the Government on the question of radicalism, but otherwise preserved their independence, more, it must be said, because of Grenville's reluctance to turn his coat so completely than from any similar scruples on the part of his relatives and followers. It might still be possible to bring them back into the Whig fold after the turmoil over coercive legislation had died down. And unless they could be brought back the prospects of a Whig administration would be indeed remote.

The Grenvilles preserved an ambiguous attitude till the end of 1821. They then, with the exception of Lord Grenville, formally identified themselves with Lord Liverpool, receiving their due quota of offices and emoluments. For the future Grey had no cause to study their prejudices. But in the meantime trouble had arisen in another quarter. He was confronted with the prospect of a further schism in the Whig party if he made parliamentary reform an urgent question. Tierney, the leader in the Commons, the younger members, and the *Edinburgh Review*, desired that he should do so; and Sir James Mackintosh so far relapsed from the political philosophy of Burke as to encourage and assist these hotheads.[2] In the autumn session of 1819 Russell declared himself in favour of disfranchising rotten boroughs and reducing the duration of Parliaments; and in 1820 he introduced the first two of his measures for disfranchising named boroughs of particularly ill repute. Both passed the House of Commons, and the second of them, for disfranchising Grampound alone, was eventually accepted by the House of Lords.[3] Late in the autumn session

---

[1] *Hansard*, xli. 481-2.

[2] See the article on 'The State of the Country' in the *Ed. Review*, October 1819; Butler, *Great Reform Bill*, p. 33 (for Tierney), and Mackintosh's letter of 14 October to Lord John Russell in *Early Correspondence of Lord J. Russell*, i. 206.

[3] In 1821; 1 & 2 George IV. c. 47.

Mr. Lambton, Grey's son-in-law, gave notice of motions for shortening the duration of Parliament, extending the franchise and disfranchising rotten boroughs.   This scheme at once elicited strong protests from Lord Fitzwilliam and Lord Holland, the political heirs of Rockingham and Charles James Fox.   It would, Lord Holland remarked, be as bad as a revolution if it were carried.   Grey was exceedingly perturbed.   He told Lambton that, however popular reform might be in the country, there was no reasonable hope of carrying a Reform Bill through Parliament 'in my lifetime, or even during yours'.   To press the subject in Parliament would mean the dissolution of the Whig party, which was 'the only defence for the liberties of the country'.   His own wish was to keep the party, as a party, uncommitted.   He desired that individuals who thought strongly on the subject should pursue their object by methods which would not divide the party.   Taken by itself this letter reads like the renunciation of a cherished ideal.   But at heart Grey was on the side of Lambton.   Mr. Trevelyan has published the two remarkable warnings which Grey gave to Lord Holland in the course of this dispute.   No party, he told Holland, which depended upon public opinion, would ever succeed until it produced some measure of reform more direct and more comprehensive than the half-measures of Lord John Russell.   At the end of 1820, when the Liverpool Government appeared to be tottering, Grey presented Holland with his own private views. The minimum with which public opinion would be satisfied was, he thought,

'Shortening the duration of Parliament at least to five years; admitting copyholders to vote for counties, and adding 100 members to be divided between the large towns and the most extensive and populous Counties; taking the same number from the representation of the most obnoxious boroughs.'[1]

He was still uncertain whether this plan should be made a condition *sine qua non* of accepting office.   But, if that course were adopted, he hoped that it would unite a majority of the Whigs, and that the Crown would ultimately be obliged by public opinion to admit the Whigs to office on these terms. What Holland thought of the proposal we can only guess.   But

[1] S. Reid, *Life of Durham*, i. 129–31; Trevelyan, *Lord Grey*, pp. 371–3.

Grey's scheme remained a secret; Lambton and Russell, Aber-cromby and Lord Archibald Hamilton, were left to ventilate the subject of reform in their own fashions, and Lambton wearied of the business after making one brilliant speech in 1821. When he became silent there was no one in Grey's immediate entourage to revive his flagging interest.   In one way and another the subject was raised annually up to 1827.   But Grey kept his own counsel.   Not that he had changed his mind.   In 1822, while it seemed possible that the death of Castlereagh would lead to a change of ministry, he told Brougham that he would only accept office on condition of being allowed to introduce a moderate scheme of reform, but he would pledge himself to resist anything more.[1]   At that time, and indeed up to 1830, his thoughts were chiefly occupied with Catholic Emancipation and foreign policy; with the Catholic question because it was still, as it had been in 1806, the question on which Whig opinion was united, while Tory opinion was divided.   He attached so much importance to this question that he would have condoned Lord Lansdowne's coalition with Canning in 1827 if the terms of alliance had effectively com-mitted Canning and the whole administration to some prompt and substantial measure of relief.   Foreign policy, however, he regarded as his own peculiar *métier*, and he was uniformly critical of Tory policy, whether directed by Castlereagh or by Canning.

Grey's opinion of Castlereagh was already stereotyped in 1815.   He believed that Castlereagh was essentially hostile to political freedom, in England, in Ireland, on the Continent.   He assumed that Castlereagh was committed to the principles of the Holy Alliance and desired to see Europe purged of revolution by Alexander I and Metternich.   In the session of 1821 he developed his indictment with special reference to the Congress of Troppau and the Austrian declaration of war upon the liberal government in Naples.   He was shocked by the Troppau Declaration in which the Eastern Powers arrogated to them-selves the right of suppressing revolutions.   He was also shocked that Castlereagh had admitted the special claim of Austria to provide in her own fashion for the maintenance of Italian peace.

[1] Brougham, *Memoirs*, ii. 444.

He jumped to the conclusion that Castlereagh's protest against the Troppau Declaration was no more than a handful of dust thrown in the eyes of Parliament. Sublimely contemptuous of the Treaty of Vienna, he denounced Austrian rule in Lombardy and Venetia as a monstrosity. In defence of the Neapolitans he quoted the classical doctrine of Intervention which he and Fox had so often invoked against Pitt and Grenville. Were the Neapolitans to be regarded as enemies of European peace for no better reason than that their example might serve as a precedent for risings of oppressed peoples in Silesia or the Prussian Rhineland? With what face could a British minister break off friendly relations with the Neapolitans on account of a revolution which like our own of 1688 was produced solely by misgovernment. It was the speech of a man who was inevitably ignorant of many of the facts. It was notably unjust to Castlereagh's methods and intentions. Like most statesmen of his time Grey erred in supposing that Alexander's Holy Alliance was anything more than a pious aspiration. But he divined accurately enough that in Italy at least the Vienna settlement was doomed, and that Castlereagh was doing his best to delay the day of doom, with very unfortunate consequences for Italy.[1]

With Canning it might seem more difficult for Grey to quarrel. For in 1822, when Grey took stock of his own ideas of foreign policy, he found that the three points on which he laid most stress were : no intervention with the affairs of France or any other country; a benevolent attitude towards the Greek Revolution, but not such benevolence as would involve us in a war; a voice in the settlement of Eastern Europe, whenever the Turkish Empire should break up, to be used for the purpose of keeping Russian power within due limits.[2] These were all points to which Canning would have cordially subscribed, and yet Grey would never allow that any step of Canning's was right or profitable. In 1825 Grey wrote to Holland that Castlereagh was a better man than Canning, but there was nothing to choose between their policies. Yet Grey held that Castlereagh was one of the meanest of mankind, and the most purblind of foreign ministers. He could never do justice to Canning, either as a

[1] *Hansard*, N.S. iv. 742 ff. (18 Feb. 1821).
[2] Brougham, *Memoirs*, ii. 452.

man or as a statesman.   It was not merely a case of incompatibility of temper.   Grey hated Canning as a wolf in sheep's clothing, as an inveterate Tory who had the art of concealing his obscurantism behind a screen of principles which he had borrowed from the Whigs and for which he had no real affection.   How much of truth there was in this verdict the biographer of Canning must decide.   Grey was not rancorous, but neither was he easily induced to change an opinion which he had once deliberately formed.   Perhaps he never realized that Canning at the height of his career was a wiser politician and a better man than the Canning of the Napoleonic period.

To Grey it seemed that Canning was a bungler who had gained a reputation through his worst mistakes.   The first of these mistakes he held to be the passive attitude which Canning assumed towards the French invasion of Spain; and here we discover in Grey's mind, not for the first time, the deeply rooted belief of a Foxite Whig that strong language which is not supported, and cannot be supported, by armed action, is enough to intimidate a wary and sagacious opponent.   The strong language in this case was not altogether wanting, as we know, and as Grey must have known.   What the Government had not in readiness was an army available to co-operate with that of Ferdinand VII.   To say, as Grey said a little later, that the game had been in our hands but was badly played was to betray a complete misunderstanding of the situation.[1]   A few years later, when himself Prime Minister, we find Grey applying to the case of Poland the remedy which he had prescribed for the case of Spain, and trying to save the Polish constitution by a strong remonstrance (Nov. 1831), which it was not possible at that time to support by the only argument which might have influenced Russia.   Nesselrode answered the complaint curtly enough, knowing, as Grey also knew, that there was no prospect of the British navy appearing in the Baltic.[2]

In Canning's management of the Greek question we should have expected Grey to find less cause for complaint, since Canning did in the end take energetic measures to secure for the

---

[1] *Correspondence of the Princess Lieven and Earl Grey*, i. 34.

[2] The dispatch was written by Palmerston, but it appears to have been Grey who inspired it.

Greeks self-government under the suzerainty of the Sultan, and did so in concert with Russia, a power for which the Whigs, despite their abhorrence of the Holy Alliance, still felt considerable respect and sympathy. To help Greece by detaching Russia from the influence of Metternich was a step for which any Whig statesman would have been proud to assume responsibility. Yet Grey regarded the Treaty of London, which was the consummation of Canning's Greek policy, as a capital mistake.[1] If we ask the reason of this strong judgement, it appears to be that the secret article of the Treaty led directly to the battle of Navarino, and Navarino to the treaty of Adrianople. The arbitrament of force was so repulsive to Grey's mind that he would hardly ever admit it to be justifiable; he used the 'untoward incident' of Navarino to enforce the moral that those who sanction the use of force will probably find themselves obliged to condone a breach of international law. An illegality which gave Russia leave to cross the Pruth, and to dictate her own terms to the Porte, seemed to him, as it seemed to Wellington, a mere ineptitude. Yet, if Grey had fairly asked himself what better means of settling the Eastern question could have been devised, and what arguments could have converted the Turk to a sweet reasonableness, he could hardly have avoided admitting that Canning's plan of co-operation with France and Russia was preferable to the plan of competing against Russia for the privilege of liberating the Greeks. The battle of Navarino cleared the air by showing that the Allies were in earnest. The Russian advance on Constantinople drove home the lesson of Navarino, and the Tsar did not in fact abuse his success to secure any of the illegitimate gains which the critics of Canning's policy had foretold.

Grey's correspondence with Princess Lieven, which began in 1824, did not influence his views so much as that vivacious lady hoped. But it was undoubtedly of great value to him. It gave him considerable opportunities of learning the trend of Russian policy, not so much because he received secret information, as because his correspondent rarely failed to set before him the Russian view of every notable event. It was something to have first-hand information about the sympathies and antipathies of

[1] *Op. cit.*, i. 308.

one of the great powers ; and Russia was, from 1824 to the end
of Grey's active career, the great enigma of continental politics.
Nor was this his only obligation to the Princess. She kept him
au courant of diplomatic gossip through a period when he had
few opportunities of learning the *dessous des cartes* from any
other professional diplomatist. It was largely due to Princess
Lieven that Grey was prepared for the July Revolution when
it came, that he understood thoroughly the character of the
party which established Louis Philippe. Already in December
1829 she warned him of the design to abrogate the *Charte Con-
stitutionnelle*. Within four days of the *coup d'état* of July 25
she was able to assure Grey that Charles X would not be supported by Russia, and that Polignac had not been acting in
concert with the Duke of Wellington. She acted as a channel
of communication between Grey and the Duke of Orleans. She
conveyed to the latter Grey's warning that the next ruler of
France would be expected, in this country at least; to dissociate
himself from the plans of conquest or foreign intervention which
were generally ascribed to the French Liberal party ; and she
brought back to Grey the assurance that Louis Philippe desired
nothing so much as friendly relations with foreign powers. But
she also warned Grey that one of the ministers of Louis Phillippe,
Sebastiani, was in favour of a forward policy. The information
which she gave him about the Belgian Revolution was good so
far as it went, and had the effect of showing him that in the
Netherlands, more than in Germany or Italy, the July Revolution
was likely to have consequences very menacing to the peace of
Europe. When Grey took office he was tolerably well acquainted
with the character and dimensions of the European crisis.[1]

The only other correspondents from whom Grey obtained
foreign information at this time were Lord Holland, Lord Ponsonby, Flahault, and Lady Keith ; and the information to be
obtained from the two last named was likely to be coloured by
enthusiasm for the House of Orleans.

But if Grey was becoming better acquainted with the *carte
politique* of Europe, he was in these last years before his final
triumph grievously out of touch with most of his natural sup-

---

[1] *Correspondence of Princess Lieven and Earl Grey*, i. 392 ; ii. 30-1, 40,
50, 55, 73, 100, 105.

porters. Owing to the bad health of his wife he was much in
Devonshire during the years 1823-6.[1] In the year 1824[2] he
handed over the leadership of the Opposition to Lord Lansdowne ; and Duncannon, one of the party whips, told Grenville
in 1827 that for a long time past Grey had declined all invita-
tions to take an active part in politics, and had told Duncannon
to refer all questions to Lord Lansdowne as he himself meant to
withdraw altogether from public life.[3]   He was even ceasing to
write to his old friends.   Hence he was naturally not consulted
when some of the Lansdowne Whigs opened communications
with Canning.   Grey arrived in London while the negotiations
were in progress, totally unaware that there was any talk of
a coalition.   He was seriously annoyed when he learned the
true state of affairs.   Apart from his personal dislike of Canning,
and his objections to Canning's foreign policy, he was influenced
by the conviction that no loyal Whig would ever find a basis of
principle on which to combine with a politician who was hostile
to parliamentary reform and Laodicean on the subject of Catholic
relief.   Having explained his personal position to the House of
Lords he retired to Northumberland 'unconnected with any
body but the very few who took the same line I did in the last
session'.[4]

For the next year or two he consistently referred to his lost
supporters as the Lansdowne party and professed the most complete ignorance of their intentions.   They were at first disposed
to treat his secession as due to wounded *amour propre*, and
credited him with an unreasonable aversion to George Canning.
But their experiences as followers, first of Canning, and then of
Goderich, went far to justify his strictures upon the policy of
compromise into which they had been seduced.   Unable to advance any cause which they had at heart, treated with more or
less civil contempt by their Canningite colleagues, obliged to
serve, after Canning's death, with two such obstinate Tories as

---

[1] *Life and Opinions of Earl Grey*, p. 422.
[2] *Op. cit.*, p. 424.   Sir R. Wilson gives the date as two years before the
formation of the Canning ministry ; but the evidence of Grey's son is to be
preferred.
[3] *Grenville*, 17 June 1827.
[4] *Correspondence of Princess Lieven*, i, p. 87.

Herries and Huskisson, the Lansdowne Whigs realized too late that they had sacrificed reputation without obtaining power. Meanwhile Grey was applauded as the one Whig leader who had stood fast by his principles. The Duke of Wellington came to the conclusion that Grey was the one Whig whom it might be worth while to conciliate, or to whom the position of first minister might safely be entrusted. His verdict had important consequences. It seems at least probable that, if the Whigs had been left to choose their own Prime Minister at the end of 1830, they would not have selected Grey, who for the best part of three years had sedulously separated himself from them in public and in private. The King sent for Grey on the advice of the Duke of Wellington, and the Lansdowne Whigs were obliged to accept him with a good grace.

During those three years Grey stood in an uncomfortable position. Clear-sighted spectators, like his old friend the Princess Lieven, felt certain that his day would come ; but he himself felt assured that George IV would never allow him to be brought into any Cabinet. Gossips differed as to the motives of the King's hostility, some of them tracing it back to the distant days when he and Grey were both in love with the beautiful Duchess of Devonshire, others, more reasonably, dating it from the trial of Queen Caroline. But the hostility was patent, as Wellington discovered in 1828 ;[1] and it may have been one of the reasons why Grey was deserted in these years by many of his oldest political friends. There were a faithful few, in particular Lord Holland and the Duke of Bedford, Lord Lauderdale, Mr. Thomas Creevey ; but such was his isolation at the beginning of 1830 that he knew nothing about the intentions of either the Whigs or the Canningites.[2] Lady Grey, the gentlest of women, seems never to have forgotten or forgiven some of the desertions of those years. Her husband was more philosophical, in spite of passing fits of bitterness.

In the summer of 1830, as the health of George IV and the situation on the Continent became more critical, he began to

---

[1] *Creevey Papers*, p. 493, for Wellington's explanation, transmitted to Grey through Lord Lauderdale, of his omission to approach Grey in 1828.

[2] *Correspondence of Princess Lieven and Earl Grey*, i. 459, 470.

take stock of the political situation. In the spring of 1830 he came up to London for the latter part of the session, and found that Wellington's majority was crumbling. Cautiously he re-opened communications with personal friends in both branches of the Opposition. The results were satisfactory. On 30 June (four days after the death of George IV) he wrote to his old friend, the Princess Lieven, that he found himself regarded with favour by ' all the parties not connected with Government ', and that he had thrown down the gauntlet to ministers by moving in the House of Lords ' that this Administration is not capable of conducting the Government with advantage to the country '. It only remained to see what would be the result of the general election (necessitated by the demise of the crown) which took place in August and September. He waited quietly for the results at Howick. They were not overwhelmingly favourable to the Whigs, since many of the successful candidates could not be labelled with any confidence. But the experts felt little doubt that the Duke's majority had disappeared or would do so very shortly.

It is just possible that the Duke might have saved himself at the eleventh hour by taking in the Canningites and introducing a moderate measure of reform. Rumour predicted up to the 15th of September that he would take this course. But the accidental death of Huskisson on that date put an end to what-ever *pourparlers* had been opened. Melbourne, who found himself, after Huskisson's disappearance, the undisputed leader of the Canningites, had already committed himself to co-opera-tion with Lord Grey. The fall of the Tory Government was therefore inevitable ; and Wellington's much-criticized declara-tion against reform, at the beginning of the autumn session (November 2), only precipitated the crisis. Within a fortnight ministers were defeated in the House of Commons on the question of the Civil List, and on 16 November Grey was sum-moned to form a ministry.

The two facts which most impressed his critics in the next few months were that Grey formed a Cabinet of the most aristo-cratic description, and that his Home Secretary, Lord Melbourne, proceeded to suppress disturbances with a severity which threw the performances of Lord Sidmouth quite into the shade. Grey undoubtedly believed that he had come to power in a time of grave emergency, when it was necessary to allay the excitement in the country by large constitutional concessions, but also necessary to show that ministers would not endure the slightest hint of rebellion or intimidation. The cause of reform had suffered in the past from the excesses of Radical fanatics. The time had come to prove that reforming statesmen had no sympathy for those who desired to subvert the existing order of society.

What is fairly open to question is the assumption—which was common to politicians of every shade of opinion—that a social crisis was imminent in the autumn of 1830. The facts which might be held to justify such apprehensions were partly economic and partly political.

The economic position was undoubtedly bad in 1830–1. Since 1826 the export trades as a whole had been in a trough of deep depression, deeper even than the depressions of 1837 and 1840. Employment was still brisk in the coal and iron industries, which continued year by year to show an increased output; and the cotton-spinning industry had begun to revive in the course of 1829;[1] but this revival had produced a new agitation for higher wages; a General Union of Operative Spinners, covering all the cotton districts in Great Britain and Ireland, had been founded at the end of 1829, and in July 1830 a still more ambitious organization, the National Association for the Protection of Labour, was launched by James Doherty, the secretary of the Manchester Spinners' Union. Masters and men of the cotton industry organized themselves for industrial warfare, the operatives organizing strikes, and some important mill-owners combining to cut prices in defiance of a recent price agreement. There were simultaneous disturbances on the Tyne among the mining population. It was thought advisable, in consequence, to keep a force of soldiers at Manchester, and to send ships of war to the Tyne.

But the most dangerous symptoms of unrest were those that appeared in certain agricultural counties of the South and Midlands, especially those in which wages were exceptionally low,

---

[1] See the report by Mr. G. Cowen (in the *Wellington Despatches*, second series, vi. 502), dated 12 February 1830.

and the Speenhamland system of poor relief contributed to keeping wages down. For, if we can believe Cobbett, the 'parish wage', which was considered so intolerable a burden on property, did not afford to the workless families as much bread as they would have been allowed in gaol; and the man in full work earned no more than 7s. to 9s. a week.[1] A small spark was quite sufficient to set alight this mass of poverty. The threshing-machine, which took from the labourer the main chance of employment in the off-season, was in many districts the immediate cause of the riots of November 1830. These were widely spread, in South Hampshire and in Berks the magistrates were 'completely cowed', and in each of these districts a regiment had to be brought upon the scene to deal with the rioters who marched from one country house to another, levying contributions on each.[2] But in most cases these inconvenient symptoms of poverty and discontent were repressed by improvised patrols, raised by the Lords-Lieutenant of the counties and formed of the yeomanry with the local gentry and their retainers. Greville has much to tell at second hand of these encounters, and is at all events a good witness to attest the excitement which this pitiable attempt at a jacquerie roused in London drawing-rooms. The main centres of disturbance were Bucks., Hants, Wilts., and Berks. Nine years later the Duke of Wellington put on paper his recollection of the Hampshire *bellum servile* :—

'I induced the magistrates to put themselves on horseback, each at the head of his own servants and retainers, grooms, huntsmen, gamekeepers, armed with horsewhips, pistols, fowling pieces and what they could get, and to attack in concert, if necessary, or singly, these mobs, disperse them, destroy them, and take and put in confinement those who could not escape. This was done in a spirited manner, in many instances, and it is astonishing how soon the country was tranquillized, and that in the best way, by the activity and spirit of the gentlemen.'[3]

The Duke might have added that the work of pacification

---

[1] This was the range of wages in Berks., Hants, Sussex, Wilts., according to Cobbett's evidence in *Rural Rides*.

[2] Duke of Buckingham to Duke of Wellington, 22 November 1830 (Torrens, *Melbourne*, i. 348).

[3] *Wellington Despatches*, second series, viii. 388.

was completed by the indictment of 700 Hampshire rioters before a Special Commission, sitting at Winchester. Beside this outburst the other riots of the time, at Bristol, Derby, Nottingham, pale into insignificance; although the Bristol riot of October 1831 showed how easy it was for a few hundred rioters to throw a great city into confusion when the local magistrates were faint-hearted or taken by surprise.

It is quite probable that the disturbances would have blazed up over a much wider area, and with disastrous results, if there had existed any revolutionary organization to take advantage of the situation. Individual incendiaries there may have been. The Duke of Wellington, who attended the sittings of the Winchester Commission, reported to a friend that hardly one of the indicted persons belonged to the distressed classes. 'They were generally artificers in the receipt of from 18s. to one guinea a week, some publicans and persons certainly not of the honest classes of society.'[1] These of course were the ring-leaders. The Duke was inclined to see in them the instruments of a Jacobin club possibly situated in France:

'We have in this country, unfortunately, a very numerous class of men, well educated, who have no means of subsistence and who have no employment. These are the gentlemen who go about in gigs. . . . How are the gigs paid for?'[2]

The Duke was obliged to admit that, when in office, he and his colleagues had failed to discover any confirmation of these remarkable suspicions. But the suspicion was deeply rooted in his mind and in the minds of his friends. They felt that in resisting reform they were doing their best to neutralize the baneful influence of foreign ideas, possibly promoted by French conspirators. With the impression of the Hampshire riots still fresh in his mind he wrote to Mr. Gleig, his future biographer:

'I see in thirty members for the rotten boroughs thirty men, I don't care of what party, who would preserve the state of property as it is; who would maintain by their votes the Church of England, its posses-sions, churches, and universities; all our great institutions and corpora-tions; the union with Scotland and Ireland; the dominion of the

---

[1] *Wellington Despatches*, second series, vii. 388. But the evidence is conflicting. See Butler, *Great Reform Bill*, p. 133.
[2] *Op. cit.*, vii. 373.

country over its foreign colonies and possessions ; the national honour abroad and its good faith with the King's subjects at home.   I see men at the back of the government to protect individuals and their property against the injustice of the times which would sacrifice all rights and all property to a species of plunder called general convenience and utility.   I think that it is the presence of this description of men in Parliament, with the country gentlemen and the great merchants, bankers, and manufacturers, which constitutes the great difference between the House of Commons and those assemblies abroad called Chambers of Deputies.'[1]

The nearest approach to a political conspiracy that we can detect in the England of 1830 is the small body of middle-class Radicals, chiefly to be found in London and Birmingham, who organized the Political Unions, magnified Hampden Clubs, each claiming to represent 'the respectable and industrious classes' of a considerable area.   The leaders of the unions stoutly and, no doubt, sincerely professed their abhorrence of the argument of force.   Some of these leaders played with dangerous schemes. Attwood of Birmingham at one time suggested that the Tories might be driven out of power by a general refusal to pay any taxes.   Place thought that, if Lord Grey were turned out of office to make way for the Duke of Wellington, the appropriate reply would be to organize a run on the Bank of England. Attwood began in November 1831 to arrange that his followers should be organized in districts and sub-districts, under their own officers, to do the work of a volunteer constabulary and also to show the Tories that English Radicals could not be oppressed with impunity.[2]   It is no wonder that Melbourne and Althorp and Grey himself watched the activities of the Political Unions with some uneasiness even when the unions were working at high pressure to influence public opinion in favour of the Whig Reform Bill.   They thought it quite possible that the unions would survive the crisis which had called them into being, and become the nucleus of a self-constituted National Guard.   In fact the unions proved unexpectedly amenable.

[1] *Op. cit.*, viii. 21.

[2] It was stated in 1832 by Thomas Young, Melbourne's Radical secretary, that the Birmingham P. U. intended to invite Sir William Napier, the historian, to take command of their forces, if the Duke of Wellington had formed a ministry.

They had no French conspirators behind them. Nor were there any home-grown Lafayettes and Baboeufs to be found in their ranks.

Grey did not misconceive the situation so thoroughly as the Duke of Wellington; for Grey had colleagues who knew pretty accurately the measure of men like Attwood, Parkes, and Place. But Grey had a certain fellow feeling with the Duke. The main difference between them was that Grey hoped to save much of the old order of things by moderate concessions, and Wellington feared that the slightest concession would let in a flood of undiluted demagogy.. Grey was hopeful because he believed that the driving power of the Radical movement was supplied by the middle classes, who after all were men of property. Wellington was pessimistic because he imagined that the real leaders were those crypto-Jacobins, the penniless and voluble 'men in gigs'. Grey did not like the prospect of middle-class rule, but he regarded its approach in a spirit of fatalistic resignation. He told the King, in May 1831,

'that it was the spirit of the age which was triumphing; that to resist it was certain destruction; that nowhere would the King find any support for a backward step; that even Russia was unable to resist a handful of rebels.'[1]

He developed his views more fully in a letter to the Knight of Kerry, which Mr. Trevelyan has printed. There had been, he told this correspondent, a great change in the distribution of property since the Napoleonic wars. If a revolution was to be averted, a corresponding change must be made in the representative system. Greater influence must be given to the middle classes, 'who have made wonderful advances both in property and intelligence'. To refuse them this influence would be suicidal. If a moderate reform were refused, a republic would come into being and all established institutions would be destroyed.[2]

This attitude explains much, if not most of Grey's conduct during the political crisis of 1830–2. He was doing his best to save the old order, and he felt confident that he would receive

---

[1] *Letters of Princess Lieven* (ed. Robinson), p. 302.
[2] Trevelyan, *Lord Grey*, p. 237.

the support of many moderate men who had supported Wellington and Peel. Indeed he was surprised that these moderate men
had not compelled the Duke himself to become the sponsor of
a moderate Reform Bill. To satisfy his own followers, and to
honour the pledges that he himself had given in the past, he was
obliged to make more sweeping proposals, particularly with
regard to rotten boroughs, than any Tory statesman would be
likely to offer. But it was necessary to conciliate all waverers
in either House who could be mollified either by the respecta-
bility of the administration or by concessions on points of
secondary importance.

The ministry which Grey brought together was, politically
speaking, composed of the most incongruous elements---Lans-
downe Whigs, Canningites, Tory deserters, and semi-Radicals.
The bond which held them together was certainly one that
transcended party ties. None of the Canningites and few of the
Lansdowne Whigs felt the slightest enthusiasm for the one
measure which they were all pledged to support. But, with a
few exceptions, they were sound and respected members of the
ruling class, representing families which were deeply rooted in
the soil. On the day after his list was approved by the King,
Grey told Princess Lieven that his first object in compiling it
had been,

'to show that in these days of democracy and Jacobinism it is
possible to find real capacity in the high aristocracy—not that I wish to
exclude merit, if I should meet with it in the commonalty ; but, given
an equal merit, I admit that I should select the aristocrat ; for that
class is a guarantee for the security of the State and the Throne.'

Brave words! But it would be interesting to know what 'real
capacity' he had discovered in Lansdowne, Holland, Carlisle,
Goderich, and Charles Grant, all of whom were in the Cabinet.
Brougham and Durham were, in their several fashions, men of
great ability, but they were not well fitted for the work in hand.
There remained the Canningites—Palmerston, Graham, Melbourne—competent as administrators, but lukewarm towards
reform. Althorp in the Cabinet, Russell and Stanley outside
it, were the trio whose capacity would make or mar.[1]

---

[1] Creevey, 576, 639.

In private Grey showed a keen and perhaps too indiscreet appreciation of the foibles of his colleagues. 'Everybody told me there was nothing to be done without the two Grants, and they have never been worth a farthing.' 'Lord John Russell— very obstinate, very pert, and can be very rude.' 'Abercromby a perfect humbug.' 'It is not usual', writes Creevey, 'to amuse a Prime Minister by jokes upon members of his own Cabinet', but Creevey took the unusual course with the most complete success.

Yet the fact remains that Grey did hold together, for three years and a half, this curiously assorted ministry. Moreover he earned their loyalty, and in some cases their affection, in spite of frequent collisions between his old-fashioned views and the rather ruthless temper of his more energetic colleagues. He could be querulous, despondent, peevish when the fit was on him. But in a crisis he was bold and wary, as soon as the moment came for action ; and he held tenaciously to the essential features of his Reform Bill, when a man of less fore-sight and courage would eagerly have sought for peace in any kind of compromise.

Grey's share in the preparation of the Reform Bill can hardly have been considerable. He gave the instructions upon which the Drafting Committee worked, and these are precise enough so far as they go. The bill was to be sufficiently comprehensive to satisfy public opinion and to afford a sure ground for resist-ing further innovations ; in other words, the policy which Brougham favoured, of reform by instalments, was ruled out. Finality was not a word of Grey's invention, but a lasting settle-ment, 'an arrangement on which we can stand',[1] was what he most desired. Next he enjoined that the measure should be 'based on property and existing franchises' ; in other words, manhood suffrage was inadmissible, and no one was to lose the vote which he already possessed, unless indeed the constituency in which he voted was scheduled for extinction. Thirdly the measure was to be based on 'existing territorial divisions', the counties and the towns: the Radical demand for equal consti-tuencies was to be ignored.[2] When the Drafting Committee

---

[1] *Correspondence of Earl Grey and William IV*, i, p. 65.
[2] Parker's *Sir James Graham*, i. 120.

produced their scheme,[1] it was probably more sweeping than
Grey had contemplated.   For its chairman, Lord Durham, had
troubled his head little about Grey's susceptibilities, although
appointed as the minister most likely to know and to respect
them.   The Prime Minister accepted the scheme, but with
reservations which were by no means unimportant, some dictated
by respect for the King's scruples, others by his own convictions.
So voting by ballot disappeared; and the Septennial Act
remained unaltered, though the Committee had desired to limit
the duration of any Parliament to five years.   On the other
hand, Grey stood fast when Brougham pleaded for the preservation of a few close boroughs, without which ' there would be no
safe means of getting seats for persons in the Government.[2]

When the time arrived for negotiating with the waverers, it
was Grey who undertook to define the possibilities of compromise, and his definition was admirable.   Schedule A must
stand ; there must be no tampering with the ten-pound householder franchise, and no whittling down of the representation
provided for the great towns ; everything else was open to discussion.[3]   Once, in the great debate on the third bill in the
House of Lords, Grey declared (12 April, 1832) his readiness to
abandon, as a last resort, even the first and second of these
points ; but by that time he was certain of the waverers and can
hardly have expected to be driven to this sacrifice.   For, a
month later, when the Lords voted for the postponement of
Schedule A (7 May), he immediately resigned, leaving to his
opponents the responsibility, if they dared to assume it, of forming their own ministry and passing a truncated, one might even
say a decapitated bill.   Nothing could be more judicious than
his conduct at this juncture, when it was quite possible that the
folly of the Opposition combined with the folly of the King
might have led, not indeed to the rejection of the Whig scheme,
but to its acceptance under threats of mob violence and civil
war.   In that case the Reform Bill would have been not an
eirenicon, but a capitulation imposed at the sword's point.

It is possible that Althorp or even Lord John Russell would

---

[1] Text in *Correspondence of Earl Grey and William IV*, i, pp. 461-3.
[2] *Correspondence of Earl Grey and William IV*, i, pp. 81, 114.
[3] *Op. cit.*, ii. 213.   Schedule A disfranchized the worst rotten boroughs.

have managed the campaign against the Tory peers with equal skill, and it is highly probable that they had as much to do with its organization as the Prime Minister who spoke for them and for the whole Cabinet. But neither Althorp nor Russell carried the same weight as Grey in the country or the House of Lords; and neither of them could have managed the King so dexterously. The Court did not love Grey; it positively disliked his family; and it was his invidious duty to be continually correcting the King's theory of the royal prerogative. It was necessary to tell William IV that he must not criticize his ministers and their measures before leading members of the Opposition; that the Foreign Secretary was something more than the King's private secretary; and that the Army was a national institution, not the King's personal body-guard. Discussions of this kind did not help to establish cordial relations between King and minister, and yet the Government needed from the King, in the years 1831-2, much more that a correct neutrality. They needed his personal influence; they needed a promise that he would create peers up to any number which they thought advisable. Grey rose to the occasion. With what honesty and firmness, with what tact and consideration he controlled the vagaries and soothed the alarms of his wrong-headed, warm-hearted, and altogether irresponsible sovereign, is apparent from their correspondence in those agitated years. At heart a republican of the old Whig type, Grey had imagination enough to appreciate the vitality of the monarchical idea. He realized that, for many Englishmen who were by no means ultra-Tories, the prerogative was the keystone of the arch of the constitution, and the King himself the living symbol of national unity and the whole social order. By his Reform Bill he made the House of Commons the effective instrument of the popular will. By securing the co-operation of William IV he prevented the monarchy from committing suicide.

To these great services Mr. Trevelyan has done no more than justice. But it is necessary to emphasize the contrast between Lord Grey in his great moments, and Lord Grey in his more frequent, more prolonged periods of anxiety and suspense. Old age and ill health were sapping his vitality and his self-confidence, especially in the year 1832. He was terribly afraid of the consequences of creating peers on a large scale. 'I wish to God', he writes in January, 'that it could be avoided. I sometimes think we should have done better to resign on our defeat in the House of Lords.' Suppose that Palmerston should retire on this question, what would become of our foreign policy? Would not Melbourne and Richmond, Lansdowne and Stanley follow the lead of Palmerston? And how, after such defections, could the ministry be reconstructed? Althorp's advice was precisely what Grey himself would have given, in like circumstances, thirty or twenty or even ten years previously. Althorp wrote that ministers should honour their pledges and go out, if go out they must, with their characters unsoiled. 'If the bill be lost without a creation of peers, every one of us in whom the country at present places confidence will be utterly and entirely ruined in character.' Still Grey persisted in pleading for delay, in explaining his own reluctance to take the fateful step. 'I am conscious that my feeling is stronger than my reason. It is a measure of extreme violence; there is no precedent for it in our history, the case of Queen Anne's peers not being in point. It is a certain evil, dangerous as a precedent; and, with all these objections, in my opinion very uncertain of success.'[1] These fits of despondency passed over. They did not interrupt the negotiations of the Cabinet with the King, or alter ministerial strategy. But it is difficult to avoid the conclusion that Grey was only by fits and starts the 'daring pilot in extremity'. It was well that he had younger and more audacious colleagues to remind him that other objects had to be considered besides that of maintaining or strengthening the aristocratical element in the constitution.

Over the decline and fall of the Grey administration we must pass rapidly. The great adventure being over, and the lions driven from their path, ministers felt themselves at liberty to indulge in the luxury of divided opinions. They justified their existence as a ministry by passing three useful and important measures—the Factory Act of 1833, the Act for the emancipation of slaves throughout the Empire, and the new Poor Law. These measures were not of their own devising, and were not

[1] Le Marchant, *Althorp*, pp. 386, 404-5, 413. Cf. the observations of Lord Broughton on Grey's conduct in February 1832 (*Recollections*, iv, pp. 174-9).

party questions. They were taken up by ministers with the honourable intention of proving to the nation that the reformed House of Commons would concern itself with all the problems of social reform which the unreformed House had systematically shelved.

But ministers were privately more occupied with other problems—especially with their own differences concerning foreign policy and Irish policy. Already Palmerston's colleagues were discovering the absence of any distinctive Whiggish note in his diplomacy, and lamenting his interest in Portugal, his lack of interest in Poland, and his firmness in dealing with the inconvenient aspirations of continental liberalism, whether in Belgium or in France. Grey might boast that he kept Palmerston in order and himself corrected all dispatches. But Durham and Russell were both convinced of their superior fitness for the charge of foreign affairs. Early in 1834 there was a Cabinet crisis over Portugal, on the question whether we should or should not intervene to defend the Constitutionalists against the followers of Dom Miguel. Grey and Palmerston, who favoured intervention, were overruled by the majority, although they had for once the approval of Lord John Russell. Grey was deeply mortified, since he still thought of foreign policy as his peculiar province. He was with difficulty dissuaded from resigning.[1] In this case Palmerston retrieved the situation, for himself and for his chief, by broadening his plans, to include Spain as well as Portugal, and by taking Talleyrand into partnership. His Quadruple Alliance was audaciously presented to his colleagues as a union of the constitutional governments of Western Europe against the despotic powers of the East. ' I carried it through the Cabinet by a *coup de main*, taking them by surprise, and not leaving them time to make objections.'[2]

But the problem of Ireland was more intractable, and lay outside the sphere of Palmerston's activities. Grey's views on Ireland, except where Catholic relief was concerned, did not differ substantially from those of Wellington ; he was not prepared to consider any compromise about tithes or about the Act of Union. But in April 1831 Grey did take the extra-

[1] *Letters of Princess Lieven* (ed. Robinson), p. 365.
[2] Ashley, *Palmerston*, i. 297.

ordinary step of endeavouring to come to terms with O'Connell, at a time when the Viceroy and his advisers were indicting O'Connell on a large variety of counts. The intermediary was Sir Francis Burdett, who was authorized to promise an arrest of judgement, and also to state that if the movement in favour of Repeal were suspended, 'a new state of. things would arise '. O'Connell took the offer and threw his energies for the time being into Irish electioneering, on the side of the Reformers. In the autumn Grey wrote again to Burdett to express the hope that 'a useful connexion' might soon be arranged with O'Connell.[1] A truce was in fact arranged, through Sir Henry Parnell and Bishop Doyle, to hold good until the Reform Bill was carried.[2] It lasted until the meeting of the first reformed Parliament (Feb. 1833) when it was destroyed by the decision of the Whigs to pass a Coercion Act. In the session of 1834 O'Connell inaugurated a new Repeal campaign.

The Coercion Act was the main count of O'Connell against the Whigs. This Act, passed for one year only, would expire in the session of 1834, unless it was renewed. Various members of the Government had made up their minds that it could not or should not be renewed without the omission of the clauses which restricted the right of public meeting. Althorp detested them as quite inconsistent with Whig principles and was prepared to resign if they were perpetuated. Littleton, the Chief Secretary, and Brougham, the Chancellor, thought that the Coercion Act could not be renewed without the help of the Irish parliamentary party, who would of course fight against the meeting clauses. On the other hand, Grey had made up his mind that nothing less than the whole Act would suffice to stop the Irish tithe war, and he intended to resign unless the whole Act were renewed.

Under these circumstances Brougham and Littleton appealed to the Viceroy, Lord Wellesley, for help. Wellesley had committed himself to the view that the whole bill was required.

---

[1] Grey's letters to Burdett on this subject, dated 3 April and 22 October 1831 are among the Burdett papers. They were brought to my notice by my friend the Rev. M. W. Patterson, who is engaged on a biography of Burdett.

[2] Dunlop, *O'Connell*, pp. 261-2.

His correspondents begged him to adopt their view and to inform the Prime Minister that he had changed his mind. Wellesley complied with the request, and Littleton, imprudently assuming that Lord Grey would fall into line, gave definite assurances to O'Connell that the obnoxious clauses would be struck out. But Grey was obstinate. He threatened to resign unless the Cabinet would stand by his original decision. They reluctantly agreed, and the Coercion Act was brought up for renewal without the alterations which O'Connell was confidently expecting. When he accused Littleton of bad faith, and disclosed Littleton's confidential promises, Grey realized that three or four of his colleagues, including the leader of the House of Commons, had combined to frustrate his own considered policy.[1] Grey and Althorp resigned on 8 July 1834, and the King sent for Lord Melbourne to form a new ministry.

The end of the old ministry was ignominious but not altogether accidental. It was not only on the Irish question that Grey was losing the confidence of his colleagues. At critical times they were beginning to look to Althorp for their lead. And on this occasion it could not be doubted that Althorp took up the right Whig position. Since 1792 the Whigs had been accustomed to presume that coercive laws were the last resource of corrupt or incapable governments. If the position in Ireland was still desperate after two years of terrorism, was it not high time to look for other remedies, measures not of coercion but of conciliation. Was it really impossible to defend the rights of Irish tithe owners without courts martial and the suspension of the right of public meeting ?

Lord Grey remained until his death the titular chief of the Whig party. The more Radical of its members looked on him with ill-disguised contempt. ' The more I see, the less I think of this really inferior man ', is the verdict of Hobhouse in 1836.[2] But in 1835 the Whig leaders wished to take service under him again and to put the control of foreign affairs into his hands. He refused because he had lost all desire to be in politics. He

---

[1] The relevant letters from the Wellesley papers, the Hatherton papers, and the Althorp papers are epitomized in Aspinall's *Brougham* (1927), pp. 195–6.

[2] Lord Broughton's *Recollections*, v, p. 55.

was shocked and bewildered by the newest developments of
Whiggism. The first blow was that Durham, his own son-in-
law, publicly declared his predilection for the ballot and for
short parliaments. Such a declaration amounted to a rejection
of the settlement of 1832. ' I could have anticipated nothing so
bad ', wrote Grey ; ' the measures to which he has pledged himself I feel myself bound by every obligation of honour and duty
to oppose.'[1] But worse things were to follow. The Whigs,
evicted from office by the King to make way for Peel, invited
the Irish and the Radical parties to attend a meeting of the
Opposition, and went on to conclude the Lichfield House
Treaty with the Irish. Though he was assured by his old
friends that the Treaty would expire automatically with Peel's
resignation, Grey fumed and fretted at the tacit agreement
between Lord John Russell and O'Connell which obviously continued in being long after the Whigs returned to office. Sooner
or later he predicted the Whigs would burn their fingers, would
find themselves compromised by that unnatural partnership.
' I have never had and never will have any communication with
a man whose conduct has been beyond any example, except
that of the worst man at the beginning of the French Revolution, unprincipled and brutal.'[2] Had Grey then forgotten those
pourparlers of 1831, in which Burdett had been his go-between ?
One would imagine so. At all events he did not fully realize
the straits to which his party was reduced after 1834.

It is with the new Whiggism of the 'thirties and the 'forties,
the Whiggism of Lord John Russell, that we must now concern
ourselves.

[1] Reid's *Durham*, i. 389-95 ; *Correspondence of Earl Grey with Princess
Lieven*, iii. 37.

[2] *Correspondence of Earl Grey with Princess Lieven*, iii. 184.

X

THE WHIGS AND THEIR ALLIES, 1831–1848

THE years 1831–41 are characterized by a great and even feverish activity in legislation. Russell's principle was to provide Parliament in every session with one bill of capital importance, and there were years in which the exigencies of party politics compelled the Whigs to bring forward several first-class measures simultaneously. He and most of his friends thought it a misfortune that the even progress of the legislative machine should be disturbed by debates on questions of foreign and colonial policy; and in dealing with home affairs their tendency was to think more of legislation than of purely administrative reforms. This was a new tendency, fostered by the alliance between the Whigs and Radicals which began in 1830. The Radicals believed that legislation was the supreme duty of a Parliament; even the most intelligent of them supposed that good laws and plenty of them would bring back the age of gold. The Whigs were generally less sanguine; but they realized that the ten-pound householder demanded legislation, and they were willing now and then to stretch a point of orthodox doctrine for the purpose of giving him the kind of legislation that he expected and could understand. Only the ballot, the further extension of the Parliamentary franchise, and more frequent elections were tabooed. For the plain truth was that the Whigs at all times needed a proportion of Radical votes to make their ascendancy secure. Even in 1833, after the first general election held under the Reform Act, the Parliamentary situation was precarious. The Whigs held in that year 320 seats, the Tories 150, the Radicals (including O'Connell's followers) 190.[1]

While the Radicals were still intoxicated with their new importance, the Whigs were actually driven to rely upon the

---

[1] Parker's *Peel*, ii. 209; Bulwer's *Palmerston*, ii. 212; *Edinburgh Review*, lvi, p. 543, gives the number of staunch Tories as 130 to 140, the half-hearted as 15 to 20.

contemptuous and grudging help of Peel, who had determined not to make common cause with Cobbett and O'Connell even when (as in the case of the Irish Coercion Bill) he privately shared their point of view. It seemed to Russell and to Althorp quite intolerable that they should govern upon sufferance in this way. Their first instinct was to make friends with as many as possible of the English Radicals. But in 1835 they stumbled more by accident than design into the Lichfield House Compact with O'Connell. It was in form a temporary alliance, which involved no sacrifice of principle on either side, and was due to terminate as soon as Peel should be turned out of office. Actually it survived, without being formally renewed, until O'Connell turned his attention to the Repeal campaign of 1840. While it lasted the Whigs were sure of forty to fifty Irish votes at a pinch. This was the only considerable block of votes which could always be purchased by some timely concession. The O'Connellites, unlike the English Radicals, were an organized party. By themselves the O'Connellites were not numerous enough to give the Whigs an assured majority. But any measure which satisfied O'Connell was reasonably sure to catch Radical votes in a greater or less degree.

The Parliamentary situation goes far to explain the general course of Whig legislation. Up to the end of 1835 it was framed specially with an eye to the principles and the suscepti- bilities of the English ten-pound householder. Afterwards Irish legislation had the first call on Russell's attention.

We have next to observe that, in the first of these two periods, there was no definite alliance between the Whigs and the English Parliamentary Radicals. There was no alliance because the Radical group had no organization and no recognized leader. Some of its ablest members prided themselves on being abso- lutely independent and voting as the reason or conscience of each individual might dictate. Those who looked to Lord Durham as their eventual Prime Minister were induced by his adviser, Joseph Parkes, to organize themselves in the winter of 1834–5.[1] It was hoped that seventy or eighty Radical members might be brought together in a solid block, under one acknow-

---

[1] Letters of J. S. Mill, i. 110; Torrens's *Melbourne*, ii. 66; Buckley, *Joseph Parkes*, pp. 135, 159.

ledged head. But no acceptable leader was forthcoming. Joseph
Hume had in his favour an intimate knowledge of parliamentary
procedure and public finance; Grote's was the ablest brain of
the party; Charles Buller was an acute and ready speaker. But
not one of the three had the art of leadership or could dominate
a critical assembly. Thomas Duncombe and Sir William Molesworth and Charles Villiers owed such parliamentary reputation
as they possessed to their connexions and social influence. Only
when Cobden appeared on the political scene could the English
Radicals boast of any spokesman who was capable of sitting
with credit in a Cabinet, or of inspiring the whole group with
a common purpose.

In the 'thirties and in the 'forties the Radicals were more
formidable in the country than in the House of Commons.
Individually insignificant, they represented the ideas which were
in the air, and they circulated their ideas more energetically
than the politicians of other schools. They had a firm grip on
the daily and the periodical press. They provided the *Morning
Chronicle* with its best contributors. They controlled, through
Albany Fonblanque, the *Examiner*, through Perronet Thompson and John Stuart Mill the *Westminster Review*. Their
influence on opinion was out of all proportion to their numbers
or political efficiency. But in the House of Commons they
allowed themselves to be slighted, divided, and exploited. They
were too angular, too dogmatic. Each man of them had his
infallible nostrum for the diseases of the body politic, and was
either puzzled or irritated when the subject under discussion
was one to which his small stock of dogmas supplied no key.
In short they were impractical. The Radical legislation of this
period was not their work. It was inspired by men like
Chadwick, Parkes, and Cobden, who had served their apprenticeship and formed their views in an atmosphere less rarefied than
that of Westminster. The Whigs treated the Radical parlia-
mentarians with a cold civility which was nearly akin to contempt, and looked over their heads to catch the eyes of the new
electorate. For that electorate, with the help of men who were
not professional politicians, the Whigs provided the Slave
Emancipation Act and the Factory Act of 1833, the Poor Law
Amendment Act of 1834, and the Municipal Corporation Act

of 1835. The last legislative project of this kind in the great Whig era was the Corn Law Amendment Bill which died still-born in 1841.

These well-known measures need not be described in all their details here. From our special point of view they only deserve notice in so far as they reveal the growth of a new Whiggism coloured, not to say tainted, with ideas which old-fashioned Whigs suspected or abhorred.

(1) Fox and Grey were responsible for the Act of 1807 abolishing the Slave Trade. But their party was not committed to the abolition of slavery itself. The Whigs felt, as Canning had felt, a strong reluctance to interfere in the internal affairs of colonies which possessed representative institutions. They gave no pledges about slavery at the general election of 1830, and declined, in the session of 1831, to take any action. The Anti-Slavery Society, which represented an overwhelming body of opinion in the churches and the chapels, forced the subject forward by putting up Fowell Buxton to move for total abolition (15 April), when the fate of the first Reform Bill was hanging in the balance and a general election seemed imminent. Althorp dexterously compromised with the society by offering preferential treatment to the sugar of those colonies which ameliorated the condition of their slaves by accepting the rules of the Order in Council of 1823 ;[1] and the Government ordered the immediate manumission of all slaves of the Crown. The first of these steps was denounced by the legislature of Jamaica as an un-constitutional proceeding; and the Whigs in general thought that it would be unwise to embark on a quarrel with the West India interest, although Brougham, their own Chancellor, presented a monster petition from the Abolitionists.

So matters remained until the end of 1832. But on the 23rd of November Wilberforce urged Fowell Buxton to present an ultimatum. ' I really believe ', he wrote, ' that, if you cannot get Government to concede to your wishes, you might carry the measure in the House of Commons.'[2] Buxton acted at once, and the ministers promptly opened negotiations. They were

[1] Not a single colony accepted this Order (*Hansard*, third series, xvii. 1205).

[2] *Life of W. Wilberforce*, v. 351.

on the point of a general election, and they had good reason
to know the voting strength of the Abolitionists.   Sir James
Graham, on behalf of the Cabinet, interviewed Buxton, and held
out hopes of an Emancipation Bill in the next session.   He did
more; he stated that Government would adopt as their own
any safe and practicable measure that Buxton could propose.
Buxton then asked that the slaves should immediately become
apprentices, working for reasonable hours at reasonable wages
on five days of the week; that complete emancipation should
be granted within two years, after which the negro would be
at liberty either to cultivate his own land or to work for a
master of his own choosing on such terms as he could get.   For
a short time, Buxton added, it might be necessary to impose
severe penalties on idleness and vagrancy.   He was willing that
the planters should be assisted by loans from the State, and
that the question of compensation should be discussed after five
or ten years, when the losses of the planters could be ascertained.
To these terms Graham agreed; he said that they corresponded
with his own views and those of his colleagues; and he asked
for a written statement.

Thus encouraged, the Abolitionists were energetic at the
polls, and Emancipation proved one of the most popular cries
of the Whig party.   But within the Cabinet unexpected difficulties arose, and the Abolitionists were surprised and indignant
when the King's Speech, at the opening of the new session, was
found to contain no mention of Emancipation.   Lord Grey
was the chief stumbling-block; he argued that there was no
time available; he also told his colleagues that the objections
of William IV could not be overcome.[1]   A second ultimatum
from Buxton was necessary before Grey would reconsider his
decision.   The Colonial Office was instructed to prepare a draft,
but this document (prepared by Howick, James Stephen, and
Henry Taylor) failed to satisfy the Cabinet—probably because
the authors sympathized with Buxton's demand that apprenticeship should only be enforced for a short period.[2]   On 28 March

---

[1] Le Merchant, *Spencer*, pp. 469–70.
[2] Sir Henry Taylor, *Autobiography*, i. 129, gives no details of this plan.
But we have Buxton's statement that Howick resigned because his plan was
rejected.   See *Hansard*, xviii. 157.

Stanley became Secretary of State for the Colonies in place of Goderich; Howick resigned the under-secretaryship; and Stanley proceeded to concoct a 'safe scheme' in consultation with Sir James Graham.[1]

That scheme appeared at first before the House of Commons in the form of five resolutions (14 May 1833), of which the two most important provided that every slave should serve a period of apprenticeship, to be fixed by Parliament, before receiving complete freedom, and that the planters should be assisted by a loan not exceeding fifteen millions sterling. Early in June the basis of the scheme of compensation was changed, Stanley accepting a proposal of the West India interest that a free grant of twenty millions should be substituted for a loan of fifteen.[2] Late in July Stanley balanced this concession to the planters by another to the Abolitionists; he reduced the period of apprenticeship from twelve years to seven,[3] on finding that he had a majority of no more than seven votes for the original and longer period.

More than once, in the course of the debates, Opposition speakers referred caustically to the extraordinary openness of mind which ministers displayed on questions of this magnitude. The three who were principally concerned—Stanley, Graham, and Althorp—took Abolition in hand without any special knowledge of the difficulties by which it was beset, and Lord Howick, who had been active in the earlier stages of the ministerial discussions, confessed in Parliament that, so late as 1830, he had believed that no real need existed for Parliamentary interference with the rights of the slave-owners.[4] There is no reason to doubt the sincerity of his conversion; it was the natural result of his close association with Stephen and Taylor at the Colonial Office, and of his own strong sense of justice. Stanley and Althorp, whom Howick criticized for yielding so much to the planters, were undoubtedly thinking more of the Abolitionist electorate and the West Indian interest than of the slaves whom they emancipated.

It was inevitable that Emancipation should bring the Whigs into collision with the West Indian legislatures, who had proved

---

[1] Taylor, p. 132.
[2] *Hansard*, xviii. 322, 550.
[3] *Op. cit.*, xix. 1254.
[4] *Op. cit.*, xvii. 1240.

themselves quite incorrigible when invited by Canning and by Goderich (Stanley's immediate predecessor) to mitigate the lot of their slave population. It may well be that Stanley aggravated a difficult position by his scathing criticism of these legislatures, and by his peremptory enunciation of the *arcanum imperii* which Burke had desired to shroud in obscurity :

' I do not pretend to enter into that nice discussion, or to argue that grave constitutional question which affects to settle where the power of Parliament over Colonial Assemblies terminates. Except by the authority of Parliament itself, I know of no such termination ; and if there be those who vindicate the right of Colonial Assemblies to set themselves in opposition to the laws, regulations, and avowed determinations of Parliament, I call upon them to show . . . how it is possible that a delegated authority should exceed the authority of the body from which it is derived. In 1778 undoubtedly Parliament passed that Declaratory Act which limited its own power ; it did so then, not denying or abandoning its right, but waiving it, and declaring that in the single case of internal taxation, Parliament would not make a claim on those colonies which had assemblies of their own. The right of regulating matters of trade no man will deny ; but on the right of interfering with, or of making, internal regulations some honourable Members may raise a doubt. I know not when that right of internal regulation was abandoned.'[1]

Stanley was not a final authority on Whig principles, but he undoubtedly convinced his colleagues of 1833 that they had come to a parting of the ways in imperial affairs, when they must either assert the authority of Great Britain over the Empire as it had not been asserted since 1778, or else resign themselves to watch the disintegration of the Empire. In 1839 Russell found himself faced, both in Canada and in Jamaica, with the necessity of defining the rights and powers of a colonial legislature. He took in each case the line which Stanley had indicated. With reference to Lower Canada he repudiated the principle ' that all internal affairs should be governed according to the will of the majority of the Assembly ', and added :

' It is quite impossible to allow it to be laid down, as a general principle, that any part of the government of this country, conducted by Ministers having the sanction of this House, shall be overruled by a

[1] *Op. cit.*, xvii. 1207-8.

colony, and that such colony shall not be subject to the general superintending authority of the Crown of these realms.' [1]

He qualified this general statement by the remark that on some questions it was obviously undesirable that the Secretary of State for the Colonies should overrule a representative assembly. But this saving clause was not intended to affect the principle of law. Remembering what the issues were in Lower Canada in 1839, we are bound to admit that Russell went a good deal beyond Stanley in pressing the claims of the mother-country to supervise and overrule colonial legislatures. Stanley claimed to intervene in the West Indies in the name of common humanity. Russell frankly claimed for the Colonial Secretary the last word on every contentious question.

(2) The Factory Act of 1833 raised momentous issues, some of which will be discussed hereafter in another connexion. Here we have only to notice the treatment that it received from ministers. They frankly adopted an attitude of suspense, both when the measure was in Sadler's hands, and when Ashley asked leave to reintroduce it, after Sadler's death. In the debate of 3 April 1833, when Ashley's opponents were demanding a Parliamentary Commission, Russell, acting for the moment as leader of the House, reassured Ashley by stating that the subject of the bill was one on which Parliament ought to legislate, and that the only question was how to legislate in the best manner.[2] On June 17 Althorp announced that he would not oppose the second reading as he considered that it was necessary to put some restriction on the labour of children [3] under fourteen years of age by limiting them to an eight-hours day, instead of the ten-hours day which Ashley's bill proposed. He left it to be inferred that he objected to interfering with the hours of work for all of fourteen years and upwards. In this matter Althorp followed the findings of the Commissioners (Tooke, Chadwick, and Southwood Smith) who were not the creatures

[1] *Speeches of Lord John Russell*, ii. 68–9. This doctrine was criticized in a public letter by Joseph Howe of Halifax, Nova Scotia, as a claim of unlimited prerogative (Kennedy, *Const. Docs. of Canada*, no. cxl).

[2] *Hansard*, third series, xvii. 111.   [3] *Op. cit.*, xviii. 914.

of the ministry, but very able exponents of the views of middle-class radicalism.

Althorp appears to have believed that their verdict on Ashley's bill was bound to be the ultimate verdict of the country. He was also impressed by the statement of the Commissioners that the ulterior object of Ashley's working-class friends was a ten-hours day for old and young alike, and that the ten-hours day for young persons of ages fourteen to eighteen could not be combined with a longer day for the elder hands. Althorp persuaded himself that mills running no more than ten hours a day would be ruined by foreign competition. But he was prepared to enforce a twelve-hours day and did so by an amendment which attracted less attention than it deserved. In the protection of children he was prepared to go farther than Ashley. He gave them the eight-hours day in all factories except silk-mills. He proposed the amendment which provided that every mill employing child-labour should be subject to inspection—an amendment which, as Mr. and Mrs. Hammond well remark, was an innovation of capital importance,[1] making this Act, what no Act of the kind had been before, a genuine protection to those whom it was designed to protect. Althorp does not appear to have believed that Ashley's bill, so altered by his amendments, was the last word on the subject. He reminded his hearers that it could always be extended in future, when a case for extension was established. All that he desired was to proceed with caution, lest they should inadvertently ruin the manufacturing system that they were bent on reforming.[2] Althorp would never have originated a Factory Act. But when the need for such an Act became apparent, he exerted himself to make the measure as effectual as might be within the narrow sphere in which he believed that State interference was reasonable and just.

(3) The New Poor Law for England and Wales was not exactly an extempore performance, hastily concocted from the evidence which the Poor Law Commission brought together.

---

[1] It is curious that these writers refuse to give Althorp any credit for this new departure. See his remarks in *Hansard*, xix. 223.

[2] *Op. cit.*, xix. 887.

The Whigs, as we have seen, had paid considerable attention in 1820–4 to the defects of the Old Poor Laws; and the credit of setting the Poor Law Commissioners to work belongs to three Whigs—Althorp, Brougham, Lord John Russell—who had taken part in the earlier inquiries. But the remedies proposed by the Commissioners were inseparably bound up with an innovation which was thoroughly distasteful to the average Whig. Not content with formulating general principles of action, some of which had been foreshadowed in the Russell report of 1824, they recommended that the control of poor relief should be entrusted to a permanent Commission wielding large discretionary powers, including the power to issue general orders which, in their generality, were suspiciously like Acts of Parliament. It was in vain that the Government called attention to the safeguards by which this power of making orders was circumscribed. True it was that an aggrieved body of rate-payers could appeal to the Court of King's Bench against an order which they conceived to be illegal; true also that no order could be enforced until a Secretary of State had given it his approval. These salutary restraints were, however, so little esteemed that one Radical member of Parliament bitterly complained of the new despotism. It seemed, he said, that the Commissioners had authority both to levy taxes and to legislate. What then had become of the sovereignty of the King in Parliament?[1]

Philosophic Radicals, however, such as George Grote and Edward Buller were delighted. The former urged that without the permanent Commission no reform was possible; Buller praised the idea, upon which this expedient was founded, of 'a controlling power remote from local influence, free from local prejudice, which would have the will and the ability to administer the law firmly, impartially, and justly'. But the Whigs themselves cannot have been quite comfortable. For Althorp thought it necessary to justify the appointment of the Commissioners at each stage of the discussion of the bill. On the first reading he stated bluntly that it was necessary to create some kind of discretionary power which would be guided by experience in making rules and orders. On the second reading

[1] Colonel De Lacy Evans, in the debate on the second reading of the Poor Law Amendment Bill (*Hansard*, third series, xxiii. 806).

he argued that in the past a discretionary power had been given to the justices of the peace in fixing the rate of relief, and that it was impossible to provide for all contingencies by an Act of Parliament. On the third reading he argued that it would be dangerous to introduce the new system otherwise than gradually and that the Commissioners must be allowed to decide at what time it was expedient to make the changes ordered by the Act. Althorp, always at heart something of a Radical, accepted the novel expedient of a Commission without misgiving ; and so did Brougham, who devoted himself with his usual vivacity to the task of convincing the Lords that the Commission was indispensable and was not unconstitutional. But neither Althorp's plain good sense nor Brougham's dialectic could disguise the Radical origin of the new machinery, which betrayed itself in their best arguments, and more especially in those of Brougham. It is strange to find a Whig Chancellor criticizing self-government in local affairs :

'Generally speaking I am willing to adopt that principle. . . . Nevertheless experience certainly does show that it is not universally applicable ; or rather that it is not applicable to places where the concerns of a number of persons are managed by a majority of their body and not each man's by himself; for when a certain leaven of men gets into an assembly, all of whom have a voice in the management of the common concerns, it very often happens that a combination takes place, arising from sinister and interested views ; and that this junta, by its activity and intrigues, baffles the general disposition to consult the common interest and sets it at nought.'

' The bad practices have taken such root and spread so widely that a strong hand alone can extirpate them. But it must be not only strong, it must be ever ready ; in other words all must be left to the discretion of the men intrusted.'[1]

What is this but Bentham's demand for a ruthless and omnipotent State which will make war on every corrupt interest ?

The general Whig defence of the New Poor Law was much simpler than this. ' The Poor Law Act has saved the land ', writes the Duke of Bedford in 1841.[2] Just for this reason there were influential Whigs who disliked it, amongst them Lord

[1] Brougham's speech of 21 July 1834 in the House of Lords (*Speeches*, ii, pp. 503, 511).
[2] *Later Correspondence of Lord John Russell*, i, p. 37.

Melbourne, of whom his biographer says that he only acquiesced in the new law because he had no alternative to propose. Melbourne thought that the workhouse test was a cruel one to apply to the most ignorant and helpless classes in the country.

(4) The Municipal Corporation Bill of 1835 was a considerable measure, even if it is judged in the light of its consequences, which were much smaller than either opponents or supporters expected. It reduced the number of corporate boroughs in England and Wales from 246 to 178. It endowed these boroughs with a uniform municipal franchise and a uniform constitution. The right of voting at municipal elections was given to all resident householders or shopkeepers who contributed to the poor rate. The government was vested in a town-council, composed of aldermen and councillors. The councillors were elected by the qualified ratepayers. No one could be a councillor unless he possessed the necessary qualification, which in the larger boroughs was £1,000 capital or a tenement rated at £30, in smaller boroughs £500 capital or a tenement rated at £15. A councillor was to hold office for three years, but one-third of the councillors was to retire in each year. The aldermen were to be elected by the councillors and to hold office for six years. The mayor, ex-officio chairman of the town-council, was to be elected by that body for one year, but to be re-eligible.

This constitution, which in its essentials still exists, was the outcome of prolonged discussions in both Houses of Parliament, and was in some of its features a compromise between the conflicting opinions of the Whig majority in the Commons and the Tory majority in the Lords.

The debates in both Houses were animated, because on both sides it was believed that the remodelling of the corporations might lead to far-reaching changes in the British constitution. The corporate boroughs were the strongholds of the middle-class from whom so much was feared by one political party and expected by the other. It was widely supposed that the political opinions of the middle-class would be affected by the form and spirit of the municipal institutions under which its members lived. Therefore the Radicals desired that every corporate borough should be a pure democracy, endowed with universal suffrage, or at the worst with household suffrage, electing all officials and representatives by ballot and for no longer period than one year; while the Tories demanded, more vaguely, but not less earnestly, that the aristocratic principle and the monarchic principle should be somehow recognized, and that no one should possess the municipal franchise without some property qualification.

Before it reached its final and much chastened form the Municipal Corporation Act was resented by the rank and file of the Tories as essentially a Radical measure. They pointed out that, with the trifling exception of the Scottish Corporation Reform Act of 1833, there was no precedent for parliamentary interference with the charters which the Crown had granted to municipal corporations.[1] The bill of 1835 trenched, in their opinion, both upon the prerogative of the Crown and upon the rights of the electors and the elected in the old municipalities. The wrongs of the hereditary freeman were the subject of passionate harangues. Other speakers criticized the injustice of proscribing more than two hundred corporations by a single Act of Parliament and the folly of endowing all the corporate boroughs with precisely the same institutions. The Act was denounced as a theoretical, a levelling measure; based upon the mere and unfounded assumption of the Municipal Reform Commissioners that a government controlled by the people would be more honest, more efficient, more economical than the best of the old types of corporate body. It was said to be (and no doubt it was) part of a deep-laid design for destroying the wholesome influence of property on local government. Mr. Scarlett averred, in the debate on the third reading, that the superior stability of the British constitution ' might be traced to the fact that the landed proprietors of this country had been awarded a considerable influence over the population of towns'. This happy state of equilibrium would now be destroyed:

' By this Bill the Legislature is about to establish in every town a pure and unmixed republican government, to abolish the aristocratic principle, and in short to interfere with monarchical authority.'[2]

---

[1] This point was taken by Mr. Gladstone in the debate of 20 July (*Hansard*, third series, xxix. 756), although he expressed approval of the general principle of making municipal officers elective.

[2] *Hansard*, third series, xxix. 757.

The truth is that the bill of 1835 was essentially a Radical measure. It was founded on the report of the Municipal Corporation Commission, and this document was the work of two earnest Radicals, Joseph Parkes and John Blackburne. Parkes himself states that he convinced Melbourne of the necessity for conceding household suffrage at a time when the Cabinet were doubtful; and Parkes was delighted with the bill as it emerged from the hands of the draftsman, Sir John Campbell. In this draft there were no aldermen, no property qualification was required of a councillor, and the freemen of corporate boroughs were deprived of the municipal franchise and of all exclusive rights of trading. 'We *buske* the Freemen', wrote Parkes to Durham.[1]

It is interesting to observe in these debates how thoroughly Russell identified himself with the views of his Radical supporters. On 5 June 1835 he defended with spirit the proposal that all ratepayers should have the municipal franchise. He said that even the lowest class of ratepayers were capable of taking an intelligent interest in the government of their own town. And it was equitable that they should have the vote, since they would all pay the borough rate. They ought to have a voice in the expenditure of their own money.[2] On 30 June he resisted Peel's amendment for attaching a property qualification to the office of Common Councillor. Not content with reminding the House that in London no such qualification was required, he went on to say that reason and principle were in favour of allowing the municipal electors to make an unrestricted choice. If the House had no confidence in the discretion of the electors it would be better to refuse them the right of making these elections.[3] This was a courageous line to take, for some parliamentary Radicals openly expressed the hope that this concession to their principles would prove the thin end of the wedge and that the time was not far distant when no property qualification would be required of members of the House of Commons.[4] Still more courageous was his warning to the House that the Municipal Reform Bill 'was at this time

---

[1] See J. K. Buckley, *Joseph Parkes of Birmingham* (1926), chap. 7.

[2] *Hansard*, third series, xxviii. 541.

[3] *Op. cit.*, third series, xxix. 115.   [4] *Op. cit.*, xxix. 113 (Mr. Ewart).

called for by the general voice of the Country, and that it was due to the spirit of the age—that such a Bill should become the law of the land '.[1]

The House of Lords did not venture to reject a bill which had the support of Sir Robert Peel and of most Tories in the Lower House. But the bill was considerably amended in the Lords. A property qualification for councillors was introduced ;[2] and a clause was inserted providing that one-quarter of the councillors should hold office for life. The first of these amendments was accepted in principle by the Government and the House of Commons, although the Commons were successful in persuading the Lords to accept a lower qualification than that originally proposed. The second amendment was rejected, but the Lords agreed to a counter-amendment providing that one-third of the council should be styled aldermen and should hold office for six years instead of the ordinary term of three years. The Lords were able to congratulate themselves on having bridled, to some extent, the will of the majority as expressed in municipal elections ; and it is probable that Russell himself was not displeased at the result. He had loyally fulfilled his compact with the parliamentary Radicals, and had passed a measure which gave great satisfaction to an important section of the parliamentary electorate; but he had been saved by his political opponents from endowing the municipalities with a purely Benthamite constitution, which might have furnished a new argument for a radical reform of the parliamentary franchise and of Parliament itself.

From these illustrations of the effects of the alliance with the English Radicals we may now turn to consider the dealings of the Whigs with Ireland. Some little time before the Lichfield House Compact was signed, Russell had decided to make himself specially acquainted with the needs of Ireland, and to construct an Irish policy. He had at first no intention of making common cause with O'Connell. He believed that the discontent of Ireland was a running sore, which might prove mortal to the Union unless it received prompt and sympathetic attention. He believed that it should be possible to cure this discontent by

[1] *Op. cit.*, xxix. 751.
[2] As Peel had proposed in the Commons (*op. cit.*, xxix. 99).

measures which left the Union intact and the Castle system of government unaltered. He was not satisfied with Stanley's brusque and narrow policy of the years 1831-2. That the Government should uphold the tithe-owner's rights of property, even by the use of armed force, was no doubt inevitable when the Tithe War broke out in 1831. But the presumption was, so Russell argued, that the wholesale resistance of the Irish peasants arose from some general and deep-seated sense of injustice. Stanley has assumed that the grievance would be obviated by shifting the burden of the tithe from the shoulders of the peasant to those of the landlord, and with that end in view passed the Irish Tithe Composition Act (1832). But experience soon showed that this remedy was insufficient, and Stanley proceeded to introduce the Coercion Bill of 1833—a measure which combined all or nearly all the different methods of dealing with Irish riots and conspiracies which the Tory Governments of the past thirty years had elaborated. It was passed through all its stages by large majorities, the only opponents being O'Connell's followers and a few of the English Radicals.

Russell, Althorp, and Durham had desired that this bill should be balanced by another which would appropriate to Irish education the surplus revenues of the Irish Church. They could not induce Lord Grey and Stanley to go so far. Grey thought that, even if the Cabinet as a whole could be persuaded to accept such a proposal, Parliament would turn against them and the Whig administration would be dissolved. Russell was so mortified that he tendered his resignation and was with difficulty induced to withdraw it.[1] His protest was justified by the scornful reception which the Irish party accorded to Stanley's Irish Church Bill of 1833, which abolished the Church cess, an impost as unpopular as tithes, but did not divert one penny of ecclesiastical revenues to undenominational purposes.

It is significant that Russell paid his first visit to Ireland after the session of 1833, and drew up, at the close of it, a memorandum embodying an outline of a new Irish policy. In this document he notes that the agrarian disturbances were partly due to evictions effected by improving landlords, and partly to the excessive rents exacted by the landlords of encumbered

[1] *Life*, i, pp. 188-92.

estates. For the evicted he had little sympathy, regarding them as ' bad tenants ' who after eviction became ' Whiteboys and murderers ' ; he thought at this time that an Irish poor law was not necessary to provide for such persons. For the over-rented he had more feeling; the remedy which he afterwards embodied in the Encumbered Estates Act had not yet occurred to him ; but his memorandum suggests that these estates might be bought by the State and used as a means of providing for large numbers of industrious tenants. He has in mind two expedients for diminishing religious strife—the provision of State endowment for the Presbyterian and Roman Catholic Churches in Ireland, and a partial disendowment of the Established Church. He notes that the second of these expedients could not be adopted without long and patient investigation.[1]

But it cannot have escaped his notice that a partial disendowment of the Irish Church was a measure which commended itself to the English Radicals.[2] In the session of 1834, when the commutation of Irish tithes was discussed, Russell blurted out the opinion ' that the revenues of the Church of Ireland were larger than necessary for the religious and moral instruction of the persons belonging to that Church, and for the stability of the Church itself '—a calculated indiscretion which was intended to bring to a head the issue between Stanley and himself. It had that effect. Stanley, Graham, Richmond, and Ripon resigned (May 27) when they found that Russell would neither resign nor retract, and that even Lord Grey was against them. Russell had the powerful support of Althorp, and it was moreover evident that his declaration had been received with enthusiasm by the greater part of the ministerialists in the House of Commons.[3] In a month's time Grey himself resigned on discovering that a powerful minority in the reconstituted Cabinet was involved in negotiations with O'Connell about another Irish subject—the renewal of Stanley's Coercion Act. Decidedly the tide was running strongly in favour of a ' new course ' in Irish politics. Russell himself was not involved in

[1] *Life,* i, p. 197.
[2] Joseph Hume had advocated such a measure in 1823 (*Hansard*, viii. 367).
[3] Parker's *Graham,* i, pp. 186-93 gives the fullest account of the crisis.

the revolt against Grey's system; but Althorp was, and his views on Irish matters were substantially those of Russell.

In spite of these events it seems that the Whigs had no thought of an Irish alliance until their calculations were upset by the general election at the end of 1834. In September we find Russell writing to his new chief, Lord Melbourne : ' I hope whatever independent members of Parliament may do, no member of the Government will seek any intercourse or ask for any truce from O'Connell '.[1]   But the King's arbitrary dismissal of the Whigs (November) was in effect an appeal to the Tories and to the electorate against the new policy of conciliation. William IV stated, in a letter to Sir Robert Peel:

'His Majesty could not have sanctioned the nomination of Lord John Russell to the office of Chancellor of the Exchequer without bringing into question the sincerity of his [the King's] declaration that he would resist the encroachments [on the revenues of the Irish Church] to which that individual had pledged himself.'

and again, in a memorandum of 1835, he informed Peel that,

'He considered Lord John Russell to have made up his mind to certain encroachments upon the Church which H.M. had made up his mind to resist.'[2]

Therefore it seemed to some of Russell's political friends perfectly natural and reasonable that he should invoke the help of O'Connell against the new Government,[3] which was avowedly committed to set back the clock in Irish policy. Russell, to judge from the tone which he assumed in the negotiations, was more dubious about their expediency. They meant, at the very least, an irreparable breach with Lord Grey and other Whigs of that school. They might be ill-received in the English constituencies. But he decided to take the risk because he was determined to fight the King and Peel on the ground which they had chosen. If Russell had been allowed by his colleagues to take his own course in the debates on the Address he was prepared to move an amendment to the effect that:

---

[1] *Early Correspondence*, ii. 46.

[2] Parker's *Peel*, ii. 264 ; Stockmar's *Memoirs*, ii. 264.

[3] See for instance Durham's speech of 4 October 1834, quoted by Stuart Reid, i. 381-3.

' The expectations of the country will not be satisfied with anything less than the measures which the House of Commons, recently dissolved, was prepared to adopt.'[1]

This amendment was opposed by the Cabinet and another was preferred which did not emphasize the Irish question ; on which Lord Melbourne was much less heated than were the left wing of the Cabinet.[2] But Russell found another opportunity of nailing his colours to the mast. On 20 March 1835 the new Government introduced a bill for the commutation of Irish tithes : and ten days later Russell retorted by moving for a Committee of the Whole House to consider the temporalities of the Irish Church. He carried his resolution after prolonged debates, and followed up the success by carrying others which asserted the desirability of appropriating the surplus revenues of the Church to Irish education, and of incorporating this proposal in the Government's Tithe Bill. On these defeats Peel resigned (8 April).

The debates on these resolutions raised fundamental issues, as Russell had intended. They were nearly all involved in the second resolution which ran as follows :

' That any surplus which may remain after fully providing for the spiritual instruction of the Members of the Established Church of Ireland ought to be applied locally to the general education of all classes of Christians.'

Russell took his stand on strictly utilitarian principles, though with his usual astuteness he avoided any reference to Bentham, and cited instead the honoured name of Paley to support the position that a Church Establishment owes whatever rights it possesses to its utility. The only part, said Russell, of the endowments of the Irish Church to which that Church nad any moral claim was the part actually expended on ministering to the moral welfare of the Irish nation.[3] Graham, who next to Peel was the principal adversary of the motion, spoke as the champion of the rights of property. Assuming that the motion had been inspired by O'Connell he denounced it as ' the com-

[1] *Life*, i. 217.

[2] Melbourne told William IV, in November 1834, that he had not pledged or committed himself about the Irish Church.

[3] *Hansard*, third series, xxvii. 361 ff.

mencement of a series of attacks, first on Corporation property, then on private property '. Peel preferred to insist upon the clause in the Act of Union which guaranteed the Irish Establishment. He argued that ' nothing but the strongest conviction of absolute necessity ' would justify any statesman in appropriating ecclesiastical property to other than ecclesiastical uses ', and in fact assumed that it would be wrong to use funds which had been given to one religious denomination for the benefit of any other. He was prepared to reform the Church of Ireland, and the Church of England also, by a redistribution of endowments, as for example by suppressing sinecures in order to augment poor benefices. By making this concession, which he himself regarded as the barest justice, he gave offence to some of his own party.[1] But it did not save him from defeat. The majority were set on partial disendowment.

It was a barren victory from one point of view. Defeated in the House of Commons the Tories were invincible in the Lords. An Irish Tithe Bill with an appropriation clause was introduced by the Whigs in 1835, and in 1836, only to be amended so radically by the Lords that it could not be accepted in its new form by ministers. At last in 1837 it was allowed by the Lords to pass on condition that ministers gave up the appropriation clause. By this alteration it became substantially the same as Peel's Bill of 1835.[2] Russell was wise in accepting defeat. His Irish allies had come to the conclusion that it was not worth while to agitate any longer on account of surplus revenues which would probably be too small to effect any great improvement of Irish education. Russell had to be content with the knowledge that the principle of appropriation had supplied a useful party-cry in time of need. Had he possessed the gift of prophecy, he might have comforted himself with the reflection that the Irish Church was only respited for another twenty or thirty years. He lived to rejoice that Gladstone succeeded where he himself had failed.[3]

---

[1] *Hansard*, third series, xxvii. 736 ff. ; Parker's *Peel*, ii. 284.

[2] 'The one measure of the nineteenth century affecting Ireland which completely attained the objects at which it aimed ' (O'Brien, *Ec. Hist. of Ireland*, p. 501).

[3] *Recollections and Suggestions*, pp. 415-16.

It remained to be seen whether the Whigs could pass any
Act that would be a substantial benefit to Ireland. Russell
passed two which he hoped would be beneficial—a Municipal Corporations Act and a Poor Law Act, both modelled
upon measures which had been devised for England and
Wales.

The Corporations Act, introduced in 1836, was founded on
the reports presented by a Select Committee in the previous
year. The two most obvious evils which these reports disclosed
were first that the ratepayers as a body had no influence on the
election of councillors, aldermen, and mayors; secondly, that
Roman Catholics were either excluded from the corporations or
very insufficiently represented; thirdly, that these Protestant
bodies appointed the sheriffs, recorders, and justices of the
peace in their respective boroughs, with the result that the
administration was, or was believed to be, moved by sectarian
bias. The corporate property was generally misused or em-
bezzled by those responsible for its administration. The system
was impossible to defend, and Peel discovered that the corporations, fully conscious of the weakness of their position, were
generally willing to surrender their privileges, on condition that
the corporate organization should be abandoned.[1] Their only
fear was that the introduction of the English system of popular
election would leave the Protestants at the mercy of a Roman
Catholic electorate. Peel accepted the proposals of the Irish
corporations in 1836, believing that the Irish towns would be
better governed by Crown nominees than by elected officers and
councils. The House of Lords naturally accepted Peel's proposal and amended the elective principle out of Russell's bill.
By 1837 Peel had come to the conclusion that he had been mistaken. Irishmen in general resented his scheme as an insult
to their nation. In England even Conservatives were found to
believe that some form of self-government must be better than any
form of bureaucratic administration. He therefore recommended
the Lords to give way. This course did not commend itself to
Lord Lyndhurst, who dominated over the Tory peers. He
delayed the passing of the bill until 1840. Even then he only
permitted it to pass after Russell had agreed to change its

[1] Parker's *Peel*, ii, pp. 336–47.

whole character and purpose by limiting the municipal franchise to the £10 householders in all corporate towns, whether small or great.

Such was the inauspicious origin of an extremely useful measure which Irish Nationalists criticized bitterly and not altogether without reason. It extinguished all but ten of the seventy-one ancient corporations which existed in 1835, though by way of compensation it provided that any town of more than 3,000 inhabitants might petition the Crown for a charter. It stripped the surviving corporations of all powers of control over the courts of justice; in future the sheriffs, recorders, and justices of the peace were to be nominated by the Lord-Lieutenant. It established a municipal electorate which was very small in comparison with the urban population, though larger than the old electorate composed of corporators. These were the consequences of the persistent pressure which Peel and Lyndhurst had applied to the Government for five years. On the other hand, the new electorate was now, in most of the corporate boroughs, predominantly Roman Catholic and usually elected mayors, aldermen, and councillors who professed that faith; and this revolution was accepted with resignation by the minority, who perceived that, at the worst, they were secured against judicial persecution.[1]

The Irish Poor Law of 1837 was passed with little difficulty, and without material alteration. Like the Corporations Act it was modelled upon an English measure; and was preferred to an alternative scheme which found a considerable body of support in Ireland. In 1835 an Irish Poor Inquiry Commission had proposed that pauperism should be extirpated, without any recourse to the workhouse system, by the three expedients of encouraging emigration, improving waste lands, and spending public money on useful works which would create a large demand for labour. Although supported by eminent names, this policy did not commend itself to experienced statesmen. Emigration schemes, however well devised, could not provide for more than a few thousand emigrants in each year. The waste

---

[1] See H. L. Jephson, *Notes on Irish Questions* (Dublin, 1870) for a defence of this reform. The other side of the question is stated in B. O'Brien, *Fifty Years of Concessions*, i. 640.

lands were lying waste because they were not likely to yield a livelihood, much less a profit, unless they were first improved at enormous cost and then presented gratis to the cultivator. Other public works would only afford temporary relief for an evil which was due in the main to the rapid growth of Irish population. The workhouse test, it was objected, was also quite inadequate as a remedy for a desperate situation. But there was something to be said in favour of the workhouse test as a palliative. It would unmask and discourage the idle vagrant. It would throw upon the community as a whole the burden of supporting those who were idle through no fault of their own. Irish opponents of the Poor Law argued that Ireland had so far provided for her poor by spontaneous charity. They omitted to notice that the evil was growing by leaps and bounds in spite of, or possibly because of, the readiness with which Irish compassion responded to appeals for help. They also ignored the fact that the burden of supporting the mendicants was mainly borne by the poorer classes, the small farmers and the cottiers, who proved themselves far more generous than their social betters.[1] One at least of Russell's motives in applying the English system to Ireland was his conviction that the propertied classes in Ireland ought to be held liable for the relief of Irish necessities. The Poor Inquiry Commission had alleged that Ireland could not support her poor upon the English system, which they predicted would involve an annual expenditure of five millions. But Russell's scheme was not in fact inordinately expensive before the famine. In 1844, the fifth year of working, the sum expended on workhouses and relief was only £271,334; in 1846 when the construction of workhouses was at last complete the figure was £316,026.[2]

Russell and his colleagues have been accused of introducing the workhouse into Ireland with a sinister purpose, to facilitate the eviction of the cottier tenants on the great estates. It is perfectly true that some of them, particularly those who had studied Irish conditions, thought that the cottier tenancies were unprofitable to the cottiers themselves and to every one concerned. They held that the cottiers should be transmuted as

[1] Jephson, *Notes*, p. 222.
[2] G. O'Brien, *Ec. Hist. of Ireland*, p. 194.

soon as possible into wage-earners, working under the direction of landlords and rich farmers. They thought that the cottiers, in their own interest as well as in the interest of the landlords, ought to be evicted. But the politicians who argued thus were not inhumane. They had no intention of allowing the evicted tenants to starve. They proposed that the workhouse system should maintain the unemployed until work at a weekly or daily wage was forthcoming. In 1847 they passed the Irish Poor Law Amendment Act, authorizing the payment of out-door relief to those for whom no accommodation was available in the workhouses. This was a wise and necessary relaxation of the orthodox principles of poor relief.

This Act, however, contained one proviso, the so-called Gregory clause, which excited intense indignation. The effect of the clause was that no individual who was in occupation of more than a quarter of an acre should be deemed destitute. In other words, no poor relief for sitting cottier tenants. There was much to be said for enforcing some such rule in normal times. The taxpayer cannot reasonably be required to subsidize a small holding which is never likely to support the occupier and his family. But in 1847 the cottier tenant was staggering under the blow of two successive failures of the potato crop. The Gregory clause must have driven off the land large numbers of tenants who, with some temporary assistance, might have weathered the crisis. No one can accuse Russell of consciously assisting the Irish landlords to give the *coup de grace* to un-wanted tenants. He did not foresee how unscrupulously land-lords would put pressure on the struggling cottiers, whom they should have helped.[1] Probably some of Russell's colleagues saw the situation more clearly and made up their minds that, in one way or another, the cottier must be eliminated. When, in 1848, Russell was proposing to limit the right of eviction, Palmerston protested:

'Ejectments ought to be made without cruelty in the manner of making them ; but it is useless to disguise the truth that any great im-provement in the social system of Ireland must be founded upon an extensive change in the present state of agrarian occupation, and

---

[1] Walpole, *Life of Russell*, i. 450.

this change necessarily implies a long continued and systematic ejectment of Small Holders and Squatting Cottiers.'[1]

Palmerston spoke for his own class. The Irish landowner
believed that the famine was not so much an accident as humani-
tarians presumed. Even without the potato-blight, they contended, a famine must have come sooner or later as the result
of an abnormal growth of the agricultural population and an
abnormal subdivision of the land. They were not inclined to
accept responsibility for the consequences of these fatal developments. They claimed for themselves the right of putting back
the hands of the clock by a policy of systematic and unrelenting
consolidation of small tenancies. They would save the country
and themselves by the simple expedient of compelling the State
to provide for any number of cottiers that they thought fit to
expropriate.

Russell and most of his colleagues were less inclined than
Palmerston to treat the famine as simply the last phase in the
development of an economic crisis which had been boiling up
for many years. For them, as for Peel, the famine was a stroke
of fate involving the culpable and the innocent in one common
doom. While the famine lasted the one obvious duty was to
save human lives by any means that could be devised. The cost
would have to be counted afterwards. It would be time enough
to overhaul the economic situation in Ireland when she returned
to something like her normal state. Peel had gone to work in
this spirit. Russell continued and extended Peel's operations on
such a scale that, by the end of 1848, more than seven millions
of public money had been spent on Irish relief. The figure is
less impressive to-day than it was in 1848. It must be remembered that the national revenue for 1848 only amounted to fifty-
five millions.[2]

There was no want of goodwill on the part of the Whig
Government. Nor did Russell spoil his liberality by cheese-
paring in details. His first instructions to the Lord-Lieutenant
provided that the wages given on relief works should be somewhat higher than those current before the famine, because the
cottiers had no longer any crop of their own to supplement

[1] *Later Correspondence of Lord John Russell,* i. 225.
[2] G. O'Brien, *Econ. Hist. of Ireland,* i. 257.

their wages.[1] In two points he showed more regard for economy than Peel. The latter had paid out of Government funds the cost of bringing Indian corn from America to Ireland; but Russell decided that the whole business of transporting supplies must be left to private enterprise. Peel had undertaken to pay from Treasury funds one-half of the expense of relief works; but Russell decided that in future each Irish locality must be liable for refunding to the Treasury the whole of the expenses incurred. These decisions were in strict accordance with the old Whig policy of resisting any enlargement of the sphere of State action, and with Russell's private conviction that in the last resort every landlord was responsible for the maintenance of all the labour employed upon his land. But we know on good authority that Peel himself approved of these two changes in policy. 'Peel said to me', writes Charles Wood, 'that he felt the danger of the course which he had adopted; that, if persisted in it was most dangerous, and that it was hard upon us having to withdraw.'[2] In the end Russell was reluctantly convinced that his chief deviation from Peel's course was not practical. By 1848 he had been obliged to remit half the debt due upon relief works,[3] having discovered that the alternative would be to foreclose upon the estates of a large number of Irish landlords, who could not or would not pay the quotas due from them.[4] He took a broad view of the situation. At all costs it was necessary to save Ireland from becoming a prey to cut-throats and incendiaries; and he told those of his colleagues who were less generously minded that Ireland could not be left to bear the whole burden of a national calamity. But he made great demands upon Irish landowners and farmers. A memorandum on the famine contains two or three weighty sentences:

'It is impossible to say that the land can support the people and pay rent. But in that case I think rent should be sacrificed. Proprietors and their tenants have raised up, encouraged and grown fat upon, a potato fed population. Now that the question is between rent and sustenance, I think rent must give way, and the whole rental, if necessary, be given to support the people.'[5]

He was shocked, perhaps he was surprised, that Irish land-

[1] *Later Correspondence*, i. 146.   [2] *Op. cit.*, i. 152.
[3] *Op. cit.*, i. 221.   [4] *Op. cit.*, i. 161.   [5] *Life*, i. 446.

lords did not spontaneously recognize their obligations as he saw them. He was surprised that they did not supply their own labourers with food below cost price, or start relief works at their own cost upon their own estates. He asked why they did not study improved methods of cultivation so that Irish land might once more become capable of supporting the Irish population. If they would do none of these things he was determined that they should contribute to relief work through taxation. He thought of applying the income-tax to Ireland; but he was deterred partly by want of the information on which assessments could be based,[1] partly by the reluctance of his colleagues to face the odium of this innovation. But he was determined that Irish property should pay in meal, if not in malt. As early as December 1846 he decided that Parliament should be asked to sanction the payment of outdoor relief in Ireland,[2] since the cost of this relief would fall mainly upon Irish property. He worked hard to devise a measure limiting the landlord's right of ejectment which his colleagues would accept.[3] A bill on this subject, drafted by Somerville, the Chief Secretary, was actually submitted to Parliament in the session of 1848, but shelved by the exertions of the landlord interest. But Russell desired a more drastic measure. The bill of 1848 only proposed that ejected tenants should be compensated for improvements actually made. Russell proposed that no tenant who had occupied his land for more than five years should be ejected without a payment for his tenure, in accordance with Ulster tenant right. Of this proposal he said frankly that it was ' a transfer of property ' and ' a cure objectionable in the extreme '. But nothing less would stop the landlord's habit of evicting cottiers without compensation and without prospect of employment. In 1847, to the irritation of Lord Clarendon, he tried to insist that no coercive legislation should be issued for Ireland unless accompanied by an Ejectment Act on these lines. He was overborne by his colleagues. Clarendon obtained his coercive measures—which were proved by the events of 1848 to be not

---

[1] This presumably is the explanation of his remark that, by general consent, no Irish income-tax could be imposed before 1850 (*Later Correspondence*, i. 161).

[2] *Op. cit.*, i. 164.   [3] *Life*, i. 467 ; *Later Correspondence*, i. 222 ff.

at all excessive. Russell only obtained the Encumbered Estates
Act of the same year. It was a measure designed to accelerate
the extinction of the class of insolvent landlords to whom was
ascribed the blame for the more atrocious forms of ejectment.
By 1880 about five million acres of land had been sold under the
terms of the Act, but without benefiting small tenants to the
extent that Russell had hoped and anticipated. For the frustra-
tion of his excellent intentions his colleagues and the Irish
landlords were responsible. It was left for Mr. Gladstone to
accomplish in 1870 what both Peel[1] and Russell had vainly
tried to accomplish.

The Encumbered Estates Act is a conclusive proof that
Russell had learned much in the eighteen years which he had
devoted to Irish affairs. The main decision to which his studies
had led him was

'that the political franchises on which we so long pondered and
legislated were not directed to the cure of the specific evils of Ireland,
and that the discontent of the poorer tenantry has been the pabulum
upon which agitation for repeal has fed, fattened, and flourished.'[2]

In accordance with this new method of envisaging the Irish
problem he produced, for the consideration of his colleagues,
a scheme of State-aided emigration, the funds to be raised by
a special poor rate of 6d. in the £ in Ireland and threepence in
England and Scotland. On the security of this rate a sum not
exceeding five millions was to be borrowed and expended by
special Emigration Commissioners. The Commissioners were
to advance sums not exceeding £2 a head to each member of
a family desirous to emigrate and fit for emigration. The proceeds of the emigration tax in each kingdom were to be spent
on the emigrants of that kingdom. Not more than one million
was to be borrowed in any one year. The effect of this scheme
would have been to make possible the emigration of half a
million persons in each of five years.[3] So far as Irish emigration was concerned Russell could quote the views of the Poor
Inquiry Commission, who had proposed a scheme of this kind
in 1835.[4] It may be doubted whether 500,000 persons could

[1] Peel's measure was introduced in 1845 (Parker's *Peel*, iii. 177–8).
[2] *Life*, i. 464.   [3] *Life*, ii. 79–80.
[4] O'Brien, *Economic History of Ireland*, p. 180.

have been emigrated from the British Isles to foreign and colonial destinations in any single year : and Irish emigration did in fact proceed at a rapid pace without the stimulus of a State subsidy, as is shown by the following figures :

1848	1849	1850	1851
178,159	214,425	209,054	249,721.

It was not improbable that Russell's scheme would simply have the effect of subsidizing emigrants who in any case, subsidy or no subsidy, were resolved to emigrate. That was the view of Russell's own Chancellor of the Exchequer, who was then as always a resolute disciple of *laisser-faire*,[1] and it may have been correct. But on political grounds and grounds of humanity there was a strong case in favour of making the experiment for which Russell asked, and he took the resistance of his colleagues greatly to heart.

The rest of the Whig ministry were still of the opinion that the Irish situation called for political concessions rather than for any interference with the working of economic laws. They welcomed a suggestion, which accompanied his Emigration Scheme, that the time had arrived for endowing the Roman Catholic Church in Ireland, at the expense of Irish landlords, by imposing an Irish land-tax at a rate sufficient to yield £400,000 a year.[2] Lord Lansdowne thought the proposal most important ; Palmerston thought it essential for the future tranquillity of Ireland. Russell was encouraged to expand his proposal in the shape of a formal communication to the Vatican. This document explained that the proposed grant would be permanent, and that the Government had no desire to interfere with the spiritual independence or the ecclesiastical arrangements of the Roman Catholic Church. It is probable that the offer would have been refused, like similar offers made in the past. But the scheme broke down *in limine* when it was communicated to the Irish Roman Catholics. Russell stated it in a letter to

---

[1] See Greville, 11 November 1848.

[2] Greville believed that this scheme originated with Charles Buller, who showed it to him on 2 September 1848 as part of a comprehensive scheme for dealing with Irish distress. But Russell's scheme is dated 30 March (*Life*, ii, p. 64).

Thomas Redington, the assistant under-secretary, who was himself a Roman Catholic and the recognized mouthpiece of his co-religionists. The essence of the scheme, according to this letter, was that it would establish ' a fair, though not a rigid or literal equality between the three Churches, Episcopal, Catholic, and Presbyterian '.[1] But the answer which Redington brought back from the Catholic bishops was a demand that the suggested provision should be made out of the funds of the Established Church. This was what Russell himself had once proposed. But by 1848 he had learned to fear the anti-Catholic sentiment of England and Scotland. He would not court disaster a second time by proposing an Appropriation Bill. If he had been free to decide for himself, he would have communicated with Rome over the heads of the Irish Roman Catholic bishops. But his colleagues were divided, and in November 1848 Pio Nono fled from Rome to Naples.[2]

[1] *Later Correspondence*, i. 230.
[2] *Life*, ii, pp. 65, 77–8; Greville's *Diary* for 11 November 1848.

XI

WHIGGISM 1830-1850. RUSSELL AND MACAULAY

FROM the account that has been given, in a previous
chapter, of the fortunes of the Whig party during the
French wars, it will readily be inferred that the principles to
which the party as a whole subscribed were vague and general,
leaving a large latitude of interpretation. The irreducible
minimum of principle which would qualify a politician to be
labelled at that time as a Whig is frankly stated by Lord Holland
in 1810, when he is correcting the excessive idealism of his
favourite pupil, Lord John Russell. Why, asks Holland, do you
carp at the system of close constituencies? The influence of
property must exist, and it is by no means to be deplored.
Sinecures are an evil, but an evil which is grossly overrated;
a sinecure is simply a bad, uneconomical, and uncertain method
of rewarding public services. They might be awarded with
more discrimination, but the positive harm that they do is very
small indeed. A good Whig, Holland continues, ought to feel
a certain inclination to reform the House of Commons and other
abuses. He should always aim at reducing the national expenditure. But such aims and inclinations should not be carried to
extremes. Things are not so bad as they appear to the young
and uninstructed.[1]

Holland, perhaps, is too Laodicean to be treated as entirely
typical; and it may be fairer to take the views of Romilly as
representing the creed of the moderate and clear-headed
members of his party. In an election address of 1812 Romilly
explained to the electors of Bristol what he conceived to be the
principles of a sound Whig:

'He ought to be a Man firmly attached to those principles of our
Constitution which were established at the Revolution. . . . He should
justly appreciate and be ready at all times to maintain the liberty of the
press and the trial by jury which are the great securities for all our other
liberties. He should be a sincere friend of peace. . . . He should be

---

[1] *Early Correspondence of Lord John Russell*, i, pp. 131-9.

an enemy to that influence of the Crown and of the Ministers of the Crown which has been so fatally exercised in the House of Commons, and consequently a friend to Parliamentary Reform. He should be a constant advocate for economy in the public expenditure, and a determined enemy to corruption and peculation. He should be ready, when he sees abuses arising from any of our present institutions, to inquire into the causes of them, and to suggest a remedy, notwithstanding the reproach of being an innovator. Above all he should be a man incapable of being severed from his duty by the threats of power, the allurements of the great, the temptations of private interest or even the seduction of popular favour.' [1]

The language of this definition is old fashioned and prim. The hasty reader might infer that Romilly comes forward as an apostle of the pure and undefiled Whig creed of 1688. The careful reader will, however, perceive that one-third of the creed of Romilly's ideal Whig was comparatively new. The Whigs of 1688 were not in principle averse to continental wars. They had no objection to ministerial influence, so long as that influence was lodged in the right hands. They did not feel any impulse to reform constitutional abuses in general, for their own power was based on electoral corruption. Not Romilly but Grenville and his friends were after all the most faithful guardians of this old Whig policy. But even Romilly's zeal for reform is still the zeal of an aristocrat. Speaking to an audience which contained a noisy Radical element, he plainly expresses his contempt for ' popular favour ', for the vagaries of what the Radicals were pleased to call ' the sovereign people '. He regards himself as a trustee of constitutional liberty ; he will not become a mandatory pledged to secure for the people that kind of liberty which they imagine that they need.[2] Here he is on common ground with Burke, fighting the cause of the Old Whigs ; and here he expresses a principle in which the Whig party were practically unanimous, so long as they remained a party.

The common creed is stated more fully, and in more modern language in Russell's juvenile *Essay on the English Govern-*

---

[1] Romilly, *Speeches*, ii. 466.

[2] On 3 October 1811 he wrote to Major Cartwright: 'To subscribe an article of political faith as a condition . . . would neither suit my inclination nor agree with those rules by which I have determined always to govern my conduct' (*Life*, ii. 417).

ment and Constitution (1821). Though juvenile it cannot be described as immature ; for the writer republished it in 1865 without substantial alteration. One object, if not the principal object with which he wrote it, was to define the attitude of the orthodox Whig towards the political nostrum of contemporary Radicals, and in his references to radicalism there is discernible a desire to conciliate, which Burke or Romilly would not have approved. The principles of 1688 have soaked into Russell's mind, but he sometimes gives them an unexpected turn, which shows that he has read and meditated on *Le Contrat Social*. Thus, in speaking of reformist agitation, he agrees that some regard must be paid to the wishes of the people. There is no contract between the King and his subjects which compels him to yield to a popular outcry. But if the people demand new liberties at any time, the King (in Parliament) is bound to give them, not necessarily all that they ask, but ' the species of government which the state of the nation and the knowledge of the age may demand ' (c. x). So again, Russell defines political liberty as ' the acknowledged and legal right of the people to control their government or to take a share in it ' (c. xi). But these apparently democratic principles are only an introduction to the old theory of a constitution guaranteed by checks and balances. In the well-ordered constitution, we are told, power is divided between the monarch, the aristocracy, and the people. If any one of these three powers become supreme, liberty is in danger. But in England the House of Commons is sobered and stabilized by the influence which the landed interest enjoys in it, and also by the hereditary House of Lords which revises the bills passed by the Commons, ' interposing its grave and thoughtful opinions to suspend the effect of an intemperate vote '. The King's prerogative is no danger to liberty, because it is exercised through responsible ministers, and is also held in check by the courts of law. On the other hand, the existence of the hereditary King is an invaluable barrier against that kind of revolution which originates in the craving of ambitious individuals for supreme power (c. xiv).

Russell freely admits that the popular orator and waves of political agitation may serve a useful purpose in the well-ordered state—a courageous admission to make in 1821 when the memory of Peterloo was still green. ' These discussions ', he says, ' arising out of the state of the nation, and carried on with the whole nation for audience, so far from being mischievous, tend to excite that spirit of inquiry and investigation which is necessary to the freedom of the State (c. xxx). But agitation is a drastic medicine for desperate diseases. It is to the great political parties that the nation must look in general for its views on national policy.

The party system Russell defends, in the first instance, with Burke's familiar argument. Party, he says, gives a substance to the shadowy opinions of politicians ; party attaches them to steady and lasting principles. But he proceeds to contend that party does well the work that the demagogue and his followers do badly, or fail to do at all. A proposed reform, when it is taken up by a great party, becomes the object of an organized body of men, which is prepared to pursue that object from year to year, or even from one generation to another. And the more violently the nation as a whole is agitated by any question, the more expedient it is that the views of contending factions should be debated between parliamentary parties in the calm of a legislative assembly, rather than in the streets or at the hustings. Such debates act as a safety-valve for opinions which otherwise ' would break the machine to pieces ' (c. xvii).

In 1821 Russell was already definitely committed to the cause of parliamentary reform ; and in this book we find two or three of the leading principles which he was to apply, without much modification, in solving the practical problems of 1830. In this book we find the Aristotelian doctrine, adopted without acknowledgement and without discussion, that the middle classes carry in their breasts the political conscience of the State, as being ' the most disinterested, the most independent, and the most unprejudiced of all '.[1] Russell does not yet equate the middle class with the ten-pound householders of the English boroughs and the lease-holding or copy-holding tenants in the counties ; he is thinking in 1821 of the men of moderate means who are the rank and file in the professions and the business world. It is on their behalf, and on behalf of the much smaller and weaker ' aristocracy of talent ', that he opposes manhood suffrage and

---

[1] A doctrine endorsed by Mill in his *Essay on Government* (1828).

pleads for the preservation of a limited number of close constituencies. Manhood suffrage will rob the middle class of any
influence in parliamentary elections, and among the candidates
at these elections the wealthy men will be chosen, while the
clever men are rejected. Whatever shape parliamentary reform
might assume, Russell was confident (in 1821) that only sagacious
patrons disposing of pocket boroughs would ever be able to
bring the ' man of talent' into politics without a substantial
fortune at his back.

Finally, we have in this book the idea that a uniform franchise,
high or low, will lead to a dull uniformity in the House of
Commons, and for other reasons will prove the beginning of
chaos. The arguments by which he defends this view will not
bear close examination. He assumes, in the first place, that
a uniform franchise will mean the predominance of the same
social class in every electoral district. And, secondly, he assumes
that in each constituency the majority will elect the man who
most exactly reflects their own opinions. But what he most
apprehends is the danger that, if you allow the constitution to
be reformed on some principle which the electors believe to be
a panacea for the evils of the State, you will excite expectations
of a millennium, and you will pay heavily for the inevitable
disappointment of the electors, who will demand more and more
preposterous changes when they find that a mere change in the
House of Commons has not eased their lot.

These fears and doubts go far towards explaining some of the
anomalies of the Great Reform Bill. Even Russell was infected
with the political philosophy of Eldon and Sidmouth; he was quite
capable of applying to the British constitution the eulogy which
Peacock's Seithenyn passed on the crumbling sea-wall which protected his kingdom : ' That the embankment is old I am free to
confess ; that it is somewhat rotten in parts I will not altogether
deny ; that it is any the worse for that I do most sturdily
gainsay. . . . If it were all sound it would break by its own
obstinate stiffness ; the soundness is checked by the rottenness,
and the stiffness is balanced by the elasticity.' Russell did not
believe that the constitution was in no need of improvement.
But the need was not urgent ; the constitution, even as it stood,
was not far short of being the best in the world, since nowhere

in the world was liberty, civil, personal, political, more firmly guaranteed by the law.[1]

From these expositions of Whig principle it is easy to discover the strength and the weakness of Whiggism a hundred years ago. Peace, economy, religious freedom, the rule of law, and the utmost latitude in political discussion that is compatible with social order—these were objects the worth of which could hardly be questioned by reflecting men. Whiggism was a form of political optimism ; in the last resort it was based upon the assumption that truth must prevail over falsehood wherever men are free to argue out their differences ; in other words, that the reason and the moral conscience are stronger, in the mass of men, than tradition or the instinct of selfishness or party spirit. Even those who maintained that this optimism was not warranted by the facts, that British society was endangered periodically by gusts of blind passion, by the greed or envy of the poor, by the vanity or ambition of mob-leaders, by the gullibility of the uneducated or half-educated—even these critics admitted that society would become happier and government would become more enlightened as soon as it was possible and safe to put Whig doctrines into practice. But such doctrines are more easily advocated by a party in opposition than they are applied by the same party in power. It was embarrassing, yet it was inevitable, that the Whigs, when they came into office, should find themselves driven to rely upon influence, even upon corrupt influence, when appeals to the reason of the electorate were manifestly ineffective, that they should, on occasion, pass coercive laws for Ireland, suspend trial by jury in Canada, and propose to suspend the constitution of Jamaica. They had in practice to confess that their perfect system was not altogether adapted to the needs of an imperfect world.

Another defect of Whig doctrine was the assumption that government can only cure those evils which are due to bad laws or to defects of the constitution. We do not find that Romilly or Russell, in their statements of the orthodox Whig creed, had the slightest desire to examine scientifically the national system of taxation, or the policy of the navigation laws, or the defects of central administration and local government. What

[1] *Essay*, ch. xxxii.

could be more faint hearted than the recommendations which
Sydney Smith put forward in 1820 and 1821 for the amendment of the Poor Laws ? In 1830 he holds that they are entirely
responsible for the problem of redundant population and must
therefore be abolished. But they must be very gradually
abolished. In 1820 he could only suggest two measures which
were probably useful so far as they went, but certainly not
calculated to produce any great reduction of the rates. The
first proposal was that the adult labourer's right of settlement
should be taken away, so that he could only claim relief in the
place of his birth. The second was that the single justice of
the peace should be disabled from granting relief at his personal
discretion. In 1821 he was encouraged to go farther by the
fact that a Whig lawyer, James Scarlett, had produced a
courageous, though not a well-considered, Poor Law Bill.[1]
Endeavouring to improve upon this bill, Sydney Smith suggests
that no parish shall in future years be allowed to exceed the
Poor Law assessment of the last financial year, which was the
highest on record ; and that the assessment shall be diminished
annually by one-half per cent., until poor rates have been reduced by twenty per cent. It is very curious to find him
arguing (in 1820) that it is the merest common sense to continue
the ' system of roundsmen ' under which paupers were hired out
to farmers at any wage, however low, which the farmer would
agree to pay, and this pittance was supplemented by the parish.
Sydney Smith is astonished at the ' strange assertion ' that the
farmer who pays a labourer 6d. a week under this system is committing an injustice. ' Why are the farmers not to take labour as
cheap as they can get it ? Why are they not to avail themselves
of the market price of this as of any other commodity ? ' Yet
Sydney Smith was, on social questions, the expert of the
Edinburgh Review.

It is true that in 1824 Lord John Russell took in hand the
Poor Laws, asked for a Select Committee, presided over it, and
guided it to sensible conclusions. The Report of this Committee

---

[1] *Hansard*, v. 572, &c. Nicholls, *History of the Poor Law*, ii. 221–4.
This bill was withdrawn after the second reading. In 1822 Scarlett proposed to abolish the practice of removing paupers from place to place. But
this bill also was withdrawn.

anticipated that of 1834 in condemning the roundsman system. It also recommended that able-bodied paupers should be forced to work for the parish 'with labour less acceptable in its nature than ordinary labour, and at lower wages than the average rate of the neighbourhood'. But the Committee was not purely Whig in composition. Althorp, Scarlett, and Brougham sat on it; but so did Peel and Sturges Bourne. From whose brain the Report emanated is uncertain; probably not from Russell's since its main ideas are absent from the first edition of his *Essay on the English Government and Constitution* (c. xxvi), published in 1821. Yet he took no further part in the movement for reforming the English Poor Law; the burden of introducing the New Poor Law Bill of 1834 fell upon Althorp in the Commons and Brougham in the Lords. In 1837 Russell himself sponsored an Irish Poor Law which was based on the leading ideas of the English measure. But he acted under the guidance of others and with no first-hand knowledge of the Irish situation.

The narrowness of the Whig intellect is nowhere more evident than in the field of economics and finance. Between 1830 and 1841 the policy of the Exchequer was tame and halting. Althorp, who was responsible for the first Whig budget of the period (1831) showed his usual common sense when he proposed to his colleagues that they should adopt the policy advocated by Sir Henry Parnell in the *Treatise on Financial Reform* (1830). The main features of this policy were proposals to reimpose the income-tax, to repeal the duties upon raw materials, and to reduce other duties to a moderate level. The Cabinet, however, demurred against the first of these proposals, and Althorp was obliged to substitute for the income-tax a system of duties on transfers of land and funded property, which was calculated to yield the modest sum of £1,200,000 per annum.[1] Even this proposal was thrown over by his colleagues as soon as it appeared that the great moneyed interests were hostile to the transfer duties, though Althorp held that the outcry would soon subside if Government preserved a resolute attitude. In conse-

[1] In 1815 the property-tax at 2s. in the £ was estimated to yield £15,000,000. Therefore in that year an income-tax of 2d. would have yielded £1,250,000—rather more than Althorp's transfer duties.

quence Althorp was obliged to curtail his programme of tax remission, and the honour of applying Parnell's policy was reserved for Sir Robert Peel, who introduced it under economic conditions which were far more difficult than those of 1831. Only in four financial years of this period were the Whigs blessed with a surplus revenue, and in 1840, at the end of a decennium of peace, the national debt was actually larger than it had been in 1830. It is true that considerable reductions of the taxes were affected in the years 1831–6. But they were not large enough to impress the imagination of the electors, or to stimulate trade. By 1837 it had become apparent that the chances of balancing future budgets without some drastic change of system were remote. Spring Rice, who followed Althorp at the Exchequer (1835–9), could devise no remedy for deficits. Francis Baring (1839–41) began his Chancellorship with the correct but depressing policy of raising all the indirect taxes by 5 per cent. (1840), and had the mortification of finding himself faced at the end of the year with a larger deficit than that which he had hoped to wipe off. In 1840 the taxes were yielding less than they had yielded in 1831, and expenditure was practically at the same level (forty-nine millions) in both years. It did not seem likely to decline while Palmerston remained at the Foreign Office.

To meet this situation the Cabinet approved of a new policy which was, as to one half, the work of Baring, as to the other the work of Russell. Baring proposed to reduce the preferences given to West Indian sugar and to Canadian timber, by raising in each case the duty on import from the colonies and lowering the duty on import from foreign countries. Russell proposed to abolish the sliding-scale of corn duties which had been in force since 1828 and to substitute a fixed duty.[1] Baring's proposals had a purely financial object; he estimated that they would yield an additional revenue of £1,300,000. Russell was chiefly concerned to prevent violent fluctuations in the price of corn, but claimed that there would be some increase of revenue as a result of the adoption of his measure; and Baring accord-

---

[1] He committed himself to a fixed duty in January 1839; proposed a revised sliding scale to the Cabinet in February 1841. They, however, preferred the fixed duty (*Life of Russell*, i. 366–9).

ingly relied upon the fixed duty as one of the means for giving
equilibrium to his budget, although the corn duty was not
actually proposed in the budget speech. This curious procedure
was apparently the outcome of Baring's reluctance to imperil
his whole budget by bringing into it a proposal which would
throw the agricultural interest into the arms of the Opposition.[1]
But it was a tactical mistake, since the House was left with the
impression that ministers proposed to pass their budget by
instalments.

In essence the ministerial policy was audacious; a simultaneous attack, as Russell puts it, on three giant monopolies—
sugar, timber, corn. An audacious policy should be audaciously
pursued. Instead of doing so, Government invited the Commons
to accept the revised duties on sugar and on timber before it
revealed the exact nature of the proposals about corn. Nor
was this the only error of judgement. As a national financier
Baring had good reasons for attacking the enormous preference
to colonial sugar. While foreign sugar paid 63s. a cwt. under
the existing tariff, East India sugar paid 32s. and West India
sugar 24s.; and about eighty per cent. of the total quantity
imported came from the West Indies. But the West Indian
trade had a moral claim to protection on a liberal scale. It had
been heavily hit by the abolition of slavery; it could point to
possible competitors—Cuba, Brazil, Louisiana in particular—who
still were able to rely upon slave labour. Baring might argue
that his revised duties gave the West Indian planter all the
protection that he had a right to expect; Russell might point
out that the preference to the West Indies was fraudulently
abused by the planters, who imported slave-grown sugar into
Jamaica and sent it to England labelled as colonial sugar. The
House refused to accept these arguments. The sugar duties
were thrown out, and with them the Government.

It is impossible to decide the merits of the question whether
a preference of 12s. a cwt. was or was not a reasonable indemnity
to the West India planter. But it is remarkable that, in 1844,
a Tory Government took up Baring's scheme and passed it in
a form which gave the planter a preference of 10s. only. Peel's
followers did not accept this measure without some hesitation;

[1] See *Later Correspondence of Lord J. Russell*, i, p. 32.

it was in fact once rejected (14 June 1844) by a majority composed in part of Tories; but three days later this adverse vote
was rescinded. Uneasy though they were at the free-trade sentiments which their leader sometimes expressed, they respected
him as a financier. They felt that he had in his head a coherent
and comprehensive plan; that they were not likely to fare well on
tariff questions or any other questions under different leadership.
The Whigs never felt confident to this degree when Russell or
a Whig Chancellor of the Exchequer was laying budget plans.

The Whig Presidents of the Board of Trade were uniformly
second or third rate. First came Lord Auckland, justly described
by Greville (his subordinate) as too ignorant. Even Auckland's
friends were sceptical of his abilities until, in 1835, he left the
Board of Trade for India.

Thomson came to the Board with a practical knowledge of
commerce, and is remembered as the creator of the Statistical
Department, which has since become the indispensable guide
and mentor of economic reformers. For the rest he was an
unflinching partisan of the school of *laisser-faire*. He it was
who moved in 1836 to exclude from the benefit of Ashley's
Factory Act all children between twelve and thirteen years of
age—a measure which the Whigs happily withdrew on discovering that it had imperilled their majority in the House of Commons.
A member for Manchester, Thomson represented too faithfully
the prejudices of the cotton manufacturers upon this question;
yet we have Cobden's evidence that he was not regarded as
a real business man. Like Auckland, he developed into a
statesman when he was translated to a sphere in which economic
questions were not the first consideration. In Canada he proved
a success; for in Canada his business was to manage intractable
politicians and to carry on a policy which was prescribed from
home.

Labouchere, who did nothing memorable in his first period
as President (1839–41), had the good fortune to come in again
in 1847, in time to be responsible for the repeal of the Navigation Laws. This great and salutary measure has all the appearance of an enlightened Whig reform. It relieved British foreign
trade by the mere abolition of restrictive laws. But it was in
fact a measure which had been contemplated by Sir Robert Peel,

but delayed by the objections of his protectionist supporters.[1]
The measure was based on the report of a Select Committee
which Russell caused to be appointed in 1847; but it was
strongly opposed by many Whig politicians. When it passed,
it was through the help of the Peelites that it obtained a respectable majority in the Commons and a very small majority in the
House of Lords.[2]

Russell was sufficiently impressed with the importance of the
measure to decide that he would resign if it should be thrown
out by the Lords.[3] But he had evidently not yet succeeded in
educating the rank and file of his party to his own very moderate
level of economic wisdom. He was beginning to acquire an
economic general staff. The first recruit of note was George
Cornewall Lewis, who graduated in these studies while serving
as an assistant to the Poor Law Commissioners (1834-6) and
produced at that stage his masterly essay on the causes of local
disturbances in Ireland. The second was James Wilson, founder
and editor of the *Economist*, who was returned in the Whig
interest for Westbury at the General Election of 1847, and took
office as a secretary of the Board of Control in the following
year, Lewis becoming simultaneously the under-secretary for
the Home Office. But the influence of these advisers is not
very marked in Russell's first ministry.

The leaven of Bentham began to ferment in the Whig mind
much earlier than that of orthodox political economy. Under
Bentham's influence the young Whigs of the 'thirties diverged
considerably from the doctrine of Russell's essay on the constitution. They did not as a rule read Bentham's own treatises, but
they read the works of James Mill and John Austin on the
British constitution, and they accepted practical utility as the
touchstone by which all laws and institutions must be tested,
though it need hardly be said that they refused to measure
utility by the hedonistic calculus. Macaulay is the best literary
spokesman of this new Whiggism, and for that reason the

---

[1] Graham, in supporting the bill, said on behalf of the Peelites: ' This
measure is in my opinion the capital necessary to crown the work which we
have already accomplished ' (*Life*, ii. 84).

[2] Parker's *Peel*, ii. 503-4.

[3] *Later Correspondence of Lord John Russell*, i. 193-5.

development of his political views deserves more than a passing glance.

The earlier essays of Macaulay contain hardly anything on history or politics to which Holland House could take exception. But if we turn to his speech of 1842 upon the People's Charter, we find ourselves dealing with a thinker who has learned much from the philosophic Radicals. 'I have voted for the ballot,' he says, 'and I see no reason to change my opinion on the subject.' He agrees with the Chartists that every man who has a vote at Parliamentary elections ought to be eligible for a seat in Parliament, without a property qualification. Though he dislikes the proposals that members of Parliament shall be paid, that electoral districts shall be equalized, and that Parliament shall be re-elected annually, he does not consider that these points are vital. He would be sorry to see England a republic; but he would never fight to the last gasp for the preservation of the monarchy or of the hereditary House of Lords. 'I cannot consider either monarchy or aristocracy as the ends of government. They are only means.' So far as concerned the House of Lords, Macaulay had been converted to the popular side some years before this time. While in India he had prophesied that 'in a few years the House of Lords must go after Old Sarum and Old Gatton', and he had submitted to Lord Lansdowne a scheme for re-constituting that House on an elective basis.[1] Considering the consistency of the opposition which the House of Lords offered to all legislation which the Whigs especially desired, it was but natural that many staunch Whigs should think as Macaulay did. Russell thought none the worse of him for these republican tendencies. Both in 1838 and in 1839 he pressed the claims of Macaulay to a cabinet office, and in 1852, when he himself was at the helm, he invited Macaulay to become his colleague,[2] not because of any warmth of personal friendship, but because he saw in Macaulay a Whig of his own pattern.

The last trace of the old Whiggism which we find in this speech of 1842 is the conviction, to which Macaulay had been always wedded, that private property, government of any kind,

[1] Trevelyan, *Life of Lord Macaulay*, ii. 57–8.
[2] *Melbourne Papers*, p. 385; *Early Correspondence of Lord John Russell*, ii. 247, 257–61, 264.

and civilization itself would be in danger as soon as Universal
Suffrage was conceded. Even on this question he had made
some remarkable admissions in the past. He said in 1831 [1] that
Universal Suffrage was producing no very dreadful consequences
in the United States, and might be safely introduced in any
country where the condition of the working classes was always
prosperous. It was in old countries, such as England, countries
subject at times to industrial depression, that a property qualification was needed as a safeguard. In 1839 Macaulay told his
constituents that he would stand by the Whig party while one
single shred of the old banner was still flying.[2] He took this
opportunity of characterizing Whig principles as 'immortal
with the immortality of truth'. But already at that date he
himself had done his best to tear more than one shred from the
old banner. He moved with the stream and was hardly aware
how fast the stream was flowing. Russell was in the same
case.

The life of Macaulay shows that, from his youth upwards, he
was in close contact with Radicals and a reader of Radical
literature. At Cambridge his chief friend was Charles Austin,
an apostle of Bentham and political economy. He accepted as
incontrovertible the formula of James Mill that 'Government
exists to increase to the utmost the pleasures and diminish to
the utmost the pains which men derive from one another'.[3]
Unlike a good many of the believers in *laisser-faire*, he had
already, in 1824, pushed that principle to its logical conclusion in the sphere of economics; he had decided that Free
Trade was one of the greatest blessings that any Government
could confer upon its subjects.[4] But he was repelled by some
aspects of philosophic radicalism. He hated the scholastic
methods of James Mill; he held that true conclusions in politics
could only be reached by the inductive method.[5] Like Burke
and Mackintosh, he judged the weaknesses of the existing
Government of England with the indulgent good humour of an
historian. That Government was irregular and full of archi-

---

[1] *Miscellaneous Writings* (popular edition), p. 484.   [2] *Life*, ii. 64.
[3] *Life*, i. 75–6.   [4] *Misc. Writings*, p. 91 (Review of Mitford).
[5] *Misc. Writings*, p. 82 (Review of Mill's *Essay on Government*, which
Mill answered in the *Fragment on Mackintosh*).

tectural anomalies, like an old house; but an old house is a good house if it is comfortable for those who live in it. This may be Utilitarianism, but it is not Benthamism; it is the optimistic creed of the eighteenth-century Whig. All the more remarkable is the fact that Macaulay converted the younger Mill to it;[1] nothing shows more clearly that the barriers which separated the open-minded Radical from the open-minded Whig were beginning to tumble down by the middle of the century.

Macaulay entered political life with a strong prepossession in favour of the landed aristocracy, which had ruled England from the death of William III to the battle of Waterloo:

'Even in this island where the multitude have long been better informed than in any other part of Europe, the rights of the many have generally been asserted against themselves by the patriotism of the few. . . . The people are to be governed for their own good; and that they may be governed for their own good they must not be governed by their own ignorance.'

This belief in aristocracy was tempered with the doctrine that the happiest state of society is that in which supreme power resides in the whole body of a well-informed people, and with the belief that the circle of the well informed would gradually be enlarged.[2] In 1829 Macaulay derides the assumption, which James Mill had made, that the middle classes constitute a natural aristocracy, fitted for rule both by their intelligence and by their virtues, predestined to rule whenever the classes inferior to these are enfranchised:

'There can be no doubt,' says Mill, 'that the middle rank, which gives to science, to art, and to legislation itself their most distinguished ornaments, and is the chief source of all that has exalted and refined human nature, is that portion of the community of which, if the basis of representation were ever so far extended, the opinion would ultimately decide. Of the people beneath them a vast majority would be sure to be guided by their advice and example.'

Macaulay holds, in 1829, that the rule of the middle classes would mean rule by the aristocracy of wealth, and he is not prepared to hail it with open arms.[3]

---

[1] Mill, *Autobiography*, c. v; *Logic*, Bk. VI, c. viii.
[2] *Misc. Works*, pp. 91–2.   [3] *Misc. Works*, pp. 167, 179.

In the Reform Bill debates of 1831 Macaulay supported his leaders whole-heartedly but without any sanguine expectations. He held at that time that, in England, Universal Suffrage would infallibly lead to revolution. He desired to enfranchise the middle classes because they were dissatisfied with the existing system of 'government by certain detached portions and fragments of property'; because no Government could stand unless it enjoyed the confidence of the middle classes.[1] He was perfectly certain that all the concessions which his leaders proposed were necessary. He was too much impressed with the inevitability of a broadened franchise to waste time in analysing its consequences:

'I believe that over the great changes of the moral world we possess as little power as over the great changes of the physical world. We can no more prevent time from changing the distribution of property, and intelligence from aspiring to political power, than we can change the courses of the seasons and of the tides. . . . The feeble efforts of the individuals to bear back are lost, and swept away in the mighty rush with which the species goes onward. Those who appear to lead the movement are, in fact, only whirled along before it ; those who attempt to resist it are beaten down and crushed before it.'[2]

This belief in the irresistible march of events was to some extent tempered by faith in the constant and unbroken progress of humanity. The arguments in favour of that faith do not appear to us so strong as they appeared to Macaulay. But, since the Whigs in general accepted the doctrine of progress, it is worth while to recapitulate the case, as Macaulay puts it. For about two hundred years the standard of living amongst all classes of the English population had steadily improved. Within the shorter period, for which vital statistics were available, the average expectation of life had increased. Macaulay felt certain, though he could not prove, that every class of society was better furnished with worldly goods in the nineteenth century than the corresponding class had been in the days of Queen Elizabeth. Whatever might be said against the new industrialism, it offered better wages than the country labourer could earn. If the new manufacturing towns were less healthy than country parishes, at

---

[1] Speech of 2 March 1831 (*Misc. Works*, p. 483 ff.).
[2] Speech of 16 December 1831 (*Misc. Works*, p. 525).

all events these towns were healthier (to judge from the rate of mortality) than England and Wales had been in 1780 before the age of industrialism had properly arrived.[1] These and other such improvements of the human lot were due to the progress of the applied sciences. There appeared to be no limit to the development of these sciences, founded as they were upon experiment and observation. Consequently it was reasonable to expect that the material prosperity of mankind would be progressively ameliorated for an indefinite period to come.

Captious critics of this optimistic forecast might object that material progress was worth very little unless accompanied by improvement of the moral faculty in man. But Macaulay has his answer to these critics. He thought, with Bacon, that it was possible to elaborate by inductive methods a practical science of morals, a science which would cure the diseases of the mind, and would discover how to develop character by education, by habituation, and in other ways. Macaulay believes, as firmly as Godwin and Owen believed, that human nature is perfectible.[2] More temperate, however, than Godwin and Owen, he declined to believe that human society could be purged of all the evils inherent in its present constitution. He took the side of Malthus against Godwin and Michael Sadler. The latter had protested, in the name of Christianity, that the Malthusian 'principle of population' could not be true since to believe it was tantamount to alleging that 'the law by which the Deity multiplies his off-spring, and that by which he makes provision for their sustenation are different and, indeed, irreconcilable'. To this abstract reasoning Macaulay opposes the facts of experience. The laws of nature are not all benevolent to mankind. Evil has always existed in the world. It may be that the evils which exist are necessary to avert still greater evils that might otherwise come into being; but while we may legitimately cherish this belief, we cannot prove it. All we can say from experience is that human societies never retrograde in civilization and prosperity except as the result of violent and terrible calamities. These calamities, he appears to assume, may be traced in most cases to

[1] See Macaulay's *Essay on Southey's Colloquies* (1830).
[2] See the essay on *Lord Bacon* (1837) of which Macaulay says: 'I have never bestowed so much care on anything that I have written' (*Life*, i. 452).

external causes rather than to the innate defects of the societies which they destroy.[1] The human intellect, he says, in reviewing Southey's *Colloquies*, tends naturally towards truth, and human society tends naturally towards progress.

Yet when Macaulay wrote of imperial Rome, or of the city states of medieval Italy, or of the Spanish Empire, or of the Mogul power, he came to a widely different conclusion from that which he defended against Sadler and Southey. As an historian Macaulay explains the decline and fall of the great states of the past mainly or entirely by reference to moral or intellectual defects which, as he describes them, appear to be natural and inevitable concomitants of one-sided excellence. But of his two theories it was the weaker that appealed to most of his fellow Whigs.

The theory of human perfectibility was a good theory for hard times, such as the 'thirties were in England, when nothing was so much needed in English statesmen as a sanguine confidence that the country would emerge unbroken from a long series of economic trials. It was a good theory, so long as those who held it did not assume that the best course which statesmen could take was to fold their hands and wait for the good times that must surely come. Macaulay was in that dangerous frame of mind when he criticized Southey's ideal of a paternal government. ' Is there any reason ', he asks, ' for believing that the government is more likely to lead the people to fall into the right way of themselves ? ' A very pertinent question to ask in reference to money-making;[2] but an absurd question if it is meant to imply that the Government had better not attempt to improve the minds or morals of its subjects. At this stage of his career Macaulay believed that the whole duty of Government was to defend the rights of property and the liberties of the individual. Four years and a half of official life in India led him to modify this belief. In 1839, when criticizing Gladstone's book on the relations of State and Church, he produced what he calls

---

[1] See essay on *Sadler's Law of Population* (1830), and also *Sadler's Reputation Refuted* (1831), (*Misc. Works*, pp. 226–66).

[2] As in Macaulay's Speech of 20 September 1831 : 'The business of government is not directly to make the people rich, but to protect them in making themselves rich ' (*Misc. Works*, i. 503).

'a good counter-theory'. It is a compromise between his own old views and those of Gladstone. The State exists *mainly* for the protection of property and personal freedom. But there is no reason why the State should not pursue other collateral objects—such as the encouragement of art and learning and education—when it happens, as it may well happen, that the Government can act more efficiently than any private individual or voluntary association. Indeed, in such a case, the Government not only *might* take the initiative, it *ought* to do so. Mr. Gladstone erred in assuming that Government ought to propagate the theology of any particular denomination. But to educate the people in the principles of Christian morality was one way, and a most effective way of ensuring a respect for individual rights. The genuineness of his conversion to a middle position is attested by the attitude which he assumed, in 1846, towards the Ten Hours Bill:

' I say first that where the health of the community is concerned it may be the duty of the State to interfere with the contracts of individuals. . . . Where the public morality is concerned it may be the duty of the State to interfere. . . . Can anyone doubt that education is a matter of the highest importance to the virtue and happiness of a people ? . . . It is said that this bill . . . will by an indirect operation limit also the labour of adults. Now Sir, though I am not prepared to vote for a bill directly limiting the labour of adults, I will plainly say that I do not think that the limitation of the labour of adults would necessarily produce all those frightful consequences that we have heard predicted. . . . Never will I believe that what makes a population stronger and healthier and wiser and better can ultimately make it poorer.' [1]

Macaulay was a vigorous thinker in the field of politics. He was not systematic, but he was open to new impressions, which was a valuable quality in these unsettled times. In his changes of mind, as in his stock of inherited principles, he is a good representative of his party. He was enough of a politician to avoid the habit of committing himself hastily to rigid formulas. But he was not immersed in politics to the degree of losing all respect for general principles. More even than Lord John Russell, he deserves the credit for translating the classical Whig

[1] *Misc. Writings*, p. 718.

doctrines into modern terms.   But he did not stop there.   He modified those doctrines to bring them into relation with the Benthamite principle of utility.   He taught his colleagues to think of sweeping constitutional changes as natural and inevitable consequences of all great changes in the distribution of property and the diffusion of political intelligence.   His robust confidence in the stability of the English character, his conviction that, however forms of government might change, England would still follow the lead of property and intelligence, were shared by many members of his party.   But no other Whig of his generation had the same gift of translating this new spirit into forcible and persuasive eloquence.

XII

SIR ROBERT PEEL

IN discussing Tory ideals and Tory statesmanship, we have
naturally spoken of Sir Robert Peel's ideas in more than
one connexion. He was a loyal Tory, but if he had been no
more than this, he would not stand higher in the roll of British
statesmen than Lord Liverpool, and indeed would probably be
rated lower than the Duke of Wellington. What then was the
individual contribution which Peel brought to the common
stock of his party? The answer must be—a genius for administration and a genius for finance.

At the beginning of the last century the Tories were strong,
and the Whigs very much the reverse, in the theory and practice
of administration. How could it be otherwise? The Tories
held office with only one short interval from 1784 to 1827, and
in that period every Tory statesman of distinction had the
opportunity of presiding over several of the great executive
departments, in the natural course of the shuffling and reshuffling
of the front-bench men in successive administrations. Lord
Liverpool is the classical instance of this unsystematic but highly
useful vagabondism. At the beginning of his political career
he was for six years a member of the Board of Control, for two
years Master of the Mint. From 1801 to 1804 he was at the
Foreign Office, and so had the invidious distinction of arranging
the Treaty of Amiens. In Pitt's second administration (1804-6)
he held the seals of the Home Department, and so again in the
Portland Cabinet (1807-8). He served under Perceval first as
Foreign Secretary and afterwards as Secretary for War and
the Colonies. From 1812, as First Lord of the Treasury and
Prime Minister, he exercised a light, but a watchful and judicious
control over the work of all his leading colleagues.

Furthermore, throughout the period the young men of promise
and good connexions were put through their apprenticeship in
such inferior offices as were not required to reward the seasoned
and dependable voters on the back benches whom the whips

delighted to honour.   So Robert Peel became Under-Secretary
of State for War and the Colonies in 1810, at the age of 22.
His chief, Lord Liverpool, on becoming Prime Minister, two
years later, promoted him to be Chief Secretary for Ireland.
Already in 1812 Peel was versed in the routine of office business
and well accustomed to defend the policy of his department in
the House of Commons. His new office made him responsible
for the smooth working of the Irish executive, and for all
Parliamentary business arising out of it, but left him in matters
of high policy responsible to the Home Secretary (Lord Sidmouth) as well as to the Lord-Lieutenant and the Prime Minister.
Therefore the four years during which he remained Chief
Secretary were chiefly valuable as giving him an enlarged
knowledge of official business, and an opportunity of studying
at close quarters the mazes of the eternal Irish question.   It is
difficult to imagine that Peel could have become, under any
circumstances, an idealist or an enthusiast.   But his Irish
experiences, which brought him into contact with the seamy
side of Dublin Castle politics, and with the incorrigible slackness
and inefficiency of the Irish civil service,[1] made him a reformer,
so far as it was possible to be a reformer and yet remain a Tory.
He took for granted that the system of governing Ireland from
Whitehall was the only possible system ; and, if he could have
changed it at his pleasure, he would have done so by making
the system more despotic than it was already, and practically
emancipating the Chief Secretary and the Viceroy from Parliamentary control.   This great parliamentarian, thanks to his
administrative experience, contracted very early and cherished
to the end of his career a healthy contempt for the practical
capacity of the House of Commons.   He was strongly of
opinion that the policy of executive departments should be
shaped by the responsible ministers with the minimum of
parliamentary interference.[2]

He was acutely conscious of the abuses of the Castle system,
and did what he could to reform them, even while he was using
his best efforts to screen them from the eyes of Parliament.
With his habitual indifference to abstract rules and principles,

[1] Parker's *Peel*, i. 95-6, 208-9.
[2] Parker's *Peel*, i. 211 ; ii. 409.

he made up his mind from the first that Ireland could not be
governed without bribery and corrupt transactions. What he
would not tolerate was the perpetration of jobs and other
irregularities which did not benefit the Government or his party.
When these higher interests were concerned, he seems, in his
salad days as Chief Secretary, to have stuck at nothing short of
a palpable violation of the statute law ; to evade the spirit of the
law did not strike him as disgraceful.[1] He did what the conventional code of politics allowed, and pleaded in extenuation
that, if he refrained from bribing, the Whigs would [2] pay the
bribe and take the *quid pro quo* without a moment's hesitation.
A venial error perhaps ; but such errors are apt to blunt the
conscience and to produce a matter-of-fact morality, which, if
applied to the private relations of life, would be abominable in
the eyes of all right-thinking men. In one respect, however,
Peel was honourably distinguished. He scorned the idea of
soiling his hands for his own personal advantage, or for the
benefit of needy dependents. He practised corruption in a
thoroughly disinterested spirit and from patriotic motives, as
the only means of maintaining the English Protestant ascendancy
which, even after 1829, he considered to be indispensable. With
abuses, as he understood the term—malpractices which were
both avoidable and expensive to the State—he dealt uncom-
promisingly.

The state of Ireland when Peel first went over was much
disturbed. He left the country quieter than he had found it ;
but this state of relative quiet, of which he spoke complacently
to Lord Sidmouth, was very like an armed truce. In 1815
Ireland was garrisoned with 27,000 infantry and 3,000 cavalry ;
the native yeomanry could not be trusted, and were therefore
worse than useless ; and Peel objected to the withdrawal of two
regiments for the campaign in Belgium. In 1816 the Chancellor
of the Exchequer budgeted for an Irish establishment of 25,000
regulars, and Peel, bent though he was upon economy, thought
that this force was insufficient ; a not unreasonable belief, seeing

---

[1] See e. g. Parker's *Peel*, i. 38–50 (transactions with reference to the
general election of 1812).

[2] In the Irish elections of 1812 the Duke of Devonshire showed
' incredible activity ' (Parker, i. 63).

that, in Tipperary alone, 9,000 regulars had been required to keep order during the previous autumn.[1] It is characteristic of the man that we do not find him attempting to diagnose this alarming situation. The national feeling of the Irish Catholics seems to have escaped his notice, though it was the first fact which struck that acute observer and sound Tory, Lord Redesdale, who went to Ireland as Lord Chancellor in 1802.[2] Peel's view of the causes of unrest was more circumstantial. The leaders of the Catholic Board were unscrupulous agitators, who were inciting the peasantry to madness by delusive promises; the peasantry deprived of these counsellors were too ignorant and too divided to give cause for serious alarm. Therefore it was essential to crush the Board and to make it impossible that any similar body should be formed in future. The Board was accordingly proclaimed in June 1814, and almost immediately sank into obscurity and insignificance. The propertied class of Roman Catholics, who like their Protestant neighbours lived in fear of a *bellum servile*, rallied to the Government. Peel went on to procure a Peace Preservation Act, which enabled the Lord-Lieutenant to establish stipendiary magistrates and a paid police force in districts where serious disturbances prevailed; also an Insurrection Act for suspending trial by jury, and establishing a curfew law in proclaimed districts. These measures produced a temporary suspension of outrages and disturbances;[3] the agrarian situation did not again become serious until 1822, and this may have convinced Peel that he had discovered how Ireland might be pacified. In fact he was favoured by circumstances. The Catholic Board would not have succumbed so easily if its members had been united. But in the years 1814–22 the Veto controversy paralysed the Catholic body, and deprived the lay leaders of the indispensable support of the clergy. When O'Connell succeeded (1823) in healing this feud, the Catholic Association rose phoenix-like from the

[1] Parker's *Peel*, i. 173, 206, 210.

[2] Redesdale to Eldon, 2 November 1803: 'The spirit of the Roman Catholic in this country calls itself Irish, separates itself equally from Great Britain and from English or Britons, and calls by the appellation of Englishmen or Saxons not only the inhabitants of Great Britain, but all the Protestants in Ireland' (Twiss, *Life of Eldon*, i. 433).

[3] Parker, *Peel*, i. 154.

ashes of the Catholic Board; and it found combustible material
ready to hand in all the old centres of agrarian disturbance.
Already in 1822 the peasants of six counties and the lower
classes in the cities of Cork and Limerick were in such a ferment
that it was necessary to make widely extended use of the
Insurrection Act.

Peel's Insurrection Act was, of course, no new invention, but
a well-tried expedient which had been first applied to Irish
disorders in 1796; it was a milder measure than the Courts
Martial Act of 1799 or the suspension of the Habeas Corpus
which had been employed by his predecessors in the years
1800–1 and 1803–5.   It only affected districts which had become
notorious for outrages, and the better sort of Chief Secretaries
resorted to it sparingly.   Its main provisions were inserted in
Irish Coercion Acts by both political parties throughout the
nineteenth century; and probably most statesmen of that century
who knew Ireland intimately, as Peel knew it, shared his view
that these provisions ought to be the permanent law of that
country.[1]   The Peace Preservation Act was more original, since
it first introduced into the statute-book the plan of maintaining
a permanent staff of professional peace-officers under the control
of a Government department, and also invented the stipendiary
magistrate.   The Act did not create a police for the whole
country; that reform was left to be carried out by Thomas
Drummond in the Constabulary Act of 1836.[2]   But Peel's Act,
though insufficient to deal with agrarian outrage organized on
the grand scale, did far more for the re-establishment of order
than all the coercive measures which had been passed before his
time either by the Irish Parliament or by that of the United
Kingdom.

These two unexceptionable measures were only palliatives.
They did not go to the root of the mischief.   That criticism
Peel himself would have been the first to admit.   But he would
have added that the root of the mischief was ineradicable,[3] being

---

[1] Parker, *Peel*, i. 155.

[2] Peel anticipated Drummond's idea.   Why he did not proceed to legislation is not clear (Parker, i. 179).

[3] Peel to Mr. Gregory, 24 June 1814: 'I said the [Peace Preservation]
Bill was not meant to meet any temporary emergency, but was rendered

the double dose of original sin with which Irish human nature had been, was, and always would be tainted. The doctrine of original sin had a fascination for the Tory mind, which in its revolt against the optimism of Rousseau felt far too confident of the essential naughtiness of mankind in the gross. Peel could never feel sanguine about the Irish question. This was not merely because he despaired of persuading his party to concede the measures needful for pacification, but because he was convinced that no English statesman ought to concede them. In 1815 he told Lord Sidmouth that the Irish Catholics could never be conciliated by mere Emancipation, so long as a separate Church establishment was maintained for the benefit of one-fifth of the Irish people.[1] He firmly believed that in the Catholic plan of campaign Emancipation figured as the first step towards Repeal of the Union, and that Repeal would have as its logical result the destruction of the land settlement of 1662.[2] When he was Chief Secretary even the first of these concessions was reprobated by most Tories; and when he retired from power in 1846 the second and the third were still regarded by the vast majority of Englishmen as quite unthinkable.

But from 1828 onwards Peel was acutely conscious of the danger of trusting solely to a policy of firm administration. An efficient police and an active, public-spirited magistracy were perhaps the boons that Ireland most required. Without these checks upon crime and sedition the material and moral condition of the Irish lower classes could never be improved. With them, he told the Chief Secretary in 1829, the country could be made fit, within ten years, for the trial of extensive reform, of schemes which would improve education and increase employment. But the first thing needful was to enlarge the police force created in 1814, so that police stations and police barracks could be established broadcast over Ireland. Peel, that is, suggested in 1829 the measure which a Whig Government allowed Mr. Drum-

---

necessary by the past state of Ireland for the last fifty years and by the probable state of it for the next five hundred' (Parker, *Peel*, i. 145). Peel to Lord F. Gower, 14 August 1814 : ' Tipperary is by far the most troublesome county of Ireland, and my firm belief is that the turbulence of it has become habitual and arises out of sheer wickedness ' (*ibid.*, ii. 125).

[1] Parker, i. 185.   [2] Parker, ii. 162.

mond to carry through Parliament in 1836. The second pre-requisite of reform was unhappily not capable of being provided by State action. Efficient magistrates could only be found, on the scale required for Peel's plans, amongst a public-spirited class of country gentlemen. ' If the gentlemen of Ireland would make a systematic attempt to enforce the law, my belief is that they have it in their own power to ensure their own protection and the public peace.' Ten good magistrates in each county was what Peel desired to have at his command. But apparently they had still to be discovered,[1] and the Wellington ministry fell while Peel was still exploring the conditions of the Irish problem. He did not cease to consider them when he went out of office in 1830. The conclusions to which he came were frankly communicated to his Cabinet in 1844. Ireland, he reminded his colleagues, had extorted great concessions from England in the past by means of organized agitation. First in 1792, when the franchise was granted to the Irish Catholics; secondly in 1829, when the Catholics had to be relieved of their remaining civil disabilities. A similar crisis was impending, and this time Repeal would be the issue. He asked the Cabinet to remember that, so long as trial by jury existed in Ireland, the Government might at any moment find itself unable to punish crime and sedition by process of law. ' How will you administer the law in a country in which the vast majority regard the law with disfavour?' That state of public opinion was bound to arise, unless the English Government adopted a policy of conciliation in good time. And if it arose when Great Britain was at war with a foreign power, the effect might be an enforced capitulation to Irish demands, even more humiliating and disastrous than that of 1792. Mere force would not avert these dangers. It was essential that the foundations of a better state of things should be laid without delay.[2]

How was this to be done? (1) Peel's first thought was to pro-vide, at the expense of the State, a national system of elementary education in which there should be proper provision for scrip-tural teaching; the schools to be open to the children of Roman Catholics and Protestants indifferently, with the most ample

---

[1] Parker, ii. 122–7.   [2] Parker, iii. 65,105, 116.

securities that there should be no proselytism, and with arrangements, if necessary, for handing over to the Protestant ministers
and Catholic priests the duty of giving doctrinal instruction.[1]
This scheme had been recommended by a Select Committee in
1827; and it was actually given a trial by the Whigs in 1832;
but the new schools did not become mixed schools of Catholics
and Protestants as Peel had hoped.[2]   They did, however, provide a better education than had hitherto been within the reach
of the Irish poor; and in 1844 Peel increased the annual grant
to them.   (2) Secondly, he was insistent that the government of
Ireland should respect the spirit of the Emancipation Act of
1829, by giving to Roman Catholics a reasonable share of public
offices and appointments.   He did not merely demand a renunciation of the bad old doctrine of Dublin Castle that, as you
cannot conciliate your enemies, you should give everything to
your friends.   There was to be an end of the more specious
principle that ' if Protestants are better qualified for offices that
fall vacant, Protestants ought to be preferred to Catholics.'[3]   If,
for example, special efforts were made to appoint a reasonable
proportion of Catholic judges, the respect of the Irish Catholics
for the Bench would be greatly increased.   And, moreover, a
policy of showing favour to Catholic candidates for public
appointments would have the effect of detaching from the
Repeal movement a number of educated Catholics who had
been driven into it by the disappointment of their legitimate
ambitions.[4]   By such means Peel hoped to unite the moderate
Protestants and moderate Roman Catholics into a middle party,
which should hold the balance of power in Ireland.   Thus, he
thought, but not otherwise, would it be possible to save the
Union from disruption and the Established Church of Ireland
from disendowment.[5]

   Peel might have been expected to address himself instinctively
and in the first instance to promoting the economic welfare of

----

[1] Parker, ii. 127.   [2] Parker, i. 393.
   [3] Peel to Sir James Graham, 16 June 1843 (Parker, iii. 53-4).   In this
matter Peel followed the example which had been set by Lord John Russell
in 1836 (*Early Correspondence of Lord John Russell*, ii. 169-72).
   [4] Parker's *Peel*, iii. 55-6, 61, 116-17, 182, 185-6.
   [5] Cabinet Memorandum, 17 February 1844 (Parker, iii. 106); Peel to
Lord Heytesbury, 1 August 1844 (*ibid.*, iii. 114).

Ireland. He was by no means indifferent to economic questions, although as a young statesman he took no trouble to familiarize himself with the speculations of the theoretical economists. He welcomed the Corn Law of 1815 as an unquestionable boon to Irish agriculture. He desired to stimulate other Irish industries by means of a protective tariff.[1] But it seems to have been late in his career that he acknowledged the urgent need of helping the small Irish cultivator. In 1829 he ascribed the wretched condition of the peasantry to 'the tenure of land, high rents and various other causes [*sc.* of crime], many of which are out of the control of any human authority, and scarcely one of which admits of the application of any immediate remedy.'[2]

His chief lieutenant in the forties was Sir James Graham; and Graham, who had no first-hand knowledge of Irish administration but a considerable knowledge of agriculture, pressed the case for an inquiry. It was needed, in his opinion, to discover why Irish landlords as a class were bankrupt and why the poverty of their tenants was desperate and heartrending. Graham had no great hope of remedying this state of things by legislation. But he felt that an inquiry must be made, especially as he was informed that the peasants favoured Repeal solely in the hope of improving their wretched condition.[3] Accordingly a Commission was set up, with Lord Devon as its chairman, to investigate the case which O'Connell and his party had so long proclaimed to deaf ears. In spite of the fact that Peel's Government regarded fixity of tenure as a dangerous innovation, the Devon Commission's report in favour of giving protection to the Irish tenant was so cogent that it could not be disregarded. Peel went cautiously to work. He did not accept all the proposals of the Devon Commission; and he caused the Government bill to be introduced in the first instance in the House of Lords, where it might be easier to meet and to satisfy the criticism of the landed interest than in the more heated atmosphere of the Lower House. But the bill, though warmly championed by Lord Stanley, met with so unfriendly a reception that it was withdrawn before the third reading. Graham took

[1] Parker, i. 233.   [2] Parker, ii. 137.
[3] Parker, iii. 363-4.

the measure seriously, as an integral part of the new scheme of conciliation,[1] and appears to have shared with Stanley the responsibility for its details. Peel appears to have taken no very active part. He had begun to despair of Ireland. Late in 1845 he told Sir James Graham that Ireland was in a state which seemed to preclude honest and impartial government. 'To conduct the Government on party principles ensures the support of one party at least; to administer it on any other than party principles is to forfeit the confidence of both. I am firmly persuaded that you have done whatever could be done to apply a remedy to a sad state of things.'[2]

We need not think badly of Peel because he failed, and confessed his failure, in Ireland, that 'Serbonian bog, where armies whole have sunk'. We must remember that, on the question of tenant right, he had against him the landowners of the three kingdoms; and that, if he had attempted to endow the Catholic Church in Ireland, he would have united against his Government the high Tories and Dissenters of England, the Presbyterians of Scotland, and the whole Orange interest. He is entitled to the credit of being the first responsible statesman in England who drew up a reasoned plan of conciliation. It was his misfortune that only two items of his programme, and those of secondary importance—the increase of the Maynooth grant and the increase of the grant for elementary education—could be passed through Parliament, though in both Houses he had a majority for all ordinary purposes.

If we turn from Ireland to Great Britain, we not only find in his policy the proofs of good intentions; we must admit that he rendered considerable services. It must be admitted that his conduct in regard to social legislation gave great pain to Lord Ashley, to whom he offered no practical support on the Collieries Bill (1842), although Sir James Graham had made fair promises.[3] While Peel and Graham honourably supported, as far as they thought practicable, the movement for the moral and religious education of poor children, both held out firmly against Ashley's Ten Hour Bill (1843-4), and insisted that a twelve-hour day

[1] Parker's *Graham*, ii. 13-14.   [2] *Ibid.*, ii. 19.
[3] Hodder, *Shaftesbury*, 229-31.

was the utmost concession which could be enforced without
ruining the manufacturers. Ashley in his disappointment spoke
of them with measureless indignation. ' Their speeches ingenious in argument, but wretched in principle and feeling, purely
commercial, Peel urging a decay of trade, Graham an abatement
of wages. . . Peel argued in fact against all interference. . . In
the sight of God and man he abdicated the function of government.' [1]

On this subject, at all events, Ashley was better treated by the
Whigs, the natural allies of the manufacturers, than by his own
party. Lord John Russell supported the Ten Hours' Bill both
in Opposition (1846), and when himself Prime Minister (1847).
It was another Whig, the great Macaulay, who summed up the
case for Ashley in a spirit of noble optimism. ' Never will I
believe that what makes a population stronger and healthier and
wiser and better can ultimately make it poorer.' [2] It was not
Peel's habit to call upon his supporters to run the risk of material
losses for the sake of immaterial gains. Not that his own mind
was sordid. As an individual he sympathized with Ashley over
the Collieries Act, although his own pocket was touched by it.
As an individual he subscribed heavily to causes which he did
not venture to subsidize from public funds.[3] But Peel was
acutely conscious of the selfishness of average human nature,
and terribly afraid of imposing too great a strain upon the
loyalty of the rank and file of his party. The reforms which he
liked to undertake were safe reforms, reforms which would not
give his enemies a handle, or leave any large section of his

[1] Hodder, p. 296. But Ashley does not seem to have realized that his
bill meant in effect a ten-hours' day for adult workers. ' The whole debate
proceeded and will proceed on a lie : on the lie that the Bill is directed to
the control of the labour of grown men ' (Hodder, 342). He might have
argued that grown men had no right to exercise their right of making free
contracts at the expense of the health and happiness of the young.

[2] Speech on the Ten Hours Bill, 22 May 1846.

[3] He and Graham also subscribed to Ashley's election expenses after
Ashley had resigned rather than vote for the Repeal of the Corn Laws.
They subscribed so that he might be able to look after his Ten Hours Bill.
' If I were returned, and the next night moved the Ten Hours Bill and by
success drove them from office, they should consider that it was simply within
the compass of my inevitable duty.' The money was civilly declined.
(Hodder, p. 341.)

followers with a grievance; the reform of the criminal laws
relating to theft (1825), the abolition of capital punishment in
cases where such punishment was obviously not needed as
a preventive (1830), the institution of the new Metropolitan
Police (1829), the elimination of abuses from the judicial system,
the reorganization of the national tariff.   His correspondence
shows that he was always on the alert to discover some possibility of uncontentious reform, and always both ingenious and
indefatigable in working out the details of any reform which he
took in hand.   But, as a Conservative, he could not afford to
attack abuses which had the support of powerful interests and
parties.[1]   At least he could not afford to do so unless, as in
1829 and 1846, the danger of doing nothing was greater than
that involved in taking a bold line.

We know what the sterner and more rigid Tories thought at
the time of those two great surrenders—the Catholic Emancipation Act and the Repeal of the Corn Laws.   Many good men
swallowed their doubts and even praised Peel's patriotism in
undertaking measures which he disliked, but which he felt to be
inevitable.   But it is worth noticing the attitude of Ashley, who
in Peel's time succeeded to the position which Wilberforce had
held in the days of Pitt and Liverpool, the position of keeper
of the conscience of the Tory party.   Ashley in 1829 was
a young and subordinate member of the ministry, and he
changed sides on the Catholic question when his leaders did so.
But his private conviction, from which he never departed, was
that though the measure was needed Peel and Wellington ought
not to have become responsible for it.   'They should have said
boldly to the Crown: " it is a measure that must be passed, but
it should be passed by those who agree with it.   We are not
the men to do it."   And I have often thought in subsequent
years, that their action inflicted such a deadly blow on confidence
in public men, that there has never since been a complete

---

[1] Ashley's general verdict on Tory administration 1841-3 is penetrating,
though sharpened by his own conflicts with his leaders. 'The disappointment is general; men looked for high sentiments and heard small opinions;
for principles and were put off with expediency' (Hodder, 257).   He attri-
butes to Peel 'a mighty desire to reverse the rule of the Apostle and be first
peaceable and then pure' (*ibid.*, 258).

recovery'.[1] At the end of 1845 the moral problem was the same
—Ashley, like his leader, converted to a policy which they
had long been pledged to oppose. This time Ashley decided
that he could not honestly vote against the Corn Laws without
seeking re-election. He resigned his seat, even though this
involved leaving his Ten Hours Bill, which was already before
the House of Commons, to be defended by others. His satisfaction at the Repeal of the Corn Laws was tempered with contempt for the man to whom repeal was due. In his private
diary he endorsed the biting criticisms of Disraeli's speech on
the third reading, ' bitter ', he says, ' in principle and motive,
hardly exaggerated in imputation '. Peel had denounced party
to set up a party of his own. He had led the Tories and followed
the Whigs. ' His opinions, I suspect, have ever been discordant
with his conduct.' [2] Considered as a party leader, and judged
by the standards of parliamentary generalship, Peel had displayed ' his own miserable want of foresight and discrimination '.
He had reduced Parliament, party, and men's minds to the
original chaos.

We mention Ashley's views to show how far Peel deviated
from the path which his party expected him to pursue. He was
not, at any time of his career after 1828, a man who held dog-
matically certain principles. He was prepared to argue that, as
times change, so principles must be modified. The practical
aim which he pursued, whether in power or in opposition, was
that of holding together the party in which he had grown up
and through which he had risen. The *raison d'être* of that
party was to maintain so much of the eighteenth-century constitution as it was practicable to defend. He thought of the
Tories as a beleaguered garrison, whose right and whose duty
it was to evacuate and demolish untenable positions, in order
that what remained of the fortress might hold out the longer.
And at the back of his mind there was always the assumption
that, if changes had to come, they could be more safely carried
out by the Tories, and perhaps more safely under his own leadership than in any other way. Lest it should be thought that,
in charging Peel with this obsession, we are merely repeating

---

[1] Hodder, p. 48.   [2] Hodder, p. 343.

Disraeli's indictment,[1] we will refer here to the evidence of Peel's own letters and papers.

First with regard to Catholic Emancipation. Peel tells us how, in the early summer of 1828, before the election of O'Connell for county Clare, and before such a contretemps had been anticipated, he recommended Wellington to take up and settle the Irish question.[2] In a subsequent communication he justified this advice by arguing that it was important to make a *sincere* and *honest* attempt to settle the question on *just* principles—as though the Tory party was the only one from which such an attempt could be expected. Yet almost immediately afterwards he predicts that the Duke's just measure will have to be carried mainly by the votes of members who are not committed to support the Government.[3] It does not occur to him as possible that any one but a Tory leader can safely be commissioned to rally and lead this heterogeneous majority. At this stage it was his intention to take no part in the management of this most difficult campaign ; he proposed to resign, no doubt in all sincerity, as being deeply committed against the Catholic claims by many previous votes and declarations. But, finding that the Duke, unaided, made little headway against the opposition of the King and the bishops, Peel resolved to depart from his self-denying resolution. Why this change? 'I was firmly convinced', he writes, 'that if the Duke of Wellington should fail in procuring the King's consent . . . no other public man could succeed in procuring that assent, and in prevailing over the opposition to be encountered in the House of Lords.'[4] On the strength of this conviction Peel wrote to the Duke (12 Jan. 1829) to offer that co-operation which, six or seven months previously, he had felt obliged to withhold.

Why did Peel assume that only he and Wellington could meet the crisis? He admits that Earl Grey was the natural leader of an Emancipation ministry ; since Emancipation had long been a cardinal feature, perhaps indeed the principal feature, of his political programme. Within two years Grey

---

[1] *Lord George Bentinck*, p. 32 : 'When Sir Robert Peel was of opinion that the corn-laws must be repealed, he was resolved to be the repealer.'

[2] *Memoirs*, i. 128.   [3] *Memoirs*, i. 184-7.

[4] *Memoirs*, i. 280.

was able to form a ministry strong enough in the House of
Commons and in the country to override the King and the
House of Lords, and to carry an even more contentious measure
than Emancipation. Peel, it is true, insinuates that Grey was
the last person likely to succeed in persuading George IV. But
no one knew better than Peel that none of the King's animosities
were insuperable in the last resort.[1]   To assume that Grey was
out of the question was a hazardous assumption, very soon to
be disproved by the course of events. But Peel made the
assumption, and allowed himself to be completely reassured by
a written statement that the Duke did not see the slightest
chance of getting on without him.[2]

In 1846 Peel had a stronger case for arguing that no alternative to his own Cabinet was available. The only Whig statesman of high standing who had declared against the Corn Laws
was Lord John Russell. He was the natural leader of the
Whigs, but, for one reason or another, he found himself unable
to construct a solid ministry. Failing Russell, there remained
only Cobden and the Manchester Free Traders. But Cobden
was new to Parliament ; and even Russell, who was anxious for
Cobden's support, did not think of offering him anything better
than the Vice-Presidency of the Board of Trade. If a Protectionist Cabinet had been attempted, Lord Stanley would have
been the obvious choice ; but neither he nor any other of the
ministers who broke with Peel on the question of the Corn
Laws was prepared to form a ministry. This we know from
Peel's explicit reply to a question from the Queen.[3]

We come, therefore, to the question whether Peel did all that
he could and should have done to smooth the way for a Russell
ministry. This is a question which has been variously answered.
There were several difficulties of a serious character which em-
barrassed Russell in his task. Though he had expressed himself boldly in his Edinburgh manifesto (22 Nov. 1845), advocat-
ing the total extinction of the corn-duties ' within a short period ',

[1] See Lord John Russell's remarks, *Recollections and Suggestions*, p. 58.
[2] *Memoirs*, i. 280–1, 285.
[3] Peel to the Queen, 15 December 1845 (Parker, iii. 248). Peel had put
the question to Stanley on the previous day, and wrote after the interview to
Wellington : 'he states that he could not undertake to form such a ministry
or to advise the attempt' (Peel, *Memoirs*, ii. 232).

he had not consulted with his colleagues about a fiscal policy before the Queen sent for him. He had intended gradual abolition; but he yielded to Grey's view that abolition must be immediate and final.[1] He found himself at issue with Grey on the larger question of free trade. Secondly (and this was the ostensible reason for the breakdown of his plans), Grey declined to take office if Palmerston became Foreign Secretary. But there is no reason to suppose that these difficulties need have been fatal. Grey would, on his own confession, have been more amenable if he had realized that he was endangering the formation of the Cabinet.[2] We are left with the impression that Lord John was not anxious to take office, and seized the first plausible excuse for resigning. The end of the business left him, as he wrote to his wife, 'with a great sense of relief'; he told her father that he had 'happily failed in forming a ministry'.[3] For he would have come into office as the leader of a minority in the House of Commons. His success or failure would have depended upon the attitude of the friends of Sir Robert Peel. And his attempts to obtain Peel's support had not been met in a satisfactory fashion. Peel had promised, through the Queen, 'to support in a private capacity' measures similar to those which he had advised as Prime Minister; but he stated that it would be unbecoming to make any reference to the details of such measures. His principle would have been in general accordance with that of Lord John's Edinburgh letter. But he would have wished to give some relief to landowners by the remission of onerous charges.[4] Three days later, Lord John told the Queen that he proposed sending to Peel a draft of his proposed Corn Laws Bill, in order to learn whether it would have Peel's support; he intimated at the same time that, if Peel could not promise support, he himself must decline to form a Government. Peel, through the Queen (Dec. 15), objected that

[1] Stanmore, *Sidney Herbert*, i. 56. J. R. Thursfield (from the Grey Papers) in *Eng. Hist. Review*, 1886, p. 123. Memorandum by Prince Albert, 20 December 1845, in *Letters of Queen Victoria*, ii. 59. (The third Earl Grey, not his father, the second Earl of Reform Bill fame, who had just died.)

[2] *E. H. R.*, 1886, p. 131 (Grey to Ellice, 27 December 1845).

[3] *Life*, i. 416.

[4] Peel to the Queen, 10 December 1845 (*Letters of Queen Victoria*, ii. 52–4).

it would be inconvenient for the head of a Government to frame his measures in consultation with some one who was not in the Government; he also argued that co-operation between himself and Russell would lead to more difficulties than it obviated; it would be 'distasteful to the House of Commons and embarrassing to all parties'.   Still, he renewed his general promise of support, and added that three of his colleagues—Graham, Sidney Herbert, and Lord Lincoln—were pledged to take the same line as himself.   He also gave his personal view that 'many influential peers' would support a reform of the Corn Laws.[1]   This reply was diversely construed by those whom it most concerned. The Prince Consort gently hinted that it was ambiguous and embarrassing, and would probably induce Lord John to give up his task; Peel's intentions no doubt were good, but the position of Lord John was peculiarly difficult.[2]

The request which Lord John Russell had made was of an unusual kind; but then the situation was unusual.   With a little more goodwill and mutual confidence the difficulty might have been solved.   But Peel was afraid of being entrapped into a coalition,[3] and the Whigs, as they confessed in private conversation, were afraid that his general promise of support in a private capacity meant little or even was intended to mislead. On 16 December Russell made a further effort to obtain a pledge. His measure would be for immediate repeal of the Corn Laws, not, as his Edinburgh letter had seemed to indicate, a proposal for immediate suspension with ultimate repeal.[4]   Would Sir Robert resist this proposal?   Sir Robert's reply was that he would give no promise beyond that, which he had already

---

[1] Peel, *Memoirs*, ii. 234-7; Parker's *Peel*, iii. 249.

[2] Prince Albert to Peel 17 December 1845 (Parker, *Peel*, iii. 251).

[3] Only Grey had ever suggested a coalition with Peel; all the other Whig leaders were averse from this (Stanmore, *Sidney Herbert*, i. 56).

[4] This decision was taken, on Grey's proposal, at a conclave of the Whig leaders on 16 December (Stanmore, *Sidney Herbert*, i. 56). It was communicated to the Queen on the same day, by her to Peel, who replied on 17 December (Peel, *Memoirs*, ii. 238-41). According to Macaulay this way of testing Peel's loyalty had been devised and provisionally adopted on 12 December, at a small meeting of five leaders (of whom Macaulay was one), subject to subsequent confirmation by the other leaders on their return to London (*Life of Macaulay*, ii. 164-5).

tendered, of co-operation, in his private capacity, in the 'adjustment' of the Corn Laws. For this reserve he could give an excellent reason. He had offered support on a policy of gradual abolition, that being his own policy, and also the policy indicated in Russell's Edinburgh letter. Now he was asked suddenly and peremptorily if he would go one step farther. This might seem a momentous decision to take on the spur of the moment. But was it really so momentous? The progressively diminishing scale of low duties which Peel had proposed to his colleagues a fortnight previously would be worth very little to the English agriculturist, who was far more efficiently protected by the high level of corn prices in all the chief foreign markets.[1] Peel himself believed that no reduction in the duties would materially affect the price of corn; he stated this expressly, six weeks later (27 Jan. 1848) in the House of Commons,[2] when he offered to the agriculturists the illusory concession of a low sliding-scale duty for three years only. Either measure, his or Russell's, was formidable to the landed interest, not as diminishing the incomes of country gentlemen in the immediate future, but as assuring them that, if ever foreign competition in the English market should become acute, they would not be in any way protected. Frank explanations of this kind would have cleared the atmosphere. As they were not forthcoming, Russell seized the opportunity of a breach with Grey, the principal Free Trader of his party, and announced to the Queen the failure of his negotiations.[3]

---

[1] See Peel's memorandum of 2 December 1845 (*Memoirs*, ii. 214–20), and the comments of Sidney Herbert (Stanmore's *Sidney Herbert*, i. 52–3).

[2] In reply to a question from Lord George Bentinck (Disraeli, *Bentinck*, p. 76).

[3] According to Greville, when Peel's letter was considered by the Whig leaders, ten voted for taking the Government and five against. Some of the ten were still suspicious of Peel's intentions, and Greville supports the explanation, which I have given, of the ultimate decision not to take office. 'Peel's reserve was really, then, the cause of the failure' (Greville, *Memoirs*, 21 Dec. 1845). Macaulay, who attended a Whig Conference on 12 December, lays stress on the difficulties which would be inherited by a Whig Government. 'Ireland, we fear, is on the brink of something like a servile war. . . . Foreign politics look dark. An augmentation of the army will be necessary.' But his main fear was that Peel would leave the Whigs in the lurch about the Corn Laws (*Life*, ii. 164–5). Yet later, on 20 Decem-

It is probable, though we have no proof, that Peel foresaw this result, and that he was not displeased. True, he expressed in very emphatic language his joy at the prospect of being relieved from office ; now at last, he wrote to a friend, he could conform to his own sense of the public necessities ; now he was absolved from following blindly 'certain party doctrines'. He could, it seemed, go out into the wilderness again, as he had done in 1830, and build up another, more intelligent, more enterprising party. He was also, we are told on the authority of the Prince Consort, 'much affected' by the failure of Lord John, and also hurt that Lord John had not confided in the integrity of his motives. He said that he would have supported *any* measure that Lord John should have thought fit to introduce. But in the same breath he accepted office. He had already warned his former colleagues that he should do so. They might join him again if they pleased. But only on condition of accepting the policy which he meant to lay before them.[1] His confidence in his colleagues was justified ; only Lord Stanley declined to return ; even the Duke of Wellington described the Corn Laws as 'a subordinate consideration'.[2]

If the rank and file followed the example of their chiefs, it was indeed a noble prospect that opened before him. The old Tory party, purged of its prejudices, absolved from old and inconvenient principles, should launch forth on a career of wise and even-handed fiscal reform. All readers of Disraeli's *Bentinck* will remember its inimitable dissection of the Free Trade policy which Peel outlined to an expectant House of Commons at the opening of the next session ; of the appeals to manufacturers to bear patiently the loss of protective duties which in fact were negligible ; of the trivial remissions of certain county rates assessed upon the land ; of the otiose proposal that the Government should lend money, on strictly commercial terms, to improving landlords. No doubt Disraeli exaggerates his points of detail ; but the main point, that the scheme, apart from the proposals affecting corn, was a thing of shreds and patches, is

ber (*Life*, ii. 168), he throws the whole blame on Lord Grey and Lord Palmerston, but especially on the former.
    [1] *Memorandum by Prince Albert*, 20 December 1845 (*Queen Victoria's Letters*, i. 61).   [2] Parker's *Peel*, iii. 285.

obvious and undeniable.   Yet Peel was thrilled with enthusiasm by the contemplation of his own purposes.   That enthusiasm finds an echo in one of Prince Albert's memoranda of this time :

'Sir Robert has *an immense scheme in view* ; he thinks he shall be able to remove the contest entirely from the dangerous ground upon which it has got—that of a war between the manufacturers, the hungry and the poor against the landed proprietors, the aristocracy, which can only end in the ruin of the latter; he will not only bring forward a measure upon the Corn Law, but a much more comprehensive one. He will deal with the whole commercial system of the country.   He will adopt the principle of the League, *that of removing all protection and abolishing all monopoly*, but not in favour of one class and as a triumph over another, but to the benefit of the nation, farmers as well as manufacturers.'[1]

In justice to Peel it may be supposed that he had been unbosoming himself not merely as to immediate plans, but also as to the ulterior programme which he hoped to carry out, if only his followers would stand firmly by him.   He was not by nature of a sanguine temperament; but at this moment he felt like Christian in *Pilgrim's Progress*, when the load of sin fell off his back.   The work which he now had in hand was thoroughly congenial, and by the consent even of his political opponents he was better qualified than any of his rivals for it. Cobden, for example, was heartily glad that the fight for Free Trade would be conducted by Peel rather than by Russell. Peel, he said, had the better grasp of economic questions and the juster appreciation of their importance; Peel also could judge more accurately the opinion of the public.   Peel, not Russell, ought to be leader of the middle class.[2]

But, before the Session was far advanced, Peel had to realize that his position in Parliament was weak, however favourably the country at large might be disposed towards him.   More than half of the Conservatives, 197 out of 320, were expected

---

[1] Memorandum of 25 December 1845 (*Queen Victoria's Letters*, ii. 66). Greville, who talked to Peel on 23 December, says : ' he was evidently elated at the advantage that had been thrown into his hands, and chuckling mightily at the pitiful figure which the Whigs cut ' (*Greville Memoirs*, iii. 447).

[2] Cobden to Combe, 3 March 1846 (Morley's *Cobden*, 366).

to vote against him on the grand issue. For that issue he could depend upon the Whig members; and when the Opposition had exhausted the resources of obstruction the Corn Bill passed the third reading in the Commons by 327 votes to 229. It was otherwise with the Irish Coercion Bill—a measure necessitated by the prevalence of agrarian crime in five Irish counties. Strong as the case for the bill appeared to be, the Whigs could hardly be expected to be unanimous in its favour. They still needed the alliance of O'Connell's tail; and they could boast that for seven years (1834-41) they had ruled without recourse to extraordinary powers. But Peel and Graham felt that without extraordinary powers Ireland could no longer be governed by them.[1] Much depended upon the attitude of Lord John Russell, and Russell's intentions remained obscure till June, probably through the restraining influence of the Whig peers, who were, to a man, in favour of coercion.[2] But early in June Russell decided to oppose the bill, having already ascertained that Bentinck's Protectionists would do so. Once this combination· had been formed, the days of the Peel administration were clearly numbered. Peel accepted the inevitable with equanimity, refusing to try the experiment of dissolution. There was no doubt that he had lost the support of his party. A general election, on the most favourable forecast, would only enable him to return to power as the ally of the Free Traders, and an alliance so unnatural, founded on the single point of Free Trade, could not possibly last long.[3]

[1] Peel on the position of the Government, 21 June 1845 (*Memoirs*, ii. 291).

[2] Parker's *Peel*, iii. 345 (Duke of Bedford's statement).

[3] Peel on the position of the Government, *Memoirs*, ii. 294-7.

XIII

SOCIAL REFORMERS, 1775–1852

BEHIND the religious scepticism of the eighteenth century—
a scepticism which made light of every revelation but that
afforded by the natural reason—there was a more or less explicit
faith in a providential order of the universe. Man was intended
to be perfect; he. had within himself the power of becoming
perfect; and if he fell short of perfection the failure must be
attributed to some fault in himself or in the society of which
he was a member. It could not be attributed to any handicap
imposed by his physical environment; for the physical world
was providentially adapted to his needs and his capacities.
Opinions differed upon the problem how perfection was to be
attained. Hedonists like Hartley and Helvetius offered the
simple rule that the individual should avoid pain and pursue
pleasure. Reason would naturally have to be invoked whenever it came to a choice between alternative lines of conduct,
each carrying with it a train of pleasures mixed with pains,
some intense and others faint, some long and others brief. But,
assuming the balance to be fairly calculated, the individual
would be pursuing the right and perfect course; and in doing
so he would be making his utmost possible contribution to the
happiness of his society. Utilitarians of the Benthamite school
seriously qualified this theory by demanding that 'the greatest
happiness of the greatest number' should be the object of the
legislator, and that in all calculations of the balance of pains and
pleasures 'each should count for one and no man for more than
one', thus introducing the ideal of social justice. But it was
left for William Godwin to elaborate the ideal of Justice, and to
represent the perfect state as that in which justice, as between
one man and another, as between the individual and the State,
was fully realized.

Benthamism as a theory of moral action only appealed to the
select few who were confident that their special training or their
native acumen would enable them to reach better moral judge-

ments, by means of the hedonistic calculus, than could be formed with the help of religion and tradition. As a rule of statesmanship it was more generally accepted, even in its author's lifetime, because it had long been obvious that many problems of politics and legislation could not be settled by a simple reference to accepted moral principles. But for men who had no practical experience of statecraft, and no strong desire to meddle with it, who only needed some self-evident principle by which to guide their private conduct, Godwin was a more humane and less bewildering guide. His influence is less easy to trace than that of Bentham ; for Godwin had not Bentham's art of coining aphorisms which stuck in the memory of the faithful. But echoes of the leading ideas of Godwin's *Social Justice* occur in the most unlikely quarters. His influence on the mind of Shelley has long been acknowledged. M. Halévy, in his essay on Thomas Hodgskin, has shown how some of Godwin's ideas gave a peculiar bent and complexion to the teaching of the earliest English socialists. In the bewildered mind of William Lovett, that most likeable of all the Chartists, Godwinist aspirations appear to underlie and to outlive all the long series of his practical schemes for the moral and material improvement of his class.

Godwin's style is often flat and dull, the style of a man who has read enough of French philosophy to blunt his sense of English idiom. But his matter is more inspiring than his style— and nowhere more so than when he is explaining his ideal of social service :

' How much am I bound to do for the general weal, that is for the benefit of the individuals of whom the whole is composed ? Everything in my power. . . . If the extraordinary case should occur in which I can promote the general good by my death more than by my life, justice requires that I should be content to die ' (Bk. II, c. 2).

No man, he says in another passage, has a right to do what he will with his own fortune or even with his own time.[1] To refuse assistance to a starving man is nothing less than murder. The crime is equally heinous if I deny to another the means

---

[1] A thought as old as Christianity and derived by Godwin from one of the sermons of Dean Swift.

which are required to perfect his intellectual attainments or his moral character (Bk. II, c. 5). Since all men have the same common nature, they are capable of the same kind of improvement, and in justice they have ' an equal right to be improved ' (Bk. II, c. 4).

This is the kind of social justice that Godwin desires—a justice which cannot be secured by legislation or by any forms of government. It is a sentiment of benevolence ; it is charity as described in the New Testament. When the spirit of justice has permeated the whole community there will, thinks Godwin, be no further need of law or government. ' Render the plain dictates of justice level to every capacity . . . and the whole species will become reasonable and virtuous.'[1]

In the meantime, pending the victory of the sentiment of justice, there must be a Government, to defend the community from foreign enemies and from its own criminals. For purposes of police and justice each parish can provide its own machinery. For defence against invasion, Godwin thinks, it will be sufficient that the parishes should enter into a temporary league or alliance whenever the emergency arises. It will not arise often, since most of the ordinary causes of war will disappear with the abolition of the unitary State. ' For wars do not originate in the unbiassed propensities of nations, but in the cabals of governments, and the propensities that governments inspire into the people at large.'[2] The effect of subdividing all national States into self-governing parochial republics will be to annihilate the sentiment of patriotism and to substitute for it the spirit of humanity which regards the whole human species as one vast republic. ' The love of our country, if we would speak accurately, is another of those specious illusions which have been invented by impostors in order to render the multitude the blind instruments of their crooked designs.'[3] It is unnecessary to criticize this ideal in detail. But it is, in effect, a *résumé* and a defence of the criticisms which were provoked in this period, first by the growing tendency of all governments towards increased centralization and towards enlarging the domain of the State, and secondly by the tendency of statesmen to

[1] *Political Justice*, Bk. V, c. 24.   [2] *Ibid.*, Bk. V, c. 22.
[3] *Ibid.*, Bk. V, c. 16.

regard international relations as a *bellum omnium contra omnes*.[1]

But Godwin despairs of reducing human society to this simple shape until wealth has been redistributed more equitably among the members of society.   There must be an economic revolution before there can be any political reformation.   For so long as the majority of men are condemned to lifelong poverty they will regard the social order as a contrivance for vesting all the advantages of the social compact in the hands of a few favoured individuals ; and they will regard the state of society as a state of war.   It is just, Godwin thinks, that a man should enjoy the fruit of his own labour, within reasonable limits.   But he assumes that no man becomes rich unless he is extravagantly rewarded for his services.   ' All riches, and especially all hereditary riches, are to be considered as the salary of a sinecure office. . . . Hereditary wealth is in reality a premium paid to idleness, an immense annuity expended to retain mankind in brutality and ignorance.'[2]   On the strength of such sayings we may regard Godwin as one of the founders of English socialism. In dealing with the distribution of wealth, as in dealing with the political organization of society, he pays little attention to practical difficulties.   These difficulties, he tells us, arise from the present imperfections of human nature, which will all melt away as soon as the ideal commonwealth has been erected.

So far as principles and ideals are concerned, no book could well be more revolutionary than *Political Justice*, which preaches anarchism and communism (of property) without disguise.   But Godwin believed and taught that no revolution of any lasting value could be effected otherwise than by argument and by persuasion ; it is useless to overthrow laws and institutions until society has ceased to believe in them.   He exhorted his disciples to work unremittingly at the business of converting public opinion, and he warned them that the process must in the nature of things be slow :

' In attempting prematurely to anticipate the conquest of truth,

[1] Cf. Paine, *Rights of Man*, Part II, c. 5, says that the states of Europe in their relations *inter se* ' put themselves beyond the law as well of God as of man '.

[2] *Political Justice*, Bk. I, c. 5 ; Bk. VIII, c. 2.

we shall infallibly give birth to deformity and abortion. If we have
patience to await her natural progress, and to assist her cause by
no arguments that are not worthy of her, the event will be both certain
and illustrious.'[1]

There is obviously a close affinity between the ideas of Paine
and Godwin, and it is possible that to some extent Godwin
actually borrowed from the *Rights of Man*, which he read in
manuscript some time before the publication of *Political Justice*.
The two agree in their criticisms of existing institutions, although
Godwin's criticisms are more guarded in their language, and are
not so obviously aimed at the government of Great Britain.
Paine had the greater vogue at first because he was a master of
the biting phrase. 'The Duke of Richmond alone (and there
are cases similar to his) takes away for himself as much as would
maintain two thousand poor and aged persons.' 'The crown
signifies a nominal office of a million sterling a year, the business
of which consists in receiving the money.' 'The foundation and
the superstructure of the government is bad. Prop it as you
please, it continually sinks into court government, and ever
will.' 'It is wrong to say that God made rich and poor; he
made only male and female, and he gave them the earth for their
inheritance.' 'Moderation in temper is always a virtue; but
moderation in principle is a species of vice.' Paine also had
the advantage of the man who professes that he has found
a simple remedy for an acknowledged evil. Paine produced
a whole string of remedies—government by a single chamber,
the abolition of monarchy, State-aided education for the children
of the poor, old-age pensions, a progressive income-tax on landowners—and was ready in each case to show what precise evil
was attacked, and how the remedy would work. But Godwin
held out hopes for the future which did not depend on these or
any other dramatic measures which it would require a violent
revolution to enforce.

Paine's progressive income-tax, and Godwin's pious hope that
wealth may be more equally distributed in the future, are signs
of a tendency to call in question the theories of private property
which were accepted as self-evident by all political parties.

---

[1] *Political Justice*, Bk. IV, c. 2.

This tendency in a very naïve form appears in the celebrated
pamphlet of Thomas Spence, the Newcastle schoolmaster, on
The Real Rights of Man (1775).   Spence has a place, though
a humble place, in the troublous history of English radicalism.
For he was the patron saint of the Spencean Society, which
was founded after his death (1814) to propagate his theory of
agrarian communism.   This society alarmed the poet Southey
and also Lord Liverpool by an illiterate manifesto which it put
forth in 1816.   Some of its members were involved in the riots
which disgraced the first and the second Spa Fields meetings of
that year.   It was suppressed by statute in 1817, along with all
other clubs which proposed the division of the land and the
confiscation of funded property ;   several of its members (in
particular Arthur Thistlewood) were involved in the Cato Street
Conspiracy.   The Spenceans were at no time formidable or
numerous, and Thomas Spence found the vending of his tracts
an unprofitable business, from first to last ; but the Spencean
doctrine served its turn in 1816 and 1817 as a bogy with which
to frighten men of property from dabbling in reform.

Spence's best-known work is hardly terrifying.   It has a strong
family resemblance to Robert Blatchford's *Merrie England*.   It
was suggested by a dispute between the corporation and the
freemen of Newcastle about the common lands of the town,
which led Mr. Spence, not himself a freeman, but the son of an
Aberdeen cobbler, to muse upon the theme how happy the poor
might be if every poor man had his rights.   With these musings
he astonished the Philosophical Society of Newcastle in a lecture
of which his pamphlet gives the substance.   The society expelled him for publishing the pamphlet, and his position in
Newcastle became so invidious that he removed to London.

Landlords were unpopular at Newcastle in 1775, being, in
Spence's phrase, ' haughty, unthankful men ', and he started on
his speculations by trying to imagine what would happen if the
landlord were eliminated from the social framework.   ' Let it be
supposed then ', he suggests to the Philosophical Society, that
the whole people ' in some country ' have resolved to assert
their equal property in the land, and to live together in such
a fashion that each shall reap the utmost possible advantage from
his natural rights.   He assumes that this emancipated people

will hold together in the parishes of which they are already members. Each parish will become a self-governing corporation, will be recognized as owning all the land within its boundaries, and will pledge itself never to alienate the least morsel of this common heritage. Each householder will rent from the parish his fair share of the parish soil; and the funds thus obtained will enable the parish to meet all expenses which are necessary for the common good, including a contribution to the upkeep of a national government. This national government Spence assumes to be essential, and the mainspring of it will be an elected parliament; but the State lies in the background of his thought, as a distant and not unduly interfering providence. The parish will build and repair all houses, bridges, highways, and canals. It will make and maintain convenient and delightful streets. It will plant the waste lands. It will maintain the poor and tend the sick. It will keep stores of arms and ammunition for its own militia. It will set up a lawcourt, which will be competent to enforce all laws : ' for the judgement of a parish may be as much depended upon as that of a House of Lords '.

How free a world, how merry, it will be in the new age! no standing army; no taxes; no laws of settlement to vex the migratory labourer; no excise men, no customs officers, ' nor such like ruination vermin '. The mention of roads and canals suggests the possibility of industrial life. But the parish which Spence desired to see was a commonwealth of small cultivators, ' which makes employment for a greater number of hands and makes more victualling of all kinds be raised. What he craved for himself and his fellows was the peace, the neighbourliness, the secure, unhurried routine of village life, with a small stake in the country. Adversity made him shrill and virulent—on paper—in his latter days; and he was twice sent to prison for vending seditious works. As early as 1794 he seems to have been an object of concern to the spies of the Home Office.[1] But he kept his faith in the golden age to come and was, according to Francis Place, ' very honest, simple, single-minded, but unpractical to a degree hardly imaginable '.

[1] Holland Rose, *Pitt*, ii. 187. For a sample of his later style, see the dialogue printed in Hovell's *Chartism*, pp. 33-4.

The manifesto of the Spencean Society which we have already
mentioned, written and published in 1816 by their secretary,
Thomas Evans, is entitled *Christian Policy*. It gives a sadly
devitalized and dehumanized account of the Spencean Utopia.

' Now is the time to cancel Domesday Book and establish a partnership in the land ; there is no other means to prevent the establishment
of a military despotism, or all the horrors of a bloody revolution.
Great as is this undertaking, it can be easily effected. The easy process is to declare that the territory of these realms shall be the people's
farm, thus transferring all the lands, waters, mines, and houses, and all
feudal permanent property to the people. This will injure no one and
benefit all—the alteration which is proposed being that all persons
possessed of houses or lands shall in future pay rent for them instead of
receiving it. The Government is to remain as it is ; pensions to be
allotted to the Kings, Princes, and Nobles, and the remaining balance
of the whole rent-roll to be divided among the whole people, to every
man, woman, and child, being the profit of their natural estate
without tax, toll, or custom—which would be near £4 a head
annually.' [1]

The ultimate source of these Spencean doctrines is to be
found in urbane and peaceful writers of the eighteenth century,
generally in writers who, for one reason or another, were
shocked by the conduct of contemporary landlords. The best
known of them is Adam Smith, who, in his placid fashion,
throws doubt upon the equity of a system of great estates,
founded upon mere usurpation in the distant past, and preserved
down to modern times by the law of primogeniture and the law
of entails. It is, thinks Smith, self-evident that every successive
generation of men has an equal right to the earth (Bk. III, c. ii) ;
and he considers it to be notorious that the great estate is seldom
cultivated to the best advantage. The farmer, who rents from
a proprietor, is seldom fairly treated, the laws of land being all
framed in the interests of the proprietary classes.

---

[1] Quoted in *Quarterly Review*, October 1816. Evans probably based
his calculations of the individual's birthright on Colquhoun's tables, which
estimated the aggregate income of the royal family, nobility, and gentry at
fifty-nine millions sterling, and the numbers of productive labourers at
thirteen millions. These tables were constantly used by the Socialists
of the period. (P. Colquhoun, *Wealth, Power, and Resources of the British
Empire* (1814), c. iv.

Adam Smith is outdone by his fellow countryman William Ogilvie (1736-1819), who held for fifty-seven years the Chair of Humanity in King's College, Aberdeen. No man, we are told by his pupil Sir James Mackintosh, ever translated the *Aeneid* more delightfully. Yet Ogilvie sharpened his pen against landlords, and attacked their title-deeds on the lines which Adam Smith had suggested.

Ogilvie was the heir to a small estate and became an improving proprietor on a small scale; and there is no reason to suppose that he was hostile to the system of great estates in every form. For he dedicates his essay to 'the worthy and humane landlords of England'. But it is probable that he had a much less favourable opinion of the landlord class in his own country, though he writes in general terms, without reference to any country in particular, and though the problems which vex his mind—the extinction of the small-holder, the chronic poverty of the manual worker—were by no means peculiar to Scotland. But his criticisms on the landlord class undoubtedly have special reference to the black spots of the agricultural revolution which began in south-west Scotland about 1724, and which was in full tide when Dr. Johnson paid his visit to the Western Highlands (1773). It is the landlords of Scotland that Ogilvie has in mind when he accuses landlords as a class of exacting unreasonable rents from a population which is rooted to the soil by ignorance and conservatism; of stifling the impulse to industry in the tenant-class by a persistent refusal to grant long leases; of checking the growth of population and obstructing the development of waste lands which might be improved at less expense than the forests of North America. Some of his strictures hit the improving landlord, others the landlord who is obstinately wedded to old fashions. But between these two classes he evidently thought that the industrious small-holder had little hope of making a decent livelihood.

But this seemed to Ogilvie an intolerable prospect. For he regarded the agricultural population as the soundest element in the population. 'If not oppressed by the superior orders, if permitted to enjoy competent independence and rustic plenty, remote from the contagion of intemperance, they are known to excel in strength, comeliness and good health every other class of men in civilized nations.' The artisans, the factory workers, and all other men of degraded ranks and vocations who live in great cities are, by comparison, dwarfish, deformed, degenerate. It is from the country-side that the army and the navy must be recruited, and the wastage of life in cities and manufacturing operations must be repaired. Furthermore it is the countryman who produces for the State the necessaries of life, which are the highest form of wealth ; and the wise statesman must hold that all labour which is diverted from the soil is misapplied, ' unless in so far as it is given to those liberal arts whose productions operate on the mind, and rouse the fancy or the heart '. Ogilvie, in short, brings together in his argument two favourite themes of the eighteenth century, the need for a bold and numerous peasantry, the folly of supposing that any form of industry but agriculture can add to the real wealth of the community.

How is it, then, that the landlords have been permitted to pervert the natural order of society, to oppress and all but extinguish the class which should be the main filler of the nation's prosperity ? Simply because society has forgotten the true nature, the just limits, of the right of property in land.

This right, according to Ogilvie, rests upon what he calls ' a maxim of natural law ', the principle that every man has a right to an equal share of the soil of his native land, in its original and unimproved condition. As we have seen, this ' maxim ' had already been accepted by Adam Smith, and this perhaps is why Ogilvie takes it as self-evident. The landlord is a relic of feudal system ; might and not right is the basis of his pretended title to an absolute property in the land. All that he can justly claim is the value of the improvements which have been effected by his predecessors or by himself. The State may therefore expropriate the landlord, provided that the State gives him a fair compensation for improvements. Or, in the alternative, the State may fairly impose a tax on land which represents the annual value of the land before improvement. The State, in any case, should assert its rights in the land in such a way as to bring about the disintegration of the great estates and the enlargement of the class of small-holders. Ogilvie would welcome the imposition of a special tax on undeveloped land ; or a policy of granting State loans on easy

terms to tenants who wish to buy their farms.[1] But he would
prefer the more sweeping policy which he outlines in his draft
of an ' Agrarian Progressive Law'. Give, he says, to every
citizen, on reaching the age of twenty-one, the right to demand
a holding of not more than forty acres in his own or an adjacent
parish. Let the State carve out for him such a holding from
some contiguous estate, and fix the rent which shall be due in
perpetuity from the tenant to the landlord. Compel the tenant
to reside upon his holding. Prohibit any subdivision of the
holding between the tenant's heirs until all the uncultivated land
in the country has been taken up. For the family of average
size Ogilvie thought that forty acres was the most desirable
holding. But he looked forward to a time when nearly all the
cultivable land in Scotland might be broken up, through the
natural growth of population, into holdings of six or eight acres.

Such was Ogilvie's scheme. It made some noise in his own
time. Mackintosh says blandly that it was ' not the work of
a man experienced in the difficult art of realizing projects for
the good of mankind'. But Ogilvie anticipated some features
of the Irish Land Purchase Act of 1891, of the English Small
Holdings Act of 1892, and of the Finance Act of 1909; he
founded a school of agrarian reformers, which has made a considerable stir both in Great Britain and in the United States.
He cannot be dismissed from consideration as though he were
an isolated and uninfluential eccentric. But in his own time he
attracted little notice. Perhaps his essay was saved from oblivion
by an approving reference to it in Godwin's Political Justice.[2]
But Godwin did not express an opinion on Ogilvie's project.
He regarded the Scots professor simply as a theorist who had
some glimmering of the true doctrine of the rights of property.
The Chartists, who reprinted Ogilvie's Essay, read it more
thoroughly, and it was one of the sources from which their
land schemes were derived.

The Chartist movement, however, falsified a prediction which
Ogilvie had used to frighten the landlords of his day. He had
told them that the landless classes would take advantage of the
first political crisis in these islands to attack the grand monopoly
of land. A new Pretender might appear to challenge the title

[1] Essay, §§ 53-5.   [2] Bk. VIII, c. 2.

of the Hanoverians. The Roman Catholics of Ireland might make up their minds to claim toleration at the sword's point. Or Great Britain might be attacked by a continental power. Would it not in such cases be the obvious policy of the aggressor to appeal to the poor by promises of an agrarian revolution? And, finally, he points out, the poor may be called in to turn the scale in any conflict of domestic parties:

'Whatever party shall, hereafter, in the agitations of any state, assume the patronage of the lower classes ... may entertain confident hopes of being able, by their support, to obtain their own particular object of pursuit,'

provided that such a party offers to give back to the poor their birthright in the land.[1] When Ogilvie talked in this way he was only blurting out the fears which haunted the minds of many nervous politicians; and, after 1789, it was impossible to deny that an agrarian revolution was highly probable in any state which accepted the French version of the *Rights of Man*, or allowed it to be taught to the rural population. The rick-burnings and machine-breakings of 1816 and 1830–1 appear to have excited more alarm than any of the political unions and mass meetings of urban labourers; and in 1835 the two great parties in the House of Commons united to resist a motion praying for the pardon of the Dorchester Labourers,[2] who had taken secret oaths binding them, as it was currently supposed, to the most nefarious designs. And yet the agricultural labourer remained indifferent to O'Connor's plan for dividing England into cottier tenancies of three or four acres apiece, to be rented on easy terms from the owners of the soil; such support as he obtained came chiefly from the artisans of the midlands and the north.[3]

Perhaps the earliest convert to Ogilvie's version of the rights of property was Thomas Paine, who, in his *Agrarian Justice* (1797) adopted whole-heartedly the principle that the original value of the soil should belong to the State. He added, as his own contribution to the theory of the rights of property, that

---

[1] Ogilvie, *Essay*, §§ 57–61.

[2] G. B. Hurst, 'The Dorchester Labourers', *E. H. R.*, xl, p. 63. They were, however, released in 1837.

[3] Hovell and Tout, *Chartist Movement*, pp. 267 ff.

movable property is partly acquired by the labour of society as a whole, and therefore cannot be claimed by the possessor as his exclusive property. He proposed that the injustice of the existing system of distribution should be corrected by a succession-duty of ten per cent. on all estates, and that the fund so raised, which he estimated would be, in England, not less than four millions per annum, should be employed in providing pensions for the aged and incapacitated poor, and bounties for young married couples.[1]

Neither in this work, nor in the second part of his *Rights of Man*, where other suggestions are made for State aid to the poor, does Paine propose anything like Ogilvie's scheme of colonization. He desires to give free education to the children of the poor, to give every married couple a start in life, to insure the poor against the accidents of age and sickness, but not to shepherd them into an agricultural mode of life. But he takes it for granted that the marriage-bounty (of £15) will be used by the average young couple to buy ' a cow and implements to cultivate a few acres of land ', at all events if they can find no more profitable occupation. Paine does not contend that farming is the only proper occupation for the poor; but he does assume too easily that it is the only occupation in which no family need ever starve.

This opinion was not peculiar to Paine; it lies at the root of several later social experiments which were backed by men of the most various schools of thought. In 1797 a Tory philanthropist, Sir Thomas Bernard (1750–1818), published an account of a Yorkshire cottier who had succeeded in maintaining a wife and family on the produce of one rood of waste land. This was the beginning of the movement for promoting spade-husbandry and the multiplication of small holdings for those who would otherwise be paupers on the parish rates. Tories and practical agriculturists were not unjustly sceptical as to the magic of the spade, at least in the hands of the unemployed. But the Society for Bettering the Condition of the Poor, which

---

[1] In the thirties we find William Lovett petitioning Parliament to meet the whole of the national expenditure by a tax upon the land (1833). In 1848 Lovett adopted Paine's alternative proposal (made in Part II of the *Rights of Man*) for a graduated income-tax.

was founded in 1796 with Wilberforce's aid, examined seriously
the advantages of a cottage garden or a grass paddock to the
labourer, as a means of supplementing wages. Southey gave
publicity to these discussions in an essay contributed to the
Quarterly Review in 1816,[1] and the fashion of giving or renting
out potato patches and small gardens seems to have become
firmly established soon after 1830. A Poor Relief Act of 1819
empowered parish vestries to provide allotments for the relief
of the poor, but in practice it was left to landowners to give this
boon to the labourer 'not altogether in vain', as Dr. Clapham
says.[2]

More remarkable than the help given by landlords to the
allotment policy, which was in effect an acknowledgement that
agricultural labourers did not receive a living wage, is the
sympathetic hearing which Owen found in the most unlikely
quarters for his project of covering the face of England with
communistic settlements. The truth is that Owen only disclosed
by slow degrees the more fantastic features of this scheme, and
that he proposed it as a method of relieving employment in
that critical year, 1816, when the resources of conventional
philanthropy, organized by the influential Association for the
Relief of the Manufacturing and Labouring Poor, had proved
utterly inadequate to relieve the misery of a general trade
depression. Owen invited the benevolent rich to finance a
joint-stock company which would settle the unemployed in
self-contained and self-sufficient colonies on the waste lands
of England. This was a plan with an ancient pedigree, and
Owen, when he propounded it, alleged that he was merely
reviving the proposals of the seventeenth-century philanthropist
John Bellers. Subsequently he disclosed his intention to abolish
private property within his colonies. This confession, though
it shook the faith of the two parliamentary committees to which

[1] Reprinted in his *Moral and Political Essays*.

[2] On the subject of allotments see J. H. Clapham, *Economic History of
Modern Britain*, i, pp. 115–16, 472–4. *Politics for the People* (1848),
p. 56, gives an intimate characterization of the Tory squire, in which occurs
the following passage: 'As to buying out a small landowner, the thing is
quite foreign to his nature. He daily laments over the departed yeomanry
of England and is a zealous promoter of allotments.'

it was submitted in 1817 and 1823, was accepted with surprising indulgence by most of his original supporters, the chief dissentients being suspicious Radicals who feared that the Owenite colony would be nothing but a 'pauper-barrack' in disguise. In times of general despondency it is exhilarating to come across a stalwart optimist, and Owen's optimism was not altogether unreasoning. To the economists who opened fire upon his plan in 1819, when he was appealing for a fund of £100,000, he returned a notable reply in his *Report to the County of Lanark* (1820). They attacked his plan on the general ground that he provided no remedy for the grand evils of overproduction and redundant population. His retort was to the effect that these evils were imaginary.

'Manual labour properly directed is the source of all wealth and prosperity. When properly directed, labour is of far more value to the community than the expense necessary to maintain the labourer in considerable comfort. Manual labour, properly directed, may be made to continue of this value, in all parts of the world, under any supposable increase of population for many centuries to come. Wealth will grow faster than population.'

This statement of the case against his critics is by no means satisfactory as a proof of the soundness of a communistic scheme of industry. But it was a timely and convincing refutation of the pessimistic forecasts which had been inspired by the Malthusian theory of population and by the distressful times in which Owen wrote. As a messenger of hope he deserved well of his countrymen.

But the Owenite community, as Owen described it in this same report, was an easy mark for ridicule and caricature. The working man was perhaps not competent to criticize the author's confident assumption that the communal conscience would inspire every colonist with an honest resolve to work for the good of the community without any expectation of being rewarded in proportion to his efforts or penalized if he fell below the standard of due diligence. But the working men, even though suffering from unemployment, did not appreciate the privilege of living in ' the large square or rather parallelogram ' of buildings, capable of accommodating about 1,200 persons, which Owen postulated as the central feature of each colony.

To the wife of the working man we can imagine that the prospect of a communal existence, with a single bedroom for each
family, a public refectory, and a common ward into which all
young children would be huddled, was simply terrifying.　And
there was another difficulty which confounded the wealthy to
whom Owen looked for financial support.　On his own admission the initial outlay for establishing one such colony would be
£96,000, or £80 for each individual colonist, man, woman, or
child.

Nevertheless, money was raised and experiments were tried
in the British Isles, to say nothing of the calamitous venture
at New Harmony in the United States (1825–8).　In England, as
in America, the failure may be ascribed to the circumstance that
Owen's scheme demanded a high degree of enthusiasm and self-
abnegation from all who were concerned in it; that he refrained
deliberately from making a selection from among those who
applied to be admitted; and that the minority who were willing
and competent to work for the common good found themselves
swamped by the drones who consumed more than they produced.　Communities like Orbiston (founded 1826), Ralahine
(1831), Manea Fen (1840), and Queenwood (1840) did not in
any way supply a fair test of the worth of ' manual labour
properly directed '.　Probably the Radicals were right in pro-
phesying that such communities formed of the average unemployed would never become self-supporting except under an
iron discipline which would impose forced labour on the idle
and rebellious.[1]

But, even if the scheme had been practical as an emergency
measure for the relief of distress, would it have presented any
attraction to the best type of working man who had a reason-

---

[1] It should be noticed that the rule of equal reward for all was not
invariably observed.　At Orbiston there was at first a scale of wages
ranging from 10s. to 30s. a week, according to the rates paid for different
degrees of skill ' in old society '.　Later the unskilled, who were in the
majority at Orbiston, passed a resolution in favour of equal wages for all.
At Ralahine there was a scale from first to last.　But the wages were paid,
in both colonies, in credit notes which could only be used at the communal
store ; and in neither was there any machinery for securing a fair day's work
in return for the day's wage (B. Jones, *Co-operative Production*, i, pp. 59–62,
68).

able prospect of fending for himself under the older individual-istic system? Some perhaps might have adhered to it from a sense of duty, in a spirit of self-sacrifice. But more, one may believe, would have shared the opinion of William Lovett, an opinion remarkable as coming from an admirer of Owen's personality who had at one time embraced the Owenite way of life with some enthusiasm :

'What may become of the best portion of man's nature (of his industrial, skilful, persevering, saving energies) when some aspiring hopeful individual, resolving to labour and save while youth and vigour favour him, in hopes of realising leisure and independence, or to procure some cherished object of his heart, is constrained to abandon his resolution, to conform to the routine of the majority, and to make their aspirations the standard of his own? Or what advantage to him would be spacious halls and luxurious apartments, and all the promised blessings of a community, if he must rise, work, dress, occupy, and enjoy, not as he himself desires, but as the fiat of the majority wills it ? '

This, perhaps, is stark individualism ; but it is individualism of a type which can hardly be expelled from the heart of the working man. Lovett refused to believe that he could further the interests of his class by stunting his own development. That belief raises issues of a far-reaching character, not appro-priate for discussion in this context. The important fact for us is that Lovett expressed the views of those independent, hard-working, ambitious artisans without whom no Owenite com-munity could become what Owen hoped it would become, a self-governing fraternity. Indeed Owen's ideal community appealed more to enlightened Tories, such as Southey, than to the working man.

So far we have been dealing in this chapter with fantasies ; with projects which the historian cannot afford to neglect because they exercised, both by attraction and by repulsion, some influence on the development of thought and policy ; but with projects which all subsequent experience has discredited. We have now to consider two more substantial instruments of social reform which were not invented by any one ingenious brain, but made their appearance and gathered form and con-sistency by slow degrees in the midst of economic strife. These are the Trade Union and the Co-operative Society. Each of these forms of association has established its claim to respect ; but each of them is to-day something different from what it was in the first half of the nineteenth century. Between 1825 and 1850 there were several attempts to divert trade unions and co-operative societies to more ambitious objects than had been previously suggested or have subsequently been regarded as practicable.

The repeal of the Combination Acts in 1824 offered to the working classes a simpler mode of improving their economic status than that which Owen was suggesting. Although the concessions made in 1824 were somewhat modified in 1825 by an amending Act which prohibited the intimidation of minorities and the interference of unions in the management of any factory, trade, or business, it was not the opinion of unionists themselves that these amendments had reduced the concessions of 1824 to a nullity.[1]   On the contrary, extravagant hopes were formed and grandiose projects were put in hand which failed because the unions embarked on a warlike policy without counting the cost beforehand.

Some of the wilder ambitions of 1825 are expressed by the socialist Thomas Hodgskin in his *Labour Defended Against the Claims of Capital*. Hodgskin was in revolt against Ricardo's assumption that the capitalistic system was part of the eternal order of the universe, and held, with Charles Hall of Tavistock, that the capitalist exacted an excessive remuneration for comparatively trifling services. Now that the weapon of combination had been legalized the time had come, as Hodgskin thought, to reduce or even to annihilate the profits of the ' idle capitalist '. The hope of the future was to be, not Owen's plan of peacefully superseding the capitalistic system by communist methods of production, but the yoking of capital by brute force to the car of labour.   William Thompson, the leading Owenite economist, duly reproved Hodgskin for deserting the programme of their master.   For the next few years Owen devoted all his ingenuity to the conversion of trade unionists.   He begged them to

---

[1] This opinion is nevertheless adopted by Mr. and Mrs. Hammond, who say (*Town Labourer*, pp. 140–1) that under the act of 1825 ' Trade Unions were not allowed more than a bare existence '.

abandon their struggle with employers, and to form guilds of
the medieval pattern in every trade, which should include
masters as well as men, and should fix the prices to be paid by
the consumer in such a way as to secure both to the employer
and the employed their just remuneration. His efforts culminated in the project of a Grand National Consolidated Trades
Union (1834)—a bitter disappointment from the first, since it was
joined almost exclusively by unskilled labourers.

But in the meantime the militant policy of Hodgskin had also
proved a failure. The Lancashire cotton-spinners, led by the
journalist John Doherty, endeavoured to defeat their employers
through a combination of all the men of their craft in England,
Scotland, and Ireland. Doherty even sketched the plan of a
National Association of Trade Unions (1830),[1] yet, in spite of
all, found that the cotton-masters could hold out longer than
the men. In 1837 Doherty told a Select Committee of the
House of Commons that, in his opinion, ' no individual trade
could stand against the combined efforts of the masters of that
particular trade '; the only hope lay in persuading unions which
were not out on strike to finance those that were; and this was
a kind of finance on which the ordinary trade union was not
eager to embark. Nor was it easy for any union in the late
'thirties, when trade was generally depressed and union funds
were heavily mortgaged for the relief of unemployment, to build
up a considerable strike fund.

In the experience of these years the orthodox economists
found a confirmation of their view that unions could only raise
the rate of wages by restricting artificially the supply of labour
in their respective industries. They could, that is, create little
enclaves within the general community of labour, oases in which
a higher standard of comfort might be artificially maintained;
but they could not under any circumstances improve the condition of labour as a whole. Mill was inclined to rejoice that they
could do as much as this.[2] More severely logical advocates of
the Wage Fund theory argued that the unionist merely improved
his position at the expense of his unorganized and unsheltered

---

[1] The plan of a general Trade Union (not for fighting purposes) was
advocated in the tract *Labour Rewarded*, which William Thompson
published in 1827.

[2] *Political Economy* (ed. 1848), Bk. II, c. xiv, § 6. In the edition of

fellows. Mill defended them on the ground that the unions of the 'thirties and 'forties were too small to inflict serious injury on the general mass of labour, and under the most favourable conditions could not maintain their privileged position for any length of time.[1] Not until 1871 did he recognize the justice and the substantial nature of the advantage which collective bargaining secures to the wage-earner.[2] But it is to be observed that his tardiness in acknowledging what now appears to be an obvious truth was not due to any feelings of alarm. Up to 1852, or even later, the trade union seemed to him a useless, but on the whole a harmless, institution. ' Experience of strikes ', he wrote in 1848, ' has been the best teacher of the working classes on the subject of the relation between wages and the demand and supply of labour '; and, he adds, ' it is most important that this course of instruction should not be disturbed ' by the revival of the policy of the combination laws in any shape or form.

Yet in the period of which Mill was thinking when he wrote this passage the trade unions had given unmistakable proofs of their ability to improve the conditions of labour. Ashley deserves all honour for the skill and patience with which he worked for the Factory Bill of 1833, the Mines and Collieries Act of 1842, and the Ten Hours Act of 1847, but what most impressed ministers was the organized mass of working-class opinion in the industries concerned which was controlled by the Short Time Committees and through them by Ashley. Ashley in particular, in his dealings with Government, public or confidential, was always able to speak as the mandatory of ' the operatives '; nor was his influence in that character diminished by the fact that he had assumed the office on the distinct understanding that there should be no strikes and no intimidation on the part of his following.[3] If there had been no unions among the factory hands, there would still have been enthusiasm for Ashley's aims; but there would not have been the organized

---

1852 he retracted so far as to blame the selfishness of trade unionists. In 1862 he returned to the position of 1848.

[1] *Op. cit.*, Bk. V, c. x, § 5 (ed. 1849).
[2] *Op. cit.*, *l.c.* (ed. 1871).
[3] Hodder, *Life of Shaftesbury* (ed. 1888), pp. 85, 216. For his relations

campaign of the Short Time Committees to influence wavering electors and politicians. The essential moderation of the unions was shown by the fidelity with which they kept the pledge given to Lord Ashley, even when the resistance of Government to the desired reforms was obstinate and defiant. It was also shown by that general avoidance of any connexion with the Chartist movement which led O'Connor to revile 'the pompous trades and proud mechanics who are now the willing forgers of their own fetters '.[1]

The trade unions of this period should not have been condemned *en bloc*, as they were too often condemned by political and other critics, for the occasional excesses of individual members, or even on the strength of suspicions excited by oaths of secrecy and the grotesque initiatory rites. They were, however, detested by many who sympathized with the lot of the industrial population—by Ashley, for example, and by Charles Kingsley. It was not merely the crude economics of trade-unionist leaders that repelled such thinkers. The insistence of unionists upon the antithesis between the interests of capital and labour seemed to suggest that class warfare was a necessary incident of industrial life. Moreover, the trade union was, or was in danger of becoming, an aristocratic society, the members of which intended to improve their lot by excluding fellow workmen from participation in their trade. Even Maurice, who endeavoured, like Owen, to come to terms with the trade-union movement, and who admitted that unionists were no more selfish or inhumane than other workers and other classes of society, warned them that they could never reform society until they reformed their own moral standards. ' If you have the principles of fellowship at heart, you must diffuse them as widely as possible, and thus convert the union into an association.' This language leaves us in doubt whether the new associations were to include employers as well as employed. But we gather from the remarks of Maurice about socialism that

with Peel see *op. cit.*, pp. 192, 215, 247, 294, 305-6. In 1833 he told the House of Commons that he was the elected representative of 'the operatives' (Hammonds, *Shaftesbury*, p. 21), though in principle he was hostile to trade unionism.

[1] Quoted in Hovell and Tout, *Chartism*, p. 276.

he regarded the formation of syndicalist groups as an inevitable and salutary change, bound to come about in a few years.[1]

To those who held with Maurice the Co-operative Movement appeared the most hopeful of all the experiments in industrial organization which had been tried or suggested in their time. Needless to say that they ignored or condemned the original, Owenite, ideal which was represented from 1824 by the London Co-operative Society and its leader William Thompson, the author of *Practical Directions for the Speedy and Economical Establishment of Communities* (1830). But, from the time when Robert Southey praised the modest experiments of the Brighton co-operators as ' a slip of Owenism grafted on a stock of common-sense ', Tory philanthropists looked kindly on all such schemes,[2] and on the prospect that such associations might in time win for themselves a substantial position in the industrial field.

Though there were many failures, the co-operators were in certain localities and in a limited range of undertakings successful enough to justify the hopes of their well-wishers. Already before 1848 the co-operative shop of the Rochdale Equitable Pioneers had proved a success, and had provided a model of sound management for such distributing concerns. There were in existence co-operative mills and bakeries which had behind them a long record of prosperity ; there were other more speculative undertakings, such as the Paisley Print Works and the Manchester Hatters' Association, which could show some years of profitable trade. So far as could be seen, the co-operative idea was capable of being applied to almost any trade which did not call for a large initial outlay. In 1847 a beginning was made with building societies, perhaps the most remarkable of all the co-operative experiments of this time, seeing that they were able, in the next twenty years, to spend upwards of eight millions in providing their members (who were largely drawn

---

[1] *Life of F. D. Maurice*, ii, pp. 112–17. For his views on socialism, *ibid.*, pp. 49, 93–4.

[2] In November 1829 the *Quarterly Review* published an article on the Brighton Co-operators ; it was written by Dr. Robert Gooch of Brighton, a friend of Southey. (See the *Life of Southey*, v, p. 50.)

from the working class) with freehold houses.[1] Mill said in 1850:

' There is no way in which the working-class can make so beneficial a use of their savings, both to themselves and to society, as by the formation of associations to carry on the business with which they are acquainted, and in which they are themselves engaged as work-people.' [2]

In 1852 he committed himself to a prophecy that the organization of the Rochdale Pioneers must encourage hopes of a new social order in which the freedom and independence of the individual would be reconciled with the advantages of large-scale production, and the best aspirations of the democratic spirit would be realized, without violence, without spoliation, and even without any sudden disturbance of existing habits (*Pol. Econ.*, ed. 1852, Bk. IV, c. vii, § 6). When Mill was moved to this pitch of enthusiasm it is not surprising to find that Ludlow anticipated a moral no less than an economic revolution. Drunkenness and other vices which militated against efficiency would be suppressed by the spirit of communal loyalty; and the co-operators, assured of steady and remunerative employment, would acquire a feeling of independence and security not other-wise obtainable.[3]

Parliament gave a guarded and cautious approval to the principle of the co-operative associations. An Act of 1846[4] enabled them to register themselves as friendly societies ' for the frugal investment of the savings of the members, for better enabling them to purchase food, firing, clothes, or other neces-saries, or the implements of their trade or calling, or to provide for the education of their children or kindred '. This permission was chiefly valuable as an evidence of goodwill; for in practice it was found difficult for societies to register under the Act of

---

[1] For the building societies see Ludlow and Lloyd Jones, *Progress of the Working Classes* (1867); for other co-operative enterprises see B. Jones, *Co-operative Production*, vol. i, pp. 37, 81, 151.

[2] Quoted by Ludlow and Lloyd Jones, p. 214, from Mill's evidence before the Committee on Savings and Investments.

[3] Ludlow and Lloyd Jones, pp. 143-4.

[4] 9 and 10 Vict. c. 27 (Friendly Societies). Friendly societies were first recognised by an Act of 1793 (33 George III. c. 54).

1846.[1]　Another Act, passed in 1852[2] at the instance of J. S. Mill and Robert Slaney, authorized the establishment, by working men, of enterprises 'for the mutual relief, maintenance, education, and endowment of the members, their husbands, wives, children, or kindred, and for procuring to them food, lodging, clothing, and other necessaries, by exercising or carrying on in common their respective trades or handicrafts'. The wording of the Act shows that the promoters were anxious to disarm the opposition of Tories and of capitalists ; but, in spite of its seeming narrowness of definition, the Act enabled co-operators to undertake almost any productive enterprise. Neither Act conceded the privilege of limited liability to co-operative societies, for the simple reason that the principle of limited liability was not recognized at all in English law until 1855. But the concession was duly made in 1862.[3]

The practical experiments in co-operation to which the Christian Socialists gave their support were neither numerous nor important. Maurice confessed in after years that his party had never attempted anything which was comparable in magnitude with the work of the Rochdale Pioneers. The twelve productive associations organized by the Christian Socialists in London were formed to assist certain sweated industries. The members, as was only to be expected, were generally deficient in the qualities which alone could have ensured success—and especially deficient in the sense of mutual obligation. It was distinctly rash of the 'Society for Promoting Working Men's Associations' to infer from their brief experience—as they did infer in their report of 1853—that 'working men in general are not fit for association'. They had better grounds for their second inference, that no co-operative experiment (in a productive enterprise) could succeed unless the members were carefully selected.[4] And Charles Kingsley also seems to hit the mark when he states that, in his experience, no association for manufactur-

---

[1] B. Jones, *Co-operative Production*, i. 123–5.
[2] 15 and 16 Vict. c. 31 (Industrial and Provident Societies).
[3] 25 and 26 Vict. c. 87 (Industrial and Provident Societies).
[4] Extracts from this report are given by B. Jones, *Co-operative Production*, vol. i, pp. 112, 120–3.

ing had ever succeeded unless it contained some one master-mind.[1]

The true mission of the Christian Socialists, as most of them fully understood, was not to conduct experiments but to explore the principles of social reform. The main principle which they espoused was that the democratic principle must be recognized in the industrial sphere, but must at the same time be Christianized. It was a more alluring, because a less familiar, principle than Ashley's, which was simply that the relations of capital and labour must be Christianized ;[2] but within a few years after 1850 it became evident that the industrial democracy of the future would be something radically different from the democracy which Owen and Maurice had postulated; it would be a democracy in which the subjects, having first united together in a *pactum mutuum*, would enter into a contract with a constitutional sovereign. To this new situation Ashley's formula was on the whole more appropriate than that of Maurice.

We naturally turn for further information regarding the principles of the party to that short-lived periodical, *Politics for the People* (1848). It appeared at a time when party feeling ran dangerously high, and one object of the promoters was to convince the working man that the differences of opinion between the best men of all parties were less important than the points on which they were agreed. This point is elaborated in John Townsend's portraits of 'The Old Tory' and 'The Conservative' and 'The Whig'. Maurice, in an article on 'Fraternity', asked the more searching question whether the time had not come for the best men of every party to cut themselves adrift from party cries and party programmes, in order to reflect seriously upon the true ends of social reform, and the efficacy of the means by which the Chartists hoped to secure those ends. The Chartists, he complained, proposed to bring about some kind of millennium, the true nature of which they had not yet considered; and they expected to secure that object by measures which they had accepted on the authority of others. Another writer, taking 'Sanitary Reform' as his text, reminded

---

[1] Kingsley's *Letters*, p. 179.

[2] See his article on Infant Labour in the *Quarterly Review*, December 1840 (quoted by Hodder, p. 173, ed. 1888).

the Chartists that the campaign of the health reformers against disease, and against the maladministration of local authorities, by whose negligence so much disease was caused in English towns, was something that concerned the workman more nearly than universal suffrage or annual parliaments. It is true that in July 1848 the writers deliberately decided to postpone all other inquiries till they had investigated the possibilities of Christian Socialism. The last number of *Politics for the People* contains a note on the June insurrection in Paris which sounds the call to action. The insurrection is, he says, the logical consequence of that social war ' which has been waged for ages, which is being waged around us, which will be waged in every country, so long as society is given up to the sway of self-interest'. Now or never capital and labour must be harmonized and associated. ' It is not a machinery that will do this without God's grace shed abroad in our hearts; but can it be done without a change of machinery? Is it Christian, is it human, to leave labour—that is, the nerves and muscles and life-blood of our fellow creatures— to the scientific operation of the laws of supply and demand? To deem oneself justified in paying the current rate of wages, when that current rate of wages is not sufficient to support life?'

The Christian Socialists investigated this problem to the best of their ability, and confessed that they were baffled by it. Their influence in their own time was partly due to the clearness with which they perceived, and the frankness with which they denounced, some flagrant social evils. Still more was it due to their impartial, unpretending, and disinterested efforts to search out remedies. They were not men of genius, but they brought a stream of fresh air into the heated atmosphere of party strife. Some of them, as, for instance, John Ludlow, lived to realize that the world was not so evil, nor fate so harsh, as they had imagined in 1848; all of them had the courage to admit that they had made mistakes, and yet not to weary of well-doing. Their best monument is the Working Men's College, which was founded by their leader Maurice, and which owed to them much of its practical success as a centre at which the leaders of working-class thought came into contact with all that was best in the intellectual life of the Victorian era.

INDEX

PRINTED IN GREAT BRITAIN
AT THE UNIVERSITY PRESS, OXFORD
BY VIVIAN RIDLER
PRINTER TO THE UNIVERSITY